Living Legislation

Living Legislation

Durability, Change, and the Politics of American Lawmaking

EDITED BY JEFFERY A. JENKINS
AND ERIC M. PATASHNIK

THE UNIVERSITY OF CHICAGO PRESS   CHICAGO AND LONDON

JEFFERY A. JENKINS is associate professor in the Woodrow Wilson Department of Politics at the University of Virginia.

ERIC M. PATASHNIK is professor of politics and public policy and associate dean of the Batten School of Leadership and Public Policy at the University of Virginia.

The University of Chicago Press, Chicago 60637
The University of Chicago Press, Ltd., London
© 2012 by The University of Chicago
All rights reserved. Published 2012.
Printed in the United States of America
21 20 19 18 17 16 15 14 13 12   1 2 3 4 5

ISBN-13: 978-0-226-39644-6 (cloth)
ISBN-13: 978-0-226-39645-3 (paper)
ISBN-10: 0-226-39644-4 (cloth)
ISBN-10: 0-226-39645-2 (paper)

Library of Congress Cataloging-in-Publication Data

Living legislation : durability, change, and the politics of American lawmaking / edited by Jeffery A. Jenkins and Eric M. Patashnik.
    p.   cm.
Includes bibliographical references and index.
ISBN-13: 978-0-226-39644-6 (cloth : alkaline paper)
ISBN-10: 0-226-39644-4 (cloth : alkaline paper)
ISBN-13: 978-0-226-39645-3 (paperback : alkaline paper)
ISBN-10: 0-226-39645-2 (paperback : alkaline paper)
    1. Legislation—United States.   2. United States—Politics and government.
I. Jenkins, Jeffery A.   II. Patashnik, Eric M.
KF384.A2L585 2012
328.73'077—dc23

2011032937

♾ This paper meets the requirements of ANSI/NISO Z39.48-1992 (Permanence of Paper).

Contents

PART I

Overview

CHAPTER ONE

Living Legislation and American Politics

Jeffery A. Jenkins and Eric M. Patashnik

On November 4, 2008, Barack Obama was elected president of the United States. Senator Obama ran on a campaign of "hope" and "change," generating a wave of optimism in the face of multiple wars and economic recession that had bogged down the final years of the George W. Bush administration. A key component of Obama's domestic agenda was the promise of universal health care for all Americans.

Once elected, President Obama sought to make health-care reform a reality. Progress on health legislation was slow through the early months of 2009, however, as President Obama—seeking to avoid the mistakes made by President Bill Clinton in 1993—encouraged Democratic leaders in Congress to craft the bill. Following the enactment of a $787 billion economic stimulus package, a conservative groundswell, dubbed the Tea Party movement, emerged to protest against government expansion, including health-care reform. But Speaker Nancy Pelosi (D-CA) marshaled her troops and pushed through HR 3962, the Affordable Health Care for America Act, over strong GOP opposition.[1] The House bill provided for a "public option," a government-run insurance plan to compete with those offered by private insurance companies. The Senate, however, went in a different direction. Needing the votes of all 60 Democrats in the Senate to override Republican filibuster attempts, Majority Leader Harry Reid (D-NV) was at the mercy of moderate members of his caucus. In the end, the public option was dropped, and Senate centrists extracted additional concessions. The Senate bill, HR 3590, the Patient Protection and Affordable Care Act, passed 60–39 on a straight party-line vote.[2]

But then events intruded.[3] Liberal stalwart Senator Edward Kennedy (D-MA) died and was replaced in a special election by Scott Brown, a Republican. The Democrats lost their filibuster-proof majority and the ability to pass a new bill. Thus, Democratic House leaders chose to adopt the Senate bill and fix some of its problems later. After contentious debate, the House passed HR 3590 by a vote of 219–212, with 34 Democrats and all 178 Republicans voting against it.[4]

Thus, health-care reform was a reality.[5] But the law did not enjoy wide public support, and its enactment helped energize the Republican base for its repeal. Several features of the health reform law create political sustainability risks. First, the law passed without a single Republican vote in either chamber. This is not the usual way landmark welfare state expansions have been enacted in the United States. The Social Security Act of 1935 was supported by a strong majority of Republicans in the House and Senate on final passage. The final votes on Medicare in 1965 were closer, but that law still won the support of a narrow majority of House Republicans and almost half the GOP senators. Second, the law failed to deliver large, visible benefits to the 85% of Americans who already had health insurance. It remained unclear whether the program would build a strong constituency or come to be viewed as a broad middle-class entitlement. Third, Congress back-loaded many of the subsidies and benefits to 2014 for budgetary reasons. As a result, the most generous provisions of the law were not scheduled to kick in until after the 2012 presidential election. Finally, the law relies heavily on state authorities for its implementation, but many Republican state officials viewed the law as a federal overreach and challenged its constitutionality. It seemed likely that the issue would end up before the Supreme Court—with no certainty about the outcome.[6]

The November 2010 midterm elections were not kind to the Democratic Party. Damaged by continued high unemployment and flagging support by key voting groups from their 2008 victory, the Democrats lost sixty-three seats and their majority in the House and six seats in the Senate. Emboldened by their party's resurgence and pushed by leaders of the Tea Party, Republican leaders took aim at the health-care law. Knowing they lacked the votes to repeal the law outright, they began to devise ways to derail its implementation.[7]

As this book went to press, it remained an open question whether the law would become a durable part of the American policy landscape or if Republicans would ultimately succeed in their rear-guard efforts to unravel the measure in whole or part. The enactment of the Patient Protection and Affordable Care Act was a contentious, high-visibility event—but it did not settle anything. Rather, the moment of legislative enactment was merely the first round in an unfolding political and legal battle, and what federal health reform legislation looks like when the dust finally settles is anyone's guess.

*   *   *

Legislation is a living, breathing force in American politics. Laws enacted by the U.S. Congress, if entrenched, determine the boundaries of the political community, establish the rights and duties of citizens and officeholders, and provide the vehicle through which campaign promises, party platforms, and ideological programs are translated into policy outputs. Because the stakes for democracy and governance are so high, legislation also shapes the ground on which political battles are fought and the political commitments that tomorrow's officeholders inherit and sometimes seek to abrogate or unravel.

Scholars of American politics have devoted considerable intellectual energy to examining certain aspects of the lawmaking process. A sophisticated empirical literature has developed that seeks to explain legislative voting in committees and on chamber floors. This literature has given us much insight into the influence of constituency interests, ideological preferences, public moods, and partisan pressure on the outcome of roll-call votes in Congress. In addition, political scientists have uncovered the factors that shape the rules and procedures by which the Congress debates and acts on proposed legislation.

Despite these impressive research accomplishments, scholars have left important questions about legislation unaddressed. Why do some ideas remain on the legislative agenda for years and even decades while other ideas quickly drop off of it? Why do some laws, once added to the statute books, persist for decades in their original form while other laws are repealed or substantially modified soon after enactment? How can major policy reforms, which challenge the privileges of powerful clientele groups to promote diffuse interests, survive the legislative process and significant amending activity and become embedded in governing routines? In short, what happens *before* legislative adoption and what happens *after* the dramatic moment of legislative enactment? These questions go beyond a concern with the fidelity of bureaucratic implementation or the technical competence of public administration. They speak to the broader role of legislative coalitions, partisan forces, and policy commitments in remaking the American polity.

As the brief overview of health-care reform at the beginning of this chapter illustrates, a law's enactment is often simply the opening move in a larger political drama. A preoccupation on enactment—and *only* enactment—runs the risk of directing attention away from critical features of the lawmaking process. The objective of this volume is to explore how public laws are born, how they live, how they remake or fail to remake politics, and how they mutate and die. To address these questions, the standard view of legislation as a fixed end point is inadequate. We need to look at lawmaking *developmentally*, to see it not as a static act in which a piece of legislation is conjured up in a brief moment of political deal making or policy inspiration, and then put into immediate and permanent effect, never to be modified, but rather as a complex process of governance in which the policy content and societal impact of legislation unfolds over time. Laws have a life *before* adoption, when they are merely proposals advancing on the agenda, as well as *after* enactment, when they may generate durable legacies that channel the political possibilities of the future. While a legislative measure may not carry the imprimatur of the state prior to enactment, it may embody policy ideas that have been the objects of political deliberation, gestation, and contestation for many years. And the rules, incentives, and expectations contained in legislation are given tangible meaning and effect as they intersect with and refract the evolving political process. Lawmaking is not merely the culmination of a struggle among rival interests, values, and ideas; rather it is the very medium through which this political struggle plays out.

To assemble this volume, we invited a diverse set of contributors—including quantitative political scientists, political development scholars, historians, and economists—to address some underexamined aspects of lawmaking. We have made no attempt to force our contributors to use identical theoretical frameworks or methodologies or even to define their inquiries in precisely the same terms. The contributors thus deploy a variety of concepts and approaches and stress different causal mechanisms. As a result, there are both intellectual synergies and intriguing tensions among the chapters. We believe that the juxtaposition of these competing and complementary perspectives will provide a greater stimulus to scholarship than if we imposed an artificial and premature consensus on this emerging line of research.

Changing Perspectives on Lawmaking:
The State of the Literature

Lawmaking is, and has always been, at the heart of American democracy. One reason why lawmaking has been so deeply woven into the American political tradition is the durability and resilience of the Constitution itself. As William N. Eskridge Jr. and John Ferejohn point out, the difficulty of using the formal process of constitutional amendment to undertake policy commitments, declare new rights, and address injustices has long channeled political energy into the crafting and adoption of statutes. The result of this ongoing process of public lawmaking has sometimes been to change baseline understandings of constitutional norms themselves.[8]

While lawmaking has been integral to the American Republic since 1789, the prisms through which scholars and practitioners have viewed the legislative enterprise have changed significantly over time. As political historian William J. Novak observes in chapter 2, a critical transformation in both the theoretical and pragmatic understanding of American lawmaking occurred in the late nineteenth century. With the rise of a modern administrative state, legislation came to be seen less as an end in itself, a reflection of abstract sovereignty or the embodiment of the people, and increasingly as a human construction developed for the efficient management, organization, and control of the nation's business. This conception of legislation as both an evolving and instrumental activity could be found in the writings of leading progressives such as Woodrow Wilson, who sought to make the legislative enterprise more potent and responsive to the challenges of the day. In his 1885 book *Congressional Government*, Wilson argued that lawmaking was not an authoritative act that settled political controversies once and for all but rather one step in an ongoing process of political deliberation and social experimentation, in which the adoption of each new law yielded a reaction:

Legislation unquestionably generates legislation. Every statute may be said to have a long lineage of statutes behind it; and whether that lineage be honorable or of ill repute is as much a question as to each individual statute as it can be with regard to the ancestry of each individual legislator. Every statute in its turn has a numerous progeny, and only time and opportunity can decide whether its offspring will bring it honor or shame. Once begin the dance of legislation, and you must struggle through its mazes as best you can to its breathless end,—if any end there be.[9]

Wilson's point was not that new laws are invariably superior to old ones, for he recognized and decried the many obstacles to wise and effective lawmaking in a representative democracy. Rather, Wilson's claim was that laws, once enacted, create effects that future legislators must address one way or another. As he wrote, "It is not surprising, therefore, that the enacting, revising, tinkering, repealing of laws should engross the attention and engage the entire energy of such a body as Congress."[10] Yet if Wilson possessed a keen understanding of the developmental and pragmatic nature of the legislative enterprise, his arguments were largely unsystematic and did not establish a research agenda for twentieth-century American political science.

After World War II, the study of Congress as a lawmaking body became less prescriptive and more social scientific. Many studies of Congress took on a sociological flavor that reflected the dominant intellectual currents of the age.[11] Influential political scientists such as David Truman and Donald Matthews analyzed Congress as an autonomous institution whose members were governed by the norms, folkways, and role expectations internal to each chamber.[12] The focus of research shifted from a study of lawmaking as a constructive human enterprise to a detailed examination of the politics of legislative representation. Patterns of lawmaking were understood primarily for what they revealed about how the Congress maintained its political legitimacy and organizational boundaries in a complex, pluralistic society.

With the rise of the rational choice revolution of the 1970s, scholars began exploring lawmakers' goal-seeking behavior. While congressional scholars continued to study legislation, they did so primarily as a vehicle for understanding the intentions and incentives of individual lawmakers.[13] Committees and parties increasingly became the hot areas of study, and while scholars sometimes spoke of these institutions in the context of generating "policies" or "legislative outputs," the major focus was on the procedural and structural design of Congress. Key questions included whether committees traded authority across issue jurisdictions, whether information and expertise was valued, and whether partisanship shaped legislative behavior independent of members' constituency interests or ideological preferences.[14] Moreover, for reasons of tractability and parsimony, these works were confined to a study of Congress (and often only one *chamber*); the role of other institutional actors, specifically the president, who might have an effect on the legislative process was typically downplayed or ignored.

The publication of David R. Mayhew's seminal 1991 book *Divided We Govern* rejuvenated the study of lawmaking within congressional studies. Mayhew's central question was whether divided party control of government affects legislative productivity.[15] Mayhew operationalized legislative productivity in terms of the number of "major laws" enacted and found that productivity was *not* lower under divided government than under unified party control. Although Mayhew's counterintuitive finding did not go unchallenged,[16] the overall impact of his study was considerable. First, it persuaded quantitatively oriented political scientists that lawmaking was an exciting and analytically tractable object of study.[17] Second, it stimulated research on related topics including congressional delegation, veto politics, and unilateral presidential action.[18]

Thus, by the turn of the century, a new line of political science research had emerged in which scholars formulated and tested hypotheses about the impact of institutional factors on legislative or policy outcomes. Several chapters in the present volume ably represent this style of scholarship. Jeffrey E. Cohen and Matthew Eshbaugh-Soha examine the composition of the president's legislative agenda over the 1799–2002 period. They demonstrate that the presidency plays a major role in determining the set of issues that Congress attends to, and measure the influence of key economic and political factors in stimulating and dampening the rate of legislative agenda change. Sean Gailmard and Jeffery A. Jenkins's chapter also tests hypotheses about changes in legislative outputs over time. Focusing on the passage, repeal, and amendment of significant legislation in Congress between 1789 and 2001, they find that unified coalitions produce fewer major legislative innovations as they age. When unified coalitions first take power, they bring with them numerous proposals for major policy change and enact many of them into law. But the legislative creativity of unified coalitions, Gailmard and Jenkins show, tends to decay over time as they exhaust their stockpile of policy ideas. In addition, new unified coalitions, long out of power, are often eager to repeal legislation that their partisan rivals put into place. The implication is that legislative creativity and energy is mostly a trait of young coalitions. The "age" of coalitions should thus receive as much attention from scholars and journalists as their size.

From a "living legislation" perspective, the key issue is not simply how productive a given coalition is (or even how recently it has arrived on the political scene), but also how long the coalition's enactments will endure—and what impact the enactments have when set down into the ground. A highly productive coalition could pass many laws that leave little mark on the political process because their underlying policy commitments are never consolidated. Alternatively, a relatively unproductive coalition could enact policies that reshape the terrain on which future governance and political contestation take place. The contributors to this volume are thus concerned with charting the life courses of all the major elements and products of the legislative process: agendas, coalitions, statutes, programs, policy frameworks, and the agency structures through which laws, programs, and policy paradigms are implemented and carried out. Our contributors demonstrate that some laws, such as the Civil Service Reform Act of 1978, have become deeply embedded and institutionalized while other laws, such as the 1980 Superfund Act, have been highly vulnerable to ongoing modification. The result is to open a new line of research inquiry about the reasons for variation in postenactment dynamics.

Clarifying Concepts

Several key concepts will be used throughout the book, both explicitly and implicitly, and it is important to clarify the distinctions among them. The contributors distinguish between *durability* and *policy sustainability*. *Durability* refers to the longevity of a legislative product, to how long a statute (or policy or program) persists in its original form without significant change. A law that was enacted in 2012 and is then changed through a major amendment in 2013 (even if the amendment is a friendly one) is not very durable. It lasted only one year. *Policy sustainability*, in contrast, refers to the ability of a legislative product to withstand political shocks and absorb change without being thrown off its developmental course.[19] A policy framework whose rules and norms of rightful action become deeply embedded in governing routines (even if its initial supporters no longer hold office) is highly sustainable, even if the underlying statute has been subject to repeated formal change.

So, for example, the Social Security Act of 1935 has *not* been a very durable law (it has been amended scores of times, beginning in 1939), but it became highly sustainable after 1950 (when conservatives in Congress largely conceded to the program's existence). Amendments to the 1935 Act largely reinforced Social Security's core social insurance principles. Moreover, Social Security has absorbed economic and demographic change and served as a launching pad for the development of similar policies in other arenas including disability insurance and Medicare. A contrasting case is the Banking Act of 1933, otherwise known as the Glass-Steagall Act, which erected a legal wall between commercial and investment banking. Glass-Steagall lasted on the statute books for more than sixty years until its repeal in 1999. Yet Glass-Steagall's functional effectiveness and political sustainability atrophied over time. Amendments to the law opened regulatory loopholes that allowed commercial banks to engage in securities activities. Glass-Steagall was also unable to absorb financial market innovations and shifts in business models induced by technological change and globalization.[20]

In sum, the contributors to this volume are concerned about legislative stability *and* adaptability, about policy continuity *and* change.

Other terms that show up in this volume include *agenda stability* (whether the same issues receive attention from one Congress to the next), *death* (when a legislative product ceases to exist as when a law is repealed), *mutation* (substantive changes in a law, policy, or program), and *spending cuts* (reductions in funding that cripple a law or program but stop short of killing it). The concepts used in each chapter are the product of the questions the authors ask—and the data and methodologies they use to answer them.

Clarifying Approaches

The chapters in this volume display two main approaches to the study of how laws, policies, and agencies emerge, develop, and die. The first group contains chapters that adopt a "positive political theory" perspective. They are written mostly by political scientists who use quantitative methods to analyze large-N data sets. The chapters by Christopher Berry, Barry Burden, and William Howell and by Forrest Maltzman and Charles Shipan nicely display this approach.[21] The second group contains chapters grounded in the historical-institutional tradition.[22] They are written mostly by political scientists who use a case-study or small-N comparative analysis method. The chapters by Stuart Chinn, Eric Patashnik, and Vesla Weaver exemplify this approach. Because the two approaches have distinctive strengths, there is much to be gained by incorporating both to examine how laws live and die.

The key strength of the positive political theory method is that it permits the identification of systematic empirical patterns in legislative or policy outputs, patterns that can be easily missed when the analyst focuses on particular cases or arenas. Thus, Maltzman and Shipan demonstrate that the political conditions at the time of a law's enactment—in particular, whether government is unified or divided and the level of ideological disagreement between the House and Senate—influence the likelihood that the law will be amended subsequently. They show that laws originally adopted by diverse political coalitions are less durable than those crafted by strong, unified coalitions that are in a position to entrench their policy preferences and protect them from future change. This empirical finding challenges much received wisdom and raises important questions that should receive attention in future research, such as the durability-endowing value of passage by a bipartisan majority. Berry, Burden, and Howell uncover a different but equally fascinating empirical pattern, namely, that a program is vulnerable to termination, spending cuts, and other changes when the Congress that inherits it is different in partisan terms from the Congress that created it. Their study thus highlights the key role that coalitional change plays in the post-enactment trajectories of laws and helps explain how elections shape policy outcomes even in issue areas that were not salient during the campaign. More generally, the positive political theory perspective draws attention to the role of macro political conditions and the role of elections and governing coalitions.

Historical institutionalism's unique strength is that it views politics and policymaking as unfolding historical processes in which multiple institutions structure governing possibilities and constraints. Patterns of policymaking may reflect the adaptations, expectations, and incentives stimulated by the commitments inherited from the past rather than the preferences of current political actors or a functional response to the conditions of the day. As Theda Skocpol argues in one of the earliest and most influential statements,

> too often social scientists . . . forget that policies, once enacted, restructure subsequent political processes. Analysts typically look only for synchronic determinants of policies—for example, in current social interests or in existing political alliances. In addition, however, we must examine patterns unfolding over time. . . . Policies not only flow from prior institutions and politics; they also reshape institutions and politics, making some future developments more likely, and hindering the possibilities for others.[23]

Thus, an implication of historical institutionalism, applied to lawmaking, is that the downstream effects of enactments may be linear and predictable, but they can also be circuitous and ironic. Vesla Weaver focuses on the latter in her chapter, by exploring the surprising political legacy of the Safe Streets and Crime Control Act of 1968. Signed into law by President Lyndon B. Johnson, Safe Streets established the Law Enforcement Assistance Administration to allocate federal grants to cities and states struggling to confront civil disorders and the problem of crime. As Weaver documents, although the LEAA ended in 1980, the organizational capacities, policy precedents, and institutional infrastructure it created persisted, making it easier for President Ronald Reagan and state policymakers caught up in the 1980s' "war on drugs" to ratchet up criminal penalties and punitive enforcement mechanisms. Just as leaders can sometimes shape political events beyond the grave, so too can defunct laws sometimes create pathways and adaptations that channel ensuing patterns of governance. Accounts that trace the origins of the carceral state to the 1980s, argues Weaver, fundamentally miss the way the 1968 Act, in unexpected ways, structured subsequent patterns of policy development.

Clarifying Mechanisms

As this discussion suggests, the contributors focus on different causal mechanisms to explain how laws unfold over time. Three mechanisms are particularly important: institutions, the structure of policymaking coalitions, and policy feedback.

The importance of institutions in shaping political outcomes is a major theme of political science.[24] Institutions allocate authority, enforce norms and duties, and determine the "rules of the game." It is therefore unsurprising that a law's development and downstream effects turn in part on how the law recasts, and is recast by, surrounding public authority.[25] While the enactment of a law signals the momentary victory of the law's supporters over its opponents, the losers in the initial enactment battle may choose not to end the fight but to use their access to other institutions to prevent the law's consolidation.[26] For example, if the opponents of a law cannot find a supportive majority in Congress, they may try to weaken the law's entrenchment. In the American political system, losers in the lawmaking process will often mount a rearguard action in the courts. Stuart Chinn's chapter tells one such story, documenting how business interests took their fight against the Wagner Act of 1935, which elaborated a new set of labor rights for workers, all the way to the Supreme Court. And, in the end, they were successful, as the Court defined the boundaries and meaning of the Wagner Act in ways that allowed business interests to recoup some of their prior legislative losses. More generally, Chinn shows that the substantive meaning and societal impact of landmark laws passed by Congress may be subject to contestation long after their initial enactments.

Of course, the supporters of a law are often farsighted enough to recognize that what was gained in Congress could be lost in the bureaucracy or judiciary. One design-stage strategy that legislative advocates can use to protect a law after enactment is to craft institutions that will shield the law from the interventions of current and future political enemies.

David E. Lewis's chapter provides a nice illustration of how an institutional design focus can shed light on the politics of policy durability. He uses an original data set from a survey of federal administrators and program managers to evaluate whether giving responsibility for policy implementation to independent commissions (as opposed to executive branch bureaus) offers greater insulation from future political interventions. Independent commissions have fixed terms for appointees and party balancing requirements for nominees, and they are omitted from regular Office of Management and Budget regulatory and budget review. Lewis's empirical results suggest that institutional design does indeed matter, and that strategic policymakers can promote the durability of their legislative creations through strategic delegation to independent commissions.

Institutional design would not much matter if the political composition of Congress and the executive never changed. Today's lawmakers would be the same as tomorrow's, not just in the physical sense of being the same people but in the more important sense of having the same preferences and priorities. But the American political system is dynamic. Elections, retirements, demographic shifts, redistricting, important events, and large-scale changes in economic and social conditions are continually remaking both the line-up of political leaders and the matters they attend to. It is therefore critical to look closely at the structure of political coalitions inside government, both at enactment and over time as the law is carried out. The chapters by Gailmard and Jenkins, Berry, Burden, and Howell, and Maltzman and Shipan provide important evidence that coalitional variables offer substantively and statistically significant purchase on a range of outcomes including legislative productivity, legislative durability, and programmatic modification and death.

A third key causal mechanism is policy feedback. Building on E. E. Schattschneider's claim that "new policies create a new politics,"[27] the insight is that an enactment can reconfigure the political dynamic by creating or strengthening incentives for collective action or inducing societal commitments that are quite difficult to reverse.[28] Positive feedback can generate self-sustaining cycles that not only promote a policy's reproduction but that also foreclose previously available options for change. The policy feedback literature traces its origins to Schattschneider's pioneering analysis of tariff politics and to Theodore Lowi's and James Q. Wilson's policy typologies, which showed how the costs, benefits, and allocations of authority inherent in different types of policies implied different kinds of political conflicts and patterns of interest group mobilization.[29] Strong feedback can generate political legacies that endure even after the waning of the political forces that generated the policy's original enactment.[30]

The chapters by Amihai Glazer and Eric M. Patashnik illustrate how policies can generate their own political support postadoption, making them increasingly difficult to reverse.[31] Glazer points to the importance of credibility and information in making policies stick, and both Glazer and Patashnik emphasize the sustainability-endowing influence of costly investments. In the case of airline deregulation, for example, Patashnik shows that the political commitment to maintaining a deregulated airline sector has persisted not because the legislative coalition that enacted the law in 1978 has remained intact (it hasn't) or even because airline deregulation has provided benefits for the general public in the form of lower fares (although it has), but rather because it has stimulated the emergence of new discount carriers and encouraged a host of business actors to make long-term, often asset-specific, investments in new aircraft, terminals, schedule tools, and revenue-management software. Supporting industries and suppliers (e.g., aircraft equipment suppliers, hotels, rental cars, restaurants, corporate office parks) have grown up around the new system. Each has a vested interest in the reform's maintenance, and any attempt to undo these vast economic changes would be massively disruptive not only for the airlines themselves, but also for their host business communities.[32]

Yet there is no guarantee that policies will create positive feedback. The production of positive feedback is often not a priority of enacting coalitions (who may be more concerned with winning initial passage of the law or maintaining their power and influence).[33] As David Mayhew has observed elsewhere, a nontrivial proportion of the laws passed by Congress is essentially symbolic in nature.[34] Such laws are designed *not* to change governance or society but rather to give reelection-minded lawmakers the opportunity to display their support for momentarily popular causes before largely uninformed mass audiences. Symbolic policies are often vaguely drawn and instrumentally irrational, making it unlikely that they will work when set into the ground. Their core design principle is to tread as lightly as possible on extant power arrangements while giving the appearance of action. Symbolic policies do not make a new politics; they merely refract an old one. As Patashnik's chapter suggests, even "landmark" enactments such as the Tax Reform Act of 1986 and the Freedom to Farm Act may fail to generate supportive constituencies or become entrenched features of the political landscape. As a result, celebrated reforms are often unceremoniously abandoned after enactment.[35]

Broader Implications

In the two final chapters in this volume, distinguished political scientists David R. Mayhew and Sidney M. Milkis offer their own observations about the broader implications of our living legislation perspective on

American politics. Here we wish simply to flag what we see as some of the major "take-aways" of this volume.

Our contributors offer three important substantive contributions to the study of American politics and policymaking. The first contribution is to challenge existing scholarly characterizations regarding the functioning of American political institutions and the policymaking process. Much of the political science literature on "legislative effectiveness" is based on some quantifiable measure of productivity, often simply a raw count of major legislative enactments. But as our contributors show, true effectiveness goes beyond such basic output counts. Effectiveness must be predicated on broader—if less easily measured—criteria. Does legislation have far-reaching political and policy effects? Are governing routines, and ultimately citizens' lives, profoundly affected? Do policies endure and serve as launching pads for other initiatives? Or are initial legislative achievements undercut over time, leaving no durable imprint on the polity? By moving beyond static measures and analyses, scholars can gain some traction on these sorts of questions. A living legislation perspective provides an important reminder that legislative activity is not the same as legislative achievement and that legislative productivity is different than political impact.

The volume's second contribution is to invite inquiry into the capacity of individual leaders and political coalitions to durably reshape state activities. The American political system is open and pluralistic, with a plethora of governing arenas. The existence of multiple access points, and the incentives of officeholders to reflect contemporary public opinion and interest group demands, makes embedding laws difficult. Even if a coalition can overcome the initial barriers to enactment, protecting the policy against significant amendment or outright repeal can be difficult. Thus, a successful lawmaking coalition must work to "lock in" a policy and insulate its key provisions against future challenges by building a broad base of support in the larger political-economic context. The achievement of "landmark legislation" thus comes to be seen not as a one-off triumph but rather as a multistage process. Enactment must be followed by diligent maintenance and consolidation, lest the initial legislative victory be for naught.

Our volume's third contribution is to draw attention to distinctive features of American national lawmaking at the start of the twenty-first century. In the contemporary era, lawmaking is frequently less about generating new laws from whole cloth than remaking and tweaking policy commitments and legal obligations inherited from the past. The inability to write laws on a blank slate creates different challenges than lawmaking in earlier periods of American history. Prior to the growth of the modern administrative state, coalitions had to accommodate diverse preferences and find ways to overcome the barriers to collective action. Legislative coalitions today must accomplish those tasks but also must worry about a plethora of new challenges postenactment. The growing complexity of the political world, the rising number and diversity of political and economic interests that press demands on government, the greater involvement of the judiciary in statutory interpretation, and the sheer growth in the reach and influence of Big Government—all these factors put into play forces that will shape the life of a law after its birth. At times, these pressures cause laws to generate an impact far beyond what their original architects anticipated, but they may also cause laws to collapse and become empty words, even as they nominally live on in the statute books. This new context creates greater uncertainty and makes the lawmaking enterprise, broadly understood, far more unpredictable. Thus, an awareness of the evolving macro historical context of lawmaking is crucial for understanding the micro strategies of political actors and for assessing the ease or difficulty of embedding legislation at particular moments.

Our volume also yields an intellectual achievement, by integrating both American political development scholars and quantitatively oriented rational choice scholars toward a broader understanding of the lawmaking process. We believe that methodological pluralism is important, as there is tremendous value added produced by looking at a single phenomenon from different methodological perspectives. While methodological debates may exist and generate a great deal of academic "heat," shared substantive agendas can—if we intellectually nurture them—produce considerable empirical light. Unfortunately, such complementarities are not typically realized, as scholars of different methodological persuasions do not often talk to one another. Our goal from the outset was to address this challenge head on, which we accomplished by consciously selecting authors from different disciplines and methodological backgrounds who share an interest in lawmaking and political dynamics. We hope that our pluralistic approach will promote an exciting new research program, as future editors and scholars recognize the benefits that can accrue from the contributions of many different kinds of research.

Final Thoughts

Though the contributors to this volume come at the topic of living legislation from diverse perspectives, their work conveys a common message: Lawmaking is a vital governing activity, integral to the dynamics not only of the Congress but of the American polity as a whole. Lawmaking expresses the inventiveness of electoral coalitions, demarks the legitimate scope of public action, and links the governing imperatives of the present to the political aspirations of the future and the policy commitments of the past. If the chapters comprising this volume do not suggest that consensus on a single approach to the study of lawmaking and legislation is likely any time soon, they do point to exciting intellectual agendas and begin to map their frontiers.

We wish to acknowledge the individuals and organizations that made this volume possible. We initially held a conference, "Embedding Laws in the American State," at the Miller Center of Public Affairs at the University of Virginia on May 2–3, 2008, thanks to the generous support of the Miller Center's Governing America in a Global Era program and the Department of Politics. The chapters in *Living Legislation* all began as contributions to that conference. Other conference participants included Brian Balogh and Jeffrey Legro, and we thank them for their insights. David Pervin at the University of Chicago Press has nurtured this project from our initial contact with him, and we are grateful for his wisdom and support. We also thank the anonymous reviewers who provided extremely helpful comments. In the end, our job was made easier by the contributions of so many talented individuals.

CHAPTER TWO

Making the Modern American Legislative State

William J. Novak

The essays in this volume are dedicated to two propositions. First, most generally, they aim to reinvigorate scholarly interest in the subject of legislation and bring a new level of analytical sophistication to the study of the legislature. Second, they are committed to looking at legislation developmentally, that is, legislation not as the simple static textual output of a law-drafting body, but as a dynamic social and political process—a living and breathing human activity with a distinct time dimension involving a complex pattern of beginnings, evolutions, maturations, mutations, emendations, and, of course, endings. These propositions nicely intersect with recent themes and priorities in the fields of law and American history.

One of the most persistent (if somewhat unrequited) themes in legal scholarship over the last century has been the demand for a more serious study of legislation. The call has an ancient pedigree in Anglo-American jurisprudence extending as far back as Jeremy Bentham's original critique of Sir William Blackstone's commentaries on English common law.[1] At the turn of the twentieth century, Roscoe Pound and Ernst Freund demanded that a modernizing polity required a better understanding of legislative processes and principles, advocating increased attention to the study of statutes in law schools.[2] James Willard Hurst carried this cause into the middle of the century, decrying the priority given to judge-made law in legal scholarship and endorsing a more capacious approach to legal inquiry that included legislation and public policy:

In deciding what to include as "law" I do not find it profitable to distinguish "law" from "government" or from "policy." . . . In order to see law in its relations to society as a whole, one must appraise all formal and informal aspects of political organized power—observe the functions of all legal agencies (legislative, executive, administrative, or judicial) and take account of the interplay of such agencies with voters and nonvoters, lobbyists and interest groups, politicians and political parties. This definition overruns traditional boundaries dividing study of law from study of political history, political science, and sociology.[3]

Recently, a new generation of legal scholars has again taken up this clarion call. In *The Dignity of Legislation*, Jeremy Waldron draws on democratic and political theory to challenge scholarly neglect of legislation and to reestablish the priority and value of the most democratic and representative branch of government.[4] Similarly, in casebooks as well as scholarly monographs, William Eskridge Jr., Elizabeth Garrett, John Ferejohn, and Richard Pildes have moved legislation and democratic processes from the periphery to the center of contemporary legal inquiry.[5] We live in an "age of statutes," Eskridge notes, where "nothing that is human escapes statutory interest."[6] Consequently, the essays in this volume could not be more timely from the perspective of the current study of law and society.

But timeliness also engages the second theme of this volume—the attempt to study legislation in time and over time and to more precisely account for change and continuity, durability and evanescence in legislative practice and performance. The essays in this volume are a testament to the many productive ways to approach the study of legislative transformation, persistence, and effect (or the lack thereof). Here again, the historical study of law (broadly construed as Hurst would have it) recommends itself, specializing in evaluating legal (legislative as well as judgemade) change over time. And perhaps the basic contribution of American legal history to the project envisioned by Jeffery Jenkins and Eric Patashnik might be the provision of straightforward legal-legislative histories like William Letwin's history of the Sherman Antitrust Act, David Langum's history of the Mann Act, or Charles and Barbara Whalen on the Civil Rights Act of 1964.[7] Placing particular statutes in proper social, economic, and political context and documenting historical transformations in content, cause, and effect across time certainly adds to our understanding of legislative process and efficacy. But an even more useful role for legal history might be to take a macro rather than a micro view of things, that is, to look less at the history of particular statutes and more at the history of legislation as a whole in an effort to demarcate certain structural shifts or substantive changes in the very act or conception of legislating itself. Identifying such large structural shifts in the nature of legislating or legislation—for example, the emergence of what Eskridge and Ferejohn dub "super-statutes"—might provide even greater insight into the reasons for overarching legislative durability and persistence across a wide variety of specific policy areas. After all, a cursory glance across American history seems to suggest that durable legislation frequently travels in packs—think, for instance, of the statutory innovations of the progressive period or the New Deal or the equally revolutionary initiatives of the "new social regulation" and the "rights revolution" of the 1960s and early 1970s.[8]

In taking the macro approach, several eras or topics in the larger history of American legislation seem worthy of further attention. Even before the onset of the modern period, one can identify several major periods of legislative transformation: (1) the role of charters and legislative codes in American colonization[9]; (2) the extraordinary legislative output of the First Congress of the United States, 1789–91 (dubbed a "continuing constitutional convention" by David Currie)[10]; (3) the early nineteenth-century movement for the legislative codification of American law[11]; (4) the mid-nineteenth-century proliferation of comprehensive state statutes overturning common law rules in areas like corporations, married women's property, and alcoholic beverages; and (5) the explosion of interest in legal hermeneutics, statutory construction, and constitutional limitations in the years surrounding the Civil War.[12]

But of all the distinct eras of legislative evolution and statutory innovation in the history of American political development, one era seems to stand out as especially significant: the period of great transformation between 1877 and 1932. This formative era marks the emergence of a distinctly modern form of legislative state in the United States that changed existing practices of legislation across the board and fundamentally altered the horizon of legislative possibility. The structural transformations of this critical period created the conditions for the development of the distinctly modern and more durable forms of statutory policymaking chronicled in this volume.

After Reconstruction but before the ascendancy of Franklin Delano Roosevelt, a new kind of American state was born—a modern nation-state. This revolution in American government yielded a polity far more rationalized, centralized, and bureaucratized than any anticipated by the founders or experienced in the earlier nineteenth century. And American governance began to take on some of those attributes that Max Weber defines as ideally central to modern statecraft: (1) a rationalized and generalized legal and administrative order amenable to legislative change; (2) a bureaucratic apparatus of officers conducting official business with reference to an impersonal order of administrative regulations; (3) the power to bind—to rule and regulate—all persons (national citizens) and all actions within its official jurisdiction via its laws; and (4) the legitimate authority to use force, violence, and coercion within the prescribed territory as prescribed by the duly constituted government.[13] This fundamental transformation of public law allowed a whole series of more particular public policy initiatives through which this more modern state apparatus extended its reach into daily American social and economic life.

One of the central features of this modern governmental revolution was a new approach to legislation. As C. K. Allen notes, legislation was "the characteristic law-making instrument of modern societies," and it reflected a new "relationship between the individual and the State."[14] At its core was what David Mayhew labels a new appreciation of "lawmaking as a cognitive enterprise," involving an effort to more fully and consciously embed instrumental rationality in governance via efficacious, ends-oriented, policy-driven substantive legislation.[15] Though theoretically that process sounds simple, expected, and rather matter-of-fact, historically, it was the product of two generations of social, political, and legal struggle. It required the contested upheaval of nineteenth-century common law traditions and the slow and arduous development of new ways of thinking about law, government, public policymaking, and the legislature.

The rest of this chapter outlines the historical development of three of the main characteristics of this modern transformation in American legislation: (1) the rise of legal positivism and a new conception of the nature of state-made law; (2) the redefinition of liberalism around a new state interventionism reliant on positive legislation as never before; and (3) a new conception of state police power—the legal power that undergirds most modern socioeconomic legislation and regulation in the United States. Together, these three developments ushered in the modern era in American legislation and changed forever conceptions of what

was thinkable, possible, or durable via statute. Positivism, new liberalism, and a modern conception of police power set new standards and pa-
rameters for judging the success and failure and measuring the efficacy
of legislative projects for the rest of the twentieth century.

Positive Law

As Léon Duguit first noted, transformations in the state moved hand in
hand with transformations in law.[16] So it should come as no surprise that
the creation of a modern American nation-state at the turn of the twentieth century was accompanied by new theories of law, providing new instrumentalities and legitimations of governance. With urgency and an
intense new critical spirit, American scholars, jurists, and publicists interrogated the rule of law as never before. As Roscoe Pound noted, "The
changed order of things has been felt in legal science." Modern conditions forced modern changes in American law.[17] The common law tradition that had shaped and ruled so much of public and private life through
the early nineteenth century was being quickly displaced as a principal
tool of American governance by a new regime of positive legislation and
administrative regulation.

   This transformation of American public law took many forms. And
American legal historians have deployed a wide array of descriptive labels to capture the legal ideas at its core: antiformalism, legal pragmatism, sociological jurisprudence, legal realism, among others.[18] Unfortunately, the proliferation of categories of schools of thought (together with
the legal academy's special obsession with American legal realism) has
led legal historians to underestimate the important contribution of legal
positivism to all of these debates and to the transformation of the American state and legislative policymaking.

   Legal positivism in its broadest sense refers to an understanding of
law as humanly posited—that is, law as established not by theological
gods but by historical human beings and communities. Positive law is
man-made law rooted in empirical social facts—an artifact of historical
conventions and contingent social needs. Legal positivism, in short, is a
quintessentially modern, disenchanted, anti-metaphysical way of looking at the origins and nature of law, rejecting earlier natural law theories of law's moral links to nature and the divine. The roots of legal positivism, obviously, are diverse and extensive, stretching all the way back

to the general emergence of a more humanistic, skeptical, and scientific outlook on the world.[19] But two sources in particular were more proximate to and important for the American reception of legal positivism. The first was the hugely influential positive sociology of Auguste Comte and his followers, articulating the need for the systematic and scientific study of human society liberated from theology and metaphysics.[20] The second was the more concrete legal impact of John Austin's philosophy of positive law as presented in his *Lectures on Jurisprudence*.[21] Austin's posthumously published materials revived interest in the reformist legal ideas of Jeremy Bentham and provided a classic English statement of a positivist approach to law that was rapidly spreading throughout Europe in the late nineteenth century. Approached as a starting point—as an opening argument in a great legal debate—rather than as a final analytical jurisprudence of formal legal categories (such as act, right, and duty), legal positivism had a transformative impact on American law. It was the entering wedge of legal rationalization in the United States, and it precipitated a whole range of more critical and functionalist accounts of the relationship of law to politics and statecraft.

Austin's analytical jurisprudence itself found many adherents and advocates in the United States, including John Chipman Gray, Henry T. Terry, Albert Kocourek, and Wesley Newcomb Hohfeld.[22] Austin dominated Gray's influential Columbia University lectures on *The Nature and Sources of the Law*. For Gray, it was Austin who led jurisprudence out of the bramble bush of theological and moral abstractions and toward a more scientific approach. As Gray put it, before Austin, "Law had been defined as 'the art of what is good and equitable,' . . . 'the abstract expression of the general will existing in and for itself'"[23] Austin, following Bentham's original critique of Blackstone, insisted on a harsh analytical separation of law from morality—of the Is from the Ought, so as to cleanse jurisprudence of the myth, folderol, and claptrap of medieval natural law and common law thinking. As Morris Cohen weighed this contribution, "Just as Machiavelli separated the science of politics from that of ethics and Grotius made the theory of law independent of theology, so Austin made jurisprudence a distinct science by sharply distinguishing between the legal and the moral."[24] Austin was interested not in moral law or divine law, but instead in positive law—law as it was, in fact, made and deployed by officials—law as an expression of force and power and as a tool or an instrument of authority. As he originally opened *The Province of Jurisprudence Determined* so matter-of-factly,

"The matter of jurisprudence is positive law: law strictly and simply so called: or law set by political superiors to political inferiors."[25]

The modern critical potential of this more objective and instrumental formulation of law as the command of a superior was not missed by the authors of American sociological jurisprudence and legal realism. In "The Path of the Law," Oliver Wendell Holmes Jr. acknowledged the "practical advantage" of mastering Austin and "his predecessors, Hobbes and Bentham, and his worthy successors, Holland and Pollock." Roscoe Pound began his pioneering work on a new sociological jurisprudence with an initial presentation of analytical jurisprudence, noting its multiple contributions such as (1) the idea of law "as something made consciously by lawgivers"; (2) the role of "force and constraint behind legal rules"; (3) the new emphasis on statute law; and (4) the social consequentialist perspective of utilitarian philosophy.[26] Felix Cohen later rooted the broad intellectual trend toward "functionalism" in philosophy and law in analytical jurisprudence: "If you want to understand something, observe it in action. Applied within the field of law itself, this approach leads to a definition of legal concepts, rules, and institutions in terms of judicial decisions or other acts of state-force. Whatever cannot be so translated is functionally meaningless."[27] Ultimately, Holmes, Pound, and Cohen offered fairly intense criticisms of analytical jurisprudence as a final formal theory striving for "a useless quintessence of all systems."[28] But in the end, the American theorists acknowledged the original contribution of positivism to a critical and progressive theory of law. As Julius Stone put it, it was the Austinians who first "washed the law in cynical acid" and established a basis for a more modern, realistic, and pragmatic jurisprudence.[29]

The influence of legal positivism was felt especially in public law where it transformed American thinking about the relationship of law to the state. The heart of this influence was the emphasis that analytical jurisprudence placed on sovereignty—law as the command of a duly constituted sovereign. As Gray pointed out, according to Austin, "'The State' is usually synonymous with 'the sovereign.' It denotes the individual person, or the body of individual persons, which bears the supreme powers in an independent political society."[30] By making explicit the links between positive law, sovereignty, and the state, Austin provided American jurists a model on which to build powerful new theories of the state and its positive lawmaking powers.

The themes of positive law, sovereignty, and the state came together

particularly well in the synthetic public law treatises of Westel Woodbury Willoughby.[31] Willoughby, one of the most prolific political writers of his time, joined new theories of the state and sovereignty to a historical reinterpretation of American constitutional law generally. At the
heart of Willoughby's system was the endorsement of analytical jurisprudence and a positivist conception of law as the command of a sovereign. In contrast to antebellum jurists who regularly rejected a Black-
stonian or utilitarian argument for the force of law, Willoughby drew the
nature of state sovereignty and all subsequent delineations of governing power strictly from a "conception of law as wholly a product of the
State's will."[32] "However confederate in character the Union may have
been at the time of its creation," Willoughby declared, "the transformation to a Federal State was effected." The essence of that state was not
compact or communal custom or natural rights; rather it was modern
sovereignty—that power that was "the source of all law."[33] While many
American theorists took greater issue than Willoughby with the crud-
est expressions of Austin's notion of law as the command of a sovereign,
they readily accepted more general formulations of law as "a product of
conscious and increasingly determinate human will" recognized and exercised by official "organs of the state."[34]

In this way, early nineteenth-century concerns with custom, local
self-government, compact, and evolutionary common law gave way to a
new emphasis on the positive constitutional powers of a modern nation
state. The reception of analytical jurisprudence speeded a legal movement away from the perceived absurdities, irrationalities, and inefficiencies of common law rulemaking (so vigorously criticized by Bentham)
and toward more systematic and rationalized accounts of law as a tool
of modern governance—an instrument of a sovereign people and state
that could be used to accomplish necessary social ends. Austin himself
defined the proper utilitarian end of a sovereign political government as
"the greatest possible advancement of human happiness."[35] Legal positivism thus reinforced a growing tendency to view law (and the state) not
as the brooding omnipresence of past moral restraint, but, as Rudolf von
Jhering put it, as "A Means to an End."[36] Imperative legislation, statute
law, and administrative regulation assumed greater significance on the
basis of stronger claims to legal legitimacy and policymaking efficacy.
Nineteenth-century common law and community-based conceptions of
the people's welfare were increasingly displaced by the more modern
notion of the people's government—the idea of a sovereign nation-state

positively pursuing a vision of the public good rooted in a more comprehensive rational and national calculus.

These generally positivist and realist tendencies were clearly visible
in an extraordinary text published in the early twentieth century by the
Association of American Law Schools entitled *Rational Basis of Legal
Institutions*.[37] As John Wigmore and Albert Kocourek put it in their ed-
itorial preface, "New times have been coming,—nay, are now here. The
outermost circle of that wave of scientific rationalism which began in the
Darwin-Huxley period has at last reached the Saragossa sea of the Law."
Oliver Wendell Holmes's introduction made clear the convergence of
modern legal thought around a new concern with empiricism broadly
construed—as a demand for "reasons," "figures," and "facts" in the law.
Such rationalization of law was part and parcel of an instrumental movement for "social control" rooted in the belief "that society advanta-
geously may take its destiny into its own hands—may give a conscious
direction to much that heretofore has rested on the assumption that the
familiar is the best, or that has been left to the mechanically determined
outcome of the cooperation and clash of private effort."[38] As Holmes
implied here, the end product of a more positive, rational jurisprudence
was an emphasis on policy—on the instrumental aims to be achieved by
a modern sovereign state passing positive laws for the general welfare. A
more positive and political conception of law, in other words, played directly into the hands of another group of thinkers and reformers trying
to rethink American liberalism and to expand the idea of legislating in
the public interest.

New Liberalism: Positive Liberty and the Public Good

Armed with new theories of the nation-state and the power and instrumentality of positive law, American theorists also rethought the nature
of liberalism in this critical period. Patterned after a similar effort underway in Great Britain visible in the influential work of T. H. Green,
Henry Sidgwick, L. T. Hobhouse, and members of the Fabian Society,
American thinkers consciously crafted a "new liberalism" for modern
times. In one of the most creative and prolific periods in American political thought since the founding, a plethora of theorists and publicists led
by Lester Frank Ward, Walter Weyl, Walter Lippmann, Herbert Croly,
and John Dewey reworked the foundational tenets of American liberal

thought amid rapidly changing social and economic conditions. Their "new" liberalism consisted of three principle positions: first, a devastating critique of "old" liberalism as a political and philosophical anachronism; second, a distinctly positive rather than negative conception of liberty and freedom; and third, a reconstruction of the idea of the public good and the common welfare.

One of the most common features of late nineteenth- and early twentieth-century American thought was a wide-ranging critique of some traditional ways of thinking about society, polity, and economy. As Walter Lippmann put it in "Some Necessary Iconoclasm" in his precocious *A Preface to Politics*, "If only men can keep their minds freed from formalism, idol worship, fixed ideas, and exalted abstractions," they could attain the more active, instrumental, and inventive statecraft that he felt this revolutionary period required.[39] The idols, abstractions, and formalisms most under fire were a set of old liberal ideas concerning the nature of liberty and the relationship of individuals to the state. In a relentless series of spirited critiques, talented writers like Vernon Parrington, Charles Beard, Gustavus Myers, J. Allen Smith, Louis Boudin, Frank Goodnow, and William Garrott Brown excoriated earlier philosophies of natural right, individualism, and laissez-faire. As they saw it, by the late nineteenth century, the complex and multilayered theories of Hugo Grotius, John Locke, Adam Smith, and John Stuart Mill were being radically distorted through the double impact of the social Darwinist philosophies of Herbert Spencer and William Graham Sumner and a rapidly industrializing, profoundly inegalitarian economy. What were originally liberating ideas honed in seventeenth- and eighteenth-century battles with despotic governmental regimes were distorting into a caricature of liberty and freedom as something like the bleak obligation to be left alone amid a fiercely competitive social and economic struggle for "the survival of the fittest."[40] Forsaking its crusading origins in emancipatory revolutions against political authoritarianism, religious and moral coercion, slavery, privation, and economic privilege and monopoly, liberalism was fast transmogrifying into a reactionary and truly merciless form of laissez-faire apologetics.

Outraged at how liberal ideas could be used to justify inequality, deprivation, selfishness, austerity, and inaction, liberals began an important and lasting intellectual reconstruction. Their critique of laissez-faire was unyielding. Lester Frank Ward led the way dissecting Spencer's chief American disciple William Graham Sumner's *What Social Classes*

Owe to Each Other, wherein "all attempts at social reform are unspar-
ingly condemned, and reformers of every kind are lashed and goaded in
a merciless manner." He suggested that the book, far from winning any
new converts to an "old" philosophy, instead only showed "that the laissez faire doctrine, if it could be carried to a logical conclusion, would be
nihilistic and suicidal."[41] In "Individualism, Old and New" and "Liberalism and Social Action," John Dewey had no trouble pulling together
a generation's worth of critiques for his devastating portrait of the scle-
rotic ideas passing for liberalism under the old regime. Dewey charged
that old liberalism had grown (1) too static (failing to account for dramatic changes in socioeconomic context); (2) too negative (emphasizing
a formal, legalistic liberty from the state instead of a substantive, positive commitment to human freedom); (3) too economistic (defining freedom in almost exclusively monetary terms and ignoring the importance
of cultural expression: science, art, intellect, aesthetics, romance); and
(4) too individualistic (failing to recognize human beings as fundamentally changing and growing, associative and relational creatures).[42] He
called for a new, renascent liberalism to positively meet the challenges of
the twentieth century.

Out of the sweeping critique of old liberalism and laissez-faire there
emerged a new conception of positive liberty—a conception that intersected with simultaneous calls for a more positive state and more positive
legislation. At the heart of this new idea of positive liberty was a critique
of an older liberal notion of liberty as a purely negative phenomenon.
The locus classicus of that negative definition was John Stuart Mill's influential proclamation in *On Liberty* that "the sole end for which man-
kind are warranted, individually or collectively, in interfering with the
liberty of action of any of their number, is self-protection. . . . The only
purpose for which power can be rightly exercised over any members of a
civilised community, against his will, is to prevent harm to others." Mill's
harm principle captured the essence of a negative liberty perspective—
emphasizing individual liberty as freedom *from* outside coercions or interventions by others or by the government. One is most free to the extent that others are individually and collectively limited from interfering
with one's own prerogatives. Negative liberty thus placed a first priority
on restraining outside power, particularly governmental power.

The new liberal critique of negative liberty took several forms. First,
critics built on A. V. Dicey's observation in *Law and Public Opinion*
that the world had changed remarkably since Mill penned his simple

principle separating private freedom from public coercion. In an urbanizing and industrializing world of complex business and social transactions, private and public interest appeared increasingly intertwined and interdependent. As Dicey put it, "Since 1859 almost every event which has happened has directed public attention to the extreme difficulty, not to say the impossibility, of drawing a rigid distinction between actions which merely concern a man himself and actions which also concern society. . . . Human knowledge has intensified the general conviction that even the apparently innocent action of an individual may injuriously affect the welfare of a whole community."[43] The second more substantive inroad the new liberals made on negative liberty was the idea that formal liberty *from* outside public intervention did not seem like actual freedom at all, especially when examined in real-world situations. In "Liberty of Contract," Roscoe Pound argued that the negative liberty of the worker to contract for sub-subsistence wages, long hours, and poor working conditions seemed to be turning freedom into something of its opposite. Pound attacked an overly "individualistic conception of justice, which exaggerates the importance of property and contract, exaggerates private right at the expense of public right, and is hostile to legislation, taking a minimum of law-making to be the ideal." He advocated instead a more positive, active conception of liberty *in fact*—not formal freedom *from* interference as an end in itself, but freedom of contract as a means *to*—as freedom *toward*—the more positive development of human capacities and the establishment of social justice.[44]

In his *Lectures on Jurisprudence*, Pound placed his own contribution on "Freedom of Industry and Contract" after T. H. Green's *Principles of Political Obligation*.[45] Pound's quest for a less formal and negative conception of liberty as an end in itself and a more empirical and positive conception of liberty as a means to larger human ends reflected the spirit of Green's highly influential theory of positive liberty—a theory incorporated into the broader American progressive effort to reconstruct a notion of the public good. Green presented the idea so clearly in his lecture on "Liberal Legislation and Freedom of Contract" in 1881 that it is worth quoting at some length:

We shall probably all agree that freedom, rightly understood, is the greatest of blessings; that its attainment is the true end of all our effort as citizens. . . . But when we thus speak of freedom, we should consider carefully what we mean by it. We do not mean freedom from restraint or compulsion.

We do not mean merely freedom to do as we like irrespective of what it is that we like. We do not mean a freedom that can be enjoyed by one man at a cost of a loss of freedom to others. When we speak of freedom as something to be so highly prized, we mean a positive power or capacity of doing or enjoying something worth doing or enjoying, and that, too, something that we do or enjoy in common with others. We mean by it a power which each man exercises through the help or security given him by his fellow-men, and which he in turn helps to secure for them. When we measure the progress of a society by its growth in freedom, we measure it by the increasing development and exercise on the whole of those powers contributing to social good with which we believe the members of the society to be endowed; in short, by the greater power on the part of the citizens as a body to make the most and best of themselves.[46]

In this way Green shifted attention away from formal legal measures of freedom and liberty as protection from outside compulsion to more social and positive measures of liberty as the power and ability to actually achieve something—to improve and to develop. The end of a truly positive liberty was "the liberation of the powers of all men equally for contributions to a common good."[47] Individual liberty and the common good were understood as mutually reinforcing rather than opposing forces, and freedom was viewed as having social as well as individual attributes.

American progressive thinkers built directly on this more idealist and positive notion of liberty in reconstructing the idea of the public good. The idea of the common good and the people's welfare, of course, had deep roots in American political and legal thought.[48] But new theories of positive liberty, law, and statecraft along with modern conceptions of social interdependence brought renewed attention and development. Rejecting the hedonistic, selfish calculus at the heart of traditional utilitarianism, progressives reached for an idea of the common good and the importance of the welfare of others rooted in a more social conception of human beings with inherent social ties finding their own good in union with the good of others. John Dewey developed ideas of public and social interest in a steady stream of articles and books from his pioneering text on *Ethics* to *The Public and Its Problems*.[49] Walter Lippmann and Herbert Croly incorporated elements of positive liberty and the public good in their manifestos *Drift and Mastery* and *The Promise of American Life*.[50] Jane Addams detected "a new conscience"—a "new

moral consciousness"—in this period. Walter Weyl dubbed it a "new social spirit," suggesting, "It involves common action and a common lot.
It emphasizes social rather than private ethics, social rather than individual responsibility. . . . The inner soul of our new democracy is not
the unalienable rights, negatively and individualistically interpreted, but
those same rights, 'life, liberty, and the pursuit of happiness,' extended
and given a social interpretation."[51]

In short, testaments to positive liberty and the public good were ubiquitous in the progressive period. And the links between new positive
theories of statecraft and law and new theories of liberalism and social
ethics created a potent intellectual environment for action, change, and
reform. These were the predominant ideas of the time, and they provided an intellectual foundation for rethinking American governance
and legislation. Moreover, these ideas were very much ideas in action. As
Weyl noted, the new social spirit was wholly coincident with the political
struggle for "popular control over government" and the economic quest
for "governmental supervision" of business and industry. The new democracy had innumerable manifestations in "ordinances, laws, judicial
decision, group actions, and individual labors."[52] Armed with more modern rational theories of law, the state, individual liberty, and the public
good, progressives were prepared to act. In particular, they sought new
regulatory and public interest legislation as well as the more general administrative supervision of social and economic affairs. The third crucial component in the remaking of the modern American state was a
dramatic expansion in the notion of legislative police power.

Police Power and the Modern Legislative Policymaking

One of the most unmistakable indicators of a transformation in the
American state was the veritable explosion of legislation in the United
States at both the state and federal levels between 1877 and 1932. At the
first meeting of the American Law Institute in 1923, Elihu Root added
to a frenzy of concern about the "flood of laws" when he reported that
some 62,000 statutes had been added to the U.S. and state legislative record in just the five-year period before 1914.[53] Charles Merriam counted
18,243 legislative acts and resolutions for the biennium 1899–1900 and
23,403 for 1929–30. Well before the heightened activity of the Depression and New Deal years, Congress alone was passing between 1,700 and

2,000 legislative acts per session, and larger states like New York were adding approximately 1,000 statutes to their books every two years.[54] By quantitative standards, statute law—the positively enacted law of the duly constituted popular legislature—was becoming the dominant instrument of modern American legal development.

But quantitative measures can be deceiving (especially given the number of private acts, internal administrative measures, and simple statutory amendments). Even more significant than the number of statutes being passed in this period was the radical character of some of this legislation—what some commentators started to call "the new social legislation" or "industrial legislation." For many of these statutes involved wholesale revisions of American common law and far-reaching social and economic reforms. From price fixing regulation and corporate antitrust laws to worker's compensation and state and national prohibition laws, this was an era of unprecedented statutory innovation. In 1926, John Maurice Clark offered up a sampling of the broad-based movement for social control through legislation:

> This period of fifty years has seen the growth of effective control of railroads and of public utilities; while electricity and the telephone have developed, first, into recognized public utilities, and, second, into businesses which transcend state boundaries and thus become essentially national problems. Irrigation, land reclamation and flood prevention also belong properly in the class of interstate public interests, while radio and aerial navigation have but recently been added to the list. The trust movement and anti-trust laws, conservation, the Federal Reserve system, vast developments in labor legislation, social insurance, minimum-wage laws and the growing control of public health, prohibition, control over markets and marketing, enlarged control over immigration and international trade, city-planning and zoning, and municipal control of municipal growth in general, have all come about within this period.[55]

By 1910 James W. Garner's introductory American political science text could list the following functions of the modern state (beyond the basic maintenance of peace, order, and safety) as subjects of state and federal legislation:

> The operation of the postal service; the construction of dikes, levees, canals, public roads, bridges, and irrigation works, and works of public utility gen-

erally; the maintenance of scientific and statistical bureaus; the erection and maintenance of lighthouses, beacons, and buoys; the construction of harbors, wharves, and other instrumentalities of trade and commerce; the care of the poor and helpless; the protection of the public health and morals; elementary education; . . . the conduct of railway traffic; the telegraph and telephone service; the manufacture and distribution of gas and electricity for lighting purposes; the furnishing of water for drinking and other purposes in cities; the maintenance of theatres, pawn-shops, bath houses and lodging houses; the encouragement of certain industries by means of bounties, protective tariffs, and subventions; the planting of colonies; the encouragement of immigration; the establishment of experiment stations, liquor dispensaries, banks, universities of learning, hospitals, reformatories, art galleries, museums, zoological and botanical gardens; the erection of improved dwellings for working people; the making of general loans to farmers; grants in aid of railroads; the distribution of seeds for agricultural purposes; the conduct of the business of insurance; the granting of old age pensions; the maintenance of employment bureaus; and many other activities too numerous to mention. Under this head may also be included a great volume of regulatory or restrictive legislation dealing with the conduct of certain trades and occupations which are affected with a public interest, such as: railway traffic and means of communication; mining, manufacturing; the relations between employer and employees; the conduct of dangerous, offensive, or obnoxious trades; the censorship of the press, vaccination, quarantine, and sanitary legislation; laws regarding the erection of buildings in cities; laws regulating banking, barbering, baking, plumbing, pawnbroking, slaughtering, and many other trades or businesses.[56]

Such lists could be multiplied a hundredfold and still not capture the full scale and scope of the American social and economic legislative record in this critical period.

The appearance of such sweeping social and regulatory statutes meshed well with modern instrumentalist theories of state power and legal action, but they raised fundamental questions for more traditional ideas about statute law and the extent of the police powers of state and federal legislatures to regulate in the public interest. Though we are all positivists now to the extent that we understand the legislative power as the omnibus authority of the sovereign state to pass constitutional laws, the emergence of a plenary legislative power wholly distinct from judicial power yet within a rule-of-law tradition was a complex and still little understood historical development. In antebellum America, the line between statute and common law (as well as legislature and court) was often quite murky, and the question of how early Americans actually viewed the act of legislating remains something of a legal-historical mystery. What is clear, however, is that prior to the Civil War, most jurists and political thinkers resisted a positivist conception of legislative lawmaking as simply expressing the command or will of a sovereign. Instead, they clung to a more organic, fundamental law tradition wherein even legislative power was understood as declaratory, amendatory, and interpretive within a glacially evolving, customary common law regime.[57]

From the perspective of such a fundamental common law vision, the statutory onslaught of the post–Civil War period was unsettling to say the least. In "Common Law and Legislation," Roscoe Pound perhaps overstated the tension: "Not the least notable characteristics of American law today are the excessive output of legislation in all our jurisdictions and the indifference, if not contempt, with which that output is regarded by courts and lawyers."[58] With the appearance of innovative modern statutes (the first hints of which appeared before the Civil War in comprehensive legislative experiments like married women's property acts, Field codes, general incorporation laws, and state prohibition statutes), law writers responded with an ambitious treatise tradition that attempted to reconcile the increasingly positive legislative state to a rule of law. Moving away from Blackstone-like commentaries on American common law, they developed two more modern approaches to the legal mediation of the positivist state. The first was statutory interpretation as reflected in a proliferation of treatises on the judicial construction of legislation from Francis Lieber's *Legal and Political Hermeneutics* to Theodore Sedgwick's *Interpretation of Statutory Law* to Joel Prentiss Bishop's *Commentaries on the Written Laws*.[59] These texts established a continuing role for the judiciary in the legal supervision of the new legislative output. The second closely related development was the expansion of judicial constitutional review, apparent both in the increased incidence of the practice of judicial review in this period as well as its more formal justification in treatises like Thomas Cooley's *Constitutional Limitations* and Christopher Tiedeman's *Limitations of Police Power*.[60] Statutory interpretation and constitutional review established an underlying institutional tension between dynamic legislatures and active courts— positive statutes and the rule of law—that would continue through the twentieth century, as Stuart Chinn illustrates perfectly in chapter 10 of this volume. But, as will be seen, these legal traditions ultimately were much more accommodating to the development of a modern American state than they were resistant or obstructionist. As William Eskridge has argued, statutory interpretation has become "the most important form of legal interpretation in the modern regulatory state."[61] Similarly, the judicial review of the constitutionality of legislation (particularly in matters concerning individual civil liberties and rights) has become an important vehicle of positive state policymaking in its own right. In the end, constitutional review and statutory interpretation encouraged and legitimated the modern legislative state in ways that would have been inconceivable within the earlier communal and customary regime of the common law tradition.

A modern science of legislation developed in the late nineteenth and early twentieth centuries that was far removed from antebellum and common law standards.[62] The techniques of lawmaking itself improved dramatically under the influence of reforms like legislative reference and bill-drafting bureaus, professional legislative staffs and associations, and the national movement for uniform legislation. As Pound surveyed the situation in 1908, "Modern statutes . . . represent long and patient study by experts, careful consideration by conferences or congresses or associations, press discussions in which public opinion is focussed upon all important details, and hearings before legislative committees."[63] The democratic consent and popular sovereignty evidenced in such legislative processes increasingly displaced the customary consent of the common law as a basis of legal legitimacy. Statutes began a steady and uninterrupted ascent in American law eclipsed only by the simultaneous development and expansion of administrative rulemaking authority.

One place to witness this transformation of public law concerning statutes and legislation is in the modern development of the doctrine of the police power. The peculiar language and terminology of "police power" no longer resonates today, as the idea has been fully incorporated (and thus rendered invisible) by a modern acceptance of general legislative lawmaking power. But in the late nineteenth and early twentieth centuries, discussion of the "police power" was pervasive. Economists, politicians, social reformers, and journalists were all aware of its important consequences for policymaking. For the police power was basically the American legal expression for the authority of the government to regulate private interests, property, and behavior on behalf of the public health, safety, morals, order, and welfare. The police power had deep roots in the early American Republic and beyond where it resided exclusively with state and local governments and reflected a common law vision of well-regulated communities.[64] The reason the police power was so ubiquitous in turn-of-the-century jurisprudence and public discourse was that it was undergoing a fundamental transformation. That transformation was twofold. First, the police power was becoming a formal constitutional doctrine that defined a modern conception of positive legislative regulatory power. Second, somewhat less conspicuously, the police power was going national.

One of the chief architects of the transformation of the police power was Ernst Freund, one of the great, relatively anonymous revolutionaries in American political and legal history. With German university training, a background in political science, and a long career at the University of Chicago Law School, Freund was well positioned to contribute to the redefinition of legislative, administrative, and regulatory powers underway in the late nineteenth and early twentieth centuries. He accomplished this through a range of national, state, and local reform activities, numerous scholarly articles, and four influential treatises on the key legal issues surrounding the creation of the modern legislative state: *Police Power, Standards of American Legislation, Administrative Powers*, and *Legislative Regulation*.[65] Like Roscoe Pound and Robert Luce, Freund was aware that he was living in a "new age of legislation," and his legal work can be seen as an attempt to create a science of modern legislation and regulation that would clarify the new forces and standards at work. He suggested that the course of Western history consisted largely of the "wresting of legislative power from the executive" (except in the case of administrative regulations proliferating through express delegations of legislative authority). The degree to which written statutes and codes increasingly supplanted both unwritten law and executive proclamations reflected the importance in democratic societies of having popular and representative sanction for governmental action. It also reflected an increasingly realist and functionalist approach to the nature and obligations of the state. Freund argued explicitly that modern socioeconomic change, particularly "the growing power, scope, and complexity of private industrial and social action," brought an increasing demand for positive state action in the public interest.[66] That action appropriately took the form of written, legislative enactments in areas of police, revenue, and administration that were increasingly positive and public rather than declaratory and private. These regulatory statutes were the hallmarks of a modern legislative state—a direct consequence of the "increasing complexity of the social and industrial structure" and the expansion of "the functions of government" in pursuit of "the public welfare" and "the public interest."[67]

At the center of this expansion of legislative regulation and the multiplication of the social and economic functions of government stood the police power—the only open-ended source of state regulatory authority in American public law. Together with a bevy of other commentaries in this period, Freund's *Police Power* helped to free the conception of police power from the limitations of its common law origins and to establish it as an independent constitutional basis of extended legislative regulatory authority.[68] The police power traded in its ancient common law roots in rather murky ideas like overruling necessity and Blackstone's notion of "offences against public police" and became a formal and positive category of the constitutional law of a modern state. Freund began his treatise by noting the great objects of government, most importantly, (1) the maintenance of national existence (the law of overruling necessity) and (2) the maintenance of justice (the redress of right and wrong via the administration of civil and criminal justice). To these more traditional defensive and protective functions of government (which reflected a more negative conception of liberty and the role of government), a third was quickly being added in modern states, namely, the positive promotion of public welfare through "internal public policy." As Freund put it, "the care of the public welfare, or internal public policy, has for its object the improvement of social and economic conditions affecting the community at large and collectively, with a view to bringing about 'the greatest good of the greatest number.'" It was here that an expanded conception of police power did its work, no longer primarily preoccupied with negative common law protections or the simple maintenance of civil and criminal justice, but reconstituted as an instrument for the positive promotion of public welfare. Freund summarized, "No community confines its care of the public welfare to the enforcement of the principles of the common law. The state places its . . . resources at the disposal of the public by the establishment of improvements and services of different kinds; *and it exercises compulsory powers for the prevention and anticipation of wrong by narrowing common law rights through conventional restraints and positive regulations which are not confined to the prohibition of wrongful acts. It is this latter kind of state control which constitutes the essence of the police power.*"[69]

In this way, Freund transformed the police power from a more limited

doctrine of community self-defense and protection hemmed in by traditional common law maxims and local and customary legal procedures
into a more positive and affirmative authority to legislate broadly on behalf of the general welfare. Modern legislation and regulation needed to
be instrumentally responsive to direct public policy needs rather than
constrained by traditional common law routines. Reinvented as the legislative "power of promoting the public welfare by restraining and regulating the use of liberty and property," the modern police power provided a powerful constitutional foundation for the modern legislative
state. Innumerable other commentators reinforced Freund's positivist
conception of police power. Lewis Hockheimer proclaimed, "The police
power is the inherent plenary power of a State . . . to prescribe regulations to preserve and promote the public safety, health, and morals, and
to prohibit all things hurtful to the comfort and welfare of society."[70]
And judges and courts also followed suit, linking the police power more
directly to the promotion of public welfare. Citing a host of cases up-
holding police power regulation, Justice McKenna argued typically in
Bacon v. Walker (1907) that the police power "is not confined, as we
have said, to the suppression of what is offensive, disorderly or unsani-
tary. It extends to so dealing with the conditions which exist in the State
as to bring out of them the greatest welfare of its people."[71]

By linking the police power with the general promotion of public welfare in a positive legislative state, these jurists and law writers paved the
way for the explosive growth of police power regulation in the progressive era. Regulatory statute books swelled, case numbers rose exponen-
tially, and expositions on police power proliferated. A new forcefulness
and resourcefulness crept into discussions as progressives expanded
the scale and scope of American legislative power, calling for the police power to be "more freely exercised and private property more freely
controlled to meet the needs of the changed conditions of society." Some
progressives saw in the police power "almost unlimited opportunities
for adopting whatever legislation the augmenting demands of social pi-
oneers may require."[72] The police power became the legal foundation
for the extensive legislative and regulatory experiments enumerated by
Clark and Garner. As Freund noted, the modern police power encom-
passed the whole range of public and governmental regulatory interests from the primary social interests of "safety, order, and morals" to
the regulation of economic interests in the guise of burgeoning indus-

trial legislation to the nonmaterial or ideal interests in the "cultivation of moral, intellectual and aesthetic forces" to the political interests secured via the increased regulation of the governmental machinery itself. Under these general categories, Freund arranged his 800-page encyclopedic survey of America's new legislative regulatory state.

But legislative police power not only dramatically expanded its scale and scope in this period, but also began a slow and steady ascent up the levels of American government. As Samuel P. Hays, among other historians, has noted, the period between 1880 and 1920 witnessed a thoroughgoing nationalization and systemization of American social and economic life necessitating a distinctly "upward shift of decision-making" power.[73] Leonard D. White surveyed the extent of such administrative centralization even before the onset of the New Deal in 1933: "The evidence of the last thirty years demonstrates a steady accretion of power and influence by the state governments over the administrative powers of local officials especially in the fields of public finance, education, health and highways, as well as a steady extension of federal influence over the states, particularly in the regulation of commerce."[74] In this respect, perhaps the most important development in the transformation of legislation and police power in this period was the invention of a federal police power—the extraconstitutional centralization of general welfare lawmaking in the United States. In *United States v. Dewitt* (1870), the U.S. Supreme Court adopted the clear antebellum constitutional consensus that the police power was explicitly a state and local rather than a federal power. Echoing Chief Justice Marshall's analysis in *Barron v. Baltimore* refusing to apply the federal Bill of Rights to the individual states, Chief Justice Chase held that though Congress clearly had the authority to regulate interstate commerce, it did not have a general national power to pass regulations of internal state police in the interests of public health, safety, and welfare. The police power remained with the individual states and localities, and the national government wielded nothing analogous to the general plenary authority of state legislatures to regulate liberty and property in the public interest.[75] But, of course, one of the great stories of the period after 1870 was that Congress increasingly secured the power to do precisely that—obtaining a de facto if not de jure national police power through the creative exercise of its commerce, taxing, spending, and postal powers. As Charles Evans Hughes told the American Bar Association in 1918, the most significant decisions of the recent Supreme Court involved "the extended application of the doctrine that federal rules governing interstate commerce may have the quality of police regulations."[76] In the areas of business, labor, transportation, morals, health, safety, and education, powers and issues that were once the exclusive domain of state and local governments moved up into the purview of the national government in one of the most significant expropriations of political power in American history. And as Ernst Freund argued in 1920, the role of law and the judiciary in that expropriation was pivotal: "The consolidation of our own nation has proved our allotment of federal powers to be increasingly inadequate; and had it not been aided by liberal judicial construction, our situation would be unbearable."[77]

One of the most important advocates of such liberal legal construction was Robert E. Cushman, who in a series of influential articles in the *Minnesota Law Review* laid out the progressive quest for a national police power. As Cushman noted, "The enumeration of the congressional powers in the Constitution does not include any general grant of authority to pass laws for the protection of the health, morals, or general welfare of the nation. It follows, then, that if Congress is to exercise a police power at all, it must do so by a process something akin to indirection." Cushman argued that if Congress wanted to expand progressive state police power experiments to the national level in an ambitious program to secure the general welfare, it would have to "cloak its good works under its authority to tax, or to regulate commerce, or to control the mails, or the like, and say, 'By this authority we pass this law in the interest of the public welfare.'"[78] That is exactly what Congress did in passing such important national morals, health, safety, and economic regulations as the Pure Food and Drug Act (1906), the Mann Act (1910), the Harrison Narcotics Tax Act (1914), the Child Labor Tax Act (1919), and the National Prohibition Act (1919). Through the spending power and federal grants-in-aid to the individual states, Congress was able to wield even more national regulatory authority through the incentive power of the public purse.[79] Consequently, the United States achieved a centralization of national legislative police power authority even before the Supreme Court accepted an expansive interpretation of the interstate commerce clause at the height of the New Deal.[80] Indeed, many of the central components of a modern legislative state were well established in the United States by the time Ernst Freund died and Franklin Delano Roosevelt won election to the presidency in the fall of 1932.

Conclusion

Cumulatively, the consequence of these multiple changes in the ideas of law, public good, and legislative regulation during this critical period in modern American state development was a more realistic conception of the state not as an abstract sovereignty or an embodiment of the people but as a modern governmental organization. The regal notion of raison d'etat was replaced by a more democratic and functional raison d'etre rooted in the provision of public services in the interest of the public welfare. The state, power, and rule were no longer formally viewed as ends in themselves, but more pragmatically as modern institutional means to the accomplishment of important public tasks. Any remaining traces of notions of divine right, ancient custom, and supreme command were subsumed beneath a new focus on the public duties, legal obligations, and social functions of the modern state in solving pressing social and economic problems. As Léon Duguit observed, "Government and its officials are no longer the masters of men imposing the sovereign will on their subjects. They are no longer the organs of a corporate person issuing its commands. They are simply the managers of the nation's business."[81]

This modern reorientation of a reorganized government around the provision of public services brought a new primacy to the legislature and a new instrumentality to legislation. Legal positivism, new liberalism, and a newly fortified (and nationalized) conception of legislative police power ushered in the modern era in the development of American legislation. This set of macro changes in the nature and function of legislation set new standards for what legislatures could do and ought to do. And it redefined the relationship of the legislature to other judicial, executive, and administrative institutions as well as to the people at large. Coming to terms with such broad-scale regime change in American governance is essential if social scientists are to fully reckon with the wide range of causes for change and durability with respect to any specific piece of modern American legislation.

PART II

Studying Living Legislation: Coalitions, Durability, and Change

CHAPTER THREE

Durability and Change in the President's Legislative Policy Agenda, 1799–2002

Jeffrey E. Cohen and Matthew Eshbaugh-Soha

In his first State of the Union Address, on January 8, 1964, Lyndon Johnson presented the nation with an ambitious and expansive policy agenda, yet one that was hardly novel or innovative. Rather, Johnson asked the nation to fulfill his predecessor's policy vision: "Let us carry forward the plans and programs of John Fitzgerald Kennedy." Just four years earlier, in contrast, John F. Kennedy argued that it was time to change the policies of his predecessor: "After eight years of drugged and fitful sleep, this nation needs strong, creative Democratic leadership in the White House . . . it's time for a change" (July 15, 1960). Like Kennedy, Ronald Reagan also entered office bent on altering the nation's policy priorities: "It [is] time for a change . . . we've got to go in a different direction" (January 20, 1981). Reagan altered his tune two years later when he urged Congress and the nation "to persevere; to stay the course; to shun retreat; to weather the temporary dislocations and pressures that must inevitably accompany the restoration of national economic, fiscal, and military health" (February 2, 1982).

As these examples illustrate, presidents try but do not always lead the nation in a new policy direction. This chapter looks at durability and change in the president's legislative policy agenda, defining the legislative policy agenda as the president's proposals to Congress for legislation. Our study grows out of a central concern of agenda-setting research:

how issues get onto governmental agendas, in this case the president's. Conceptually we build on this central agenda-setting question, also asking what keeps an issue on the governmental agenda and what leads an issue to fall off of it. More specifically we ask: Why do presidents sometimes try to steer policy in a new direction but at other times prefer to work on issues already on the policy agenda? How stable versus changeable is the president's agenda? What accounts for the degree of durability and change in the president's legislative policy agenda? And how does the agenda-setting stage of the policy process illustrate the dynamic and "living" nature of the legislative process?

Agenda building is a crucial phase in the evolution of legislation. If an issue does not find agenda space, government will not address the issue, and no law will be produced. Presidents are especially influential agenda-shaping actors. As David R. Mayhew observes in his concluding essay, an effort to pass a law, which might lead to the enactment of a new statute, usually begins with some actor's assertion that a problem exists, and presidents are highly influential problem pronouncers. The president's agenda is especially important to legislative development and policy production in the United States for several reasons. First, the president's agenda affects the agendas of Congress, the mass media, and the public.[1] A presidential decision to maintain or change the policy agenda may affect the policy composition of these other agendas. Second, presidential agenda decisions may affect success in Congress. Several studies contend that the president's ability to set the congressional agenda is a major source of the executive's influence in Congress.[2] Understanding how presidents build their agendas may go a long way in helping us understand the sources of presidential influence with Congress.[3] Third, agenda building is substantively important in its own right, providing insight into a consequential presidential decision[4] as well as the operation of the larger political system.[5] Indeed, the decisions presidents make concerning which policies to prioritize and whether to maintain the status quo have significant implications for whether a law will produce a durable policy legacy.

Despite the importance of agenda building, the literature has not produced consensus as to whether the president's agenda tends to be stable. In fact, very few studies even raise the problem of durability and change in the president's agenda.[6] To this end, we analyze a comprehensive data set that categorizes by policy areas all presidential legislative proposals from 1789 through 2002. We offer several hypotheses to account for the degree of durability or change in the president's legislative agenda. Our hypotheses focus on the impact of prior presidential agenda commitments, the size of government, the external environment, and Congress. To foreshadow our results, we find that prior presidential agenda commitments and larger government promote durability, yet limit change in the president's agenda. Although the external environment stimulates change in the presidential agenda, Congress seems to have little direct impact on these aspects of presidential agenda choice. The chapter's conclusion discusses the implications of our findings and suggests directions for future research.

Sources of Durability and Change in the President's Agenda

Previous research provides little guidance either theoretically or empirically on the question of durability and change in the president's legislative agenda. We begin with some assumptions about agendas and presidential decision making, and then offer some hypotheses about factors that may influence durability and change in the president's agenda.

Basic Assumptions about Presidents and Agendas

The size, complexity, and heterogeneity of the United States produce numerous issues seeking governmental attention. To be addressed by policymakers, these issues must achieve governmental agenda status. Finding space on the president's agenda is particularly important because of the president's primary influence as an agenda setter and a policymaker.[7] Presidential agenda space is not unlimited, however, because the political system produces more issues than the president can address. Presidents may expand their agendas to accommodate increased demand for access, but constraints of time, information-processing capability, and finite staff resources limit the president's capacity to accommodate all demands.[8] Consequently, many issues fail to gain access to the president's agenda.

The greater demand for access than agenda space forces presidents to be selective in choosing which issues to include on their policy agendas. Presidents will select those issues that offer the highest net benefits[9] until they have reached the maximum number of issues that they can handle.[10] Four factors may affect the net benefit of issues: prior presidential agenda commitments, size of government, the external environment, and Congress.

Prior Presidential Agenda Commitments

For a variety of reasons, presidents prefer to continue working on issues that they have already placed on their agendas. These reasons include their prior commitment to that policy, their reputation for leadership on these issues, or their policy expertise or interest in an issue. More important, the decision to change the policy agenda, which may require dropping issues from the agenda, reshuffling priorities, reallocating staff and other resources, or acquiring new expertise, is more costly than continuing the established agenda. Presidents reduce each of these decision-making costs by keeping their prior policy agendas in place. For a new issue to displace an old one, its net benefit must be greater than the old issue plus the cost of working on the new issue. At the same time, presidents do not view all issues on their existing agendas equally, but value and prioritize some issues more than others. Once presidents decide to alter the established policy agenda, they are most likely to delete less important and lower priority issues, those with lower net benefits, from their agendas to make room for new issues.

Government Size

As government grows larger, we should see less change and more durability in the president's agenda. The size of government signifies how much government is doing—how many agencies and programs there are for the president to staff, oversee, and evaluate. As Charles O. Jones reminds us, presidents make agenda decisions within the context of the ongoing activities of government, which continue over time. "Normally [the president] chooses from among a set of issues that are familiar because they are continuous. Many of these issues are directly traceable to programs already on the books."[11] This governmental context structures presidential agenda choice. As government grows in size, it generates a larger issue pool that requires presidential attention. The demands of this large pool of issues may tax presidential agenda-building resources, in effect restricting presidents' latitude or discretion in building their agendas. Thus, presidents will have fewer opportunities to alter their agendas, which leads to the hypothesis that the larger the size of government, the less change and more durability we will see in presidential agendas.

The External Environment

Presidents are likely to alter their agendas in response to changes in the external political, international, and economic environments. In other words, we can view agenda building as a representational process.[12] Changes in the political environment include changes in voters' preferences to electoral results. Fear of electoral defeat and loss of public support provide incentives for presidents to change their agendas.[13] Partisan change in the presidency and Congress is often interpreted as public rejection of incumbents and their policies, reflecting changes in the public mood.[14] Such change increases the likelihood of presidents claiming a policy mandate,[15] which will increase the likelihood of change in presidential agendas.

The international environment may stimulate change in the presidential agenda. Since war is the most serious of international events, it provides a best-case test. If wars fail to affect presidents' agendas, other types of international changes are even less likely to do so. We hypothesize that the outbreaks or cessations of wars may stimulate presidents to alter their existing agendas. From a policy perspective, the outbreak of war threatens the survival of the state. As such, it decreases the importance of other policy areas that lack implications for winning the war. The outbreak of war may also affect the public mood by increasing fear within the public and, consequently, pushing the public to look for presidential leadership during wartime. So long as winning the war is the nation's highest priority, presidents will alter their agendas as a result.

Once the war ends, both the policy and public opinion environment may change. Advocates of issues and problems that were set aside during the war may reassert themselves. Moreover, war often restructures society and the economy, altering the relative importance of different groups and economic sectors. Groups that lacked power and access prior to the war may have gained political access and influence during the war, as political leaders mobilized them behind the war effort. Such restructuring produces a different postwar environment. New issues and problems arise out of this environment, and the public mood turns toward building normalcy and a return to prewar issues. For these reasons, the end of war may lead to change in the presidential agenda.

Finally, economic change may affect presidents' agendas, especially when the economy worsens. Economic downturns should increase public pressure on the government to address the economy and relieve the nation's economic distress. Political pressures, such as upcoming elections, as well as popularity and public support provide strong incentives for presidents to appear responsive to these public concerns during bad economic times. Weak economies may affect other presidential programs, for instance, by reducing federal revenues, which may impose budgetary restrictions. A long literature, too voluminous to cite, points out the political implications of the economy. In this spirit, we hypothesize that presidents should alter their agendas in the face of economic change.

Congress and the Presidential Agenda: Expectations for Success

Congress controls whether a policy is enacted into law. It stands to reason, then, that in building their policy agendas presidents will take into account congressional receptivity to their proposals for legislation.[16] Everything else being equal, presidents should be more likely to submit proposals that they estimate have higher chances of enactment.[17] If defeat looks likely, presidents may refrain from submitting their proposals because legislative defeats are costly to presidents' reputation in Congress.[18] Expectations of defeat also incur opportunity costs, such as the presidential time and attention that could be allocated to proposals with higher chances of success. Thus, presidents are more likely to prioritize those that have higher likelihoods of becoming law. As behavior in Congress is also important to the durability and longevity of legislative enactments, pushing some agenda items at opportune times may even add to presidents' historical legacies.[19]

Coupling this observation with legislative gridlock theory generates a hypothesis with respect to change in presidents' legislative agendas.[20] Think of new presidential proposals—those not on the previous presidential legislative policy agendas—as challenges to status quo policies. According to gridlock theory, the only way that status quo policies can be defeated is if they fall outside of the gridlock regions. In general, the wider the gridlock regions, the greater the numbers of status quo policies that fall within them and that cannot be defeated by any alternatives. As such, when gridlock regions expand from one Congress to the next, the number of policies that fall within the gridlock regions also increases. Consequently, the number of status quo policies that can be defeated declines. In contrast, when gridlock regions contract from one Congress to the next, policies that were within the boundaries of the gridlock regions during the first Congress may fall outside of them during the second Congress, and thus may be defeated by new policy alternatives. Hence, we should see greater change in the composition of presidents' agendas when gridlock regions contract, and greater durability when they expand.

The Presidential Legislative Proposal Data Set

Our data provide the first comprehensive accounting of presidential legislative proposals to Congress over the entire sweep of U.S. history, from 1789 through 2002, some 13,800 submissions in all.[21] To assess whether presidents alter or maintain the policy composition of the legislative agendas, we coded each request into one of the seventy Tier 3 issue areas, using the Katznelson-Lapinski policy categorization scheme.[22] Since these data are new, we describe several important characteristics of the president's legislative policy agenda: its size and policy composition.

The Size of the President's Legislative Policy Agenda

Figure 3.1 plots the number of *discrete proposals* that the president submits to the legislature by Congress, while figure 3.2 plots the *number of issue areas* that have appeared on presidential legislative agendas by Congress. Figure 3.1 gives us a sense of the size of the president's legislative agenda, his legislative activism, while figure 3.2 suggests the policy scope of the president's agenda. (The data on figure 3.2 become the foundation for studying durability and change in the president's agenda as outlined above.) Both of these indicators tell a familiar story of increasing presidential legislative activism, albeit with some important modifications and nuance.

Clearly, modern presidents propose more legislation to Congress than their predecessors. The upsurge in presidential legislative proposal activity, however, comes a decade after the onset of the New Deal. Conventional wisdom and theories of the modern presidency would suggest the increase in legislative activity arises during the Roosevelt administration, not afterward.[23] But we find that the takeoff in presidential proposals begins with the transition from the 78th (1943–44) to the 79th (1945–46)

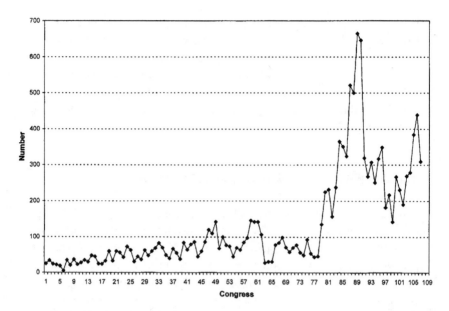

FIGURE 3.1. Number of presidential requests to Congress for legislation, 1st–107th Congresses

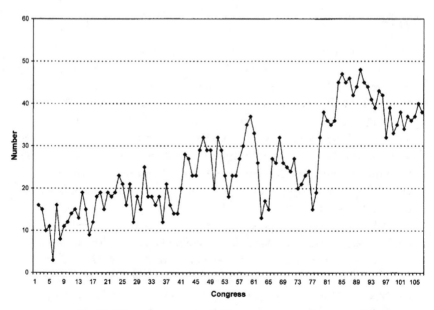

FIGURE 3.2. Number of policy areas in which the president made at least one legislative request to Congress, 1st–107th Congresses

Congresses. And although the number of presidential proposals subsides somewhat after the late 1960s, it rests at a level quite high compared to the levels prior to 1945. Our data correspond well with historical accounts of the development of the presidency in the 1930s and 1940s.[24]

Of course, presidential scholars theorize that the modern presidency begins with FDR.[25] How do we square the data in figure 3.1 with the theory of the modern presidency? First, it is useful to distinguish between substantive policy change associated with the New Deal and the development of the office, which may have begun under FDR but was only realized after his tenure. FDR radically altered the substantive composition of the legislative agenda. The Republican presidents from 1921–32 placed sixteen issue areas in at least five of the six presidential agendas of that period:[26] immigration, executive organization, judicial organization, military organization, diplomacy, international organization, maritime policy, farmers, public works, natural resources, transportation, business, fiscal matters, economic regulation, veterans, and social knowledge. FDR dropped seven of these issue areas, nearly one-half, in his four agendas of 1933–40 (using the standard that the issue area had to appear on at least three of the four agendas). The dropped areas are immigration, judicial organization, military organization, international organization, farmers, veterans, and social knowledge.

FDR also added three issue areas that never appeared consistently on the agendas of his Republican predecessors: labor policy, volunteer employment (like WPA), and social insurance. Circulation of policy areas should occur in realigning periods. We see the stark policy departure of FDR's New Deal from the Republicans' policy emphasis of the 1920s with the removal of nearly one-half of their agenda from consistent placement on FDR's agenda, as well as the addition of labor, volunteer employment, and social insurance as consistent elements on FDR's legislative agenda, issue areas that rarely were on the policy agendas of the 1920s Republicans.

From this perspective, the New Deal represents both a foray into policy areas not previously on the agenda and the elimination of a number of issues from previous presidential agendas. At the same time, FDR's legislative policy agenda does not appear larger than his Republican predecessors either in terms of discrete proposals or policy areas. Historian Adam Cohen argues that after the flurry of legislation passed in Roosevelt's famous first one hundred days, the president had a sense of accomplishing most of his legislative agenda and began sensing congressional resistance to additional legislation.[27] This strategic calculation by FDR also seems to have limited the size of his legislative agenda, measured as the number of proposals. Thus, substantive policy change, not greater presidential legislative leadership in terms of agenda size, characterizes FDR's legislative agenda and the realignment associated with the New Deal. The expansion in leadership associated with the size and scope of the president's legislative agenda comes later, with Truman, and after the conclusion of World War II.

Why the upsurge in presidential proposals in the mid 1940s, almost a decade and a half after FDR took office? First, to submit such a large number of proposals requires adequate staff and institutional resources. The presidency did not acquire these resources until the late 1940s. By the late 1930s, FDR was so administratively overwhelmed that he sought increased staff support, which finally came in 1939 with the creation of the Executive Office of the President. But it was not until the late 1940s that Truman developed legislative clearance processes, which were also necessary for this heightened level of presidential proposal activity.[28]

The Depression and the Second World War may also have depressed the number of presidential proposals when compared with what we see in the late 1940s and thereafter. During the Depression the government may not have possessed the fiscal resources to deal with many issues. The government ran high deficits during most of the Depression years, leaving little slack to deal with issues besides those that comprised the core of the New Deal. With the Second World War, prosperity arrived, but deficits mounted further. Probably as significant, attention so focused on the war that little time or energy was left for dealing with other issues. With the end of the war, we can view the great surge of proposal activity by Truman as a response to pent-up demand to address domestic issues and evidence of the nation's improved financial resources to tackle such issues.

Turning to policy areas as the unit of comparison, on average, presidents make requests in twenty-five policy areas per Congress, with a maximum of forty-eight. Early presidents make requests across a fairly large number of policy areas, too, despite comparatively lower levels of federal government activity and the historical portrait that early presidents were not very active in public policy.[29] During the first four Congresses, for example, Washington made requests in ten to sixteen policy areas. And across the first twenty-five Congresses, only three times have presidents made requests for fewer than ten policy areas.

TABLE 3.1. **Policy domain proportion by Congress, 1789–2002**

Congress	Sovereignty	Government organization	International relations	Domestic policy	Number of requests
1–10	34.69	5.31	42.86	17.14	245
11–20	28.53	5.54	48.20	17.73	361
21–30	25.82	8.48	39.88	25.82	519
31–40	33.33	5.85	44.23	16.59	615
41–50	18.37	10.35	42.09	29.19	860
51–60	17.65	8.99	30.85	42.51	901
61–70	8.78	9.88	35.12	46.23	729
71–80	3.06	9.99	24.68	62.28	851
81–90	6.80	7.60	12.05	73.54	3,999
91–100	2.63	7.29	26.35	63.73	2,619
101–107	3.19	5.28	27.89	63.64	2,101
All	9.72	7.58	26.25	56.45	13,800

Source: Presidential legislative policy agenda database, 1789–2002 (see text).

Although somewhat obscured in the figures, but more apparent from table 3.1, early presidents were more legislatively active than historical accounts portray. Presidents during the nation's first twenty years submitted on average about two dozen proposals per Congress. Each successive set of ten Congresses also reveals a general increase in presidential activity. Table 3.1 suggests that proposal activity proceeds first through an incremental, relatively steady increase in activity for approximately the first seventy-eight Congresses, followed by a surge in activity after World War II to a much higher level that persists to the present. Taking these two figures together, presidents not only increased the volume of discrete proposals that they submit to Congress for legislative consideration, but they did so for an increasingly wider span of policy areas. Historically, presidents have increased their legislative activity across a greater variety of issues.

Substantive Policy Change in the President's Legislative Agenda

Coding each presidential proposal by policy area allows us to address the composition of the president's legislative policy agenda in substantive terms. Over time the substantive mix of the president's agenda has changed. Consistent with the growth in proposals and policy areas as seen in figures 3.1 and 3.2, presidents have added new policy areas to their agendas over time. But some policy areas have also declined in prominence on the president's legislative agenda.

The first several presidents concerned themselves primarily with sovereignty and international relations issues (see table 3.1). Sovereignty issues, which comprised from one-third to one-fourth of the president's legislative agenda during three first forty Congresses, subsequently decline, occupying about one-half as much of the agenda afterward. Securing borders, defining eligibility for citizenship, and establishing the authority of the central government over its territory were vital matters only for the early Republic, while dealing with the Indians and settling the western frontier dominated post–Civil War America. Except for an occasional civil rights matter, sovereignty issues practically vanish from the presidential agenda by the early twentieth century. Unlike sovereignty, government organization almost never appears as a major presidential concern, hovering in the 5 to 10% range, and breaking 10% only once for any ten Congresses. Even at this level, government organization remains a persistent issue over the course of U.S. history.

The founders designed the presidency in part to provide decisive leadership, energy, and dispatch in foreign affairs and defense. Thus, it is no surprise that, since the earliest days, international relations has ranked among the most important policy concerns to the president. For the first one hundred years, international relations occupied on average more of the president's agenda than any other major policy area, commanding approximately one-third of the president's legislative agenda across the first seventy Congresses. Beginning in the late 1920s, international affairs occupies much less of the president's agenda, ranging from 4 to 25%, despite World War II, Korea, Vietnam, and the Cold War. Only during the onset of World War II did the percentage rise to earlier levels, at 36%, the peak until the 96th through 99th Congresses (1979–86), when about 34% of the agenda was devoted to international relations issues.

The ebbing of international relations on the presidential agenda just as the United States was increasing its involvement in world affairs presents a puzzle. The source of the relative decline in attention to international affairs can be found in the rise of domestic issues onto the president's agenda. Defined here, the domestic policy domain is the broadest in terms of the number and variety of topics. Under the Katznelson-Lapinski scheme, domestic policy encompasses agricultural, planning and resources, political economy, and social policy. With such a sweep of concerns, one would expect domestic policy to occupy a significant proportion of any president's agenda. Overall, this is the case, with presidents on average devoting nearly half (45%) of their requests to domestic issues. For only twelve Congresses does domestic policy total less than 20% of the president's agenda.

These data reveal a massive rise in presidential attention to domestic policy beginning in the late 1800s, which continues unabated into the early 2000s. Presidential attention to domestic policies account for not only the increase in the discrete number of presidential requests, but also for the relative decline in attention to international relations. Although the absolute number of nondomestic requests does increase over time, beginning with the 79th Congress, domestic policy concerns overwhelm all other policy areas in sheer quantity. Furthermore, one area of domestic policy—social policy—accounts for the bulk of increased presidential attention to domestic policy. In the post–World War II era, with from two-thirds to three-quarters of presidential proposals concerning domestic policy, it would not be too farfetched to call the modern presidency a domestic presidency—in fact, a social policy presidency.

This modern, domestic policy presidency also occurs coincident to the rise of the United States as a global power and the Cold War, which would rage for the next forty years. One might think that these international tensions would reduce presidential attention to domestic policy, at least relative to international matters. But this seems not to be the case. Several possibilities might explain the rise of presidential attention to domestic policy, especially social policy, in the post–World War II era. First, presidents may have been pursuing a type of "guns and butter" strategy, offering the public domestic policies in exchange for their support of presidents' international policies. Alternatively, presidents may have found greater unilateral power to dictate foreign policy and thus rarely needed to turn to Congress for foreign policy authority. In effect, the means for making presidential policy is specialized, with unilateral powers used to further foreign and international policy goals, and the legislative route used for domestic policy goals. Future research is necessary to sort through these alternatives.

Measuring Durability and Change in the President's Agenda

Durability and change are often seen as mirror-image concepts and measures: as durability increases, change decreases, and vice versa. However, presidential agendas exhibit two types of change, the deletion of old issues and the addition of new ones; these processes may occur independently of each other. Change too may be independent of durability as presidents may retain a large number of old items (durability) but add many new items (change). Thus, we need separate indicators of durability and change.

Conceptually and operationally, durability is relatively straightforward. Conceptually, the agenda is stable if the president retains issue areas from the first Congress of a pair of Congresses to the second Congress of the pair. However, we also need to take into account the size of the previous year's agenda in measuring durability. When the previous agenda is large, numerous issues may be carried over, yet the rate of carryover may be small. When the previous agenda is small, only a small number of issues can be carried over, even if the rate of carryover is high. For instance, consider two cases, one in which there are twenty issues on the previous agenda and a second case with ten. Suppose in the first case, twelve issue areas are retained, compared to ten for the second case. If we compare the raw count of retained issue areas, the first appears more stable (12 vs. 10), but the rate of carryover is much higher in the second than the first case (100% vs. 60%). Given that the size of the agenda can vary and presidents can expand (or contract) their agendas to some degree, the rate of carryover is the more meaningful measure of durability. Formally, we define durability as:

$$100 * (Number\ of\ Retained\ Issue\ Areas\ Congress_{t2}/$$
$$Number\ of\ Issue\ Areas\ Congress_{t1})$$

where t_1 signifies the first Congress of each pair of successive Congresses and t_2 the second. We multiply this ratio by 100 to produce percentages. Figure 3.3 plots this series.

Measuring change requires accounting for both deletions and additions of issue areas across pairs of Congresses. Formally, we define change as:

$$100 * \{(Number\ of\ Issue\ Area\ Additions + Number\ of\ Issue\ Area$$
$$Deletions)/\ (Number\ of\ Issue\ Areas\ Retained\ from\ Congress\ t_1)\}$$

Presidents do not merely replace deleted issue areas with new ones, but exhibit a slightly greater propensity to add new issue areas rather than delete existing ones, which accounts for the growth in the size of the president's agenda over time.[30] Like durability, the size of the presi-

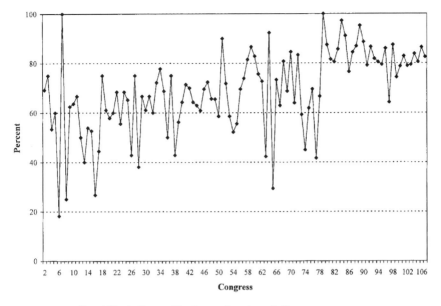

FIGURE 3.3. Durability in the president's agenda, 1st–107th Congresses

dent's agenda can affect the degree of change. As the president's agenda has grown, opportunities to add, delete, or retain issue areas have also increased, so we control for agenda size. For the ratio's base, we cannot use the size of either the past or current agendas because each contains either deletions and/or additions. Thus, we use the number of retentions. We multiply this ratio by 100 to produce a percentage, plotted in figure 3.4.

The two measures of presidential agenda dynamics, durability and change, as expected, correlate strongly but not perfectly ($r = -.80, p = .000$), confirming that the more stable the president's agenda, the less change, and vice versa. While strongly related, durability and change, as defined here, are not perfect substitutes for each other.

Independent Variable

Prior Presidential Agenda Commitments

Comparing the amount of attention that presidents pay to a range of issues indicates the relative importance and priority of issues to presidents,

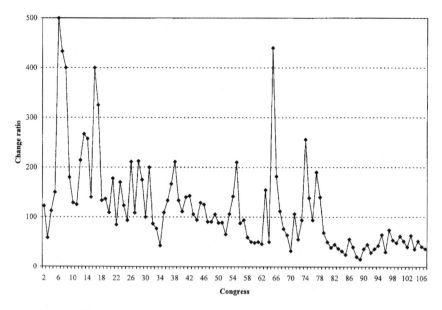

FIGURE 3.4. Change in the president's agenda, 1st–107th Congresses

such that issue areas that receive more attention are of greater importance and priority to presidents than issues receiving less attention. We
measure relative presidential attention to issue areas with a Gini coefficient of inequality, lagged one Congress. This coefficient uses the number of specific legislative requests for each issue area during a particular
Congress, which we compare across all issue areas on the president's legislative agenda. High Gini coefficients (maximum 1.0) indicate inequality in presidential attention across issues. The Gini coefficients for these
data range from .65 to .98, with a mean of .82. This suggests that presidents tend to concentrate their attention on a subset of issue areas. Hypothetically, a lower Gini coefficient should be associated with slower
rates of change and greater durability in the president's agenda.

Size of Government

The size of government should be positively related to durability and in-
versely related to change. To measure the size of government, we use federal revenues as a percentage of gross domestic product (GDP) per Congress.[31] Hypothetically, a high ratio of federal revenue to GDP should

be associated with a high level of agenda durability and a low rate of change.

The External Environment

We hypothesize that change in the political, international, and economic environments may affect agenda change. We measure change in the political environment as a dummy variable for partisan change in the presidency: 1 for change and 0 for no change in the president's party.[32] Party change in the presidency may lead to either policy change or durability. On the one hand, an issue ownership perspective suggests that alternations in the party occupying the White House will lead to changes in the legislative agenda.[33] Issue ownership theory predicts that a candidate for election will emphasize issues that their party holds a public-opinion advantage over their opponents. For instance, the Republican Party has a reputation for competence on foreign and defense policy in the post-Vietnam era. The public does not view the Democrats as being as competent on this issue. Thus, a Republican candidate should benefit by emphasizing this issue area in a campaign. The theory of issue ownership suggests a hypothesis, that changes in the party in the White House will be associated with a change in the president's legislative agenda. On the other hand, Tracy Sulkin's issue uptake concept leads to the alternative dynamic, greater durability.[34] Sulkin argues that once elected, incumbents will adopt some of the issues of their opponents to fend off future competitors and to strengthen their positions among voters. In contrast to the issue ownership hypothesis, the issue uptake perspective predicts that party change in the White House will covary not with agenda change, but with durability.

As to the international environment, we focus on the onset or conclusion of major wars with two dummy variables, 1 if war begins during the Congress and 0 for other Congresses, and 1 if the war ended during a Congress and 0 for other Congresses, for the war end variable.[35] Finally, to take advantage of the historical sweep of our presidential request data, we select the only two economic indicators available for early U.S. history, inflation and interest rates.[36] Inflation and interest rates, although broad indicators of the state of the economy, may differentially affect various sectors of the economy. The inflation rate affects consumers most heavily, although inflation may also influence investors' decisions. Interest rates, in contrast, initially affect debtors and those seeking credit. High interest rates will often lead to an economic slowdown. We hypothesize that both should lead to greater change and less durability, measured as the annual value for the first year of a Congress.[37]

Congress and the Gridlock Region

We hypothesize that expansion in the gridlock region should reduce the incentives for presidents to push for new issues, while contraction opens the possibility that new policy proposals can displace status quo policies. Thus, gridlock expansion should be associated with agenda durability and gridlock contraction with agenda change. The filibuster and veto pivots define the gridlock region.[38] Calculating the gridlock region is problematical because the filibuster was only established in the Senate in 1917 (65th Congress), when a two-thirds vote was require to invoke cloture. In 1975 (94th Congress), the Senate reduced the number of votes needed to invoke cloture to three-fifths.

Although Heitshusen and Young suggest several ways to estimate the gridlock region in the prefilibuster time period, we follow Wawro and Schickler, who show that prefilibuster the gridlock region spans from the median member to the veto pivot.[39] We use Poole and Rosenthal's DW-NOMINATE scores to identify the placement of each senator for the 1st through 107th Congresses and thus the veto and filibuster pivots. We also include a dummy variable, coded 0 for the 1st through 64th Congresses to denote the prefilibuster era and 1 for the 65th through 107th Congresses.

Findings

Time-series analysis requires careful consideration of issues such as nonstationarity and autocorrelation, which if left uncorrected may lead to false casual inferences. Diagnostics of the durability and change series indicate that both are stationary,[40] but each also exhibited autocorrelation, which Box-Jenkins series procedures identify as AR1 MA1.[41] Table 3.2 presents the results of the estimations for both series, providing both a full model, which includes all variables, and a reduced-form model, which includes only statistically significant variables. Our discussion focuses on the reduced-form models.

TABLE 3.2. **Determinants of durability and change in the president's agenda**

Independent variables		Agenda durability			Agenda change	
		Full model	Reduced model		Full model	Reduced model
New party	[−]	1.41 (3.07)		[+]	4.91 (13.24)	
War start	[−]	−5.86		[+]	49.42***	57.88*
		(4.60)			(20.19)	(28.83)
War end	[−]	−3.65		[+]	25.68	
		(4.71)			(20.55)	
Gini t-1	[−]	−32.67	−33.86*	[+]	367.77***	372.55***
		(21.93)	(21.14)		(125.81)	(115.44)
Inflation	[−]	−.31	−.47***	[+]	2.68***	3.27*
		(.22)	(.20)		(2.57)	(1.45)
Interest rate	[−]	−1.50***	−1.26**	[+]	3.57	
		(.65)	(.62)		(4.42)	
Federal revenue	[+]	1.59***	1.38***	[−]	−7.28***	−3.94*
		(.34)	(.27)		(2.28)	(.88)
Gridlock change	[+]	−14.44**		[−]	71.89**	
		(8.54)			(36.29)	
Filibuster	[?]	−3.28		[?]	49.09	
		(4.02)			(29.35)	
AR(1)		−.67***	−.69***		.64***	.62***
		(.12)	(.12)		(.09)	(.13)
MA(1)		.59***	.58***		−.42***	−.43***
		(.16)	(.16)		(.14)	(.17)
Constant		94.58***	94.05***		−90.65**	−176.99**
		(18.63)	(17.99)		(108.25)	(91.44)
R-squared		.53	.49		.65	.61
LM χ² (5 lags)		4.06	4.38		4.88	6.53
White's χ²		43.10	13.64		39.30	n/a
N		102	102		102	102

* $p < .1$ (one-tailed test); ** $p < .05$ (one-tailed test); *** $p < .01$ (one-tailed test)
Note: Standard errors are in parentheses. White Heteroskedasticity-Consistent standard errors in parentheses for the reduced agenda change

Factors Affecting Agenda Durability

Four variables significantly affect durability in the president's agenda: the lagged Gini coefficient, representing presidential preferences; federal revenue as a percentage of GDP, representing the size of government; plus interest and inflation rates, which measure change in the external environment. The gridlock change variable is statistically significant at conventional levels ($p < .05$), but points in the wrong direction. Thus, we drop it from the reduced-form estimation.

As hypothesized, equality of presidential attention across issue areas promotes agenda durability. Results indicate about 33.9% greater durability in the president's agenda when the Gini coefficient takes on its minimum value (0.0), compared to its theoretical maximum (1.0). The Gini coefficient, however, only ranges from .65 to .98. Moving from the actual maximum to minimum produces an 11.2% increase in durability. To put this finding into perspective, recall that durability ranges from 18.2 to 100%, averaging 82%, with a standard deviation of .08. Presidential preferences account for a substantively significant fraction of durability in the president's agenda.

As federal revenues grow, the president's agenda also exhibits increased durability, consistent with our hypothesis. Each 1% change in federal revenues as a percentage of GDP realizes a 1.4% increase in agenda durability. Comparing the effect from moving from the minimum to maximum level (.55 vs. 20.2) sees a 27.5% increase in agenda durability. Growth in the size of the federal establishment, an indicator of the strength of the existing national policy regime, has major implications for durability in the president's agenda. Historically, this means that modern presidential agendas, everything else being equal, will exhibit greater durability than those of earlier periods.

Two environmental factors lessen durability. Each 1% change in the inflation rate converts into nearly a .5% decline in durability. On average, inflation changes at a 1.5% rate, which leads to a small decline in durability of only about .75%. Around this average, inflation can swing much higher or lower, as the standard deviation of 5.8 indicates. A one standard deviation change in inflation thus reduces durability by about 2.9%. However, inflation topped 10%, lessening durability by 5% or more several times since World War II (1947, 1979, and 1981).

Like inflation, interest rates reduce durability in the president's agenda, but with greater force. Each one percentage point change in interest rates converts to a 1.3% reduction in durability. Interest rates seem to vary less than inflation, with a smaller standard deviation of 2.1%. A one standard deviation increase in interest rates will dampen durability by about 2.7%. Although change in interest rates from year to year tends to be small, on occasion it surges, as it did between the 96th (1979–80) and 97th Congresses (1981–82), when it grew nearly 5%. At this rate of change, the president's agenda of the 97th Congress will demonstrate about 6.5% less durability than the previous 96th Congress.

Normal changes in inflation and interest rates hardly affect durability in the president's agenda. But on occasion, either of the economic indicators may rise substantially, and once in a while they will both grow to high levels at the same time. Notably, Ronald Reagan came to office in a year of high inflation (10.4%) and interest rates (14.2%), which may in part account for the Reagan Revolution, his redirection of the nation's policy agenda.

Factors Affecting Agenda Change

Agenda change varies more than agenda durability, ranging from 15 to 500% (mean = 118%, standard deviation = 95.6). Three of the variables that affect durability also affect change—the Gini coefficient, federal revenue, and inflation—while the onset of war also significantly affects agenda change. Repeating the finding for durability, the gridlock variable is statistically significant at conventional levels, but possesses the wrong sign. Again, we drop it from the reduced-form estimation.

The Gini coefficient, which measures equality of presidential attention to issues, also affects agenda change in mirror image to its impact on durability. Comparing the lowest and highest values on this variable (.65 to .98) suggests a 123% difference in the rate of agenda change. A one standard deviation increase in the Gini coefficient (.08) results in about a 30% increase in the rate of agenda change. Large government, federal revenues as a percentage of GDP, also dampens change in the president's agenda. For example, years of maximum revenues (20.2) will lower agenda change by about 77% compared to years of minimum revenues (.55). Maximum revenue years will dampen change by 50% compared to average years (7.3). In contrast, as hypothesized, inflation stimulates agenda change. Each 1% increment in inflation produces a 3.3% increase in agenda change. Thus, a year of average inflation (1.5%) will have about 28% less change in the president's agenda than a year of 10% inflation. The onset of war also disrupts the agenda, changing the agenda by about 58% during the Congress in which war starts.[42]

Discussion and Conclusion

In building their legislative agendas, presidents must decide whether to continue working on issues already on their agendas or to turn their attention to new issues. Our study of durability and change in the president's agenda contributes to our understanding of presidential decision making and agenda building, but also raises some new questions.

First, we find several factors—the size of government, previous presidential attention to an issue area (Gini coefficient), the state of the economy, and, in some circumstances, war—*systematically* affect durability and change in presidents' agendas. The presidential agenda appears quite responsive to these factors, resembling Charles O. Jones's insight that presidents have little discretion in building their legislative agendas. Much of presidents' legislative agendas is handed to them, coming in particular from the ongoing activities of government.[43] The apparent lack of presidential discretion in legislative agenda building also bears on the debate in the literature between *president* and *presidency* theoretical perspectives, the results reported here lining up more with the latter than the former perspectives.[44]

Still, the impact of prior presidential attention on durability and change in the agenda opens a door for president effects and presidential discretion in agenda building. To make such an argument, however, requires that we identify why presidents concentrate their attention on some issue areas as opposed to others. Some of this may come from the election campaign, the promises made in the campaign to attract groups of voters. But presidential talents, skills, backgrounds, and personal preferences may lead them to focus their attention and energies on some policy areas but not others. We need more research into these *pre-presidential* processes to understand how presidents come to concentrate on some issues rather than others.

Continuing these themes, the findings reported above have important implications for our understanding of the evolution of the presidency into its modern form. Political institutions can evolve incrementally, but sometimes they undergo remarkable change in a short period of time. The theory of the modern presidency suggests a sudden transformation of the office.[45] Our results lend some support to that understanding of the presidency but with important modifications. First, both the total number of discrete proposals and the number of issue areas on the president's agenda incrementally grow from the office's earliest days, but we see a sudden surge in both in the late 1940s. FDR is usually credited with being the first modern president. But at least with regard to legislative proposals, the regime transformation from the tradition to the modern presidency occurred a decade or more after FDR assumed the office, and almost all of this increased legislative activism in the social policy area.

Second, studies like ours are good at exploring the statistical relationships among variables, but less helpful in isolating the causal factor(s) that lead to sudden breaks or transitions when they occur. Above we suggested some elements of that casual story: changing system expectations for presidential legislative leadership, the need for staff resources to allow for greater presidential leadership, and the impact of the Depression and Second World War on the size and composition of the policy agenda. But we still need to learn how the bones of this story causally connect. Did increased staffing allow for the higher number of presidential proposals, or did presidents enlarge their staffs because they wanted to increase their legislative leadership potential? And why did so much of this increased leadership focus on social policy, especially in a time when the United States emerged as the leading international power?

Finally, we found that Congress has little impact on the degree of durability or change in the president's agenda. Perhaps presidents look to Congress more when deciding on the substantive details of their policy proposals, rather than on which policies to focus their attention on. In addition, the president and Congress may respond alike to the structural factors identified in this study, leading both institutions to produce similar substantive agendas. We cannot say for certain whether Congress has no impact on presidential agenda-building decisions because our study does not incorporate all potential aspects of presidential-congressional relations. For instance, we do not model the impact that presidential success in Congress has on the decision to continue working on an issue area or move on to another. Just as legislative enactment of a presidential proposal may lead a president to cease efforts in that policy area and work on another, such success may instead lead presidents to pursue more legislation in the same issue area.

Whether legislative success leads to agenda durability or change may depend on how much of the presidents' proposals Congress adopts into law. Almost universally, presidents receive somewhat less than they ask for when Congress enacts legislation on their policy proposals.[46] But does that "success increment" satisfy the White House? Do presidents think that they can receive more from Congress by proposing additional legislation on the issue at hand, or do they conclude that they have received as much as Congress is willing to enact on the topic? Furthermore, might congressional defeat or inaction lead presidents to move onto other policy areas that they think have better prospects for enactment? And, reviving Jones's insight about the impact of ongoing government activities, might the enactment of legislation keep policy areas on presidents' agendas as issues of implementation, bureaucratic organization, policy reforms, and the like continue to required presidential attention? Answering these questions is well beyond the scope of this chapter, but we encourage others to build on our findings concerning policy durability and change in presidential legislative policy agendas to do so.

CHAPTER FOUR

Coalition Structure and Legislative Innovation in American National Government

Sean Gailmard and Jeffery A. Jenkins

A merican political institutions parcel out the power to initiate as well as block policy changes among a multitude of actors. Separation of powers and bicameralism are two crucial and constitutionally specified power divisions. Internal rules of each chamber of Congress add more veto players. Yet despite this profusion of veto points, actors do find enough common ground to pass several major new policy innovations through the legislative process in almost every session of Congress.

Analysts of the political determinants of policy innovation in the legislative process have focused extensively on the effect of ideological harmony among various institutional actors in the form of unified government. Typically, empirical analysis of this question treats instances of divided government alike and instances of unified government alike. Yet it is not clear that coalition structures fall into these broad equivalence classes. A coalition with fixed preferences may be able to effect major policy changes when it first obtains power, if the policies on which it can agree are very different from policies either enacted or left in place by predecessor coalitions. As the coalition acts on these possibilities for

An earlier version of this chapter was presented at the 65th Annual Meeting of the Midwest Political Science Association, Chicago, IL, April 12–15, 2007. We thank Chris Den Hartog and William Howell for thoughtful comments. Jenkins thanks the Bankard Fund for Political Economy at the University of Virginia and the Dirksen Congressional Center for grants in support of this project.

major innovation, it may move policy closer and closer to a "core point" given the ideological makeup of the coalition, a point from which no further major policy changes or movement is possible.

In this chapter, we explore the effects of coalition structure on major policy innovations in the legislative process, with a special focus on a coalition's "freshness" as well as its ideological composition. We use retrospective evaluations of major legislation that have not been used before in the literature as a stand-alone measure of policy innovation. We statistically model enactments of major legislation as a function of coalition structure and other control variables. We then disaggregate major legislation into types—(1) foundational acts that create policy out of whole cloth, (2) major acts that amend prior major acts, and (3) major acts that repeal (or kill) prior major acts—and estimate models on them separately.

Our results indicate that duration in power for a unified governing coalition significantly reduces enactments of major legislation in a Congress. Conditional on coalition duration, unified party control of both chambers of Congress and the presidency significantly increases enactments of major legislation. These findings apply to a restricted data set from 1969 to 2001, and also in a data set aggregating all Congresses seated from 1789 to 2001. Overall, it takes about twelve continuous years in power for the negative effect of time in power for a unified coalition to equal the negative effect of divided government, all else constant. Similarly, time in power significantly reduces the prospects for amending major legislation—a finding that is increasingly important, since (as we note below) more and more major acts are themselves amendments of previous major acts. On the other hand, the duration since a unified coalition last controlled the House, Senate, and White House is not significantly related to either the passage of foundational acts or the amendment of prior major acts, but it is significantly related to the repeal of previously enacted major legislation. Overall, if passage and amendment are taken as "constructive" legislative activity, unified coalitions tend to be less constructive as they age, while they tend to be more "destructive" of previous acts the longer they have been out of power.

Coalition Structure and Legislative Activity

A hallmark of separation of powers as well as checks and balances is that for legislative initiatives to succeed, coalitions must reach across institutions. Naturally scholars have explored how ideological agreement across institutions affects legislative activity or "output." Generally this literature has focused on divided versus unified government, following David Mayhew's initial landmark study.[1] And while scholars have not all reached the same conclusion about whether unified government matters,[2] clearly Mayhew has raised critical questions about any conventional wisdom that divided government reduces major policy innovation through legislative channels.

Although divided government, or more generally ideological disagreement, is a natural suspect to reduce policy innovation, it is not obvious that it should have any effect. There are many bargaining models in which delay in reaching agreement is inefficient and does not occur in equilibrium regardless of how strongly actors' interests are opposed.[3] Thus, ideological conflict might change the content of policy but not affect the prospects for changing it from a status quo. On the other hand, in spatial models with supermajority requirements, increasing the diversity (and therefore conflict) of preferences among institutional actors expands the core and diminishes prospects for policy change.[4] Therefore, whether unified government affects policy innovation through the legislative process clearly depends on the nature of the policy choice.

It is equally clear that not all occurrences of unified government, or any given coalition structure, are from a homogenous class. For example, the three most recent two-term presidents have spent the final two years of their second terms mired in scandals or controversies rather than advancing major new policies. While scandals arising for independent reasons may damage presidents' "political capital" and make significant new policy initiatives more difficult, it is also possible that indiscretions and distractions in the executive branch garner relatively more attention late in a second term because, simply put, the governing coalition has run out of ideas for new policies that can command sufficient agreement to pass the gauntlet of vetoes in the lawmaking process. Indeed, in the Iran-Contra case from the Reagan era, the administration's inability to find policy alternatives that could win approval through normal lawmaking channels is exactly what induced politically insulated White House staffers to push them through illegal channels. Clearly, if passing major policy changes becomes more difficult for a coalition as it ages, there are important implications not just for policy change but for the stability of institutional arrangements themselves.

In the context of policy stasis or "gridlock," this argument about the effect of coalition age on policymaking is clearly explicated by Keith Krehbiel.[5] In the pivotal politics model, a governing coalition moves policy to the point in the "gridlock interval" most preferred by the proposer (the median voter in Congress given a one-dimensional policy space) at its earliest opportunity. Policy, by definition, cannot be changed further for a given constellation of preferences. Therefore, as long as the enacting coalition remains in power, no further policy movement is possible. The implication is clear: Major policy shifts happen early in the lifetime of a coalition covering the House of Representatives, Senate, and president, and taper off later in the lifetime of that coalition.

Another source of difference among instances of unified government is how long a newly unified coalition had been out of power. For parties long shut out of simultaneous majority status across lawmaking institutions, it is possible that ideological demands become "pent up," resulting in a deluge of new policy initiatives when the party finally holds a unified coalition. On the other hand, a new unified coalition that had been in the opposition for only a short time since it most recently held a unified coalition may not have had much time to develop demands for major new legislation. This argument is made cogently by Sarah Binder, who finds empirical evidence in support of it.[6]

The common theme in all these theoretical arguments is that coalition structure—the ideological makeup and duration in and out of power—affects coalition activity. Yet no analysis of legislative activity has addressed these arguments together. Indeed, the time-in-power argument has never been the focus of sustained empirical exploration in the literature. In our analysis, we examine these arguments simultaneously, so that associations among the explanatory variables cannot undermine the estimated relationship between any one of them and legislative activity. Moreover, we perform this analysis with a previously unused measure of major legislative activity, which is important for the literature because no one measure has ideal properties of construct validity, and over a longer time span than has been analyzed by scholars thus far.

Measurement of Significant Legislation and Coalition Structure

To explore the relationships discussed above between coalition structure and legislative innovation, we use retrospective evaluations of legislative significance ("major acts") as compiled by Stephen W. Stathis of the Congressional Research Service.[7] This measure has several useful features for the questions we address. First, it applies a common evaluation metric to *each* Congress from the 1st (1789–91) through the 107th (2001–2). Thus, it allows us not only to analyze relationships over a longer time horizon than all previous treatments in the literature, but to do so without mixing sources. Second, this measure is readily available: Each major act is listed and discussed in a single publication. Third, the measure is readily interpretable because it is simply a tally of significant acts.[8]

In addition to its own unique benefits, it is useful for the literature to have arguments tested on related but different measures of legislative activity than have been used in prior work. The reason is because no one measure ideally captures the concept of "major legislation," an issue in research design sometimes referred to as construct validity.[9] Since no one operationalization of the concept is uniquely best, building a set of findings on one measure risks creating a dependence on the idiosyncrasies of a single operationalization rather than the concept itself. On the other hand, when a finding emerges from analyses of several different operationalizations of a single concept, it suggests that the finding is tapping into something about the concept itself. The Stathis measure we use has been a component of other analyses in the literature.[10] These analyses have typically combined the Stathis data with other sources that do not stretch as far back in time, so generally only part of the Stathis data series has been used in analysis of coalition structure and significant legislation.[11]

We score government as unified in a Congress if each chamber of Congress and the presidency is controlled by the same party, and divided otherwise. A unified coalition is either new or continuing. A new unified coalition occurs in any Congress with unified government, and with divided government or a unified coalition of a different party in the previous Congress. A continuing unified coalition occurs in any Congress in which government is unified, and was unified under control of the same parties in the previous Congress.

The time out of power for a new unified coalition is the number of Congresses since that same party held its previous unified coalition. For a party experiencing its first unified coalition (e.g., the GOP in 1861), time out of power is dated from the founding of the party (1854 in the case of the GOP). Time out of power is 0 for Congresses with divided coalitions or with continuing unified coalitions.

The time in power for a continuing unified coalition is the number of consecutive Congresses for which the party in power has maintained a unified coalition, starting at 1 for a new unified coalition. For divided coalitions, time in power is 0.

We also score each Congress with a dummy for the "party system" in which it falls.[12] Congresses seated in 1789 to 1823 are part of the first party system (Federalist and Democratic-Republican); 1825 to 1853 are part of the second (Democrat and National Republican/Whig); 1855 to 1895 are part of the third (Republican and Democrat I); 1897 to 1931 are part of the fourth (Republican and Democrat II); and 1933 to 2001 are part of the fifth (Republican and Democrat III). The fifth party system is further subdivided into one part from 1933 to 1967 (New Deal Democrat), and another from 1969 to 2001 (resurgent Republicans).[13]

Analysis

The major-acts data series, from the 1st through 107th Congresses, appears in figure 4.1. On average about 10.3 major acts are passed each Congress. The distribution is right-skewed with a standard deviation of about 6.6 and a range of 1 (both Congresses for Quincy Adams, one Con-

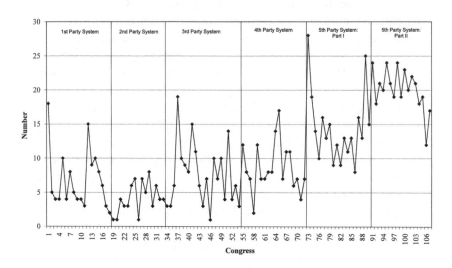

FIGURE 4.1. Major acts of Congress, 1st–107th Congresses
Source: Stephen W. Stathis, *Landmark Legislation, 1774–2002* (Washington, DC: CQ Press, 2002). Treaties not included.

gress each for Van Buren and Hayes) to 28 (FDR in 1933). The measure
is strongly trended over time; a bivariate regression of major acts on a linear time trend yields an R^2 of .47 (and a coefficient of .15). Nevertheless,
Dickey-Fuller and Phillips-Perron tests strongly reject the null hypothesis of a unit root in the time series, even without a time trend. Therefore,
while our models typically do include a time trend as a control (especially because divided government, like major legislation, trends upward
over time), we set aside issues of stationarity or trend-stationarity of the
time series.

Main Results

Our first model is in the first column of numbers in table 4.1. It specifies major acts as a function of coalition structure and control variables
for each Congress from 1st to 107th in which the largest party in both
chambers held a strict majority of seats, as opposed to a mere plurality
less than 50%. The three coalition structure variables are unified government, time in power for unified coalitions, and time out of power for
unified coalitions. The model also includes a time trend, and indicator
variables for the party system in which a Congress falls.[14] Because un-
modeled factors that make a given Congress especially innovative may
persist for more than one Congress, serial correlation of the error term
is a potential concern. Our baseline estimates are from an ordinary least
squares (OLS) model[15] with Newey-West standard errors. These standard errors are correct in the presence of first order serial correlation
(and arbitrary heteroskedasticity if present).[16]

Our main new finding of theoretical importance is that unified coalitions become less productive of major policy innovations as they age.
Time in power for a continuing unified coalition has a negative and
strongly significant effect on major legislative enactments in Congress:
One extra Congress in power for a continuing unified coalition results
in about .68 fewer major acts in that Congress, or about one-tenth of the
standard deviation of the dependent variable. This supports the argument that unified coalitions gradually work through the available major
policy changes as they age, but in the course of making major changes to
more and more policy issues, they exhaust their stock of feasible agreements. This is, in essence, the argument advanced by Krehbiel.[17]

The results also reveal a positive, strong, and significant effect of
unified government. Unified government results in about 4.3 more ma-

TABLE 4.1. **Regression results, major acts, and coalition structure**

Explanatory variable	Model 1 1789–2001	Model 2 1969–2001	Model 3 1789–1967
Unified government	4.31*** (1.05)	5.28*** (.68)	4.87*** (1.22)
Time in power for unified coalition	−.68*** (.19)	−2.50*** (.29)	−.43** (.20)
Time out of power for unified coalition	−.07 (.13)	−.02 (.09)	.05 (.28)
Indicator, party system 1 1789–1823	2.31 (6.93)		−10.08 (8.74)
Indicator, party system 2 1825–53	−4.04 (5.67)		−12.17* (6.79)
Indicator, party system 3 1855–95	−2.76 (4.21)		−7.42 (4.65)
Indicator, party system 4 1897–1931	−5.20* (2.92)		−7.23** (3.06)
Time trend	.16* (.08)	−.30 (.18)	−.03 (.12)
Constant	2.33 (7.72)	49.84** (17.15)	14.82 (9.59)
F statistic (No. obs.)[1]	34.43*** (94)	4581.30*** (17)	10.54*** (77)

Note: Each column is a separate model of major legislation. Entries are OLS estimates with Newey-West standard errors in parentheses.
* denotes significance at α = .10 or less; ** at .05 or less; *** at .01 or less
[1] N in the overall model is 94 rather than 107 because we exclude the thirteen Congresses in which the largest party in some chamber held a plurality but not a majority of seats.

jor acts per Congress, all else constant. This is about two-thirds of a standard deviation of the dependent variable. Thus, ideological disagreement among institutional actors as proxied by partisan divisions impedes the development and passage of major legislation, at least with this retrospective measure over the whole time span since 1789. This is consistent with the conjecture that policymaking entails the sorts of conflicts captured in spatial models rather than distributive bargaining models, or at least bargaining models without delay in equilibrium. More specifically, like the time-in-power result, this result is consistent with the pivotal politics model, insofar as divided government captures one aspect of the "gridlock zone" in that model. Specifically, and especially in any cases in which the president's ideal point is closer to the median in Congress than the veto pivot's ideal point is, as divided government rises the width of the gridlock zone rises. For a status quo in this region, policy cannot be changed in equilibrium by definition, and as the gridlock zone widens the status quo is generally more likely to fall within it.

All the results above are for the entire range of Congresses from 1st to 107th. Thus, it might be argued that the findings uncovered above might apply to an earlier era, but that changes in the political process (e.g., apparent weakening of party control over presidential nominations) have rendered them inapplicable to contemporary politics. In other words, the results above might simply be a mix of an earlier period in which the conclusions hold true, and a contemporary period in which they do not. To explore this, we estimated the model on the restricted time period from 1969 to 2001 (Congresses from 91st to 107th). We chose this period to mark the "current" political era because the Republican Party's resurgence began at this time and the power of the New Deal coalition, having made its strongest stands in economic and social policy, had begun to wane. The mean number of major acts by Congress in this period is more than 20, almost twice as large as for the whole time series, and the standard deviation is about 3, less than half as large as for the whole series. The results are in the second column of numbers in table 4.1.

Any differences between these results and results for the whole time series would suggest that the principal effects of coalition structure identified above have intensified. Unified government is still significant and positive, and time in power is still significant and negative. Because the standard deviation of major acts is smaller, the coefficients suggest an even larger impact in substantive terms. Unified government increases occurrence of major acts by about 1.75 standard deviations, and a single extra Congress in power for a unified coalition reduces major enactments by about four-fifths of a standard deviation. Moreover, in this political era, it takes only a little more than two Congresses for the negative effect of time in power to outweigh the positive effect of unified government. In other words, reelecting the president in a unified coalition reduces enactment of major legislation by more than electing a president of the opposite party.

Similarly, we also estimated the model for the restricted time series from 1789 to 1967 (Congresses from 1st to 90th). The mean number of major acts by Congress in this period is 8.4 and the standard deviation is about 5.3. The model results are in the last column of table 4.1. They are similar to the results from the whole time series, both for substantive effects and statistical significance. Unified government is positive and significant, and the marginal effect is more than nine-tenths of a standard deviation. Time in power is negative and significant, and the marginal effect is about one-twelfth of a standard deviation. In this time period, however, it would take more than eleven Congresses for the negative effect of time in power to outweigh the positive effect of unified government. The only occasion in U.S. history when a unified coalition served for so many Congresses was the Era of Good Feelings at the end of the first party system.

The results have interesting implications for the political determinants of major policy innovation. Aggregating over most all of American history since 1789, relatively young unified coalitions of Congress and the president tend to be the most innovative, at least in working through the legislative process. The creativity of unified coalitions tends to decay over time: After about six Congresses (twelve years), the negative effect of time in power on major acts about equals the positive effect of unified government. Thus, an electorate seeking enactment of major new legislation would do well to install a unified party coalition in power, but not return it to power too many times. On the other hand, a unified coalition does not appear to be significantly more productive if it spent a long time out of power.

Probing the Main Results

The dependent variable in our models is a count, and the Poisson and negative binomial distributions are natural probability models for count data. Therefore, we replicate all the findings above in a negative binomial regression model of the tally of major acts as a function of the same covariates.[18] Marginal effects of covariates and significance test results are very close to the OLS results. We omit the model estimates for brevity, but it is not too surprising that the models match up closely. While the dependent variable is a count, its overall mean is about 10 major acts per Congress. The right-skew of canonical count distributions starts to disappear at these levels, and they look more and more like normal distributions as the mean grows.

The effect of unified versus divided government shown in table 4.1 is supported in part by the other covariates in the models in table 4.1. In a model of major acts (all Congresses) as a function of only unified government and the time trend, without the other covariates in table 4.1, unified government has a positive effect, but it is insignificant at the .05 level. In the bivariate model of major acts as a function of the unified government indicator and a constant, unified government has a p-value of about .67. These findings from restricted models are consistent with Mayhew's principal finding that divided government has no significant relationship with legislative productivity. By the same token, given the theoretical foundation for the time in power and other variables, Mayhew's celebrated result may stem from model misspecification.

One interpretation of the divided government result is that an indicator variable is a coarse measure of policy disagreement among factions in national political institutions. With legislative "ideal point" estimates based on revealed preferences in roll-call votes, it is arguably possible to obtain a more refined measure of this disagreement. A natural candidate for such a measure is polarization among parties at the national level, as reflected by differences in median party ideal points in the House of Representatives. Rather than the crude binary measure of divided government across institutions, this measure reflects the extent of policy disagreements between parties. Nolan McCarty argues that this variable has a significantly negative effect on major legislative enactments.[19] However, adding House party polarization to model 1 in table 4.1 has no substantively important effect on any results. Polarization has a p-value of .89, while unified government and time in power have the same signs and rough magnitudes as in table 4.1 and continue to be highly significant.

It is interesting to note that the effects of coalition structure on major legislative acts do not carry over to all public acts. We estimated the same models in table 4.1 on a time series of *all* public laws enacted from 1789 to 2001.[20] For the whole time series as well as the restricted time series of the contemporary party system, neither unified government, nor time in power, nor time out of power is related to legislative activity in general. The covariates that stand out are the party system dummies. They imply that conditional on other covariates, significantly fewer public laws were enacted in a given Congress in each of the first four party systems. This is interesting because the raw (unconditional) count of public acts has actually declined over time, especially since 1933. This suggests that the downward trend of the entire series of public acts is spurious, and that other conditions conducive to passage of laws in general are not as prevalent today as before the New Deal.

Amendment and Repeal

While almost all of the literature on legislative "output" has focused on the enactment of major statutes, this obscures important subcategories of legislative activity. Further insights on the effects of coalition structure on major legislative acts might be gained by disaggregating the Stathis data. Two substantively important categories are (1) major acts that amend earlier major acts and (2) major acts that repeal earlier major acts, as compared to "foundational" acts that are created out of "whole cloth" (i.e., ones that do not amend or repeal previous major acts). Viewed in this way, one facet of legislative innovation is a type of "creative destruction,"[21] whereby policy change occurs by eliminating (repeals) or revising (amendments) prior policy enactments. By disaggregating, we can determine whether important variation in the data is explained by different mechanisms.

A typical Congress amends 3.13 major acts (standard deviation: 4.11); 28 of 107 Congresses in our data set amended none while the 104th Congress amended 17. By comparison, recall that a typical Congress passes just over 10 major laws, with most of those being foundational acts (mean: 6.87, standard deviation: 4.40). Repeals are much more binary, with only five Congresses repealing more than one major law (none more than two); about 23% of Congresses repealed at least one major law. Repeals of major laws have become marginally more common in recent years. Since 1969 about 35% of Congresses have repealed at least one major law, compared to about 21% before 1969, but the z statistic on a two-sided difference in proportions test is only 1.27 ($p = .21$).

Even more strikingly, since 1969 the average number of major laws that represent amendments is about 11.47 per Congress, while it is about 1.56 before 1969 (t statistic from two-sided homoskedastic difference in means test is 19.54).[22] This confirms an impressionistic sense about policy innovation in Congress: We have transitioned away from a period in which Congress takes up broad new categories of public policy that it had not previously touched, and entered one in which Congress's major policy work tends to alter the legislative infrastructure already in place. In other words, amendments and repeals of major laws are an important aspect of legislative innovation, and increasingly so over time.

To analyze the behavior of amendment and repeal of major legislation, as compared to foundational acts, we estimated statistical models with the same set of covariates we used in modeling the number of all major laws in table 4.1. In each case, as before, the unit of observation is a Congress. For foundational acts, we once again estimated an OLS model with Newey-West standard errors. For amendments, we estimated a negative binomial regression model[23] rather than OLS, since the dependent variable is small on average and equal to zero in a fairly large share of the observations. For repeals, we estimate a probit model of the dichotomous variable of whether or not a Congress repealed any major laws.[24] The results appear in table 4.2.

The results for foundational acts are similar in some respects to those for major acts in general (reported in table 4.1). Unified government results in about 3 new acts per Congress, an effect statistically significant at

TABLE 4.2. **Regression results: foundational acts, amendments, and repeals**

Explanatory Variable	Foundational Acts (OLS)	Amendments (Negative binomial)	Repeals (Probit)
Unified government	3.07***	.44*	.05
	(.89)	(.23)	(.51)
Time in power for	−.27	−.10*	−.09
unified coalition	(.19)	(.06)	(.09)
Time out of power for	.01	−.04	.18**
unified coalition	(.11)	(.03)	(.09)
Indicator, party system 1	−14.17**	1.34*	2.49**
1789–1823	(6.60)	(.81)	(1.23)
Indicator, party system 2	−14.86***	.98	1.00
1825–53	(5.31)	(.68)	(1.05)
Indicator, party system 3	−10.00**	1.26***	.85
1855–95	(3.92)	(.46)	(.79)
Indicator, party system 4	−6.94**	.09	[dropped]
1897–1931	(2.84)	(.31)	
Time trend	−.13*	.05***	.03*
	(.08)	(.01)	(.02)
Constant	20.08***	−3.07***	−3.02**
	(7.17)	(.84)	(1.44)
χ^2 statistic (No. obs.)	6.22***	137.71***	15.00**
	(94)	(94)	(94)

Note: Entries in first column are OLS estimates with Newey-West standard errors in parentheses.
* denotes significance at α = .10 or less; ** at .05 or less; *** at .01 or less

the .01 level, while time in power is negative but falls just short of conventional levels of statistical significance ($p = .16$). However, there is also a significant downward trajectory in foundational acts across time, picked up by the time trend variable as well as the party system indicators. This confirms the initial unrestricted results presented earlier, as more major acts in recent years are "derivative" of ones passed in earlier eras.

Our results indicate that unified government also increases the number of amendments to major laws in a Congress by about .7, an effect statistically significant at about the .05 level. When a unified coalition spends an additional Congress in power, the number of amendments to major laws falls by about .17, an effect statistically significant at the .10 level. Thus, four consecutive Congresses in power for a unified coalition inhibits amendment of major legislation by about the same amount that installing unified government increases it.

We also find that the elapsed time since a given unified coalition last held power (time since holding power) does not have a significant effect on amendment of major laws (though the p-value for the amendments model, .22, is not large enough to be completely comfortable that the null result is not a false negative). On the other hand, time since holding power does have a significant, positive effect on the probability that at least one major law is repealed in a Congress. In a probit model, the effect is significant at $p = .042$; one Congress more than average out of power increases the chance that a unified coalition repeals a major law by about 5.3%.[25] Yet for repeals, neither unified government alone nor the time in power for a unified coalition has a significant effect on the probability of repeal ($p = .92$ and .31, respectively). Overall, these models suggest that the effect of "pent-up demand" for legislative innovation depends on the type of legislative activity. A unified coalition that has spent many years out of power correspondingly inherits laws that it thinks never should have passed and sets about repealing them, but does not have a similarly long list of items that it can turn into original legislative action immediately.

Conclusion

Mayhew's analysis of landmark legislation posed a simple, compelling question that spawned a literature. Scholars have pushed this literature in a variety of different directions, but in each case have asserted arguments about how the structure of coalitions holding power in national lawmaking institutions affects the output of the legislative process. In this chapter, we have brought several strands of this coalition structure argument together for empirical analysis. We have included a unified coalition's "age" or time in power as an explanatory factor, a variable highlighted in previous theoretical work. We have simultaneously analyzed the effect on major legislative enactments of several different aspects of coalition structure, and done so with a new measure of major legislation covering a longer time span than previous analyses.

The major new findings are that time in power has a significant and negative effect on both overall enactments and amendments of major legislation. When unified coalitions first take power, they identify feasible policy changes on major issues of the day and enact those changes— whether foundational acts or amendments of prior major acts—into law. With the new policy at an equilibrium point with respect to coalition preferences, such major changes are harder to find as the coalition ages, thus reducing major legislative activity over its life span. Furthermore, once coalition time in power is taken into account, divided government has a negative effect on major legislative activity generally—at least with the measure we use. On the other hand, time out of power, which might allow a coalition time to build up a stockpile of policy issues to address, increases the chance of repeal of a major law, but not passage of a new foundational law or an amendment of an existing major law.

In general, these findings support natural theoretical arguments about the policy effects of coalition structure based on spatial models of American lawmaking institutions. They also point to many directions for future work, to explore the robustness of these findings with different measures of major legislation and new theoretical arguments about the effect of coalition structure.[26] For example, greater connections to arguments raised in this volume by Maltzman and Shipan, who explore the determinants of significant amendments of major legislation in the post–World War II era, and Berry, Burden, and Howell, who examine the mutation (amendment) and death (repeal) of federal programs during the second portion of the fifth party system, might further expand our understanding of the transition from foundational lawmaking to "interstitial" lawmaking in the latter part of the twentieth century.[27]

CHAPTER FIVE

The Lives and Deaths of Federal Programs, 1971–2003

Christopher R. Berry, Barry C. Burden and William G. Howell

If government's fundamental task is, as Harold Lasswell famously asserted, to decide "who gets what, when, and how," then we should add, "and for how long."[1] While much recent scholarship has focused on the production of legislation, relatively little has considered what happens to a program once elected officials have enacted it. It is not enough to characterize the course that a particular group of policymakers initially set. Scholars need to identify the enduring effects of policymakers' actions. We need to know whether their footprints were quickly washed away or left lasting imprints. Unfortunately, existing research yields few and often misleading conclusions about the trajectory of government programs.

This chapter analyzes the durability and size of government programs, focusing on the effects of changes in the partisan composition of Congresses over time. When the composition of the Congress that enacted a program differs markedly from the Congress that sits in its judgment, a program should be especially vulnerable to cuts, restructuring, or elimination. Conversely, when the partisan compositions of the enacting and current Congresses look much alike, a program should be less susceptible to legislative tinkering. However intuitive this logic might be,

This chapter is a slightly modified version of our article, "After Enactment: The Lives and Deaths of Federal Programs," which appeared in the January 2010 issue of the *American Journal of Political Science*.

it runs against a long literature in public administration and so deserves careful empirical scrutiny.

We therefore examine the size and survival of all federal government domestic programs established between 1971 and 2003 (2,059 programs in total, yielding 20,159 program-year observations). Consistent with our predictions, we find that changes in the partisan composition of Congresses have a strong influence on both program durability and spending levels. Moreover, these effects are asymmetric: Program life spans are regularly shortened by partisan losses, but lengthened by partisan gains; similarly, programmatic spending predictably declines after partisan losses, but increases after partisan gains. We thus dispel the dominant notion that federal programs are "immortal" while providing a plausible coalition-based account of their varying life spans and spending trajectories.

We proceed as follows. The first section summarizes the existing literatures on legislative productivity and relevant research on programmatic durability. The second identifies partisan turnover as a core element of distributive politics and program inheritance. The third section tests the effects of partisan coalition changes on program life spans. The fourth concludes.

Existing Literature

The bountiful literatures on program *creation* systematically examine how different rules, structures, and incentives determine the prospects for different policies to be enacted. Scholars, for instance, have shown that productivity—at least from the perspective of the president—is driven by such things as public approval or the size of the president's party in Congress.[2] Others have examined how changes in the ideological composition of Congress affect the production of legislation.[3] A related literature examines the effects of divided government on lawmaking.[4] And scholars continue to scrutinize Congress's variable willingness to enact elements of the president's foreign and domestic policy agendas.[5]

For all contributors to research on legislative productivity, the analytic enterprise is promptly suspended the moment that a law is enacted. But by investigating "what happens after a bill becomes a law,"[6] literatures on policy implementation implicitly pick up where these previous scholars left off.[7] Scholarship of policy implementation, though, tends to focus on the bureaucracy as distinct from Congress and the president, and it typically treats the governing legislation itself as fixed.[8] For example, to scrutinize the behavior of elected and appointed officials within the bureaucracy, much of this research holds constant the governing statute without allowing for the possibility that the law itself may change over time. Indeed, this research typically views the possibility of a governing statute being modified by later legislators as entirely outside its analytic domain.

Taken as a whole the research on both legislative productivity and policy implementation says precious little about how successive and overlapping generations of legislators and presidents deal with a program *after* its creation. This is not to say that scholars explicitly deny the importance of programmatic durability. The running debate over how to categorize legislation as "significant," for instance, points our attention not only to whether something was enacted but whether its impact proved lasting.[9] And other scholars have made much of the effects of "political uncertainty" on legislative processes.[10] An operating assumption of such research is that politicians, despite their best efforts, have difficulty committing future policymakers to their chosen enterprise. Uncertainty about the actions of ensuing coalitions can be defended by insulating policies with bureaucracy, these scholars note, but that strategy is costly and offers no assurance of success. Because there is "no guarantee that the legislation will stick,"[11] both policymakers and scholars need to understand the conditions that influence program durability. As Patashnik analogizes, "losing weight is hard, but the real challenge is *keeping* it off."[12]

Rather than developing a systematic analysis of program life spans, most of these works offer what amounts to a call to arms. Indeed, only a relative handful of studies actually analyze the durability of federal programs and agencies directly. Those that do can be categorized into three groupings. The first emerges from the public administration literature and presents case studies of particular programs. Although each is interesting in its own right, these cases fail to cumulate into a coherent whole. Frantz's study of the demise of the National Hansen's Disease Center, Mueller's description of the end of the National Health Planning and Resources Development Act, and Behn's analysis of the closing of reform schools in Massachusetts are informative narratives, but they do not form a general account of program longevity.[13]

The second assembly of studies argues that once created, federal government agencies and programs are essentially permanent. In his land-mark study, *Are Governmental Organizations Immortal?*, Herbert Kauf-man found that only 27 out of 421 agencies created since 1923 had been eliminated by 1973.[14] Even among these 27 agency deaths, many in fact saw their functions persist in other parts of the bureaucracy. Kaufman's conclusions that "government organizations enjoy great security and long life" and that "governmental activities therefore tend to go on indefinitely"[15] constitute the received wisdom to this day.[16] By this ac-count, life after enactment is uninteresting because it does not vary; agencies (and by extension programs) simply continue to exist and tend to grow at a steady rate the longer they are on the books.

So rare is program death that individual cases can only be chalked up to random factors. Echoing Kaufman's original claims, deLeon sug-gests that the reason program "termination has received such sparse critical attention is that there are simply not enough cases upon which one can begin to generalize."[17] Not surprisingly, then, Kaufman's later work on organizational survival argued that "survival of some organiza-tions for great lengths of time is largely a matter of luck" and that "lon-gevity comes about through the workings of chance."[18] Whether one be-lieves that programs are eliminated in an unpredictable fashion or not at all, this line of scholarship leaves little room for systematic thinking on the matter.

A final and more recent group of studies, some of which appear in this volume, has begun to challenge these assumptions: first method-ologically, by moving beyond case studies; and second substantively, by demonstrating the regularity and predictability of programmatic and bu-reaucratic terminations. Corder and Lewis, for instance, find that more than half of the federal tax credit programs and agencies that they an-alyzed were eliminated.[19] Bickers's analysis of the size of government programs similarly highlights program mortality.[20] Stein and Bickers in-dicate that programs are regularly created, restructured, and even de-stroyed.[21] Comparable findings emerge in Maltzman and Shipan, who track the mortality of landmark legislation; Post and Pierson, who an-alyze tax law; Ragusa, who documents repeals of legislation; and Car-penter and Lewis, who like Lewis, focus on agencies.[22] Although each of these projects is focused on a subset of federal programs, collectively they document how factors such as divided government and national economic performance systematically shape program durability.

Building on this third group of studies, we offer a general account of programmatic growth, decline, restructuring, and death—one that focuses on coalition change as the key explanatory variable. Our study makes at least three contributions. First, unlike existing studies that focus on programmatic durability within a single policy domain, we provide a systematic and comprehensive analysis of Kaufman's seminal "immortality" thesis. So doing, we resolve some confusion in the literature. Whereas Kaufman's project and the work that followed were too often vague about what constitutes a "program," we rely on the same program definitions and classifications used by lawmakers and analyze a comprehensive database of government programs.

Second, we analyze an aspect of programmatic durability that the existing quantitative literature largely overlooks: congressional turnover. For the most part, the existing literature pays scant attention to the partisan and/or ideological relations among successive and overlapping generations of policymakers. Because they restrict their focus to political alignments at the time a law is enacted and/or a new Congress considers overturning it, Maltzman and Shipan and Post and Pierson do not account for the possibility that today's Congress is more likely to support bills enacted by previous Congresses with similar preferences and priorities.[23] Carpenter and Lewis recognize that "political turnover" affects the lives of agencies, but they only estimate the effect of changes in majority party on the durability of federal agencies.[24] As we demonstrate below, majority party status in Congress is but one way in which turnover may be realized—and it turns out not to be especially important in contributing to programmatic (as compared to agency) longevity.[25]

Finally, we go beyond the old question of "immortality" to examine multiple kinds of changes made to programs. Our analysis examines the durability of programs until their death, but also identifies the correlates of program restructurings and changes in program spending. And so doing, it takes advantage of the most comprehensive database of federal government programs ever assembled, one that comprises virtually all of the federal government's discretionary commitments spanning more than three decades.

Program Inheritance and Coalition Change

As this volume makes clear, newly elected Congresses do not face blank policy slates. Rather, each Congress inherits the full history of policymaking that preceded it. This includes some laws that have been on the books since the early days of the Republic, but also many that were created by the Congresses that recently preceded it. At any given point in the contemporary era, more than a thousand federal discretionary programs are on the books, each of which carries a financial commitment from Congress. As the literature on "path dependence" has made clear, all policymaking is done in the context of what already exists.[26]

The situation, we suggest, is like that of a person who inherits an old house from a departed relative. She must decide whether to accept the house as it currently stands, to begin minor or major renovations, or to tear down the house and build a new structure. The likelihood of each of these actions is determined by both the costs involved and the similarity in preferences between the original builder of the structure and its current inhabitant. We would expect the new homeowner to consider demolition more seriously if the costs are low or if her preferences are quite different from those reflected in the current home. Likewise, the preferences of the current Congress must be sufficiently different from those of the Congress that built the program to justify the effort required to kill or restructure it.

This view of policymaking departs somewhat from standard scholarship on Congress, but is buttressed by recent research in the American Political Development (APD) tradition. This work has a deep appreciation of temporal orderings in analyzing political change. Although this research focuses much more on formal institutions rather than on programmatic activities, its rich theoretical treatments inform our own analyses. APD scholars have aptly noted that the thickening of institutions over time creates inertia and makes programs remarkably resilient to change.[27] As a result, institutions are not wholly recreated when a new coalition comes to power. Rather, in most cases new elements are layered on top of old ones, creating complex and often internally contradictory features.[28] As James's recent review essay eloquently concludes, "Current politics is the dynamic expression of multiple interactions among institutionalized vestiges of a country's political past. . . . The political present is an amalgam of 'multiple orders' rooted in a nation's political history."[29]

How should we characterize the different kinds of programs that are passed from one Congress to the next? At any given time, we stipulate, new federal programs emerge from larger legislative bargains over the allocation of distributive benefits among the president and members of Congress. The overall benefits of these programs, however, are not distributed either randomly or uniformly among districts,[30] but rather in accordance with the distribution of influence and preferences among representatives. For instance, members of the majority party might be expected to receive larger shares of the distributive pie;[31] similarly, legislators from districts and states with different ideological leanings should enact different kinds of programs.[32] Collectively, then, programs created in any given legislative session tend to reflect the partisan and/or ideological distribution of legislators holding office at the time. And as the distributions in Congress change, due to electoral replacement or other factors, then the allocation of distributive spending, as implemented through federal programs, should follow suit.

This view of legislative inheritance generates straightforward predictions about the life of programs after enactment. When a new Congress inherits a portfolio of existing programs, it will tend to cut, modify, or kill those programs created by those prior Congresses with different priorities and preferences. By contrast, a sitting Congress will preserve or, better yet, enhance existing programs enacted by preceding Congresses with shared priorities and preferences. In other words, the greater the difference between the governing coalitions of current and enacting Congresses, the more likely a program is to shrink or die; the more similar are the two Congresses, the more likely a program will be preserved or expanded.

Updating of the policy status quo will not be perfect or immediate. With many programs in existence and other demands on policymakers' time, monitoring will be imperfect. The enduring policy agendas of bureaucratic agencies and interest groups, each with varying degrees of political power and autonomy,[33] may further limit the opportunities for a given Congress to amend or overturn the existing slate of policy programs. And each congressional coalition, like the consecutive heirs of a family home, incurs costs for altering the legacies it inherits. Consequently, we can expect policy change to be "sticky."[34] But on the margins, we expect changes in the policy preferences of Congress to be consequential. Both program durability and the sizes of programs should fluctuate according to Congress's changing composition.

Program durability also may be influenced by factors beyond partisan politics. Sometimes a program will simply outlive its usefulness. This may happen when exogenous environmental changes such as the emergence of new technologies or a crisis event demand the replacement of an outmoded program with a new one, what John Kingdon would call "policy windows."[35] On other occasions, expert evaluations show that particular programs are simply not working well.[36] More generally, Kaufman's theory of organizational change points our attention to volatility in the environment in which a program finds itself.[37] We acknowledge that new resources, technologies, values, and priorities may influence program durability. Such factors, though, are largely orthogonal to the political variables on which we focus, and hence we leave to future research a systematic evaluation of their importance.

Data and Empirical Implementation

To test predictions about the effects of congressional turnover on programmatic livelihood, we constructed a comprehensive panel data set of federal programs created between 1971 and 2003. The data come from the *Catalog of Federal Domestic Assistance* (CFDA), a government-wide compendium of federal programs.[38] Originally published in 1965 in an effort to provide a single comprehensive source of information on the federal government's programmatic activities, the CFDA has been updated annually since 1969. It contains information about "any function of a Federal agency that provides assistance or benefits for a State or States, territorial possession, county, city, other political subdivision, grouping, or instrumentality thereof; any domestic profit or nonprofit corporation, institution, or individual, other than an agency of the Federal government."[39] "Assistance or benefits," the catalog further notes, include the transfer of almost anything of value from the federal government to a domestic beneficiary.[40] In short, the CFDA accounts for nearly all of the domestic programs that comprise the federal government.

In addition to being nearly comprehensive, the CFDA data also allow us to employ the same program definitions and classifications that are used in the lawmaking process. Each program was created by a public law, an act, or an executive order.[41] In addition, each program has its own line item and account number in the federal budget. Each observation in our data set corresponds to a specific program as created and funded by lawmakers. We therefore are working within the same framework by which politicians create, manipulate, and terminate federal programs.

Massive amounts of money are appropriated each year through domestic programs created during our study period. In 2003, fully $230 billion were disbursed through the 1,006 programs created since 1971; and average spending among these programs was $237 million, and the median was $14 million. These allotments range from the miniscule and obscure, such as Vocational Training for Certain Veterans Receiving VA Pension ($1,438) and the Morris K. Udall Fellowship Program ($44,922), to the massive and familiar, such as Supplemental Security Income ($31 billion) and Pell Grants ($12 billion).

To transform the CFDA into analyzable data, we refine and extend Bickers and Stein's monumental programmatic database that tracks programs from 1971 to 1990. The Bickers and Stein database has been a valuable resource for the discipline, supporting not only the work of its creators[42] but of many others who have used the data in their own work.[43] These data contain a wealth of annual information on all programs appearing in the CFDA, including each program's function, administrative agency, beneficiaries, and expenditures. The complete, integrated data set, which we extend through 2003,[44] thus represents a compilation of the programs contained in all editions for the CFDA over a thirty-three-year period. All told, we have 2,059 unique programs and 20,159 program-year observations, the most complete accounting of the federal government's activities ever assembled.

Tracing the life spans of programs proved to be a painstaking endeavor. When a program that appears in one edition of the CFDA does not appear in the next, it has not necessarily died. Over time programs can undergo a variety of transformations, from mundane renaming and renumbering to more substantial consolidations, splits, and transfers between agencies. To deal with such complications, we traced the entire history of each program created from 1971 onward, including all of its structural alterations. We compiled these programmatic histories based on the historical profiles and cross-walk tables included in CFDA, which also allowed us to bridge program histories across the original Bickers and Stein data and our extension. We then distinguished instances of program restructuring from program death. Taking a conservative approach, we coded as "mutations" all programmatic consolidations, splits, and transfers, but not simple renumberings or renamings. We coded as deaths only those programs that were deleted from the CFDA and did not continue on in any other form. The programs in our sample mutated 1,056 different times, and we were able to document 197 instances of actual program elimination.[45]

Figure 5.1 presents smoothed hazard estimates based on two different thresholds of programmatic alterations for the observations in our

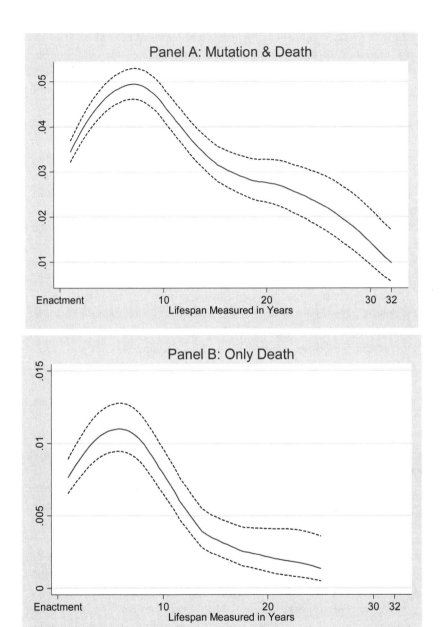

FIGURE 5.1. Program Hazard Functions

The top panel identifies both programmatic mutations and deaths; the bottom identifies only deaths. In both, the vertical axis represents smoothed hazard estimates. The horizontal axis represents time. Dashed lines depict 95% pointwise confidence bands.

sample.[46] These estimates are drawn from the raw data and indicate the instantaneous likelihood of an event occurring, given that the program has survived to that point. Panel A presents the estimates based on both mutations and deaths, and panel B identifies only deaths. Both have dotted lines indicating the 95% confidence intervals. Contrary to previous scholars' claims about the "immortality" of federal programs, we find that a substantial number of programs change over time, and a nontrivial number of programs actually die. In its first ten years of life, a program has a 4 to 5% chance of either mutating or dying, and a 1% chance of outright termination *every year.* Having survived for roughly a decade, however, programs become increasingly likely to continue without alteration. Over time, these spontaneous hazards quickly add up to sizable cumulative effects. Within twenty years of creation, every program can be expected to either mutate or die; and fully 15% of programs can be expected to actually die.

Basic trends in these data are consistent with our theory. Consider, for starters, the shape of the hazard functions, which demonstrate that mutation and death are most common in the first ten to fifteen years. During the period we analyze, the partisan composition of the House and Senate typically changed rather dramatically within any given fifteen-year period. Having survived five to seven Congresses, and thereby demonstrated an ability to satisfy members from both the Democratic and Republican parties, a program then appears to be in the clear. It is also possible, though, that programs require roughly a decade to build the support they need from interest groups, bureaucratic agencies, and expert evaluators to withstand subsequent congressional scrutiny.[47]

Similarly, the years that experienced the highest rates of programmatic death tended to coincide with high levels of congressional turnover. For instance, the first year of the Reagan administration saw a disproportionate number of program deaths, at the same time that Democrats lost thirty-five seats in the House and control of the Senate. In 1981 alone Congress dismantled programs including the Meat and Poultry Inspection Loans administered through the Small Business Administration and the Department of Education's Incentive Grants for State Student Financial Assistance Training. For similar reasons the mid-1990s saw a jump in program deaths as a new conservative majority took the axe to programs viewed as too liberal. And other programs were terminated by Democratic Congresses when the distribution of preferences shifted leftward, as when the emboldened majority did away with the

Export Market Development program for agricultural products following the 1974 landslide. In short, simple examinations of these raw data cast doubt on the contention that programs are immortal, and also reinforce our emphasis on political coalitions as agents of programmatic change.

Mutation and death, however, are not the only fates awaiting a program. Existing programs undergo continual fiscal tinkering, some growing in scope and others withering as ensuing Congresses see fit. Controlling for inflation, the average program grew by 2.6% annually over our study period. The 90th percentile of annual program growth was positive 59%, while the 10th percentile was negative 20%. Indeed, budgetary cuts in real terms constituted fully one-third of all program spending changes. So if one considers changes in the dollars spent on programs, it seems even less appropriate to view federal activities as immutable.

Modeling Program Survival and Spending

These basic descriptive results illustrate just how eventful life after enactment can be. Programs grow, decline, and even die with astonishing regularity. We now take the further step of relating program size and longevity to congressional politics, specifically the disparities between the preferences of the Congress that enacted the program and those of current members.

We start by considering the impact of changes in the partisan composition of the enacting and the current Congresses. To do so, we posit program evolution as a general function of the form $S_{ijk} = f((C_k - C_j) X_i, Z_k)$, where S_{ijk} denotes the size or survival of program i, which was enacted by Congress j and is currently under the control of Congress k. The primary quantity of interest, $(C_k - C_j)$, represents differences between the current majority coalition and the coalition that enacted program i, which we explain below. X_i is a vector of program attributes, and Z_k is a vector of attributes of the economic and political environment at the time of the current Congress, k. We estimate hazard models to predict program death, and we use panel ordinary least squares to estimate program spending.[48]

Our unit of analysis is a program-by-year observation. Using data on federal domestic programs, we match each program created since 1971 to attributes of the Congress that enacted it.[49] In each year following its creation, we compute differences between its enacting Congress and the Congress currently in power. We then use these differences to predict program survival and size during the current year. For example, in 1980 Republicans held 158 House seats and 41 Senate seats (an interchamber average of 38.7%) but by 1996 had increased that to 230 in the House and 52 in the Senate (a 52.5% average). We expect that in 2000, Congress, with an average of 50.7% Republican seats between the two chambers, would be more likely to cut or kill a program enacted in 1980 than a program enacted in 1996, all else equal.

To measure the relative distance between a Congress that creates a program and a Congress that subsequently decides its fate, $(C_k - C_j)$, we calculate the net percentage of seats that changed parties between the enacting and current Congresses, averaged across the House and Senate. We expect that the effects of $(C_k - C_j)$ depend on whether the majority party has gained or lost seats between the time when the program was created and the current Congress. Seat losses may improve the likelihood that a program is altered, is killed outright, or has its appropriation decreased. In contrast, when a majority party gains seats from the time of a program's enactment, we expect mutation and death to be less likely and spending on that program to increase. To reflect this asymmetry, our models therefore include separate measures of seats gained and lost by the majority party in the enacting Congress. That is, we calculate $(C_{km_s} - C_{jm_s})$, where m identifies the majority party at the time a program is enacted and the subscript s denotes the share of seats that this party holds for the Congress specified by k or j, and then introduce a spline with a single a knot at zero.[50] Of course, a governing coalition includes the legislative branch as well as the executive. We expect changes in the presidency to work in a similar fashion, so we include a dummy variable for whether the party of the president changed between the enacting and current Congresses.

Second, we allow for the marginal effects of partisan turnover to depend on the age of the program. The true marginal effects associated with changes in our main covariates of interest, after all, may vary during the course of a program's life span. Over time, external interest groups and internal bureaucracies can be expected to grow around a program, insulating it from political and economic disturbances. Consequentially, the relevance of a given value of $(C_{km_s} - C_{jm_s})$ for survival may depend on whether a program was just recently created or whether it has sat on the books for decades. In different ways, the models below explicitly account for this time dependence.

Background Control

Although the existing literature does not provide much guidance, it seems plausible that multiple factors beyond turnover affect the durability of programs. We therefore estimate models that control for characteristics of the programs themselves, X_i, as well as economic and political indicators at the time each Congress considers a program's fate, Z_k. The time invariant program attributes are of two types. First is a control for (the log of) spending on that program during its initial year of existence, which distinguishes large from small programs. The second set of program controls is an array of program types indicating how funds are allocated. Here we follow Stein and Bickers, who demonstrate important differences among programs that spend in traditional ways, underwrite loans, rely on formulas, support specific projects, or insure against risk. Although our project is not immediately interested in how durability varies across these types, they serve as important controls since the mix of types has varied over time.[51]

Other time-varying controls in our models account for the environment in which programs were initially enacted and then subsequently evaluated. These are drawn in part from the literature on government productivity cited earlier. First, to evaluate effects of national economic performance on program durability, we include measures of both the level (in trillions of 2000 dollars) and year-to-year percent changes in gross domestic product (GDP).[52] Our expectation is that program spending and longevity should be greater when the nation's economy is larger or experiencing growth, if only because it produces more tax revenue for elected officials to spend.[53] Second, to account for the possible budgetary trade-offs between "guns" and "butter" during war, we include an indicator variable for times of war.[54] Third, we include a dummy variable for divided government.[55] Because most of the literature suggests that divided party control impedes production of legislation, we allow for the possibility that it may also impede program death or increased spending. Fourth is a dummy variable for the first year of congressional term, which has been shown to produce more legislation than the second year of the session. Finally, we incorporate public opinion toward government activism in the form of Stimson's "public mood" measure.[56] The first dimension of this measure has been shown to influence legislative productivity since it indicates the public's desire for government action. We might thus expect higher (more activist) levels of public mood to be associated with greater durability and spending increases.

The purpose of these particular controls is to ensure that the coefficients we observe on the coalition change variables do in fact represent the effects of these factors rather than spurious attributes of the program or legislative environment. As we discuss further below, however, alternative models that include either subsets of these variables, presidential fixed effects, or additional characteristics of the economy and politics at the time of a program's enactment yield comparable findings. Moreover, we do not claim that these particular background controls amount to an exhaustive accounting of all factors that influence a program's life span after enactment. Technological innovations, a program's objective success or failure, geographic distributions of programmatic benefits, the particular policy mechanism by which a program was created, and demographic changes may also influence the probability that a program is killed, restructured, or cut. Future studies would do well to investigate their impacts on programmatic durability and growth. As previously noted, though, these factors are expected to be orthogonal to changes in the partisan composition of Congress, and hence are excluded from the models presented below.

Survival Results

We estimate two companion sets of models predicting program survival and size. The first concerns the effect of congressional turnover on a program's life span, which we estimate via Cox hazard regressions, which have the benefit of making no assumptions about the functional form of the hazard. We test the proportional hazard assumption for each covariate, and we interact those covariates that have been shown to violate standard proportionality assumptions with a linear measure of program age.[57] We expect that the marginal probability of either mutation or death in any given year, conditional on having survived until then, will increase as the majority party loses seats between the enacting and

TABLE 5.1. **Predicting program life spans, 1971–2003**

Explanatory variable	Mutation & death		Only death	
Majority party seat gains	−2.24	[1.95]	−15.93***	[5.15]
Majority party seat losses	8.46***	[1.61]	7.17***	[2.42]
Change in party of president	−0.21	[0.14]	0.16	[0.18]
Majority party seat losses × Program age	−0.34**	[0.14]	—	
Change in party of president × Program age	0.06***	[0.02]	—	
Spending in enacting year (log)	−0.07***	[0.02]	−0.12***	[0.03]
Formula	−0.13	[0.14]	0.05	[0.34]
Project	0.01	[0.12]	0.21	[0.26]
Direct spending (specified)	−0.20	[0.17]	0.05	[0.38]
Direct spending (unspecified)	0.04	[0.31]	0.66	[0.66]
Direct loan	0.26	[0.19]	0.97***	[0.27]
Guaranteed loan	0.00	[0.21]	0.88**	[0.36]
Insurance	−0.97*	[0.59]	0.95	[0.66]
Other	−0.42***	[0.12]	−0.28	[0.25]
GDP, levels (trillions)	−0.10***	[0.03]	−0.25***	[0.08]
GDP, year-to-year percent changes	0.01	[0.02]	0.05	[0.04]
War	0.62***	[0.12]	−0.05	[0.36]
Divided government	0.03	[0.10]	0.95***	[0.28]
First year of congressional term	0.23***	[0.06]	1.01***	[0.19]
Public mood (first dimension)	−0.09*****	[0.02]	−0.18***	[0.05]
Number of observations	18,739		19,169	
Log pseudo-likelihood	−6,685.91		−1,130.48	

Note: 2,130 total programs, 858 mutations, and 197 deaths recorded. Model 1 identifies both programmatic mutations and deaths; model 2 identifies only deaths. Standard errors clustered on program are reported in brackets. Cox regressions estimated with Breslow method for ties. Interactions with linear characterizations of analysis time included in model 1 to account for violations of proportionality assumptions; tests of non-zero slopes of the scaled Schoenfeld residuals of time for all other covariates in this model, and all covariates in model 2, yield null effects.
* sig $p < .10$, two-tailed test; ** $p < .05$; *** $p < .01$.

the current Congresses but will decrease as the enacting majority party's seat share increases.

Table 5.1 presents the results. We model program mutation and death together in the first model and then death independently in a second model. As explained above, *mutation* identifies any substantive change in a program (including a split, consolidation, or transfer), whereas *death* refers to the subset of cases where a program actually ceased to exist. Table 5.1 reports the results. We find evidence that changes in partisan coalitions do affect program durability; moreover, and as we anticipated, the effects are asymmetric. Seat losses by the enacting majority party increase the hazard in models that set the threshold for a spell's termination at mutation (column 1) and death (column 2), while seat gains sharply decrease the hazards. These results suggest that changes in congressional coalitions have important impacts on the mutation and death of programs, despite the stickiness of public policies and the resistance of the interests they serve. Changes in the party of the president, however, do not appear to increase the hazard.[58]

In column 1, two covariates (majority party seat losses and change in party of the president) did not satisfy the proportional hazard assumption, and therefore we allowed their effects to covary with the age of the program. Their interactions provide suggestive evidence that over the life span of a program, the marginal effects of majority party seat losses attenuates; that is, seat share losses early in a program's life span have a greater impact on the probability of death than do seat shares later in the program's life span. Interestingly, the marginal effect of changes in the party of the president would appear to increase over a program's life span.[59]

In column 2, both global and individual tests of proportionality yield null results, indicating that all covariates satisfied the proportional hazard assumption. This model suggests that when the enacting majority party loses an average of 10% of seats across the two chambers, the marginal probability of death approximately doubles; when the enacting majority party gains 10% of seats, the marginal probability of death drops by 80%. To put this in perspective, when keeping all other variables at their means, the estimated impact of a one standard deviation increase in majority party losses is over twice as large as that of a one standard deviation decline in the GDP. The estimated impact of a one standard deviation increase in majority party gains is approximately one-third as large as that observed for a one standard deviation increase in the GDP.

The effects associated with our control variables are generally consistent across both sets of models. Programs are less likely to be altered or killed if their initial appropriations are substantial—that is, smaller programs are easier to dismantle. We find only minimal differences among programs that allocate funds in different ways. There is evidence that loan programs are more likely to die but insurance programs are less likely to be altered or killed. Otherwise, though, there do not appear to be large differences in the durabilities of different types of programs.[60]

All programs appear more vulnerable to both mutation and elimination when GDP is low. Year-to-year changes in GDP, however, do not significantly affect either hazard rate. As one might expect based on our theory of program inheritance, programmatic changes and terminations are especially likely to occur during the first year of a congressional term just as a new coalition of legislators takes office. Programs are more likely to be altered or killed during times of war, perhaps reflecting trade-offs in budget priorities. Consistent with the literature on lawmaking, we find mixed evidence that divided government influences program mutation or death. Divided government appears to increase the hazard of death in model 2. Finally, program durability is quite sensitive to public opinion, captured here in the form of "public mood." When the public calls for less government activity, programs are in fact more likely to be altered or eliminated.

We also have estimated models that use alternative background controls and that focus on subsamples of the universe of programs created between 1971 and 2003. For instance, when using the federal deficit in place of GDP in all of the models or dropping baseline spending from any of the models, all the main results hold. We also have estimated models that exclude loan and insurance programs, whose spending is more difficult to measure. Once again, all the main findings hold.

Spending Results

The results presented thus far pertain to the discrete outcomes of program death and mutation. To facilitate a more subtle understanding of how programs change over time, table 5.2 presents analogous models of program spending. For comparability, the model specification matches those in table 5.1, with the exception that the dependent variable is now the change in logged, inflation-adjusted spending on programs between the enacting and current years.[61] Additionally, to account for the possibility that older programs tend to have a stronger contingent of political allies to advocate on their behalf (something we do not observe directly), we control for each program's age.[62]

The results, by and large, mirror those observed in the mutation and death models. As before, losses in congressional seats for the enacting majority correlate with spending decreases, and gains correlate with increases. When an enacting majority party loses 10% of the seats, on average, in the House and Senate, spending on its programs declines, on average, by one-tenth of one percentage point; and when the ma-

TABLE 5.2. **Predicting programmatic spending, 1971–2003**

Explanatory Variable	Spending	
Majority party seat gains	5.68***	[1.14]
Majority party seat losses	−1.42*	[0.82]
Change in party of president	0.01	[0.04]
Spending in enacting year (log)	−0.25***	[0.03]
Formula	0.79***	[0.17]
Project	0.21*	[0.12]
Direct spending (specified)	0.37	[0.23]
Direct spending (unspecified)	0.85	[0.53]
Direct loan	0.07	[0.18]
Guaranteed loan	0.83***	[0.25]
Insurance	0.38	[0.59]
Other	−0.17	[0.11]
Age of program	0.03***	[0.01]
GDP, levels (trillions)	0.05***	[0.02]
GDP, year-to-year percent changes	0.01***	[0.00]
War	0.24***	[0.04]
Divided government	−0.01	[0.03]
First year of congressional term	−0.01	[0.01]
Public mood (first dimension)	−0.03***	[0.01]
Constant	5.39***	[0.59]
Adjusted R^2	0.14	
Number of observations	17,988	

Note: The dependent variable is the difference in a program's logged, inflation-adjusted spending in current and enacting years. Standard errors clustered on program reported in brackets.

* sig $p < .10$, two-tailed test; ** $p < .05$; *** $p < .01$.

jority gains 10% of seats, spending increases by six-tenths of a percentage point. With average spending growth of 2.6 percentage points, these effects translate into a 4% decline and 23% increase in the rate of growth, respectively. Substantively, the estimated impact of a one standard deviation increase in majority party losses is roughly 70% as large as the estimated impact of a one standard deviation decline in the GDP growth rate. The estimated impact of a one standard deviation increase in majority party gains is almost twice as large as that observed for a one standard deviation increase in the GDP growth rate. Consistent with the hazard results, though, changes in the president's party do not appear to influence spending levels.[63]

Programs with larger initial endowments also tend to see smaller percentage increases in their budgets. To some degree this is because small percentages still translate to large numbers when computed on large initial appropriations, but also because smaller programs tend to be more volatile.[64] As in the hazard models, we find only modest evidence that program type affects spending. While formula-based and guaranteed loan programs see more spending increases, there are no differences among other kinds of programs.

Also as expected, a larger GDP and larger increases in GDP both tend to facilitate more spending, presumably because more tax revenue is available to policymakers. Perhaps counterintuitively, war increases spending. Rather than a trade-off between domestic and defense budget priorities, war appears to stimulate spending on many types of programs. Again, divided government has no effect on spending patterns once programs have been created. Spending is no lower in the first year of a congressional term than it is in the second. Age correlates positively with spending, perhaps because of the organizations that build up around programs over time and make them more effective at advocating for additional state resources, or because weak and unsuccessful programs (qualities we do not observe) die off, while stronger and more popular ones perpetuate. Finally, public opinion runs counter to what one might expect, as a more activist public mood translates to less spending, but that might reflect the "thermostatic" or countercyclic nature of public mood, which tends to move in the opposite direction of government policy.[65]

These results also are robust to a wide variety of alternative specifications. As in the hazard models, the main results hold when including alternative background controls and focusing on various subsamples of programs. Additionally, we have estimated models that substitute year fixed effects for all year-specific covariates. These models yield estimates that are comparable in magnitude to those presented above.

Alternative Measures and Model Extensions

In tables 5.1 and 5.2, we identify the average number of House and Senate seats that the majority party either lost or gained between the time of a program's enactment and the current Congress that stood in its judgment. There are obviously alternative ways of characterizing turnover.

TABLE 5.3. **Alternative measures of turnover**

Explanatory variable	Mutation & death		Only death		Spending	
House only						
Majority party seat gains	−0.77	[1.37]	−10.36***	[3.79]	4.45***	[0.91]
Majority party seat losses	5.96***	[0.90]	8.67***	[2.29]	−0.92	[0.72]
Senate only						
Majority party seat gains	−5.73	[3.79]	−23.52***	[8.10]	1.96	[1.25]
Majority party seat losses	5.92***	[1.27]	7.42***	[3.09]	−0.97	[0.89]
Majority party seat gains × Program Age	0.95***	[0.34]	2.55***	[0.88]	—	
Majority turnover Number of institutions that change party control	0.29***	[0.04]	0.47***	[0.12]	−0.03*	[0.02]
NOMINATE						
Shifts to extremes	−1.27	[0.94]	−7.34***	[2.34]	1.82***	[0.52]
Shifts to center	1.93***	[0.49]	2.59**	[1.21]	0.00	[0.30]

Note: The first two models include the covariates shown in table 5.1; the third model includes the covariates shown in table 5.2. Results presented only for key covariates of interest. Standard errors clustered on program reported in brackets. Interactions with linear characterizations of analysis time included in the Senate-only section results to account for violations of proportionality assumptions; where needed, interactions between other unreported covariates and analysis time were included.
* sig $p < .10$, two-tailed test; ** $p < .05$; *** $p < .01$.

For instance, one might worry that aggregate measures of congressional turnover mask important chamber-specific trends. Table 5.3 presents results that substitute measures of House and Senate turnover for those on overall congressional turnover. Though the estimates attenuate somewhat, the basic pattern holds. To conserve space, we only report the main covariates of interest in table 5.3, although we include the full set of control variables in all the models.

In a variety of ways, we have explored the possibility that changes in majority party status between the current and enacting Congresses, rather than changes in individual seats, drive programmatic duration and spending. Following Erikson, MacKuen, and Stimson,[66] we construct a counter that runs from zero to three that identifies the number of institutions (House, Senate, and presidency) to have switched party control. As table 5.3 shows, when substituting this counter for all the other turnover variables, we find that majority party changes increase the hazard in both the mutation and death models and decrease appropriations in the spending models. Notably, though, when including the counter along with our measures of seat change, the former is significant in only the mutation models, while the estimated effects of the latter remain unaffected in all of the models.

Rather than consider partisan seat shares, one might instead examine changes in the ideological composition of Congress. To wit, we have estimated models using DW-NOMINATE scores. Rather than identify whether the majority party gained or lost seats, however, we identified whether the median of either chamber as a whole shifted in a more moderate or extreme direction. The findings presented above would suggest that shifts to the extremes of the ideological spectrum (that is, conservative Congresses at enactment becoming more conservative, and liberal Congresses becoming more liberal) should decrease the hazard and increase spending; moderating shifts (that is, conservative Congresses at enactment becoming more liberal, and liberal Congresses becoming more conservative) should increase the hazard and/or decrease spending.

The results, for the most part, comport with our expectations. When the prevailing ideological leanings of the enacting Congress are strengthened, the marginal probability of mutation is unaffected, the marginal probability of death is decreased, and spending increases significantly. By contrast, when the prevailing ideological leanings of the enacting Congress are weakened, the marginal probability of both mutation and death increase, while spending is unaffected.

Additional Model Extension

On the whole, then, there appears to be solid empirical support for the claim that partisan turnover increases the odds of spending cuts, program mutation, and program death. It is less clear, however, which of the various options a particular Congress will choose. How, for instance, does Congress decide between mutation and death? And are structural changes and spending cuts mutually exclusive options?

We estimate the probability that Congress kills a program rather than restructures it, conditional on having decided to do one of the two. A simple logistic regression that includes all of the main descriptive variables identified above shows that gains in the majority party size decrease the probability of death (and increase the probability of restructurings), while losses increase the probability of death (and decrease the probability of restructurings). The estimated effect of majority party gains is significant ($p = .09$), while the effect of losses is not ($p = .30$).

We also investigated the trade-offs between mutation and spending cuts. In any given Congress, the decision to kill a program, by definition, requires setting programmatic spending to zero. It is less clear, though, what relationship (if any) might emerge between simple restructurings and spending. We therefore add to the main spending models a variable that identifies whether a program was restructured in a given year. We find that restructurings tend to accompany spending cuts of, on average, 43% ($p < .01$). As one might expect, the magnitude of the relationship between restructuring and spending varies according to whether the majority party at the time of a program's enactment subsequently gained or lost seats. Decisions to restructure a program in the face of losses coincide with spending cuts that are 50% larger on average than those decisions that occur in the face of gains.

Our analyses to this point have unearthed considerable evidence that the probability that a program is cut, transformed, or killed is increasing in differences between the current and enacting Congresses. It is likely, though, that other twists and turns in the makeup of the institution during the intervening years matter as well. A sitting Congress, after all, typically is not the first to inherit a particular program; rather, the sitting Congress is simply the latest in a succession of Congresses, each of which had the chance to have its way with programs that it found objectionable. When the 106th Congress revisits a program enacted by the

TABLE 5.4. **Between the current and enacting Congresses**

Explanatory variable	Mutation & death		Only death		Spending	
Majority party seat gains	−3.48*	[1.91]	−17.91***	[5.19]	5.63***	[1.16]
Majority party seat losses	7.13***	[1.58]	5.28***	[2.35]	−1.45*	[0.85]
Survived more hostile Congress	−0.45**	[0.17]	−0.84***	[0.26]	−0.02	[0.03]
Majority party seat losses × Program age	−0.42***	[0.13]	—		—	
Survived × Program age	−0.03**	[0.02]	—		—	

Note: The first two models include the covariates shown in table 5.1; the third model includes the covariates shown in table 5.2. Results presented only for key covariates of interest. Standard errors clustered on program reported in brackets. Interactions with linear characterizations of analysis time included in model 1 to account for violations of proportionality assumptions; where needed, interactions between other unreported covariates and analysis time were included.
* sig $p < .10$, two-tailed test; ** $p < .05$; *** $p < .01$.

94th, it does so after fully eleven other Congresses had the opportunity to restructure or eliminate it.

Table 5.4 presents the results of models that include an indicator variable that identifies whether a program has already survived a more hostile Congress (measured by relative seat losses of the majority party) than the current one. In the hazard models, the estimated effects of our main variables of interest (measures of partisan turnover) remain significant and in the expected direction. And as one would expect, having survived a more hostile Congress tends to decrease the hazard; and as the interaction with age indicates, its effect is magnified over a program's life span. In the spending models, however, the added indicator variable is not significant, and the estimated effects of our measures of partisan turnover remain virtually unchanged.

Conclusion

Until quite recently, scholars had set their sights almost exclusively on the politics surrounding the enactment of programs and other legislative initiatives. Along with the other chapters in this volume, we show that there is life, alteration, and indeed death after enactment. Using a novel data set on spending, mutation, and termination, we present the first quantitative study of the postenactment lives of all federal discretionary programs enacted over a twenty-two-year period.

Our hazard and spending models demonstrate that life after enactment is not invariant nor is it so idiosyncratic as to be unexplainable. Rather, changes in the ideological and partisan character of Congress help explain why programs are more or less likely to survive. We find that a program is vulnerable to termination, spending cuts, and other changes when the Congress that inherits it is different in partisan terms from the Congress that created it. Allowing for asymmetric effects of partisan change, we find that programs are particularly imperiled when their enacting majority loses seats in future Congresses but are more likely to survive and increase their funding when a majority gains seats.

Research on this topic should not end here. This chapter presents only the average effects of partisan turnover on programmatic spending, mutation, and death. But such estimates may mask considerable variation. It is possible, for instance, that Congress is more likely to revisit programs with sunset provisions when the programs are up for reauthorization; or that during times of economic expansion, congressional turnover may not bode so poorly for programs as during times of economic decline; or that the effects of partisan turnover interact in important ways with a program's size, policy domain, or other program-specific characteristics; or that the marginal effects documented here are occasionally overwhelmed by larger patterns of historical growth and decline in the state. More generally, it is important to extend analyses of program duration beyond the period we have examined, 1971–2003. The specific period we studied is characterized by relatively large partisan turnover, moderate programmatic expansion, increasing administrative capacity, dramatic growth in entitlement spending, and a mature welfare state. Our results may not generalize straightforwardly to, say, the New Deal period or earlier eras. Though lack of comparable data may prohibit similar quantitative analysis, more research into program evolution and death in other periods is clearly warranted.

Recognizing that the policy slate is never clear, this chapter (and this volume, more generally) establishes a foundation for future empirical studies of programmatic life spans. In addition to deciding what new legislation to enact, every Congress must revisit the thousands of programs that reside on the books. What these members decide to do about each of these programs, we suggest, fundamentally depends on their partisan affiliation with those who first enacted the program.

CHAPTER SIX

Beyond Legislative Productivity: Enactment Conditions, Subsequent Conditions, and the Shape and Life of the Law

Forrest Maltzman and Charles R. Shipan

The importance and influence of public policies depend on their durability. Whereas some laws guide policy for decades, others have only a transitory influence on policy. Soon after enactment, they are swiftly amended and superseded by new law. Despite such variance, our understanding of the stability of public laws and the conditions that foster such variation is limited. What forces help to shape whether initial agreements among legislators endure or unravel? This question has received scant attention from legislative scholars, whose studies of policymaking typically focus on the dynamics of enacting laws rather than on what happens after enactment.

We explore the political conditions that influence whether a law be-

This chapter is a greatly expanded version of an article published in the April 2008 issue of the *American Journal of Political Science*. The authors gratefully acknowledge the advice of Scott Adler, Sarah Binder, Fred Boehmke, Barry Burden, Will Howell, John Huber, Eric Lawrence, Gerald Loewenberg, Bill Lowry, David Mayhew, Dan Morey, Eric Patashnik, Paul Pierson, Alison Post, Elizabeth Rybicki, Paul Wahlbeck, and Matt Whittaker; the willingness of Sarah Binder, David Epstein, David Mayhew, Sharyn O'Halloran, and Jim Stimson to share their data; and Ken Moffett's and Karen Ramsey's research assistance. Maltzman acknowledges National Science Foundation grant SES-0351469, Shipan acknowledges the financial assistance of a University of Iowa Faculty Scholar Award, and both authors acknowledge National Science Foundation grant SES-0962203.

comes amended in future years. In contrast to most legislative studies, which examine how political conditions affect the probability of enacting major policy change, we explore the conditions that increase the likelihood that major laws will be reviewed and changed in the future. And in contrast to public policy scholars, who have produced theoretically informed studies of the ways in which postenactment politics (e.g., policy feedback loops and changes among organized interests) sustain new laws after enactment, we take a step back to focus on the ways in which political conditions at the time of enactment may affect the life of federal law. Our central theme is that variation in the character of political conditions at enactment has long-lasting consequences for the duration of the law. More specifically, we argue that conditions at the time of enactment determine whether a law is crafted in such a way that it accomplishes its sponsors' objectives and is immunized against subsequent revision; whether a law fails to secure its advocates' objectives and needs to be strengthened; or whether a law is left vulnerable to subsequent legislative attacks.

Substantive changes to the original agreement are important for two main reasons. First, the longer a law lasts before it is amended, the greater its potential to shape the nation's economic, social, and political welfare. Second, much of the value of laws—to interest groups, legislators, and so on—comes from the original agreement. When this agreement is revised, regardless of whether the revision weakens or strengthens the law, such changes affect the value of that law to the original participants. Indeed, subsequent amendments provide the opponents of a bill another opportunity to enact provisions that may undermine, if not cripple, the original intention of the law. Likewise, subsequent amendments that strengthen or expand a bill suggest that the original law failed to accomplish the policy objectives of at least some of its advocates.

For these reasons, members of the original coalition—members of Congress and the president—will want to write laws that both accomplish their policy objectives and bind future lawmaking coalitions. We will contend, however, that they are better able to do so under certain conditions. Because legislators are frequently unable to constrain future policymaking coalitions, federal laws vary in terms of their stability.[1] Although some laws, such as the Civil Service Reform Act of 1978, become institutionalized in such a way that no meaningful changes are made and their effects are felt for decades, other laws, such as the 1980 Toxic Wastes Superfund Act, are dramatically amended soon after enactment. Such amendments can enhance or diminish the effectiveness of the original law. Regardless of the nature of such amendments, the amendments themselves are evidence that members of the initial coalition were unable to craft a law that secured the policy outcomes they desired into the future.

To test our model of legislative stability, we examine the fate of major laws enacted between 1954 and 2002. First, we show that not all of these laws are equally enduring. Second, we identify the factors that influence whether a major law will be amended and develop an empirical model that accounts for why and when some prominent laws are amended by other major pieces of legislation. We show that initial conditions of enactment—along with later conditions, features specific to the law itself, and the actions of the judiciary—have systematic and predictable consequences for the sustainability of the original versions of public laws.

The Life and Value of the Law

As the chapters in this volume by Lewis, Patashnik, and Berry, Burden, and Howell demonstrate, scholars recognize that new public laws are not immutable.[2] Policies and organizations that many once viewed as entrenched (e.g., the welfare state, airline regulation, and the Interstate Commerce Commission) have been dramatically recast or even dismantled. As Pierson has noted, it is commonly believed that "policies, unlike formal institutions, are relatively easy to change (or 'plastic'), they are essentially epiphenomenal."[3] Policy scholars who focus on the outputs of the legislative process have been attentive to the stability of public policy, since the lifespan of a law is essential to assessing its initial value.[4]

The political value of stable law has encouraged some to focus on the forces that promote legislative permanence. Some argue that constitutional features of the American political system help promote legislative continuity. Landes and Posner, for example, claim that an independent judiciary helps to ensure policy stability, thereby increasing the value of legislation to groups and members of Congress.[5] Supermajority requirements,[6] the presence of multiple veto points,[7] and bicameralism[8] are also credited with making legislative enactments difficult to achieve, and thus potentially more stable over time.

Public policy scholars also have explored the ways in which well-designed policies can be preserved. Institutional provisions embedded in specific legislative acts may ensure programmatic stability, as seen in Patashnik's demonstration that winning politicians use federal trust funds as a vehicle for reducing uncertainty about future commitments to the programs and for binding their successors.[9] The durability of laws that create agencies can be enhanced by removing the agency from OMB budget review, giving appointees a fixed term, and imposing a party-balancing requirement for nominees.[10] Policies also can be extended by mobilizing groups and shaping interests so that the public and dominant interests seek to preserve the status quo. For example, Hacker and Pierson argue that the emergence of the welfare state altered ideas about the capacity of the state and about preferred policy choices, thus constraining future generations.[11]

A winning legislator's central goals are both to lock in policy gains and to secure programs that automatically will be revised in ways consistent with his or her preferences as conditions change. Thus, legislators concerned about greenhouse gasses routinely lobby for emission standards that are strengthened automatically as technology improves. Likewise, advocates of Social Security support indexing the payments to an inflation index. This incentive to lock in policy successes is especially strong in a system (such as the United States) where no party has clear dominance. At the same time, losing legislators have the opposite incentive: They want enacted policies subsequently to fail. This failure can occur through either the complete revocation of a law, significant amendment of its basic parts, or even the enactment of policies that alter or fail to satisfy the long-term objectives of the initial law's advocates. For example, the failure of the 1974 Federal Elections Campaign Act to index contribution limits undermined the act and led, in part, to the 2002 Bipartisan Campaign Reform Act.[12]

In the American political context, tools available for losers seeking to either cripple or expand existing laws are plentiful. One strategy is to work to craft the law in such a way that invites review by the judiciary—for instance, by pushing for the inclusion of vague, inconsistent, or even unconstitutional provisions. Accompanying unconstitutional provisions with an inseverability clause can force the Court to declare unconstitutional a new law favored by the president and a majority of Congress. This was precisely the strategy pursued by opponents of the 2002 Bipartisan Campaign Reform Act.[13] Opponents of new policies can also advocate inclusion of sunset provisions, temporally limited reauthorizations, or other provisions that are likely to encourage the public and organized interests to lobby against successful implementation.

Legislative scholars have been attuned to these dynamics of the legislative process, paying keen attention to the ways in which political and institutional forces shape the likelihood of major policy change.[14] These studies have advanced our understanding of the policymaking process by delineating the conditions that make the enactment of major laws more likely. Central to many of these studies is the debate over the influence of interbranch and intrabranch policy differences on the likelihood of enacting new law.[15] Still, such studies essentially end at the stage of enactment. Given the substantial variation in the longevity of public laws, we need to ask whether the politics of enactment have discernible consequences for the durability of new laws.

Determinants of Stability

What factors can account for the variation in the stability of newly passed laws? First and foremost, the political environment at the time of passage influences the length of time until a law is amended. Second, subsequent political conditions also will determine whether a law is amended. Third, characteristics of the law itself will affect its longevity.

Enactment Political Conditions

Political competition over the shape of a new public law has predictable consequences for the likelihood of crafting law that is less susceptible to subsequent amendment. Because the character of such competition is strongly influenced by the political conditions that prevail during the period of enactment, we explore the ways in which these initial conditions affect a law's stability, shaping both the capacity and incentives of legislators to seek durable outcomes.

As noted in the previous section, legislative scholars have devoted considerable time and energy to examining the effects of divided government on the passage of legislation. Most of the arguments and analyses, however, have focused solely on whether divided government increases or decreases the likelihood of initial passage. And while there exists disagreement about the effect of divided control on the passage of laws, scholars have little sense of how divided government—or more generally, ideological disagreements among the House, the Senate, and the president—might affect the future of laws that *do* pass.

At first blush, one might expect that if it is more difficult for politicians to pass laws under divided government (because it is harder for them to reach agreement on the principles that should be embodied in a law), then the laws that *do* pass would be more likely to live long lives, undisturbed by future Congresses and unamended by future laws. According to this view, laws that pass in the presence of disagreements between the House and Senate, or in the presence of disagreement between the branches, require compromises that will bring both Republicans and Democrats on board and that then should increase the likelihood that the original bargain will last well into the future. This conventional view is captured by Niskanen's assertion that "the probability that a major reform will last is usually higher with a divided government, because the necessity of bipartisan support is more likely to protect the reform against a subsequent change in the majority party."[16]

In contrast to this view, we find more persuasive, albeit perhaps also more counterintuitive, the argument that laws will be more stable, and that the original agreement will last longer, when control of government is *unified* at the time of enactment. In other words, we contend that laws passed under divided government are more, not less, likely to be amended than laws passed under unified government. Three lines of argument support this contention.

First, laws passed under unified control will be more coherent and internally consistent, due to the shared policy interests across institutions.[17] Laws passed under divided government, on the other hand, require compromises that can take the form of vague or internally inconsistent provisions or that can result in a broader (and less coherent) range of provisions. Such compromises work to bring enough legislators and the president on board, allowing the bill to pass, but these compromises completely satisfy few of these actors. Consequently, laws passed under unified control provide a narrower target for opponents than laws passed under divided control.

Instances of laws that fit this description are easy to find. For example, the Energy Policy and Conservation Act of 1975, passed under divided government, was described as "an awkwardly stitched-together compromise"[18] that "satisfied no one."[19] It was also an act that had a number of provisions that virtually ensured Congress's continued involvement in

U.S. energy policy. Perhaps the most controversial provision was the creation of a unicameral legislative veto over executive branch decisions regarding the price for domestically produced oil. After a great deal of uncertainty, President Ford signed the bill. The act was significantly amended only a few years later, in 1980.

Second, laws passed under unified government are more likely to contain self-executing provisions that enable the law to evolve to current circumstances. Examples of self-executing provisions include an automatic cost of living adjustment or a funding mechanism, such as the domestic-segment tax on air transportation, which automatically adjusts to changing needs (e.g., increased air traffic).[20] Likewise, laws passed under divided government may lack the sort of self-executing provisions that immunize laws from necessary revisions or may contain provisions that specifically open the laws up to future changes. That is, legislative fragmentation induced by divided government creates an incentive to craft measures in such a way that encourages future legislators to revisit the law—for instance, through the inclusion of sunset provisions, such as those found in the 1996 Welfare Reform law, or short authorization periods.[21] Under unified government, on the other hand, we would expect legislators to seek to protect their policy choices from political intrusion.

Third, recent theories and findings from studies of legislative delegation also support the argument that the original agreement will be more specific and less flexible for laws passed under divided control than for laws passed under unified control. In particular, legislators are more likely to attempt to limit executive branch discretion during periods of divided government by adopting laws that spell out in detail which policies should be implemented.[22] Although these kinds of laws provide certain benefits to legislatures, such as potentially preventing bureaucrats from using their informational advantages to implement policies that legislators do not like, they also come with some costs. The most relevant cost from the standpoint of our analysis is that the sorts of precise, detailed laws that divided government produces are less likely to provide bureaucrats with the flexibility they would need in order to respond to exogenous shocks. When conditions do change in the future, the specific provisions in the original law may no longer be adequate and may even be inappropriate. Thus, a detailed law is more likely to need a legislative fix than is a law that provides bureaucrats with the flexibility to adapt to changing circumstances; and divided government is more likely to produce detailed laws.

Taken together, these arguments suggest that unified government will produce longer-lasting laws. Thus, our first hypothesis captures the idea that original legislative agreements will last longer when Congress and the president are controlled by one party; and conversely, that laws passed when parties share control of government are more likely to be amended:

> *Divided Government at Enactment: Laws enacted during periods of divided government are more likely to be amended than those enacted under unified control.*

Research on the influence of bicameralism on lawmaking suggests that the alignment of preferences in bicameral legislatures may also make policy change more difficult.[23] Correspondingly, the chances of overturning the policy status quo are strongly shaped by the policy differences between chambers of bicameral institutions.[24] In that context, successful policy adoption depends on finding an overlap in preferences between pivotal players in both chambers. By broadening the scope of policy views that must be incorporated into final policy choices, the potential for writing durable law is compromised. This leads us to the following hypothesis:

> *Bicameral Differences at Enactment: The greater the policy disagreement between the House and Senate, the greater the probability of amendment.*

Subsequent Political Conditions

Our main focus so far has been on the effect of political and institutional factors at the time of enactment. Of course, the probability of a law being amended will depend on more than just the political conditions at the time of enactment. Conditions that exist after enactment also are likely to affect the chances that Congress will succeed in passing another major law that revises the initial law. Although, as we noted earlier, findings on the relationship between divided government and the passage of major laws have been mixed, several recent studies have demonstrated that many types of major laws are more likely to be passed under unified government than under divided government.[25] Hence, successful amendments, being laws themselves, should be more likely to occur under unified control.

Similarly, the degree of bicameral differences will shape not only the likelihood of initial enactment of a stable law, but also subsequent efforts to revise earlier decisions. Two chambers that are ideologically distant from each other will have more difficulty reaching a consensus to pass a new law than will two chambers that share similar preferences and consequently will be less likely to pass laws that amend existing laws. Overall, then, we would expect that subsequent political conditions, in addition to the conditions at the time of enactment, will affect the stability of public laws. The following two hypotheses capture this idea:

> *Subsequent Divided Government: During periods of divided government, existing major laws are less likely to be amended.*

> *Subsequent Bicameral Differences: The greater the policy differences between the two chambers, the less likely that existing major laws will be amended.*

The probability of congressional action also is likely to depend on the prevailing public mood.[26] As Mayhew has described, these moods act as "stimulators of legislation."[27] Similarly, Kingdon has argued that "changes in mood or climate have important impacts on policy agendas and policy outcomes" and that this national mood can either push items for change onto the agenda or serve as a constraint.[28] Based on this logic, we predict the following relationship:

> *Policy Mood: During periods when the public favors government action, existing major laws are more likely to be amended.*

The probability that public laws will be amended may depend in part on the treatment of new laws by the judicial branches. As many scholars have observed, interactions between Congress and the courts often guide the development of public law. Congress often takes the courts into account when writing laws, either by anticipating judicial actions or, perhaps less commonly, by responding directly to judicial decisions.[29] But another way the Supreme Court can influence Congress is by signaling the emergence of a policy problem. For example, the meaning of a public law can be so ambiguous that the Court's interpretation of the law encourages congressional revision.[30] Given the interaction of the Court and Congress, we would expect to find a systematic influence of Court activity on Congress's treatment of public laws:

> *Subsequent Court Intervention: The greater the attention of the Supreme Court to the policy area of a public law, the more likely the law will be amended.*

Law-Specific Characteristics

Factors specific to a law also can affect its longevity. We begin with the law's complexity. Some laws, such as the Financial Institutions Reform, Recovery, and Enforcement Act of 1989, clearly are complex in nature, while others, such as the Public Health Cigarette Smoking Act of 1969, which banned cigarette advertising on radio and television, are relatively straightforward. Generally, more complex bills have more provisions, they touch on more issues and policy areas (which present more targets for future amendment), and their effects are more uncertain. As such, both opponents and proponents of the initial law are more likely to pursue future amendments. Hence, we propose the following relationship between complexity and durability:

> Complexity: Major laws that are more complex are more likely to be amended.[31]

In addition to the effects of a law's complexity, a law's contentiousness may affect the likelihood that it will be amended. Simply put, laws that encounter greater opposition when they originally pass are more likely to be amended than laws that command broad support. Divisive laws are more prone to amendment for several reasons. First, because support is shallow, modest turnover in Congress can cause this support to erode. Second, when a law passes with a small majority, it is more likely that narrowly tailored provisions are incorporated into the initial law as a vehicle for appeasing a necessary supporter. Such provisions may have little to do with the broad goals of a bill and thus may be more likely to be vulnerable to a future coalition that no longer needs the support of the legislator who was initially enticed to join the majority. Finally, the absence of overwhelming support at the time of adoption may have prevented supporters of the original law from securing provisions that would enhance stability. Based on these factors, we expect that laws that are more contested and that narrowly pass will be more susceptible to future revisions:

> Divisiveness: Major laws adopted by slim majorities are more likely to be amended.

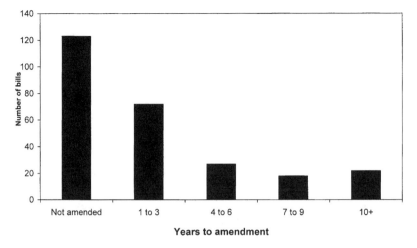

FIGURE 6.1. Number of years until amendment of major legislation

Data

To test our conjectures about the conditions that increase the stability of laws, we need to identify a set of laws and then determine whether these laws have been significantly revised. We begin by using the list of major laws identified by Mayhew in *Divided We Govern*, focusing on the laws enacted between 1954 and 2002.[32] We then use LexisNexis's "statutes at large" module, which lists all future laws that amend any given law, to determine whether and when these major laws have been significantly revised. If the amending law itself was judged by Mayhew to be a major law, we judge it to be a significant amendment. We focus on significant amendments to ensure that we are examining cases where a major law was subject to a serious amendment, rather than a minor or technical amendment or merely a reauthorization of an expiring law.[33] As shown in figure 6.1, of the 262 landmark laws included in our analysis, 139—over half—were significantly amended in subsequent years. On average, for those laws that were amended, just over five years elapsed before the original law was subject to a significant amendment.

Dependent Variable and Method

Our data set consists of a series of observations for each law, one for each year from the initial enactment until the law is significantly revised.

The first observation for each law occurs in the year in which it was enacted, and in this first observation the dependent variable takes a value of 0. The dependent variable then continues to hold a value of 0 until the year in which it is amended, at which time it takes a value of 1. Once a law is amended, it is dropped from the data set in the following year; and if a law has never been amended, the dependent variable remains equal to 0 for the length of the time series.[34] For example, a law like the Civil Service Reform Act of 1978, which has never been altered by a major amendment, is coded 0 from 1978, which is the year of enactment, through 2002, when our data is right censored. Superfund, enacted in 1980, receives a value of 0 from 1980 through 1985, and then receives a value of 1 for 1986, the year in which it was first significantly expanded. After 1986, there are no more observations for the 1980 Superfund law. However, the 1986 toxic waste dump cleanup law that amended the 1980 act is included in our data from 1986 until it is amended in 1990. Figure 6.2 shows the distribution of amendments. Although the figure demonstrates that there are no major "clumps" of amendments (i.e., periods in which a high proportion of the amending activity took place, and which therefore might be driving our results), there is a slight increase over time, as would be expected since the number of "targets" increases every year.

Because we are interested in the duration of laws—more specifically,

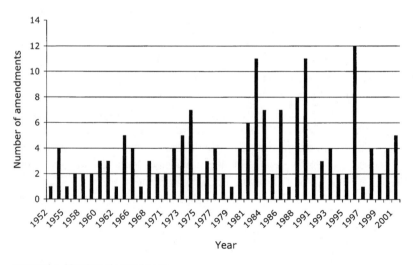

FIGURE 6.2. Number of amendments per year

the amount of time an original agreement lasts before it is subjected to a significant change—we run a Cox regression to estimate our model. In effect, each law has a life, and the failure—when the dependent variable switches from 0 to 1—occurs when the law is revised by a future law. We utilize a Cox regression to estimate the hazard or "risk" of amendment, rather than an alternative hazard model, since the Cox model does not require us to make strong assumptions about the shape of the underlying hazard.[35] With this method, a positive coefficient indicates an increased risk of amendment (and thus a less durable law) and a negative coefficient indicates a lower risk (and thus a longer lasting law).

Independent Variables—Enactment Political Characteristics

First, to test the hypothesis that laws adopted during periods of divided government are more likely to be amended than those adopted during unified control, we create a dummy variable called *Divided government at enactment*. This variable identifies laws that were enacted during a period when the party that controlled the White House did not also control both the House and the Senate. We expect this variable to have a positive coefficient.

Second, to test whether laws are less durable when the House and Senate hold distinct preferences at the time of enactment, we use Binder's measure of bicameral differences. This measure, *Chamber differences at enactment*, records the difference in the proportion of the House and Senate voting aye on passage of a conference report, averaging over the set of conference reports voted on each Congress. Each year of a two-year Congress receives the difference score for that Congress.[36] Higher scores indicate more disagreement; hence, our hypothesis predicts that the coefficient for this variable will be positive, with greater levels of disagreement increasing the likelihood of future amendments.

Independent Variables—Subsequent Political Characteristic

Our first two hypotheses about subsequent political conditions examine whether laws are less likely to be amended when partisan control over the current government is divided and when there is greater policy disagreement between the House and Senate. First, to test whether laws are less likely to be amended when control over government is divided, we create a dummy variable, *Subsequent divided government*, to denote whether the current year—that is, each year in which a bill could be amended—features divided control.[37] Whereas *Divided government at enactment* is constant for each observation associated with each law, *Subsequent divided government* is updated for each annual observation. Second, to test whether laws are more likely to be amended in periods of House-Senate agreement, we create *Subsequent chamber differences*, which is a current-year version of *Chamber differences at enactment*. We expect both of these variables to produce negative coefficients, which would show that laws are less likely to be amended when partisan control of government is divided and when the House and Senate have distinct policy preferences.

For each year in our data set, we also include Stimson's measure of the public mood. Calculated from public opinion polls, *Policy mood* shows the extent to which the public favors a more liberal, activist role for government. The scores range from 0 to 100, with higher scores indicating a more liberal mood.[38] Higher scores in subsequent years should be associated with a higher likelihood of amendment.

We also created a dummy variable, *Court attention*, to denote whether the Supreme Court made a decision pertaining to each major law during the three years previous to the current year.[39] Thus, for any law amended in 1969, for example, we utilize Court activity between 1966 through 1968. To determine whether a landmark law was central to a signed opinion of the U.S. Supreme Court, we use the LAW variable in Spaeth's Supreme Court database, which categorizes the policy content of Court decisions and thus allows us to match Mayhew's major laws to the content of the Court's opinions.

Independent Variables—Law-Specific Characteristics

As a measure of complexity, we determine the length of each of the Mayhew laws, using as our measure the number of pages for each law as it appears on LexisNexis. To confirm that the number of pages is a consistent measure of the length of laws during the period we examine, we counted the number of words per page for a large number of randomly chosen laws. Six of the laws that we use appear in a different format; for these laws we calculated the number of words per page and adjusted the length so it would be consistent with those of all other laws in our data set. Because we expect that complex laws will be more likely to be amended, the coefficient for the *Law complexity* variable should be positive.

Our next measure taps the divisiveness of the law. To measure *Divisiveness*, we first calculate the percentage of the House and Senate that voted in favor of the bill on final passage.[40] We then identify the chamber in which the majority coalition was smaller and treat that chamber's percentage yea as a measure of divisiveness. Because smaller values of this variable indicate a higher level of divisiveness, we expect it to produce a negative coefficient.[41]

Results

The results of our basic model are shown in table 6.1. The overall fit of the Cox regression model is good, as we can reject the null hypothesis that the coefficients are jointly zero beyond the .001 level. More impor-

TABLE 6.1. **Significant amendments of major legislation, 1954–2002**

	Expected sign	
Enactment political conditions		
Divided government at enactment	+	0.55***
		(0.21)
Chamber difference at enactment	+	34.14***
		(7.29)
Subsequent political conditions		
Subsequent divided government	−	−0.03
		(0.25)
Subsequent chamber difference	−	−30.11***
		(9.37)
Policy mood	+	−0.001
		(0.03)
Court attention	+	0.35*
		(0.26)
Law-specific characteristics		
Law complexity	+	0.002***
		(0.0003)
Divisiveness	−	−0.011**
		(0.005)
Sunset provision	+	—
Nonproportionality controls		
Chamber diff. at enactment * *ln(t)*		−11.71***
		(4.21)
Subsequent chamber diff. * *ln(t)*		9.37**
		(4.64)
Number of observations		4169
Wald Chi-square		94.81***

Note: Cox regression, Breslow method for ties.
* denotes $p < .10$, ** denotes $p < .05$, and *** denotes $p < .01$, one-tailed tests.

TABLE 6.2. **Marginal effects for statistically significant variables in model 1**

Independent variable	Change in variable (from, to)	Percentage change in the hazard rate
Divided government at enactment	0→1	73.6%
Chamber difference at enactment	.06→.08	39.2%
Subsequent chamber difference	.08→.10	−29.2%
Court attention	0→1	41.4%
Law complexity	39.9→125.6	16.6%
Divisiveness	66.9→82.5	−15.8%

Note: When calculating the marginal effects, the change represents one standard deviation from the mean for continuous variables and from 0 to 1 for dichotomous variables. We hold all other variables at their mean or, for dichotomous variables, their modal values, and set time at its average value for laws that have been amended.

tant, the results show strong support for our hypotheses, with most of our variables significant at $p < .05$ or better (one-tailed tests).[42] Because the coefficients in a hazard model cannot be interpreted as straightforwardly as those in a linear regression, in table 6.2 we use the parameter estimates from the table to calculate the percentage change in the hazard rate of amendment for each of the statistically significant variables in table 6.1.

Consistent with our expectations about the relationship between the conditions at the time of enactment and the stability of laws, we find strong support for both hypotheses about enactment conditions, with positive and significant coefficients for both variables. The result for the first of these variables, *Divided government at enactment*, shows that laws enacted under conditions of divided government are more likely to be amended at any given point in time than those enacted in a period of unified control. More specifically, as shown in table 6.2, the hazard rate of a law being amended increases by 73.6% when the original law was enacted during a period of divided government. Similarly, the *Chamber differences at enactment* coefficient is positive and significant. Because the effects of this variable are nonproportional, we must take into account the coefficient for the interaction of this variable with *ln(t)*. The combined effect of these terms is positive until almost nineteen years after enactment, after which the effect is indistinguishable from zero. Furthermore, as table 6.2 shows, when the chamber difference score increases from its mean to one standard deviation above the mean, the hazard increases by 39.2%.

Conditions after enactment also play a significant role in affecting the original law's longevity. The combined effect of *Subsequent cham-*

ber differences and the interaction of this variable with *In(t)* is negative, as predicted, until approximately twenty-five years after enactment.[43] This finding lends support to the idea that major laws are less likely to be amended—and thus are more stable—when the two chambers are ideologically distant from each other. In substantive terms, the change in the hazard of amendment when the difference between the chambers moves one standard deviation above the mean is −29.2%. This pattern is consistent with the claim that bicameral differences regularly account for the gridlock that can occur.

In contrast, the coefficient for *Subsequent divided government* is insignificant, indicating that the likelihood of amending a previously adopted law is not greater during periods of unified government. Such a pattern is consistent with observations that the probability of congressional action is consistent across periods of unified and divided government. Likewise, we find no support for the hypothesis that Congress is more likely to amend existing laws when the public is in a more activist mood; indeed, the *Policy mood* variable takes on a negative sign, rather than a positive sign. We suspect our null finding stems from two factors. First, our dependent variable does not capture the direction of the amendments. Some amendments may expand programs, while others may curtail policies previous embraced, and the *Policy mood* variable accounts only for a favorable view toward more government activism. Second, starting in the 1980s, conservatives themselves had ambitious legislative agendas (e.g., the Contract with America in 1995).

We also hypothesized that the relationship between the executive and legislative branches was not the only way that the separation of powers system influences a law's continuity and durability. In particular, we hypothesized that the Supreme Court's involvement in a policy area shapes the likelihood that Congress will amend a previously enacted law. Our *Court attention* variable is positive, as expected, and significant, although only with a very lenient standard of significance ($p < .10$, one-tailed). Still, this finding provides us with at least a modicum of support for our hypothesis and is consistent with other studies that have found that Court involvement influences Congress.[44]

Finally, our results show that some characteristics of the laws themselves matter. First, longer bills (*Law complexity*) are less durable. Indeed, laws that are one standard deviation more complex than average are approximately 17% more likely to be amended in the future. Given that such bills contain more sections and provisions—in other words, more targets—for potential amendment and are likely to include specific instructions for implementation that future legislators may desire to rewrite, this finding is highly intuitive. Second, the result for *Divisive* shows that when a law is more highly contested, it is more likely to be amended.

Sunset Provisions

Table 6.1 demonstrates that the political conditions at the time a law is enacted influence the probability that a law will be subsequently amended. In particular, laws enacted during periods of divided government and during periods when compromise between the House and Senate is difficult to achieve are more likely to be amended than those enacted during periods when partisan and bicameral differences are relatively inconsequential. This outcome suggests that in periods of bicameral and partisan differences, policy opponents can extract concessions that require that a law be revisited or that hinder a law's ability to fulfill the long-term objectives of its primary advocates. One of the most important vehicles for encouraging a law to be revisited is sunset provisions. Although these provisions can be used for a variety of reason (such as the uncertainty of a policy's effectiveness), these provisions are frequently employed as a mechanism for building coalitions.

Sunset provisions mandate that a law either be amended or allowed to die. Inevitably, this leads one to ask whether our findings in model 1 are driven exclusively by these provisions. To control for this possibility, in table 6.3 (model 1) we add a dummy variable to denote those laws that have a key provision that expires in the current session of Congress because of a sunset provision.[45] This variable is set equal to 0 initially and then changed to 1 at various times, as spelled out in the table, for models 1 through 4. As expected, the coefficient for this variable is statistically significant, indicating that laws enacted with a sunset provision are more likely to be amended. More important, the main lesson one draws from table 6.3 is that our principal finding still holds: Enactment conditions broadly and significantly account for the probability that a law will be subsequently amended. Similarly, we find continued support for the effects of features specific to the law and for subsequent political conditions, and also find stronger support for the effect of *Court attention.*

TABLE 6.3. **Significant amendments of major legislation: alternative versions of sunset measures**

	Expected sign	1	2	3	4
Enactment political conditions					
Divided government at enactment	+	0.52** (0.23)	0.52** (0.23)	0.53*** (0.22)	0.52** (0.23)
Chamber difference at enactment	+	38.20*** (9.71)	38.37*** (9.75)	37.99*** (9.76)	38.02*** (9.76)
Subsequent political conditions					
Subsequent divided government	−	−0.01 (0.26)	0.03 (0.26)	0.02 (0.26)	0.01 (0.26)
Subsequent chamber difference	−	−34.34*** (10.99)	−34.46*** (11.04)	−34.88*** (11.09)	−33.53*** (11.04)
Policy mood	+	0.01 (0.03)	0.01 (0.03)	0.01 (0.03)	0.01 (0.03)
Court attention	+	0.42** (0.25)	0.41** (0.25)	0.41* (0.25)	0.45** (0.25)
Law specific characteristics					
Law complexity	+	0.002*** (0.0004)	0.002*** (0.0004)	0.002*** (0.0003)	0.002*** (0.0003)
Divisiveness	−	−0.011** (0.006)	−0.011** (0.006)	−0.011** (0.006)	−0.010** (0.006)
Additional tests					
Sunset provision (dummy = 1 in *year of* sunset)	+	0.52*** (0.21)			
Sunset provision (dummy = 1 starting in *year of* sunset)	+	−	0.64*** (0.22)	−	−
Sunset provision (dummy = 1 starting in *year after* sunset)	+	−	−	0.58*** (0.25)	−
Sunset provision (dummy = 1 starting in *year before* sunset)	+	−	−	−	0.64*** (0.19)
Nonproportionality					
Chamber diff. at enactment * ln(t)		−13.80*** (5.13)	−13.86*** (5.13)	−13.62*** (5.18)	−13.71*** (5.11)
Subsequent chamber diff. * ln(t)		12.49*** (5.14)	12.75*** (5.17)	12.88*** (5.23)	12.13*** (5.16)
Number of observations		4026	4026	4026	4026
Wald chi-square		86.38***	87.89***	85.32***	97.92***

Note: Cox regression, Breslow method for ties.
* denotes $p < .10$, ** denotes $p < .05$, and *** denotes $p < .01$, one-tailed tests.

TABLE 6.4. **Significant amendments of major legislation: party change**

	Expected Sign	1	2
Enactment political conditions			
Divided government at enactment	+	0.47**	0.62***
		(0.24)	(0.24)
Chamber difference at enactment	+	39.99***	39.10***
		(10.30)	(10.04)
Subsequent political conditions			
Subsequent divided government	−	−0.021	−0.028
		(0.26)	(0.26)
Subsequent chamber difference	−	−34.58***	−35.73***
		(11.05)	(11.33)
Policy mood	+	−0.009	−0.010
		(0.03)	(0.03)
Court attention	+	0.43**	0.40*
		(0.25)	(0.25)
Law-specific characteristics			
Law complexity	+	0.002***	0.002***
		(0.0004)	(0.0004)
Divisiveness	−	−0.010**	−0.011**
		(0.006)	(0.006)
Sunset provision	+	0.51***	0.49***
		(0.21)	(0.21)
Additional tests			
Change in party of president	+	−0.27	—
		(0.22)	
Republican Congress	+	—	−0.56
			(0.45)
Nonproportionality controls			
Chamber diff. at enactment * ln(t)		−14.25***	−12.36***
		(5.33)	(5.24)
Subsequent chamber diff. * ln(t)		12.50***	11.73**
		(5.20)	(5.33)
Number of observations		4026	4026
Wald chi-square		86.96***	83.80***

Note: Cox regression, Breslow method for ties.
* denotes $p < .10$, ** denotes $p < .05$, and *** denotes $p < .01$, one-tailed tests.

The President and Partisanship

Of course, our system of checks and balances affords the president a role in an enacting coalition. Given that the president is frequently portrayed as one of the major engines of policy change in the United States, one might believe that change in partisan control of the White House is sufficient to induce a policy amendment. In table 6.4, model 1, we explore this hypothesis by including an additional variable that accounts for a change in partisan control of the presidency. In particular, we add a dummy variable that indicates that the president in the current period is not from the same party as the president who signed the bill into law. This variable, *change in party of president*, is not significant.

Likewise, one might suspect that many of the amendments stemmed from Republican efforts after 1994 to undo policies implemented by the Democratic majorities during the second half of the twentieth century. To test this, table 6.4's second model includes a *Republican Congress* dummy. This variable takes on the value of 1 following the Republican takeover of Congress in 1994. Again, the result is insignificant.

Alternative Vehicles for Changing the Law

Because we are interested in changes to the letter of the law, rather than programmatic changes, our dependent variable is limited to statutory amendments. Nevertheless, there are other vehicles that can be used to induce programmatic changes and thus ameliorate the need to amend a law. One of the most prominent tools available to Congress is the appropriations process. For example, many of the 810,000 public housing units promised in the 1949 Housing Act were never built because of the success that the pro-growth business community had in lobbying the House Appropriations Committee to defund previously authorized public housing.[46]

Because our dependent variable fails to capture programmatic changes that result from the appropriations process, one might wonder whether our results are driven exclusively by laws that are not dependent on federal appropriations for their implementation. In table 6.5, we examine whether laws that are especially dependent on appropriations are more susceptible to amendment. To explore this possibility, we exploit the fact that whereas some programs (such as a law setting a minimum wage) are virtually immune from the appropriations process, others (such as the 1949 Housing Act) are more susceptible to changes via appropriations. Although it is difficult to systematically discern whether changes in appropriations are designed to alter the nature of a program, in the four models in table 6.5, we rely on the *Congressional Quarterly Almanac* descriptions and/or the Mayhew (2005) policy codes to add a variable that controls for those laws in which spending is likely to play a prominent role.[47]

If these laws are systematically amended via the appropriations process, rather than by formal amendments, we would expect laws where domestic spending is prominent to be less likely to be subject to a formal

Table 6.5. Significant amendments of major legislation: expenditure laws susceptible to appropriations

	Expected sign	1	2	3	4
Enactment political conditions					
Divided government at enactment	+	0.58*** (0.23)	0.57*** (0.22)	0.53*** (0.23)	0.57*** (0.23)
Chamber difference at enactment	+	39.79*** (9.60)	39.70*** (9.52)	38.62*** (9.72)	40.61*** (9.70)
Subsequent political conditions					
Subsequent divided government	−	−0.02 (0.26)	−0.02 (0.26)	−0.0002 (0.26)	−0.02 (0.26)
Subsequent chamber difference	−	−36.79*** (11.05)	−36.89*** (11.02)	−33.62*** (10.84)	−36.05*** (10.92)
Policy mood	+	0.02 (0.03)	0.02 (0.03)	0.01 (0.03)	0.02 (0.03)
Court attention	+	0.49** (0.25)	0.50** (0.25)	0.51** (0.26)	0.48** (0.25)
Law-specific characteristics					
Law complexity	+	0.002*** (0.0004)	0.002*** (0.0004)	0.002*** (0.0003)	0.002*** (0.0004)
Divisiveness	−	−0.012** (0.006)	−0.011** (0.006)	−0.011** (0.006)	−0.012** (0.006)
Sunset provision	+	0.47** (0.21)	0.48** (0.21)	0.50** (0.21)	0.42** (0.21)
Additional tests					
Expenditure law (dummy=1 if law mentions specific domestic projects or programs)	−	0.49† (0.19)	—	—	—
Expenditure law (dummy=1 if law mentions specific domestic or foreign projects or programs)	−	—	0.48† (0.19)	—	—
Expenditure law (dummy=1 if a distributive policy area)	−	—	—	0.38† (0.20)	—
Expenditure law (dummy=1 if law mentions domestic spending)	−	—	—	—	0.58† (0.20)
Nonproportionality					
Chamber diff. at enactment * ln(t)		−14.39*** (5.03)	−14.32*** (5.04)	−13.56*** (5.02)	−14.68*** (5.10)
Subsequent chamber diff. * ln(t)		13.08*** (5.26)	13.16*** (5.25)	12.15*** (5.09)	12.80*** (5.24)
Number of observations		4026	4026	4026	4026
Wald chi-square		87.24***	86.80***	89.86***	88.76***

Note: Cox regression, Breslow method for ties.
* denotes $p < .10$, ** denotes $p < .05$, and *** denotes $p < .01$, one-tailed tests. † denotes significant at $p < .01$ in the positive direction (contrary to initial expectations).

amendment. Contrary to this view, all of the expenditure coefficients in positive and significant, suggesting that these laws are more, and not less, likely than other laws to be either expanded or contracted by a formal amendment.[48] Most important, the inclusion of the expenditure law variables does not change our finding that the political conditions that shaped the enactment process shaped the durability of the law.

Conclusion

Others have assessed the importance of institutional constraints and policy feedback loops in explaining the stability of public laws. In contrast, we offer a perspective on legal durability that also looks to the political conditions that underlie the original construction of public laws. Our analysis suggests that this durability is shaped not only by characteristics of the law, but also by initial and subsequent political conditions and by interactions across the branches of government. Ideological and partisan alignments across branches and within Congress indelibly shape the prospects for stable laws by molding both the initial configuration of the law and its subsequent chances of revision. By moving away from the more customary "snapshot" views of the legislative process, our focus on changes to the law allows us to examine the evolutionary character of lawmaking, an aspect of laws that is often left unexplored by legislative scholars.

Our analysis also shows a previously unnoticed effect of divided government. When unified government prevails, the majority party is able to use its governing powers to craft legislative agreements that are more likely to endure. Party alignments thus make a difference for policy choices, a finding underscored decades ago by Schattschneider and Key.[49] Still, more than party politics matter: Bicameral differences shape not only the likelihood of enacting new law, but also the chances that such laws will endure. To the extent that amendments are driven by inconsistencies or defects in the underlying law, our findings suggest that legislation enacted during periods of conflict between the chambers have provisions that are either flawed or incapable of responding to exogenous shocks.

More generally, the adoption of large-N quantitative analysis to explore the determinants of durability offers a chance to draw generalizable conclusions about legal stability and change. Our approach has its limits as well. First, although we know when landmark laws have been amended, we treat all types of changes alike, regardless of whether the amendment expands, contracts, or fundamentally alters existing public law. Although identifying whether an amendment strengthens or weakens an underlying law requires the sort of subjective analysis that is difficult given that laws frequently have multiple goals and ambiguous policy consequences, it is an important step in understanding why laws enacted by weak coalitions are more likely to be amended in the future. Without knowing whether an amendment weakens or strengthens the underlying law, we do not know whether the amendments were provoked because of the initial law's failure or because its popularity led proponents to extend the law.

Second, we limit our analysis to amendments contained in laws that were identified by Mayhew as being significant. We have no doubt that on occasion such a constraint may obscure important changes in the law. Indeed, many of the most important developments in the evolution of the law occur through bureaucratic and judicial interpretation, not formal legislative action. Finally, although we draw on Stimson's policy mood measure to determine whether the public favors a more or less activist role for government in general, we have no good indicators of when Congress's attention is focused on a particular law and its need for revision. Previous studies have demonstrated that sharp changes in attention can induce radical policy and budgetary shifts.[50] These shortcomings create plenty of room for improving large-N analyses of durability.

Still, our most striking finding gives us confidence that our approach taps an important and unrecognized relationship between enacting conditions and durability. Major laws enacted in periods of divided government are significantly more likely to be amended subsequently, compared to major laws adopted in periods of unified control. This finding increases our confidence that the political compromises required to pass legislation under divided control undermine policy proponents' abilities to entrench their view of the new public law, to sink their policy goals into legislative concrete. The influence of subsequent electoral and policy alignments on the likelihood of revisiting public law also suggests that political conditions have a lasting imprint on the character of policy compromises.

CHAPTER SEVEN

How Unpopular Policies Become Popular after Adoption

Amihai Glazer

Many have studied why, or under what conditions, government adopts a particular policy. This chapter addresses a related, but different, question: Under what conditions will government reverse or instead maintain a policy? Examples of both types abound.

Sometimes government explicitly reverses policy. Thus, the U.S. Congress passed catastrophic health insurance in one year and abolished it the next year. In Britain, successive Labor and Conservative governments nationalized and privatized industries. In the late 1940s, the British Labor government nationalized production of coal, transportation, electricity, gas, iron, and steel. A later Conservative government privatized road haulage and denationalized iron and steel, and still later some Labor governments undid these changes and nationalized the aircraft and shipbuilding industries. The Conservative Thatcher government then reversed Labor policy, privatizing firms such as the British Gas Corporation, British Airways, British Steel, the British Transport Docks Board, and the National Freight Company.[1]

We also observe that support for a policy can increase after it is adopted. Consider three examples of policies that drew increased popular support after they were enacted. Erikson looks at public opinion polls from the 1960s both before and after passage of Medicare in June

I am grateful to Stef Proost, Esko Niskanen, Eric Patashnik, and two anonymous reviewers for their comments.

1965.[2] In a February 1965 Harris Poll, 62% answered affirmatively when asked "Do you favor or oppose President Johnson's program of medical care for the aged under Social Security?" Following passage in June 1965, support for Medicare increased further. By December 1965, the percent who told Harris they "approved" of Medicare rose to 82%. Ever since, public support for Medicare has been strong. For another example, Winslott-Hiselius et al. study attitudes toward congestion tolls in Stockholm.[3] A full-scale congestion charging trial was carried out in 2006. Almost half of respondents in a survey stated that they changed their attitudes toward congestion charges during the trial, with most becoming more favorable. Reduced opposition to road charges, after they were introduced, was also found in Bergen, Oslo, and Trondheim. Another interesting example is the Japanese constitution imposed by the U.S. occupation forces in 1947, which in Article 9 included the renunciation of war. After the end of the occupation, Japan did not revise the constitution.[4]

Clever politicians can introduce policies that create interest groups benefiting from the policy. Alexander Hamilton, the first American Treasury secretary, showed the way. In 1790 he had the federal government assume the debts incurred during the Revolutionary War by the thirteen states, thereby giving claimants of the debt a strong incentive to support the success of the new federal government. In this book, Weaver (chapter 11) discusses how the creation of a major federal crime bureaucracy, the Law Enforcement Assistance Administration, led to the creation of interest groups that lobbied for continuation of federal support of local law enforcement, long after the Law Enforcement Assistance Administration ceased to exist.

Other policies may generate support by creating valuable financial assets that would lose value were the policy reversed. Consider tradable permits for emissions of sulfur. In anticipation of regulations limiting emissions, some firms may invest in equipment that reduces their emissions, allowing them to sell their emissions permits. Were government to relax these regulations, the price of these permits would fall, creating a capital loss to firms that had invested in emissions reductions. That is, the implementation of the policy creates special interests that support the policy.[5] Not all policies will generate support; for example, a tax on emissions creates no financial assets, and therefore does not generate a set of investors who favor the tax.[6]

Or consider a genius of American politics, Franklin Roosevelt. A management consultant criticized the inefficiency of the new Social Security system in recording the contributions of each worker. Any contributor could request a statement of his total contributions and an estimate of his eventual benefits. Thousands did so and were courteously answered, although the benefits were determined by Congress rather than by any insurance contract. Roosevelt justified the costs of maintaining the individual accounts on policy grounds: "That account is not to determine how much should be paid out, to control what should be paid out. That account is there so those sons of bitches up on the Hill can't ever abandon this system when I'm gone."[7] Social Security has the added feature that if people expect to receive benefits from it, they will save little for their old age, and therefore bitterly oppose reductions in Social Security benefits once retired.

This chapter examines other conditions, less closely related to interest group politics, that make a policy more popular after it is adopted,[8] looking at two mechanisms. The first is that once the policy is adopted, consumers or firms make investments that make the policy more attractive to them. The second mechanism concerns revelation of information. The adoption of the policy provides information about the preferences or characteristics of politicians or other political actors, which changes the political pressures favoring or opposing the policy.

This approach complements others' chapters in this volume, which emphasize political considerations. These studies show that a policy is more likely to be sustained over different Congresses when the partisan compositions change little over time.[9] Other work argues that changes in agency structure (such as elimination of the Civil Aeronautics Board) can reduce political pressures for policy reversal, and that the policy itself (such as airline deregulation, which fostered the growth of firms profiting from unregulated markets) can create supporters for the policy or reduce the number of its opponents.[10] My consideration of how investment responding to a new policy can generate support for the policy similarly relates to endogenous political support. Conditions at the time of enactment can also affect policy durability, with divided government (where the House and Senate differ in ideologies, or the presidency and Congress are controlled by different parties) at the time of enactment making later policy reversal more likely.[11]

Investment

Investments That Induce Political Support for Policy

Investment decisions can increase the political support for a policy after it is adopted.[12] Consumers and firms may respond to a new policy by undertaking actions to benefit from the policy or to reduce the costs the policy imposes: Firms may install equipment that reduces emissions, firms may invest in low-polluting industries instead of in high-polluting ones, and so on. These actions in turn can increase support for the policy in the future. Brainard and Verdier explore this mechanism as an explanation for the persistence of protection from imports to declining industries.[13] They argue that if protection is granted in the current period, less adjustment will be undertaken, increasing the demand for protection in future periods. Accordingly, future protection can be expected to increase with current protection.

Multiple Equilibria

When behavior by consumers generates network externalities, or when economies of agglomeration exist, multiple equilibria can appear. That can make economic agents prefer continuation of whatever policy is in place. Consider the success of policies designed to reduce smoking of cigarettes. An important characteristic of smoking is that persons are likely to find smoking more attractive if others around them also smoke. Smokers will be socially accepted, hear fewer complaints by fellow consumers, find it easier to borrow a lighter or a cigarette, and face fewer restrictions at restaurants, airlines, and other places. The process can work in reverse. When government reduces smoking by some persons, it will induce reduced smoking by others, and so generate increased support for the restrictions.

Credibility of Policies

The existence of multiple equilibria relates to the credibility of policy, which in turn affects private investments. If a policy is adopted with bipartisan support, then consumers may rationally believe that support for it is greater than they had initially thought. Consumers and firms who think that the policy is likely to be continued may make investments that in turn make the policy more attractive, and thus more likely to be continued. Consumers and firms who expect the policy to be changed will be unwilling to make investments that would make the policy effective.[14] Under some conditions, beliefs about future government policy may be unpredictable, or may vary with beliefs about future economic conditions. Nevertheless, some policies will be more credible than others. In particular, a policy will be credible if, when people expect it to be adopted and make choices accordingly, a government indeed benefits by adopting the policy.

The essential idea that policy may not be credible appears in works on trade protection.[15] The discussion of commitment in public policy relates to work by several authors who show that current decisions of economic agents depend, in part, on their expectations of future policy.[16] Phelps and Pollak apply the principle to determine optimal savings decisions.[17] Alesina and Tabellini extend these insights by showing that voters may favor budget deficits that constrain future public policy.[18] Glazer applies these principles to demonstrate that collective choices will show a bias toward durable projects.[19]

Related studies examine how expectations of a change in policy may change behavior in a way that increases political support for the policy under consideration. Cassing and Hillman show that a declining industry may suddenly collapse when its small size reduces political support for protective tariffs.[20] Obstfeld shows that a balance-of-payments crisis can be self-fulfilling if agents expect a speculative attack to set off an inflationary domestic-credit policy.[21] Rodrik claims that trade liberalization will succeed if it induces the growth of firms that support such liberalization.[22]

Policies with the same immediate result may yet differ in whether they build political support. For example, in the 1970s Congress required power plants to install smokestack scrubbers rather than to burn low-sulfur coal. Both policies would reduce sulfur emissions. But whereas burning costly low-sulfur coal instead of cheap high-sulfur coal raises costs each time the substitution is made, continued operation of scrubbers can be cheap. So firms that use expensive low-sulfur coal have a greater incentive to lobby for reversing the regulation than do firms that had installed scrubbers.

Political institutions can also affect expectations. Elected officials with short terms of office may find it difficult to impose environmental regulations that would hurt consumers. In contrast, politicians who are secure in office may be willing to impose unpopular regulations, stick with them, change expectations of consumers, induce investment, and eventually reap the rewards of increased welfare. Government's financing decisions can also affect expectations. Government, for example, may allow localities to sell tax-free bonds to finance sewerage treatment plants, thereby inducing bond holders or investment bankers to pressure government to regulate sewerage.

Information

A different class of reasons for why a policy is more likely to be continued than to be initially adopted is informational. These effects mean that the hardest part of policy reform may be the one-time problem of introducing the policy, rather than the continuing problem of generating continual support. The effects described below may also suggest what information, or what ignorance, may be likely to generate support for a policy. The results show that improved information can have counterintuitive results. Support for a policy can be greater when no one knows the identities of the beneficiaries than when the identity of most becomes common knowledge. And officials may be less willing to continue a policy the better informed is the public about the competence of officials.

Updating Beliefs about Political Pressure

People who observe that the policy was adopted have new information— the policy was adopted. This observation should affect their beliefs about the politics surrounding the policy; for example, they may believe that the special interest that favored the policy is more effective than they had initially thought. Given these updated beliefs about the power of the special interest, people may rationally believe that the policy will likely be maintained, though initially they thought it was unlikely to be adopted.

I illustrate this effect with a simple model of political pressure. Suppose two special interests compete. One special interest group favors the policy, the other opposes it. The appendix shows that under some plausible conditions the amount of lobbying by each special interest will be unaffected by its belief about how effective its lobbying is, or will be the same after the reform is introduced as before. But adoption of the reform makes people believe that the lobby that favored the reform is more effective than they had previously thought. This in turn means that people believe that political pressures in the future are more likely than before to favor the policy. This change in beliefs can reinforce the investment effects discussed above: If people expect the policy will be continued, they will make investments that are profitable only if the policy is continued, which in turn increases the political support for the policy. This illustrates one theme, that having a reform adopted may be more difficult than generating support for a policy once it has been adopted.

Resolving Uncertainty about the Identity of Winners and Losers

When some people are unsure about who will benefit and who will lose from a policy, a majority of voters may oppose adoption of the policy, but were it adopted, a majority may favor its continuation. I illustrate with an example, based on Fernandez and Rodrik.[23] Suppose a country has 100 voters. A proposed reform would benefit each of 51 voters by \$10, and would hurt each of the remaining 49 voters by \$5. Aggregate benefits of the reform are therefore $(51)(10) - (49)(5) = 265$. So the reform should be adopted. Suppose further that some voters are uncertain about who will win and who will lose from the reform. Let 49 voters know for certain that they will be among the 51 who gain. Let all voters know that these 49 people will gain. Each of the remaining 51 voters thinks that he is as equally likely as any of the other 51 voters to be a winner. Since only 2 of these 51 voters can be winners, the expected benefit to an uninformed voter is $(2/51)(10) - (49/51)(5) = -4.41$. Therefore, these 51 uninformed voters, a majority, oppose the reform. Note that they vote against the reform though aggregate benefits are positive. But were the policy adopted, 51 of the 100 voters would benefit, and each of these 51 people would know that he benefited. Therefore a majority would favor continuing the policy. In short, a majority votes against the reform though it will benefit a majority of voters, and though once adopted, a majority will favor continuing it. The example also illustrates the more general result that more voters may oppose a reform when the identities of many of the winners are known than when their identities are not.

A related result appears when risk-averse voters fear that a policy adopted today may induce a majority of voters to adopt a policy that creates excessive risk as viewed from today's perspective.[24] But once the city has a richer population, a majority may vote for policies that hurt the original poor. Suppose that in each of two periods a policy, say zoning rules that allow gentrification, is adopted if a majority of voters favors it. The policy in each period will generate gains for some voters (say those who sell houses at higher prices) and losses for a few (say those who used to shop at a cheap supermarket that has gone upscale), with each voter unsure how he will be affected. That is, after the first policy is adopted, more people see an increase in their wealth. If people are more willing to take risk the wealthier they are, this means that persons who ex post benefit from the policy are more willing to take additional risks in the future. But the persons who were hurt by the policy (say those who pay higher grocery prices) oppose further adoption of the policy (which could lead to even higher grocery prices). The collective decision made in subsequent periods can therefore differ from the choice that would be preferred by specified individuals, thereby reducing the expected gain from risky policies. Moreover, each voter realizes that the policy chosen in the initial period can influence the choices of the voters in later periods, and will consider this effect in her vote in the initial period. This bias in collective decisions applies even if in the initial period all people have identical preferences; it shows a bias against risky policies. That is, even if each and every individual would favor the policy when the decision is hers alone to make, all voters may vote against similar risky policies if decisions in the future will be made collectively. But once the initial policy is adopted, a majority of voters may favor its continuation or the adoption of a similar policy. In addition, the analysis yields the surprising result that a majority of the voters may prefer policies that, ex post, are expected to benefit few persons, over policies that, ex post, are expected to benefit many voters. After the policy is adopted, it will therefore appear that the public voted for a policy that benefits special interests.

Reputation

I so far considered the behavior of firms, of consumers, and of special interest groups, but not that of public officials. The concern of public officials with their reputation can exacerbate the status quo bias discussed above. Suppose voters have incomplete knowledge about the effects of implemented policies. But voters do see if a policymaker reverses his previous position. Such reversal can signal to voters that the policymaker had previously erred. More specifically, define the policymaker's competence as the probability that he designs an effective policy. Since a policy failure is more likely to occur under an incompetent policymaker than under a competent policymaker, policy reversal signals low competence.[25]

More explicitly, suppose that an official can be either Smart or Stupid. An official serves for two periods. In each period he estimates the state of nature. If the state of nature is more likely A, then the optimal action is α. If the state of nature is more likely B, then the optimal action is ß. A Smart official is more likely to observe correctly the state of nature than is a Stupid official. Let an official correctly observe the state of nature with probability $\pi_1 < 1$ in period 1 and with probability $\pi_2 < 1$ in period 2. The values of π_1 and of π_2 are larger for a Smart official than for a Stupid one.

Suppose the official attempts to take the optimal action in each period. If the state of nature is A, then with probability $\pi_1\pi_2$ he will take action α in both periods. And if the state of nature is A, then with probability $(1 - \pi_1)(1 - \pi_2)$ he will take action ß in both periods. The probability that he will take the same action in both periods when the state of nature is A is thus $\pi_1\pi_2 + (1 - \pi_1)(1 - \pi_2)$. The same expression holds when the state of nature is B. For $\pi_1 > 1/2$ and $\pi_2 > 1/2$, the value of $\pi_1\pi_2 + (1 - \pi_1)(1 - \pi_2)$ increases with π_1 and with π_2.

Thus, the probability that an official who acts sincerely takes the same action over the two periods increases with π_1 and with π_2. That means that it cannot be an equilibrium for an official who cares about his reputation to adopt the policy in period 2 that he thinks best matches the state of nature in that period; he instead has an incentive to adopt the same policy in period 2 as in period 1.

Such reputational considerations generate a general status quo bias—an official who had opposed environmental regulations has a continuing incentive to oppose it. But if the official did impose pollution controls, then she has an incentive to continue those controls. Moreover, as long as the preceding official was viewed as more likely competent than not, these biases can arise even when one official replaces another.

Conclusion

The ideas explored above yield implications about conditions that will make policy reversal unlikely. First, for reasons of reputation or of information revelation, the longer a policy has been in effect, the more likely it will continue to be in effect.

Second, the models suggest a trade-off between the cost of a policy and its permanence. Opposition to a policy will likely be lower the less costly the policy. But a policy requiring or inducing investment would make reversal of the policy impose large capital losses on economic agents who had made the investments; these people will therefore oppose reversal of the policy. Indeed, measures such as compensation schemes and side payments intended to reduce political opposition to a policy may undermine the credibility of the policy by making special interests skeptical that the policy will continue.[26]

Third, the allocation of responsibility across different levels of government can affect the confidence of consumers or of firms that a policy will be continued. In particular, though joint responsibility of a central and local government, or of different groups within a government, makes adoption of a policy more difficult, it also makes reversal of policy more difficult. Indeed, detailed studies find that parliamentary systems with party governments (rather than with coalition governments consisting of multiple parties) exhibit more policy instability.[27] Lewis finds that when the U.S. Congress and the president share the same party, the probability that an agency will be terminated is about double what it is under divided government.[28] Policies approved at both the local and central levels may be especially effective, as they demonstrate a broader political consensus than those produced by a unified regime. Economic actors should form appropriate expectations and be more willing to behave in ways (e.g., investment) that make the policy succeed and that also induce added support for the policy. By contrast, economic actors may hesitate in responding to policies passed by unified governments because they may expect large future swings in policy.

Fourth, attention to the credibility of policy also leads to a different view of whether policies are better enacted at the local or at the national level. For statistical reasons, local support for policies may, on average, be more stable over time than support for corresponding national policies. For instance, the longevity of a policy may be questionable if it is initiated at the national level following a landslide favoring one legislative party. As comparable idiosyncrasies at the local level may work in opposite directions, they may cancel one another and lead to little change over time in the aggregate effects of such policies. Firms operating in many localities may expect the actions of various localities to lead to a stable demand for their services. Put another way, local policies may be more reliable in the aggregate, and, given that such expectations may make policies more successful, such reliability allows local governments to succeed with policies that would fail for the national government.

Appendix: Lobbying

Label the two special interests Y (for "Yes") and N (for "No"). If the policy is adopted, Y's utility is 1/2; otherwise Y's utility is −1/2. Thus, Y gains utility 1 if the policy is adopted rather than not. Make symmetric assumptions about N: its utility is −1/2 if the policy is adopted and is 1/2 if the policy is not adopted. Interest group i spends xi on lobbying. Let the effectiveness of interest group i's lobbying be captured by the parameter γi. The probability that the policy is adopted is $\dfrac{\gamma_Y x_y}{\gamma_Y x_y + \gamma_N x_N}$, and special interest i maximizes $\dfrac{\gamma_Y x_y}{\gamma_Y x_y + \gamma_N x_N} - x_Y$. It turns out that in a Nash equilibrium, at any solution with positive levels of lobbying, each of the two groups chooses the same level of lobbying, equal to $\gamma_Y \gamma_N / (\gamma_Y + \gamma_N)^2$.

For a numerical example, suppose that $\gamma_N = 1$. Let the prior probability be that $\gamma_Y = 0$ with probability 1/2, and that $\gamma_Y = 2$ with probability 1/2. The two lobbyists know the value of γ_Y, but the public does not. If $\gamma_Y = 0$, then $x_Y = 0$ and x_N is an infinitesimally small number. If $\gamma_N = 1$ and $\gamma_Y = 2$, then $x_Y = x_N = 2/9$. Thus, in period 1 the probability that the policy will be adopted is $\dfrac{1}{2} 0 + \dfrac{1}{2} \dfrac{2(2/9)}{(2/9) + 2(2/9)} = 1/3$. But if the policy is adopted, then everyone knows that $\gamma_Y = 2$. The probability that the policy will be continued is then $\dfrac{2(2/9)}{(2/9) + 2(2/9)} = 2/3$. The probability that the policy will be continued is far greater than the probability that it will be adopted in the first place.

Why Some Reforms Last and Others Collapse: The Tax Reform Act of 1986 versus Airline Deregulation

Eric M. Patashnik

A key challenge for the federal government is to sustain policy reforms that serve general or diffuse interests rather than narrowly concentrated ones. There are two stages to the reform process. The first phase involves getting reform proposals on the policy agenda, overriding or neutralizing interest group opposition, and building a winning political coalition. The second phase of reform begins the moment *after* the curtain falls on the high drama of legislative enactment. The second phase has received far less scholarly attention than the first yet is no less important, for it is then that reform plans meet the tough realities of democratic politics. All the political compromises and trade-offs that were denied or papered over during the enactment phase will show themselves, sooner if not later. Why do some policy reforms "take" and become embedded in the American state while other reforms are eroded or reversed? How do reforms evolve over time?

In this chapter, I examine the political sustainability of the Tax Reform Act of 1986 (TRA) and airline deregulation to provide a window into these questions. By political sustainability, I mean not the length

This chapter draws together material presented across several chapters of my book, Eric. M. Patashnik, *Reforms at Risk: What Happens After Major Policy Changes Are Enacted* (Princeton, NJ: Princeton University Press, 2008). The material is reprinted here with the permission of Princeton University Press.

of time that a policy reform continues in its original form before it is amended, but rather, following Hugh Heclo, the capacity of a reform to maintain its structural integrity and use its core principles to guide its course amid inevitable pressures for change.[1] Policy reforms face tremendous "political risk." They are vulnerable, Heclo points out, to "being destabilized as time passes, unexpectedly rendering the plan's original design unsustainable in its promised operations and purpose." Such political riskiness "is not the same as uncertainties about the future in general." Uncertainties, such as an unexpected economic crisis or a scandal that causes the incumbent party to lose seats, can undermine any policy. The forces of political riskiness have to do with pressures "that are fashioned and put in play by a particular policy approach."[2] These pressures, I claim, are not reducible to the influence of macro partisan tides or election trends. They affect the potential for a specific reform to become self-reinforcing and the *direction* (not just the probability) of subsequent policy change.

The TRA and airline deregulation are clearly not "average" or "typical" federal laws. They are, rather, canonical examples of nonincremental, efficiency-oriented legislation: elite-driven reform thrusts intended to change the direction of public policy and generate benefits for millions of American citizens. The TRA collapsed the number of tax brackets from 14 to 2, and eliminated or curtailed dozens of shelters, loopholes, and other narrow tax breaks enjoyed by business corporations and well-heeled investors. By withdrawing tax preferences from a favored few, the government was able to sharply lower tax rates for millions of low- and middle-income taxpayers without increasing the federal budget deficit. The airline deregulation law removed anticompetitive government regulations that boosted industry profit margins, but also coddled inefficient carriers, stifled many innovations, and imposed huge costs on ordinary air passengers.

A fascinating political science literature has emerged on the conditions under which general interest reforms can be adopted in the face of strong interest group opposition. This literature stresses the role of expert ideas, political entrepreneurship, and the strategic framing of the policy debate.[3] But how have these hard-won reforms unfolded after enactment, and what factors have shaped their long-term sustainability? Neither the TRA nor airline deregulation has been repealed. The postenactment trajectories of the two reforms, however, have been remarkably different. Although important vestiges of the TRA remain on the books, "the tax code has been allowed to revert in many ways to its pre-1986 form and politicians of both parties are eager to push it back further."[4] Since 1987, more than 15,000 changes have been made to the Internal Revenue Code. Both rates and targeted tax breaks have increased, and the number of tax brackets has multiplied. As a result of TRA's unraveling, many experts have argued that the tax code is broken. Blue-ribbon fiscal commissions under both Presidents George W. Bush and Barack Obama have called for the enactment of comprehensive tax reform legislation to restore the principles of tax simplicity and horizontal equity that have been squandered.[5] In contrast, there have been no serious proposals for returning to the pre-1978 airline regulatory regime, even though the airline industry has remained in an almost constant state of financial turmoil.

A Historical-Institutional Perspective on Sustainability

As I argue in my book *Reforms at Risk*, these patterns are best understood from a historical-institutional perspective. The targets of general interest reforms are the inefficiencies and policy distortions of the day before yesterday. The long-term sustainability of reform projects, however, depends on what happens to them *tomorrow*.[6] There is no guarantee that reforms will prove sustainable over time. The losers at the moment of reform enactment cannot be counted on to vanish without another fight. They will press their particularistic demands up to a point where the organizational costs in effort exceed the expected benefits of winning. Over time, new concentrated interests may arrive on the political scene that would also seek to undo a reform to further their own aims. The winners from a reform may fail to repel such second-phase attacks. Because reforms offer low per capita benefits to many people, beneficiaries may have a far weaker incentive to mobilize than the actors who would profit from a reform's unraveling.

The adoption of a reform is thus only the beginning of a political struggle. Reform enactment *could* indicate a sharp, permanent break with prior patterns of governance. It *may* signal that political dynamics have permanently shifted. By itself, however, the passage of a reform law may settle rather little. In contrast to the functionalist argument that reforms endure merely because they are socially efficient, I argue that reforms must continuously generate political support if they are to stick.

Theoretical Framework: Institutions and Policy Feedback

Although reform consolidation cannot be taken for granted, it is certainly possible for a reform to become so deeply rooted in political practice and culture that its dismantlement becomes all but unthinkable.[7] Why do some reforms become sustainable while others unravel? Because reform is best understood as a dynamic process, attention must be directed to the factors that determine the willingness of policymakers to promote or frustrate an extension of a given reform's line of policy development. Two factors require careful attention. The first is the extent to which *political structures* propel a reform forward, supply necessary administrative supports, and protect it from inhospitable policy change. The second factor is the extent to which the reforms generate a self-reinforcing dynamic through the creation of *policy feedback effects*. The two factors are analytically distinct but relate to one another in practice. Institutions influence the credibility of policy commitments and, in so doing, shape the expectations and behavior of social actors.

Political Structures

While current policymakers always retain the legal authority to revise existing laws, a reform has better odds of sticking if its passage occurs simultaneously with supportive shifts in its structural environment. Four kinds of shifts may be important.

First, reforms may strengthen governing capacities.[8] This may occur through changes in administrative authority to better align the incentives of bureaucrats, through the hiring of new staff with relevant policy expertise and through the elimination of "red tape" that frustrates the appropriate exercise of administrative discretion. Second, reforms may raze the structural foundations of "cozy policy subsystems" and "iron triangles." Their destruction may be necessary to prevent inefficient patterns of governance from reproducing themselves postenactment. A reform may constrain future decision making through administrative procedures or even bring about a bureau's termination.[9] Alternatively, reforms may weaken policy subsystems by empowering actors with broader perspectives on governance, such as executives or budget guardians in Congress. Third, political transaction costs can be raised or lowered to make a reform more sticky.[10] This might be done to promote credibility and give actors confidence that movement along a reform path will continue. Transaction costs might be raised, for example, to block the adoption of inefficient policies (e.g., budget rules that require a supermajority for the adoption of a tax expenditure benefiting a small number of people). Finally, control over a given policy arena can be shifted to a political venue in which reform coalitions enjoy privileged access.[11] For example, reformers may seek to relocate policymaking authority from one congressional committee to another or from the regulatory process back into Congress or even into the courts.

Some long-lasting reforms have been reinforced through multiple structural mechanisms. An illustrative example is the Reciprocal Trade Agreements Act (RTAA) of 1934, a landmark trade policy reform that successfully collapsed logrolling coalitions supportive of high tariffs. The reform shifted the locus of trade decisions from the tax arena (in which Congress considered each tariff separately) to treaty negotiation (in which the president negotiated comprehensive tariff packages with other nations); "bundled" foreign tariff reductions and domestic tariff reductions into one legislative package (which legislators had to vote up or down on without amendment); and created special voting rules that avoided the need to obtain supermajority support for tariff reductions in Congress.[12]

Yet if the development of a reform is shaped by its structural environment, future policy outcomes rarely can be "locked in."[13] One reason is that political structures are not infrequently the products of political compromise. They may be little more than "common carriers" of multiple interests.[14] Tensions and contradictions among these goals may limit any clear sense of purpose or mission. Second, efforts to "stack the deck" can backfire, even when institutional designers have shared goals. Institutional design is an inexact science. Even the cleverest and most farsighted reformers cannot wholly escape the law of unintended consequences. Finally, it is hard to compel outcomes in a free market system in which sustaining a reform and implementing it successfully typically requires the endorsement—or at least the acquiescence—of private actors, who possess some capacity to withdraw their support.

Policy Feedback

Sustaining a reform is a *constructive* process as well as a destructive one. Once enacted, reforms may create new political facts on the ground.

Here, I draw on the literature on "policy feedback," the study of how policies, once passed, influence political dynamics going forward. This literature has demonstrated that policies are not only the result of ongoing political struggles. They also reshape the identities, interests, and goals of individuals and constituency groups, allocate political resources, encourage or discourage political mobilization, and create—or fail to create—expectations among individuals and groups that make it difficult or unattractive for leaders to reverse course.[15]

While policy feedback effects are often complex, it is possible to suggest hypotheses about the *general* conditions under which reforms will be most sustainable and about the kinds of postenactment dynamics that should be expected to arise under different circumstances. Two overarching feedback effects are crucial. The first is the way reform affects the *identities and political affiliations of relevant group actors.* After reform, the scope and composition of the interest group environment may be generally stable, and the identities and alliances of preexisting interests may undergo relatively little change. Because the sector is not being continually penetrated by new groups with diverse preferences and incentives, interest group cohesion in the sector will be relatively high. There may still be areas of conflict on particular issues, but the fact that group memberships and patterns of interaction are reasonably stable facilitates the emergence of a sectorwide consensus on major counterreform efforts, meaning that politicians will face strong pressures to undo the law. Alternatively, group dynamics may change dramatically after reform enactments. A sector may see the entry of an ever-changing constellation of groups, each of which finds itself in a somewhat different economic and strategic situation. Lobbying in the sector will be characterized by rapidly changing coalitions, as allies on one issue become adversaries on the next. The fragmentation of the emerging "issue network" will tend to inhibit organizational mobilization around a common antireform agenda, leaving each group to pursue its own narrow goals. Politicians will be cross-pressured, making explicit repeal of the reform less likely. Such dynamics are more likely to emerge in very broad policy sectors like taxation.

A second important feedback process is the effect of the reform on actors' *investments.* As Amihai Glazer's chapter 7 also stresses, societal interests can make extensive economic and organizational commitments based on the expectation that a reform will be maintained. This suggests an increasing returns process in which groups develop assets that are

Group investments	Group identities and affiliations	
	Stable (Identities and group affiliations remain stable; many clienteles have common policy preferences)	**Fluid** (New groups emerge; coalitional alignments undergo rapid change; interest group cohesion is low)
Modest (Social actors fail to make large-scale investments; organizational adaptations to the reform are minimal)	*Reversal*	*Erosion*
Extensive (Groups make large-scale, often highly specific investments based on the expectation that the reform will continue)	*Entrenchment*	*Reconfiguration*

FIGURE 8.1: Policy feedback and post-reform dynamics

specific to the new policy regime. There is no guarantee that reforms will induce complementary public or private investments, however. In sum, reforms potentially *may* generate path dependence, but it is an empirical question whether they actually do so.[16] This implies a simple two-by-two matrix in which both the stability and cohesion of group identities and the level of investments vary (see figure 8.1). Four post-reform paths can be specified.

In the upper-left quadrant, where affected groups fail to make significant investments and the interest group environment is stable and cohesive, there is a high probability of reform *reversal*, meaning an implicit or explicit repeal of the reform, leading to a return to the status quo ante. Both governmental and nongovernmental actors can play key roles in the reversal process.

In the upper-right quadrant, where passage of a reform fails to promote significant clientele investments but the interest group environment is very fluid, the *erosion* of reform should be anticipated. This is a more subtle and usually more gradual process than outright reversal. The reform statute itself remains on the books, and some of its substantive policy achievements may even stick, but the logic of the reform is not extended over time. Continual micro-level pressures are applied by various rent seekers to erode the reform after enactment because the policy sector features a diversity of unvested interests. A common dynamic is "death by a thousand cuts," which obtains when policymakers repeatedly adopt incremental amendments that undercut the previous reform. While each amendment constitutes only a marginal departure from the status quo ante and might be justified by the need to make a "special exception" to the reform's overarching rules, the cumulative effect is very large. The reform gradually loses its coherence and integrity, and its particularistic exceptions swallow its more general rules.

In the bottom-left quadrant, patterns of interaction among relevant groups remain stable, and the organizational cohesion of the sector is fairly high, but actors make large-scale investments based on the reform's expected maintenance. Here, the *entrenchment* of a reform is predicted. Reform gains are consolidated because group actors adapt to the new facts on the ground. But the constellation of actors in the sector does not significantly change. Preexisting coalitional alignments remain intact, but the reform is now something that groups must deal with.

Finally, in the lower-right quadrant, political dynamics experience a *reconfiguration*. The creative destructiveness of the market or other powerful forces causes new producer or consumer groups to join or replace preexisting interests in the policy arena. The diversity of interests raises the transaction costs of organizing a sectorwide counterreform effort. Coalitional patterns undergo rapid change, upsetting previous alliances and patterns of political mobilization. Each group actor faces a different strategic situation, but is nonetheless stimulated to invest heavily in ways complementary to the reform's maintenance. Blame-avoiding politicians will be loath to upset those investments. The defining feature of reconfiguration is the difficulty of going back to the pre-reform status quo. Political dynamics can no more easily be reversed than "scrambled eggs" can be unscrambled (an image that politicians sometimes invoke to describe the vast societal transformations wrought by airline deregulation).

How the Reforms Passed

While this chapter focuses on the aftermath of reform, it is important to understand the factors that come into play at enactment. The TRA

(P.L. 99–514) passed Congress by wide margins (292 to 136 in the House and 74 to 23 in the Senate) in 1986 despite overwhelming opposition from powerful economic interests.[17] Only a few consumer organizations, wholesalers, and electronics firms supported the measure. As Timothy J. Conlan, David R. Beam, and Margaret Wrightson argue in their insightful study of the passage of the TRA, "had Congress been a mere referee [among contending economic interests], the TRA would have lost in a lopsided game."[18]

Several factors were crucial to the stunning reform victory. First, skilled political entrepreneurs like Senator Bill Bradley (D-NJ) invested their time and energy in the reform project when it was unpopular and used the media to draw attention to the cause. Media coverage of tax reform was highly favorable, framing it as a symbolic battle between special interests and the public good. Second, political leaders gave reform their public support. In his January 1984 State of the Union address, President Ronald Reagan asked the Department of Treasury to prepare a "plan for action to simplify the entire tax code."[19] Reagan's early support, along with that of House Ways and Means Committee chairman Dan Rostenkowski (D-IL), pressured other leaders, such as Senate Finance Committee chairman Robert Packwood (R-OR), to get on board.

Despite the Reagan administration's endorsement, tax reform's fate was very much up for grabs. As R. Douglas Arnold observes in his superb book about how general interest reform laws are enacted in the first place, coalition leaders such as Rostenkowski and Packwood, "employed virtually every strategy in the book" to hold the reform coalition together in Congress.[20] They targeted a large number of tax preferences for repeal, rather than chiseling at only a few at time, in order to generate the savings needed to permit dramatically lower tax rates, which were integral to the measure's appeal. They insisted that the whole bill be revenue and geographically neutral to avoid exacerbating ideological or regional conflicts. They manipulated legislative procedures to protect lawmakers from clientele pressures. Lawmakers met in secret, avoided recorded votes, and used restrictive rules to keep the bill from being picked apart on the floor. Finally, coalition leaders strategically used side payments ("transition rules") to lubricate the package's adoption.[21]

The enactment of airline deregulation was no less remarkable. The Airline Deregulation Act of 1978 provided for the gradual removal over six years of virtually all entry restrictions into the airline industry,[22] all restrictions on the selection of routes, and all constraints on pricing. The

mass public was not clamoring for airline deregulation when the issue
first emerged on the policy agenda in the 1970s. Nor did interest group
pressure compel the law's adoption. Rather, as Martha Derthick and
Paul J. Quirk have shown in their excellent study of deregulation, policy entrepreneurs like Civilian Aeronautics Board (CAB) chairman Alfred E. Kahn and Senator Ted Kennedy (D-MA) *created* the political
conditions that made the reform's enactment possible. They did so by establishing a compelling linkage between the airline industry's anticompetitive behavior and salient issues like inflation and concerns about big
government.

Most of the big carriers adamantly opposed deregulation and waged
a fierce battle against it.[23] The airlines argued that the removal of regulatory controls on entry into and exit out of markets would lead to destructive competition. Opponents included financially strapped airlines
such as TWA and Eastern, which feared entry into their most profitable
routes,[24] but also industry powerhouses like American and Delta. Late
in the battle, a few carriers modified their position and signaled their
willingness to accept deregulation. The industry's eleventh hour political
retreat reflected less a sudden realization that deregulation would be ad-
vantageous for existing carriers than the political momentum of reform
and the fear of ending up with the worst of both worlds—government
regulation without market protections.[25] Organized labor also fought
hard to preserve regulatory projections of their rents. Unions representing pilots, flight attendants, transport workers, and other employees argued that deregulation would reduce wages and job security.[26] But Congress overcame this strong interest group opposition. The Senate passed
the deregulation bill by a vote of 83 to 9. The House vote on final passage was 363 to 8.[27]

The Evolution of the TRA

The TRA has not been repealed, and a number of its policy accomplishments live on. Nonetheless, the reform has been substantially eroded.
Tax expenditures have crept back into the tax code, and tax shelters have
reemerged in a new guise. Rather than embedding the reform's core
principles of tax neutrality, simplification, and base broadening, post-
1986 tax legislation has honored them mainly in the breach. These developments have been demoralizing to many reform supporters. "The

Tax Reform Act of 1986 was a great leap forward," said former Congressional Budget Office director Robert D. Reischauer in 1994. "Now we're slowly undoing the good that we did then."[28] "I feel like crying," said Senator Bob Packwood (R-OR), who chaired the Finance Committee when the TRA passed.[29]

Hard Promises to Keep

Taxation is a particularly difficult policy area to reform, in part because resource mobilization is so central to governing authority. Tax decisions are made annually, and Congress is notoriously reluctant to delegate control over the tax code to the executive. In addition, taxation is an exceptionally broad policy tool. It can be used as an instrument not just of fiscal policy but also of social and economic policy. Sustaining tax reform required Congress (and the president) to avoid the temptation to use the tax code as a vehicle for particularistic favor provision and servicing of the organized. While the major parties to the deal pledged to honor this commitment—chairman Rostenkowski famously announced he would hang a "Gone Fishing" sign on the Ways and Means Committee door after the TRA was signed into law to give individuals and businesses time to get accustomed to the new rules—they proved unwilling or unable to do so.[30] *Tax reform unraveled, then, not only because its enacting coalition was replaced by coalitions with different preferences, but also because many of the original drafters failed to keep their reform commitments.*

Political sustainability challenges were bound to emerge after enactment, even if the TRA's bipartisan enacting coalition had remained intact, not only because manipulation over the tax code is deeply woven into legislative routines but also because the TRA failed to provide a credible solution to the key fiscal policy challenge of the mid 1980s— rising federal budget deficits. The 1986 Act was a marriage of "Democratic tax reformers who wanted to eliminate tax preferences and treat all income alike regardless of its source," and Republican supply-siders and deregulators who were "principally interested in lowering tax rates."[31] But this political marriage was troubled from the start. Just six months after the TRA's enactment, in March 1987, Ways and Means chairman Rostenkowski announced that he and his panel would support tax hikes to reduce the deficit, even though it was clear that doing so would anger Republicans.[32] Democrats argued that the recent closing of corporate tax loopholes had made tax hikes more palatable by increasing public confidence in the fairness of the system. In contrast, President Reagan and most GOP lawmakers maintained that the budget deficit should be liquidated through spending reductions. The enactment of the TRA thus papered over an ideological conflict regarding tax fairness and the future of activist government.[33]

Unraveling the Tax Reform Bargain

If one test of reform sustainability is whether policy designers defend their legislative creations from attack, another is whether successor politicians feel bound to honor past agreements. Politicians essentially acted as if the TRA had never been enacted. President George H. W. Bush was Reagan's vice president when the TRA passed. But Bush had not been a tax reformer during his earlier congressional career. During the debate over the Tax Reform Act of 1969, then Representative Bush expressed his support for tax breaks as a method for the government to encourage business investment. "I favor tax credits and tax incentives as the way to answer many of our problems as opposed to direct government subsidy or starting some new bureau on the Potomac," he said.[34] As president, Bush never bought into the 1986 reform bargain of lower tax rates in exchange for fewer tax breaks. Bush called for restoration of preferential treatment for capital gains, claiming it would boost economic growth. Rostenkowski argued that Bush's capital gains proposal would only encourage other special interests to seek narrow tax breaks, and Senate Majority leader George Mitchell (D-ME) blocked the plan from coming up on the Senate floor.[35] But Bush pressed the capital gains issue throughout his four-year term of office. The president also called for new tax preferences for child care, oil exploration, and enterprise zones.[36] Bush would later anger many Republican supporters of the TRA by agreeing to the 1990 deficit-reduction deal, which raised the top income tax rate from 28 to 31 percent.

President Clinton also did not feel bound to leave marginal tax rates alone. In 1993, Clinton signed an omnibus budget package that raised the top marginal income tax rate to 39.6 percent. The measure passed without a single Republican vote in either chamber.[37] When Republicans accused Clinton of "breaking faith" with the 1986 reform bargain, the administration argued that Clinton wasn't a party to the reform deal and that he had his own economic agenda. "The President campaigned on a promise to restore some of the progressivity to the tax system," said Laura D'Andrea Tyson, chair of the Council of Economic Advisers. "That may be different from what was decided in 1986, but that's what he was elected to do."[38]

By the mid 1990s, the GOP had adopted a strong tax-cutting position. President George W. Bush in 2001–3 pushed through a series of major tax cuts that ratcheted the top marginal tax rate back down to 35 percent. In all, the top marginal tax rate changed five times between 1987 and 2003. Many of the Bush tax cuts were subject to sunset provisions and therefore likely to fluctuate in the future, "undermining the durability of the tax code and the certainty that taxpayers need for planning."[39]

Creating New Tax Breaks

The collapse of the TRA has been driven as much by the creation of new tax breaks as by fluctuating marginal rates. The tax breaks eliminated in 1986 were similar in terms of their political character to the tax breaks repealed in other years.[40] What gave the TRA the appearance of being a political earthquake was the sheer *number* of credits and deductions it killed. But the TRA did not penetrate into governing routines any more deeply than other tax changes.

During his eight years in the White House, Bill Clinton found he could pursue his activist domestic policy agenda more effectively through the creation of tax expenditures than through more visible spending bills. In his first presidential news conference, Clinton boasted that his proposal to restore the investment tax credit would create "over a half a million private sector jobs in the first year alone."[41] Many of Clinton's tax proposals came under fire from key sponsors of the 1986 Act. Senator Bill Bradley called some of the proposals a "rejection of the principle of tax reform."[42] "In 1986, we tried to clear up the tax code to make it as neutral as it could be to reflect economic decisions. And we want to keep it that way," added Senator Daniel Patrick Moynihan (D-NY).[43]

No doubt these protests were sincere. Yet even as Bradley and Moynihan were coming to the reform's defense, pressure was intensifying on Capitol Hill for the TRA's unraveling. Between 1987 and 1998, more than seven hundred tax bills were introduced in Congress. Nearly all of these measures would have restored or added particularistic tax breaks.[44] According to a 1989 *Business Week* survey, nine in ten members of the Ways and Means and Senate Finance committees (the majority of whom had been in office when the TRA was enacted) said they would use the tax code to encourage saving and investment. Five in ten favored tax incentives for specific industries, and eight in ten sponsored or cosponsored legislation in the previous two years to provide such incentives.[45] The logic of collective action worked against the reform's durability. While preserving a clean tax code may have been in the government's collective interest, each individual politician had a strong incentive to pursue his or her pet cause. To be sure, the cost of opening any single new loophole was not large. The cumulative effect of the process, however, was to bleed the reform to death, one nick at a time. It was hard for budget guardians to control this process, particularly when key TRA supporters like Senator Packwood were among those abandoning ship.[46]

The 1990 and 1993 budget packages expanded some existing tax preferences and created a few new ones. The Taxpayer Relief Act of 1997 opened the floodgates. The new tax breaks contained in the 1997 bill were expected to cost the Treasury $275 billion over the first decade and "vastly higher amounts" in the out years.[47] Since 1986, Congress has passed more than 100 different laws changing provisions of the tax code.[48] The number of major tax expenditures on the books of the Treasury has grown from 115 in 1986 to 161 in 2006. The estimated revenue loss to the Treasury from federal tax expenditures in 1986 was $598 billion (in 2004 dollars). The estimated revenue loss fell by 28% over the first two years of TRA's implementation. From 1989 to 2006, however, revenue losses from tax expenditures climbed to $810 billion (in 2004 dollars), an increase of 76%.[49]

Rather than destroying the TRA at one legislative stroke, the tax policy changes made by Congress since 1986 have resulted in the reform's erosion. This is a more gradual and subtle process than formal repeal. So many tax laws with conflicting goals have been layered atop the TRA that it is increasingly hard to discern evidence of the reform's enactment. Most of the tax breaks eliminated or curtailed in 1986 benefited the oil industry, realtors, and other business-oriented interests. The TRA was a rare moment when Congress was willing to withdraw benefits from powerful private interests. To some degree, Congress has backslid on this reform promise and has again begun to dole out tax goodies to business clienteles. The American Jobs Creation Act of 2004 (P.L. 108–357), for example, established tax incentives for tackle box makers, Native Alaskan whaling captains, restaurant owners, makers of bows and arrows, and importers of Chinese ceiling fans.[50]

Yet with the exception of a preferential tax rate for capital gains, most have the business-oriented tax breaks slashed in 1986 have not been resurrected. Instead, politicians have created a host of new tax expenditures for *social purposes*. The Taxpayer Relief Act of 1997 (P.L. 105–34), for example, introduced a tax break for a new individual retirement account (Roth IRA) and created various education credits. The Economic Growth and Tax Relief Reconciliation Act of 2001 (P.L. 1907–16) enlarged the child credit, softened the impact of the "marriage penalty," and created new tax breaks for retirement savings and education. The Job Creation and Worker Assistance Act of 2002 (P.L. 107–147) extended credits for the purchase of electric vehicles. The Jobs and Growth Tax Relief Reconciliation Act of 2003 (P.L. 108–27) expanded child-care credits to $1,000 per child. As a result of these and other laws, social tax expenditures climbed from $363 billion (in 2004 dollars) in 1988 to $717 billion in 2006.[51] Shortly after TRA's enactment, economist Milton Friedman predicted that the improvement in tax policy would prove to be temporary. "Nothing has changed," he wrote, "to prevent the process that produced our present tax system from starting over. As lobbyists get back into action, and as members of Congress try to raise campaign funds, old loopholes will be reintroduced and new ones invented."[52] History has largely borne out Friedman's predictions.

After Airline Deregulation

If tax reform has unraveled, airline deregulation has persisted. This is a genuine puzzle for several reasons.[53] First, the issues and social pressures that led to deregulation have faded over the past thirty years. The political climate is much changed, and coalition behind deregulation no longer governs. Second, the transition to a competitive market has been much slower and more painful than most experts predicted.[54] Contrary to the expectations of reform proponents, airports today are congested, planes are crowded, airline service has become a national joke, and the airline industry is in financial turmoil.[55] If airline deregulation had not already occurred, it seems very unlikely the reform would be enacted today, especially given the political aversion to free market solutions after the financial crisis.

It could be argued that airline deregulation has endured because it has increased economic efficiency. The best-available econometric evidence confirms that deregulation's social benefits (including lower fares for consumers) have vastly exceeded its costs.[56] This is clearly part of the story. It matters whether policies work when set on the ground. As Michael E. Levine observes in an outstanding study of the reform's post-tenactment path, however, the diffuse efficiency gains from deregulation do not offer a *political* explanation for why concentrated interests (which for decades had successfully used anticompetitive regulations as a ve-hicle to transfer rents to themselves from poorly organized consumers) have been unable to "reorganize to achieve reregulation or minimize or eliminate the costs that deregulation has imposed on them."[57] My central claim is that airline deregulation has stuck not simply because the policy has delivered broad economic gains, but because the airline industry and its politics have been thoroughly *reconfigured*.

Changes in the Political Economy of the Industry

This reconfiguration can be seen in the remarkable fluidity of clientele identities, resources, and coalitional patterns since deregulation. While some of the "trunk" airlines that predated deregulation still exist, the surviving "legacy carriers" are the product of so many corporate mergers and restructurings that many are the same firms in name only. After government controls on entry into the industry were lifted, a slew of new discount carriers began operations. Many of the start-ups quickly failed or were swallowed up under the Reagan administration's accommodative antitrust policies, but their entry forced the big carriers to change their industrial organization and business plans. Many of the top carriers of the 1970s—such as Braniff, Eastern, and TWA—were unable to compete and disappeared. In the 1990s, a second wave of smaller entrants emerged, including Frontier, JetBlue, and ValueJet.[58] These new entrants were much better capitalized than their predecessors and sought out underserved cities (Oakland, Baltimore, Providence) and provided no-frills, point-to-point service. By 2004, low-fare carriers accounted for about 25% of the domestic air market.[59] Deregulation also prompted sweeping changes in the internal governance of surviving carriers. Prior to deregulation, carriers largely organized themselves like regulated firms or utilities on dimensions such as CEO pay, concentration of equity, and board size. Once deregulation occurred, the carriers' internal governance structures began gravitating toward the governance models of unregulated firms. This organizational adaptation process was protracted.[60] Once these governance shifts occurred, however, the carriers could not easily revert to their pre-deregulation forms. In sum, the deregulation process generated shifts in the identities, governance, and strategies of clientele actors. Those carriers who were unable to carve out a stable market niche eventually disappeared. *Rather than the big carriers obtaining the market rules and governmental frameworks they desired, the deregulated airline market has structured the character and identities of the business actors that could survive.*

Creation of Hub-and-Spoke Networks

The legacy carriers constructed hub-and-spoke networks with huge fixed costs to serve decentralizing cities and suburban areas. American established hubs at Dallas–Fort Worth and Chicago, United at Denver and Chicago, and Delta at Atlanta and Dallas–Forth Worth. The construction of the hub-and-spoke system shaped firms' investment decisions and thus their public policy agendas. Carriers developed "yield management systems"—sophisticated techniques and models to extract the maximum revenue per seat by charging different rates to different kinds of passengers. The fares were constantly being updated in response to changes in supply and demand. Competition in price became so fierce that some carriers were making 80,000 airline fare changes each day.[61] Implementing these complex yield management systems required firm-specific investments in both human and physical capital. The carriers also spent heavily on marketing. They developed or expanded frequent flyer programs to build customer loyalty. The first major carrier to create a frequent flyer program was American Airlines in 1981. Within five years, virtually every other carrier offered one.[62]

Reregulating the Airline Industry?

As passenger loads increased, so did complaints about poor service and concerns about anticompetitive behavior.[63] Beginning in the 1980s, some officials argued that the government needed to play a more active supervisory role in the industry. There have been some policy responses to these issues, but government actions have largely confirmed the legitimacy and embeddedness of the existing policy regime.

Back in the 1970s, pro-reform advocates like Ted Kennedy linked deregulation to the consumer movement and to the public's desire for low prices. While ticket prices have fallen dramatically, the major consumer groups have become disenchanted with certain outcomes of the competitive market, arguing that it has resulted in a deterioration in air service quality and a loss of consumer "rights."[64] In an era in which the airlines have become fodder for late-night comics, it is no surprise that entrepreneurial politicians like Senator John McCain (R-AZ) pushed for tighter federal controls over the industry. Nor is it a shock that airline managers struggling to deliver profits to their shareholders would seek the security of government regulation. Certainly the carriers have not been shy about exploiting remaining vestiges of the pre-1978 regulated system to capture economic rents. The big carriers benefit, for example, from exclusive long-term gate-leasing arrangements and dominate airport investments at their hubs. Finally, if bureaucrats seek more power and larger budgets, then reregulating the airlines would seem to have a natural constituency in the executive branch as well. Yet the old iron triangle relationship among carriers, lawmakers, and government regulators has not reconstituted itself.

Predatory Pricing

After deregulation, the government must maintain a competitive environment and provide the physical and legal infrastructure necessary for market activity. But if government is essential after deregulation, and in any event *inevitable*, its residual presence in a policy sector with a long history of rent-seeking behavior and overregulation constitutes a serious threat to reform durability. There is fundamental political tension here. A government strong enough to make beneficial midcourse policy adjustments may also be strong enough to prevent the creative destruction and chaotic experimentation essential to a dynamic industry.

As it has turned out, policymakers have largely erred on the side of nonintervention. They have accepted the outcomes from market competition, even when competition has been nasty, brutal and not wholly fair. A case in point is the failure of the Clinton administration's "competitive guidelines" in the late 1990s. The airline industry underwent considerable consolidation over the 1980s and 1990s as government antitrust authorities permitted mergers between former competitors. At some hubs, the big carriers controlled 80% or more of all flights. Critics argued that the big airlines were driving out their competitors through unfair practices. As soon as a new carrier enters their hub, the big carriers were said to flood the routes of the upstart rival with rock-bottom fares. After the intruder is killed, the big airlines allegedly jacked up their prices again.[65]

The Clinton administration took the position that the government needed to stop such "predatory pricing" practices. The administration in 1998 drafted competitive guidelines to give the Department of Transportation (DOT) the authority to begin enforcement proceedings against any major established carrier that responded to a new entry into one of its local hub markets by selling seats at abnormally low fares. The administration's proposal guidelines received strong support from some struggling new entrants. But big carriers vehemently opposed the guidelines, which they claimed represented a misguided attempt to "reregulate the industry." The airlines mounted a multimillion dollar lobbying campaign and ran ads in leading newspapers that characterized the proposals as an unwarranted government takeover of the airline business. One featured a photograph of a DOT bureaucrat with the words, "Flying this summer? Meet your new travel agent."[66] After heated negotiations with the Air Transport Association, House Speaker Newt Gingrich (R-GA) and other congressional leaders decided to delay implementation of the DOT's recommendations until after it heard from an expert panel of the National Academy of Sciences that was studying the issue. The panel was chaired by Harvard economist John R. Meyer and included former CAB chairman Alfred E. Kahn; Roden Brandt, president of the failed start-up carrier Air South; and Randall Malin, a former executive vice president of marketing for US Airways. The panel ultimately failed to reach consensus on the merits of DOT's plan to protect start-ups, and the administration abandoned its efforts.[67]

Unable to win the support of either Congress or outside experts for its competitive guidelines, the Clinton administration took its case to the courts. In 1999, the Department of Justice (DOJ) brought a predatory pricing suit against American Airlines, accusing the carrier of seeking to drive three new entrants—Vanguard Airlines, Western Pacific Airlines, and Sun Jet—out of its hubs by flooding its routes with below-cost seats. According to the Justice Department suit, once the new entrants reduced their services, American reestablished high fares. This was the first predatory pricing action brought by the government against an airline since deregulation. American Airlines claimed it had done nothing illegal. The trial court dismissed the case, arguing that American had merely responded to market forces. "There is no doubt that American may be a difficult, vigorous, even brutal competitor. But here, it engaged only in bare, not brass-knuckle competition," ruled the Court.[68] The decision was upheld on appeal.

Passenger Service

Policymakers have also considered imposing new rules to mandate quality improvements in airline customer service. As U.S. airports and planes became increasingly crowded during the late 1980s, and flight delays and late arrivals occurred more often, many people complained about poor service. After a New Year's snowstorm in 1999 left thousands of Northwest Airlines passengers trapped inside aircraft on the Detroit tarmac for 11 hours, Congress began considering legislation to enshrine in law passenger "rights," such as being quoted the lowest available fare, receiving accurate information about flight delays, and getting larger awards for lost baggage. The effort was supported by the American Society of Travel Agents, the Consumers' Union, and the National Airline Passengers Coalitions. The major air carriers vigorously protested the need for the legislation. An airline spokesperson warned that "all the economic and social benefits of deregulation we take for granted will be at risk."[69] The congressional measure was forestalled after the airlines promised to institute a voluntary program to reduce flight delays and improve service.[70]

Small Community Service

Another issue policymakers have periodically expressed concern about is the level of service in small and medium-sized communities around the nation. "Deregulation has been an unmitigated disaster for most rural areas and smaller communities," claimed Senator Bryon L. Dorgan (D-ND) in 1999.[71] "I voted for airline deregulation, and I apologize publicly," Senator Ernest F. Hollings (D-SC) said in early 2001.[72] When Congress deregulated the airlines, it established the Essential Air Service Program to provide subsidies to air carriers servicing small communities not located near major airports. The program was supposed to be transitional, giving small communities and airliners a decade to adjust to the competitive market. While the subsidies were supposed to end in 1988, Congress has kept the program going. The costs of the program rose from $37 million in 1995 to $113 million in 2002, but total passenger enplanements per subsidized community declined from 592,000 to 477,000 over the same period.[73] In 2000, the median number of passengers of each EAS-subsidized flight was just three.[74]

The continued existence of federal subsidies for small community service more than a quarter-century after deregulation is not surprising. Politicians from rural areas like the program, and most taxpayers are indifferent to it—the costs are too diffuse for them to notice. While federal subsidies are arguably inefficient, they do not jeopardize the sustainability of the reform itself. On the contrary, the provision of the subsidies is premised on a basic acceptance that route and pricing decisions should be made by the marketplace. The transition payments were always intended for marginal communities, and the eligibility criteria have been tightened over time.

The program has not expanded for two main reasons. First, commuter airlines are increasingly reluctant partners in the small community program. The program is dependent on small fifteen- to nineteen-seat propeller planes, but the commuter lines are more and more using fifty-seat regional jets. In addition, high labor turnover has resulted in periods of heavy flight cancellations, which in turn have harmed the program's reliability. As one analyst notes, the natural incentives of the commuter lines are to "find ways to escape the program" rather than to put energy into developing small community markets.[75]

Second, deregulation has *not* in fact been an unmitigated disaster for small communities. While some small communities have been losers, many others have been winners. Some cities that initially attracted low-fare carriers later lost them. Others that were losers later gained when discount carriers began operations at relatively proximate airports. With carriers largely indifferent to the program, and a constantly changing set of affected communities, the subsidy program has generated enough support to maintain itself but not enough to undermine the basic commitment to the market process.

The 9/11 Attack

A key test of the sustainability of a reform is what happens when there is an unanticipated shock that suddenly transforms the political environment. Do policymakers abandon the reform, pushing a new line of policy development? Or is the continued maintenance of the reform taken for granted even as other policy arrangements are fundamentally revised?

For airline deregulation, the key test came on September 11, 2001. The terrorist attacks forced the government to temporarily shut down the nation's airports for several days. After the airports were reopened, many Americans were reluctant to fly, and the airlines suffered heavy financial losses.

Within weeks of the terrorist attacks, Congress passed a $15 billion assistance plan to help the airlines recover. Airlines would have to document their direct losses from the attacks to qualify for a share of a $5 billion federal grant. The federal government also agreed to provide up to $10 billion in loan guarantees to help airlines gain emergency access to capital. The DOT directed the grant program. The loan guarantees would be managed by a four-member Air Stabilization Board consisting of officials from the DOT and Treasury, the Federal Reserve, and the General Accounting Office. The House passed the airline aid bill 356 to 54, and the Senate cleared it by voice vote.[76] The speed with which Congress approved this package was a tribute not only to the ability of American government to move quickly in times of crisis, but also to the political skill of the airline lobby, which extracted more money from taxpayers than their industry lost during the shutdown. While the airline industry is usually internally divided, the bailout package demonstrated that it remains a formidable actor when it is united. The airlines drew on the resources of twenty-seven in-house lobbyists, supplemented by lobbyists from forty-two Washington public advocacy firms.

The Air Transportation Stabilization Board was given an almost impossible mission. Before it could issue a loan guarantee to a carrier, it had to determine that the applicant was an important part of the national air network, that the loan would be prudently incurred, and that the applicant could not easily raise the money privately. In sum, the Board could assist only strong carriers with sound business plans, but if a carrier's business was strong and sound, it would have little trouble raising capital privately, rendering it ineligible for government assistance. While some experts complained that the existence of the Board had reinforced the industry's dependence on Washington, the government's assistance ultimately offered no reprieve from competition for the struggling big carriers. While they suffered heavy losses after the terrorist attacks, American, Continental, Delta, and Northwest all decided not to apply for loan guarantees because they wanted to avoid the Board's scrutiny and having to give the government a stake in their businesses. US Airways received $900 million in loan guarantees, more than any other carrier, yet was unable to escape bankruptcy. The main airlines that were helped by the loan guarantees were America West and Frontier, which already had low costs and good business models.[77] Frontier repaid its $63 million loan early in 2003. In addition to the original $15 billion bailout package, Congress also offered carriers some money after September 11 to help with insurance coverage and security costs. But John Mica, chair of the House Transportation Aviation Subcommittee, told airline executives in mid-2004 that they should not expect any additional federal aid, and that they had to be prepared to "fend for themselves" in the current marketplace.[78] In the end, the program guaranteed only $1.6 billion in loans and actually earned a profit for the U.S. Treasury of more than $300 million.[79]

Explaining the Patterns

What accounts for the contrasting paths of the TRA and airline deregulation after reform enactment? I argue that two factors help explain these patterns: political institutions and policy feedbacks. In brief, shifts in political institutions have shielded airline deregulation, but not tax reform, from inhospitable policy change. Airline deregulation has also stimulated powerful interest group feedbacks that have created a new politics. Economic changes unleashed by the reform have destroyed the political cohesion of the industry while stimulating private actors to make economic investments based on the reform's expected continuation. The policy feedbacks from tax reform, in contrast, have been weak to nonexistent.

Institutions

The key institutional shift in the airline deregulation case was the termination of the CAB, the independent agency that had long governed the industry. The importance of this change has been twofold. First, since 1978 the government has lacked an agency whose central mission is to regulate airline routes and fares. When problems have emerged in the airline industry, the government has been forced to work through the DOJ and DOT, both of which have many other issues on their agendas. Executive policymaking with respect to the airline industry has consequently been episodic and ad hoc. More important, the termination of the CAB meant that there was no longer an *independent commission* with the political autonomy to control the industry. As Michael Levine (a former CAB senior executive) persuasively argues:

> The change in institutions was subtle compared to the change in legislation. About 450 of the CAB's 800 employees went over to the Department of Transportation and became the core of the DOT's airline group. Only now are they beginning to retire out. The policy preferences of that group didn't change much. . . . [They] liked deregulation as long as there was a proliferation of entrants and prices were declining and became worried about it when the opposite was the case (often because the market had been previously oversupplied for a period). What was different was that the Department was officially and overtly part of the Administration and thus explicitly subject to political and broad policy considerations. . . . As an example, when in 1998, the DOT staff [developed competitive guidelines to prevent large carriers from lowering their fares to drive out new entrants] . . . opposition came from many directions and the matter was unceremoniously dropped when the Republicans took the presidency.[80]

In sum, the federal government no longer possesses an independent commission with the autonomy and capacity to supervise routes and prices on an ongoing basis. Had the CAB remained in existence, it is conceivable the airline industry's evolution over the past two decades would have been markedly different, especially during the Clinton administration when federal regulators took a more aggressive stance toward the industry.

In contrast, no significant institutional changes were enacted to dislodge the tax policy subsystem. The TRA did not raise the political transaction costs of creating or expanding tax loopholes. There were no rules changes or procedural reforms to insulate tax policymaking from group pressures or partisan battles over fiscal policy. Authority to shape tax legislation remained firmly in the hands of Congress. More radical shifts in jurisdictional authority, such as the delegation of certain aspects of tax policy to an independent agency comparable to the Federal Reserve Board were never considered. Tax reform also failed to alter the balance of power within the Congress. If the TRA had established a credible commitment to tax neutrality and base broadening, the value to members of serving on the tax writing panels might have been expected to decline since one of the central issues the committee handles (doling out special tax favors) would have been rendered less important. Yet a seat on the Ways and Means and Senate Finance committees continued to be highly prized by lawmakers as a way to raise campaign funds from actors who seek tax favors.[81] When the TRA was being developed, interest groups gave huge sums to members of the tax panels in hopes of preserving their privileges. Ways and Means members on average received a 24% increase in donations during 1985–86 over the previous election cycle.[82] But the fund-raising bonanza did not end when the reform was passed. Chairman Rostenkowski, for example, collected $1.3 million in contributions in the 1991–92 election cycle, almost as much as he received during the entire decade of the 1980s.[83]

Policy Feedbacks

The policy feedbacks from airline deregulation have been profound. Deregulation has destroyed the interest group cohesion of the industry and uprooted long-standing coalitional patterns. The heterogeneity of interests in the policy sector increased significantly as new carriers entered and legacy carriers adapted in different ways to the pressures of market competition. Since 1978, airline carriers have sought to obtain economic rents through anticompetitive regulations, just as they did before 1978. The difference is that now there is nearly always an opposing airline to exert counter pressure on Congress.[84] As Levine observes, the Air Transportation Association, the industry's most powerful trade association, no longer can reach consensus on regulatory issues.[85] The interests of municipalities, airline industry employees, and even consumers have also fragmented since deregulation.[86]

As important, deregulation has created constituencies with a vested interest in reform by encouraging long-term, often asset-specific investments in new aircraft, terminals, scheduling tools, and revenue-management software. "Fortress" hub operations were constructed at airports around the nation. Supporting industries and supplies (e.g., aircraft equipment suppliers, hotels, rental cars, restaurants, corporate office parks) grew up around them, creating strong but conflicting local constituencies. Any attempt to undo these changes would be massively disruptive not only for the airlines but for their host business communities. As Michael E. Levine writes: "The enormous growth and expansion in scope of the route system under deregulation has created many opportunities for complementary investments in hard assets and human capital, even including the location of plants and offices by actors with no other connection to the industry. . . . This has been a very important force for policy conservatism, almost like a spontaneous and uncoordinated version of the effects of deliberately placing contracts for key defense systems in many congressional districts."[87] "You can't unscramble the egg," said Senator Jack C. Danforth in 1987. "We've set in motion forces that aren't going to be reversed."[88]

Again, the contrast with the tax reform experience is striking. No interest groups have come to the reform's defense. Even actors who had been relatively enthusiastic about the law's rate cuts in 1986 had no compunction about abandoning its base-broadening framework. For example, the National Association of Wholesaler-Distributors, which had endorsed the enactment of the TRA in 1986, began lobbying just three years after the reform's passage for cuts in the estate tax for family business owners.[89] Not only did the TRA fail to generate support among organized groups, it did not build a clientele among ordinary taxpayers (who were supposed to be the reform's main beneficiaries). In a 1988 survey, only 15% of respondents thought the reform had had a positive effect on the economy, and 67% of respondents found the new tax law more confusing than the old one.[90]

What about Macro Political Factors?

My account has stressed the role of the pressures put into play by reform policies themselves. To what degree can these patterns be explained by macro political factors? In their chapter, Forrest Maltzman and Charles R. Shipan demonstrate that laws enacted under unified government are more likely to persist in their original form than laws enacted under divided government, because strong, unified government coalitions are in a better position to entrench their preferences and because laws passed during periods of unified control are more likely to be coherent and internally consistent.[91] The trajectories of the two reforms are consistent with the expectations of this model. The TRA was enacted under divided government and has unraveled. Airline deregulation was enacted during unified government and has persisted.

One can still ask how much difference the political conditions at the time of enactment made in the tax reform and airline deregulation cases. It is a good bet that airline deregulation would have been enacted in approximately the same form even if President Gerald Ford had defeated

Jimmy Carter in the 1976 election (which he nearly did) and control of government had remained divided. Airline deregulation was driven more by the fusion of expert analysis and symbolic politics than by typical party contestation. In 1975, the Ford administration had already proposed an airline deregulation bill that had gained significant Democratic sponsorship in the Congress. The Maltzman-Shipan model might lead one to argue that the reform's elimination of the CAB reflected an attempt by a unified Democratic regime to entrench its preferences. Yet many Democrats were reluctant to include this sunset provision, viewing it as a diversionary tactic that would give the bureaucracy an excuse for postponing the lifting of regulatory controls. The provision made it into the final bill in part due to its political ambiguity.[92] The unintended consequences of reforms can be as important as strategic design choices at the moment of enactment. As for the TRA, it is certainly an example of a law passed by a strange bedfellow coalition. The reform's provisions may have pleased many academic economists, but they did not completely satisfy either liberal or conservative elected officials.

What about the effect of changes in macro political conditions *after* enactment? Christopher R. Berry, Barry C. Burden, and William G. Howell demonstrate that changes in the partisan composition of coalitions affect programmatic durability.[93] This is an important argument, and it has an empirical basis. Yet macro-level coalitional changes may not always produce their anticipated effects because they are mediated by specific policy contexts. One would have expected, for example, that the shift from unified to divided government in 1981 would weaken the political sustainability of airline deregulation. Yet the election of President Reagan (and the Republican takeover of the Senate) if anything had the opposite effect. It enabled the new regime of market competition to become thoroughly embedded under the protection of an ideologically sympathetic administration. The initial transition to a deregulated market was painful for both the airline industry and labor unions. By the early 1980s, competition over fares and routes was already rooted enough that it seems unlikely that the old system would have been restored. The pressure on a unified Democratic government to modify some of the effects of deregulation, however, might have been strong.[94]

By the same token, George H. W. Bush's election in 1989 "should" have strengthened, not weakened, the sustainability of the TRA. The Republicans, after all, retained control of the White House, and Bush had even been vice president at the moment of the TRA's enactment. As we have seen, however, Bush undermined the TRA through his support for business tax breaks and willingness to embrace higher tax rates. A case can be made that the fragility of the TRA would have become apparent under *any* plausible set of post-1986 partisan conditions—the reform's weaknesses were "baked in." This is not to suggest that macro political factors have no influence on reform paths. Clearly they can be quite important. But an understanding of how, and why, *specific* reforms unfold as they do frequently requires attention to political and economic factors much closer to the ground. Reforms can collapse even when the partisan composition of Congress remains stable. By the same token, reforms can sometimes "take" so quickly that their repeal quickly becomes unthinkable.

A Few Concluding Observations

Two brief case studies of this sort cannot, of course, provide rigorous tests of alternative theories of durability, sustainability, and change. But the analysis presented here does suggest several general conclusions.

First, it is crucial to distinguish between the *existence* and the *direction* of change. Some highly sustainable policies (e.g., the Social Security Act) have been amended many times without any evident harm to their development. Indeed, frequent legislative activity can arguably help embed a policy regime in governing routines while a lack of attention to a policy from Congress might signal that the policy is a political dead letter, no longer worth worrying about.

Second, we need to examine the impact of the full *range* of policy changes that can affect a policy's durability and sustainability over time, and not only the influence of formal amendments. New policy commitments can often be "layered" atop old ones without formal revisions to the original policy itself. These commitments may use the prior law as a model, platform, or springboard, reinforcing the legitimacy of the original policy regime. Or they can make it impossible for the original law to achieve its core goals by imposing new mandates and incentives with conflicting values.[95] These are not easy variables to code, but they demand attention nonetheless.

Third, we need to study the development of public policies as a distinct process in its own right.[96] The long-term fate of policies is shaped by the strategic and substantive choices made during the adoption phase, but downstream political developments matter a great deal as well. Some of these later events are predictable, but many are not. Would the tough 1990s welfare reform law have become deeply embedded without the economic boom and low unemployment of that decade? Would the CAB have been allowed to expire if the World Trade Center attacks had occurred on September 11, 1979? Implementation is not merely a continuation of the politics of enactment. It is, or can be, a new and different game.

Finally, durability, sustainability, and change cannot be understood without examining the material, organizational, and cognitive impacts of public policies on key societal actors, including clientele groups, program beneficiaries, and service providers. In the long run, the trajectories of reforms depends as much on the reactions, expectations, and adaptations of private actors as on the ideological preferences and partisan ties of public officials.

CHAPTER NINE

Policy Durability and Agency Design

David E. Lewis

A key concern for policymakers is ensuring that policy changes they enact endure.[1] One strategy policymakers use to ensure the durability of policies they enact is to delegate their implementation to independent commissions rather than executive branch bureaus.[2] Independent commissions have fixed terms for appointees and party balancing requirements for nominees, and are omitted from regular Office of Management and Budget (OMB) budget and regulatory review.[3] These structural features insulate agencies from the direct influence of the president and his staff agencies since they blunt the primary means of presidential influence—appointments, removals, budgets, and regulatory review. Independent commissions are also arguably more insulated from congressional influence since commissions are corporate bodies rather than individually led. This makes it harder for Congress to hold one single person accountable. In addition, the same features that limit presidential influence hinder Congress's ability to the influence the commissions. For example, the fixed terms of commissioners make it hard for Congress to pressure presidents to fire commissioners members oppose. Finally, some commissions such as the Board of Governors of the Federal Reserve and the Securities and Exchange Commission are partly self-funded through assessments. This diminishes the ability of Congress to influence agency behavior by appropriations. These features collectively

I thank the Princeton Survey Research Center (PSRC) for their work on the survey that provides the basis for this chapter. Comments provided by the PSRC and participants at the Embedding Laws in the American State Conference were very helpful.

increase the durability of policies commissions implement by partly shielding the policies from the effects of changing presidential administrations or shifting congressional majorities.[4]

While a significant amount of empirical evidence confirms that delegation decisions are influenced by the configuration of political interests in Congress, the presidency, and agencies, very little empirical work has been done to evaluate whether the strategy of delegating to independent commissions enhances policy durability. This chapter uses evidence from a survey of federal executives to evaluate whether independent commissions are more insulated from political intervention and influence than executive branch bureaus. It finds that independent commissions are more insulated from executive and legislative branch influence and that the relative influence of the White House, congressional committees, and interest groups differs by type of agency. Executive branch bureaus are most influenced by the White House, followed by congressional committees, and interest groups. Independent commissions are most influenced by congressional committees, particularly because members of Congress are more likely to give input on the selection of appointed and career executives in commissions. Interest groups exercise influence because of the frequency with which former commission employees go to work for firms doing business with or regulated by the commission.

The chapter is divided into three sections. The first section reviews existing theoretical and empirical work on policy durability and agency design and argues that more work needs to be done to determine whether delegation to independent commissions enhances policy durability. The second section presents the data and describes the variables and methods used to evaluate the influence of political actors on agency policymaking. The final section discusses the results and concludes.

Policy Durability and Agency Design

The literature on delegation and policy durability is comprised of a large theoretical literature that explains how policies delegated to administrative agencies can be altered after enactment. It also includes a thinner empirical literature evaluating various correlates of agency and program durability. This empirical work focuses largely on the formal termination of federal agencies rather than programs.[5] The work that does examine changes in laws and programs short of termination does not differentiate these laws and programs by whether bureaus or commissions implement them. This makes it difficult to assess whether the strategy of delegating authority to commissions is an effective means of enhancing program durability.

Policy Durability and Independent Commission

The argument that concerns for policy longevity lead politicians to delegate responsibility for implementation to independent commissions comes in a variety of forms. Lewis and Moe, for example, argue that interest groups reward politicians for policy changes.[6] Rewards are bigger when politicians can guarantee their durability. An important way politicians make policy durable is to delegate implementation of the policy to bureaucracies that are insulated from political control.

One threat to a policy's durability is the expected longevity of the enacting coalition itself. When political coalitions enacting important policy changes worry about their own longevity, they try to lock policy changes in by spreading benefits broadly, creating bureaucratic agencies insulated from political control, or generally implementing devices such as trust funds that tie the hands of future politicians.[7] Regular elections make it difficult for Congress and the president to credibly commit to not intervening in a policy in the future. McCubbins, Noll, and Weingast argue that structure and process can be a way of solving this credible commitment problem.[8] In their view, the only way that the House, Senate, and president can enact policies that will be an improvement for all when their preferences diverge is for each to commit to not influencing policy postenactment. One credible way for the chambers of Congress and the president to guarantee that they will not unilaterally change policy after enactment is to design structures and processes in advance that limit ex post political influence. Independent commissions are one type of structure that provides this type of guarantee against political intervention.

Testing Influence of Independent Commissions on Durability

While there has been a significant amount of empirical work evaluating how delegation decisions are influenced by the preferences of the actors receiving the delegation, very little work has evaluated the assumption that independent commissions are more insulated from political influence than executive branch bureaus.[9] If independent commissions are just as subject to political intervention and influence as executive branch bureaus, this calls into question both the wisdom of delegating to commissions to enhance durability but also our theories of delegation.

Among the work that focuses on policy durability, most of it examines the formal termination of programs and agencies.[10] Lewis, for example, argues that agency structure is more malleable than previously believed. He demonstrates that 62% of agencies created between 1946 and 1997 had been terminated and that one primary cause was political turnover.[11] This calls into question whether agency structure is a good guarantor of policy durability. In a later article, however, Lewis finds that while agency structure is more malleable than previously believed, independent commissions were significantly more durable than other types of agencies.[12] He suggests that policies produced by commissions are more likely to satisfy the congressional median than those implemented by other executive branch agencies more subject to presidential influence. He concludes that delegation to independent commissions does protect policies from political intervention.

The durability of agencies, however, is not direct evidence of the durability of policies they implement. Corder, for example, finds that federal credit programs located in independent agencies have a higher risk of termination than programs located in cabinet agencies.[13] In addition, the formal termination of federal programs is only one form of influence over federal programs and probably the most extreme form.[14] Federal programs persist, but the content, funding, and ultimate success of these programs can vary dramatically over time. If federal programs are changed beyond recognition to those that enacted them, we should not consider these programs durable. The fundamental question is whether federal programs persist in the form their supporters envisioned at the time of enactment. Maltzman and Shipan, for example, evaluate the durability of laws enacted by the U.S. Congress and find that political conditions at the time of enactment and current political conditions influence the likelihood that laws are amended.[15] Their analysis, however, generally does not disaggregate programs by efforts to insulate them from political intervention.[16] This is an important consideration since a substantial literature on agency capture argues that policies independent commissions were created to carry out were not durable. Independent regulatory commissions that were created to regulate the marketplace became captured by the interests they were supposed to regulate.[17] As Melnick explains, "Such 'capture' of the commission by the regulated is inevitable because dispersed, unorganized citizens cannot sustain the effort needed to counteract the power of organized interests."[18]

Whether or not federal programs delegated to independent commissions are more durable than other programs is an empirical question. One way to get purchase on this question is to evaluate the political environment of the federal programs to determine whether political actors have more influence with executive branch bureaus or commissions. We can also evaluate how much influence these actors are perceived to have in each type of agency.

2007–8 Survey on the Future of Government Service

To evaluate the political environment of executive branch bureaus versus independent commissions, this chapter relies on data from the 2007–8 Survey on the Future of Government Service.[19] This survey was conducted by the Princeton Survey Research Center during the fall and winter of 2007–8.[20] The survey included a variety of questions on the backgrounds, experiences, and political views of government executives. The questions included provide a means of evaluating the relative influence of different political actors on agency decisions in executive branch bureaus as compared to independent commissions.

The survey was sent to the population of federal administrators and program managers in the various departments and agencies.[21] In total, the survey was sent to approximately 7,448 government executives, both career professionals and political appointees.[22] The target population included cabinet secretaries; deputy, under-, and assistant secretaries; as well as independent agency heads, bureau chiefs, general counsels, and key deputies in the government bureaucracy. The overall response rate, once potential respondents included incorrectly were excluded, was 33% (2,225/6,690).[23] While the overall number of respondents is large, the sample of respondents may differ in important ways from the population as a whole.[24] This is something I return to below.[25] In the entire population, there were 557 potential respondents who worked in independent commissions.[26] Of the 557 executives in independent commissions, 218 responded to the survey (39%). The remainder of the population is comprised of executives working in the cabinet departments or other independent agencies that are not commissions. Of this group, 2,007 responded to the survey (31%).

Political Influence over Policy Decision

Importantly, the survey included questions evaluating patterns of political influence with administrative agencies. Specifically, the survey asked respondents, "In general, how much influence do the following groups have over policy decisions in your agency?" and included the following political actors: White House, members or staff of congressional committees, and interest group representatives. Respondents were given fixed-choice response possibilities of "a great deal, a good bit, some, little, none, don't know." In figure 9.1, I include graphs comparing the political influence of the White House, members or staff of congressional committees, and interest group representatives. Notably, the figure shows that executives in the independent commissions are less likely to report that political actors have a great deal or good bit of policy influence. This is important evidence that the strategy of delegating policy implementation authority to independent commissions may enhance policy durability since political actors have less direct influence over policy decisions in these types of agencies.

Interesting patterns of influence also emerge when agencies are examined by type (figures 9.2 and 9.3). In executive branch agencies, the

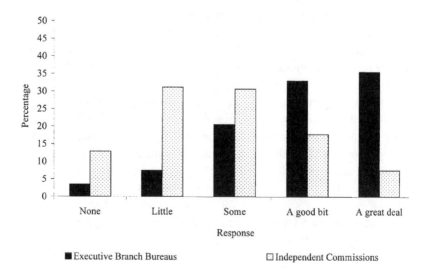

White House is reported to have the most influence over policy decisions, followed by members of Congress and committee staffs, and interest group representatives (figure 9.2). Respondents are most likely to report that the White House has a great deal or a good bit of influence over
policy decisions (68%) in the agency as compared to Congress (62%) or

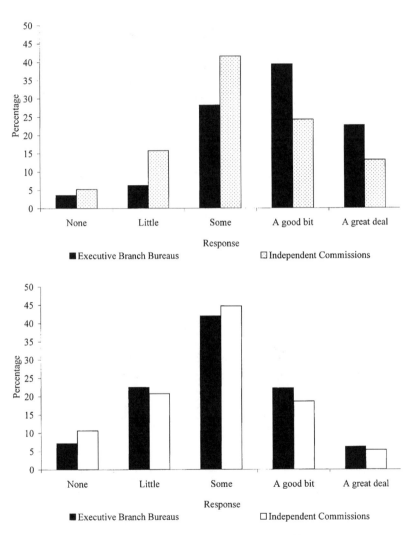

FIGURE 9.1. Political influence of the White House, Congress, and interest group representatives by agency type

Note: Responses to the following question in the 2007–8 survey on the future of government service: "In general, how much influence do the following groups have over policy decisions in your agency?"

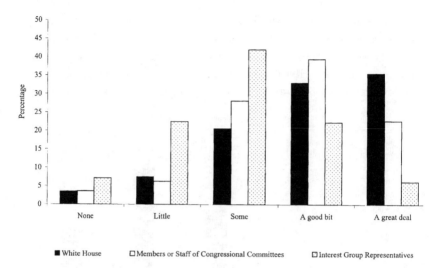

FIGURE 9.2. Reported political influence by different political actors—executive branch bureaus

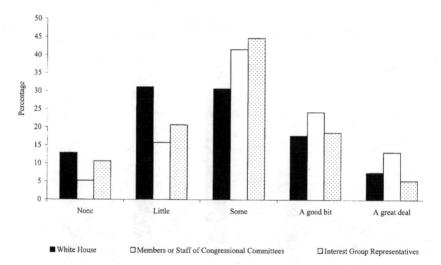

FIGURE 9.3. Reported political influence by different political actors—independent commissions

interest groups (28%). Respondents working for independent commissions, however, report that members of congressional committees and their staffs are the most influential political actors with 37% reporting that members of Congress or their staffs have a good bit or great deal of policy influence. The White House and interest group representatives are perceived to be less influential with only 24%– 25% of respondents reporting that each had such influence. Independent commissions are more insulated from political influence overall, and the relative power of key political actors is different. Whereas the president is most influential in executive branch bureaus, Congress is most influential in the independent commissions. This is consistent with the arguments of Lewis, who argues that independent commissions are designed specifically to limit the influence of presidents.[27] When presidents are the biggest threat to program durability, independent commissions may be a good place to locate those programs.

Of course, the simple bivariate relationships included in figure 9.1 could be misleading if the characteristics of respondents are systematically different between executive branch bureaus and independent commissions. For example, it is possible that respondents in independent commissions are less likely to report White House influence because a higher percentage of the management teams in independent commissions are civil servants excluded from the highest levels of policy deliberation. To control for this possibility, I estimate a series of ordered probit models controlling for key characteristics of the respondents and their agencies that could influence their perceptions of political influence. The dependent variable is the ordered categories of none (0), little (1), some (2), a good bit (3), and a great deal (4).[28]

These specifications include controls for different levels in the administrative hierarchy (Senate-confirmed appointee, SES Appointee, Schedule C appointee, SES/SFS, other civil service) and a control for years of experience each executive has in his or her current agency (mean 18.7 years; standard deviation 11.7).[29] My expectation is that those higher in the hierarchy will be most likely to report political influence and those with longer experience will be the least likely to report political influence since they have seen more administrations come and go.[30] I also include controls for whether or not executives have worked for other agencies (0,1; 51%) and whether or not respondents self-identify as Democrats (0,1; 54%). Those who have worked in other agencies are less likely to overestimate the extent of political influence. Democrats

TABLE 9.1. **Ordered probit models of respondent perceptions of political influence**

	White House	Members or Staff of Congressional Committees	Interest Group Representatives
Agency Type			
Independent Commission (0,1)	−1.07**	−.47**	−.11
Respondent Characteristics			
Senate-Confirmed Appointee (0,1)	−.01	−.25	−.10
Appointed SES (0,1)	.25*	−.11	−.13
Schedule C Appointee (0,1)	.55**	.00	−.25
SES/SFS (0,1)	.30**	−.02	.03
Civil Service (0,1)	.08	−.04	.12
Years in Agency	.00	.00	.00
Worked for Other Agencies (0,1)	−.13**	−.09*	−.08*
Democrat (0,1)	.14**	−.00	.26**
Agency Characteristics			
Regional Office (0,1)	−.06	−.16**	.11
Inspector General's Office (0,1)	−.12	−.25	−.24
General Counsel's Office (0,1)	.27	.25*	.49**
Minor Independent Agency (0,1)	−.23**	−.60**	−.38**
N	1806	1810	1760
χ^2 (13, X, X df)	639**	563**	109**

Note: Standard errors adjusted for clustering on agencies. Cut point estimates are −1.69, −1.00, −.22, .64; −1.93, −1.37, −.35, .68; and −1.24, −.31, .83, 1.82, respectively, for the three models.
** significant at the .05 level, * significant at the .10 level in two-tailed tests.

and Republicans are distributed unevenly throughout government, and Democrats are arguably the most likely to perceive White House political influence.[31] Finally, I control for a series of agency-specific factors including whether the respondent works in a regional office (as opposed to headquarters; 0,1; 19%), the office of the inspector general (0,1; 1.5%), or general counsel (0,1; 2.6%) of a larger agency, and whether the agency is a minor independent agency (0,1; .8%).[32]

Table 9.1 includes estimates from three ordered probit models.[33] The estimates generally confirm what emerges in the figures, namely that administrators and program managers in independent commissions report less influence by the political branches. Thus, even when controlling for differences among respondents such as place in the hierarchy, experience, and partisanship, commission executives report less political influence. The estimates indicate that working in an independent commission decreases the probability of saying that the White House exercises a great deal or good bit of influence by 28 and 13 percentage points, respectively. The effect, while still significant, is notably smaller for members or staff of congressional committees. Working in a commission decreases the probability of reporting that Congress exerts a great deal or good bit of influence by 18 percentage points total. This again confirms the relative insulation of independent commissions from executive or legislative branch influence relative to executive branch bureaus. This implies that policies delegated to independent commissions are probably more durable than other policies.

Interestingly, independent commission executives reported about the same amount of influence from interest group representatives as their executive branch bureau counterparts. I could not reject the null of no difference between the independent commissions and executive branch bureaus. This is an interesting finding given the prominent role that interest groups play in the literature on agency capture. While interest groups appear equally influential in both types of agencies, it is possible that interest groups would normally exert even less influence in commissions if not for extraordinary efforts to influence these agencies.

In total, the estimates suggest that the political branches exert less influence over policy in independent commissions. Independent commissions limit the president's influence the most, followed by Congress, and interest group representatives. This makes sense given that the distinctive features of independent commissions—commission structure, party balancing limitations, fixed terms, omission from OMB budget and regulatory review—are targeted at the primary means of presidential influence rather than congressional or interest group influence.

Several other model estimates are worth noting. First, those highest in the administrative hierarchy are the most likely to credit the White House with influence over agency policy. The appointees and the career professionals—with the exception of Senate-confirmed appointees—who work with top appointees most directly are the most likely to see the White House's involvement. Second, administrators and program managers who had worked in other agencies were generally less likely to report high levels of political influence from any political actors. Such executives have a better basis for comparison. Third, Democrats in the agencies are more likely to report both White House and interest group influence over agency decisions. There are several possible explanations for this finding. It is possible that partisans are more sensitive to the actions of the Republican president and the interest groups associated with the Republican Party. It is also possible, however, that agencies populated with large numbers of Democrats are the most likely to be targeted by the Republican administration and the constellation of groups that support it. Finally, respondents in general counsel offices are more likely to report political influence while those in minor and advisory agencies are the least likely to report influence. Some presidential personnel officials have referred to general counsel offices as one of the "choke points" in government, and it is possible that particular political attention is paid to these offices.[34]

Why the Different Patterns of Policy Influence

Overall, the models confirm the bivariate relationships described above. They raise the question, however, of why there is variation in the patterns of political influence between the executive branch bureaus and independent commissions. Here, again, the survey can provide some leverage because it asks executives about three potential sources of influence in agency policy decisions—direct contact, influence over personnel selection, and the prospect of future private sector employment. These sources of influence are not exhaustive since political actors have other means of exerting influence, but a focus on direct contact, personnel and future employment can give hints as to the causes of variation in influence.[35] The differential responses by agency type to these questions suggest explanations for why patterns of influence are different across agencies.

Contact by Political Actor

With regard to direct contact by political actors, the survey asked federal executives, "How often do you have contact with . . . ?" and includes several categories of political actors including the White House, members or staff of congressional committees, and interest group representatives.[36] Respondents were given a fixed choice of "daily, weekly, monthly, rarely, never, don't know." In figure 9.4, I graph the responses by political actor with the White House being the top panel, Congress the middle,

FIGURE 9.4. Reported frequency of political contacts of the White House, Congress, and interest group representatives by agency type

Note: Responses to following question in the 2007–8 survey on the future of government service: "How often do you have contact with:"

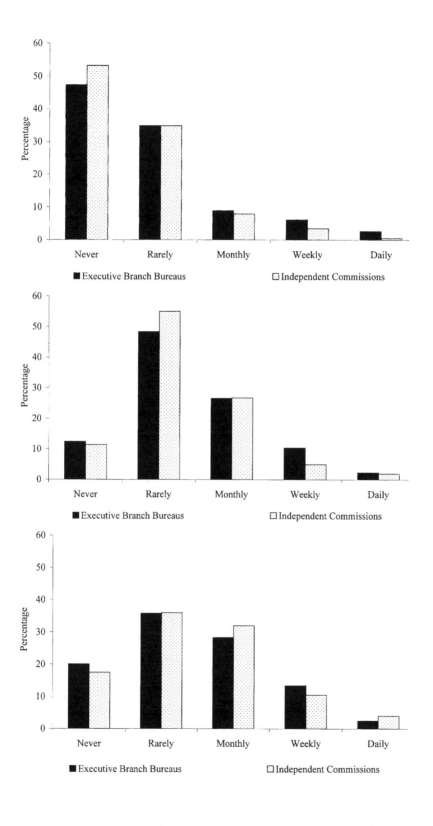

and interest group representatives the bottom panel. The figure has several notable features. First, agencies of both types are receiving contact from interest group representatives and members or staffs of congressional committees with greater frequency than the White House ($p < .00$). Among respondents, 8%–9% report weekly or daily contact with the White House compared to 12%–16% for Congress or interest groups. Close to half of all respondents report that they "never" hear from the White House, but only 12% and 20% of respondents report the same for Congress and interest groups, respectively. Second, White House contacts are more frequent in executive branch bureaus than independent commissions ($p < .02$). Twice as many respondents in executive branch bureaus than commissions report weekly or daily contact with the White House (9% vs. 4%). It is possible that the structural features of commissions that limit presidential influence over appointments, budgets, and regulation also diminish the opportunities for direct contact. This is one possible explanation for why Congress and interest group representatives are more influential in these agencies.

Of course, political actors may contact agencies for a variety of reasons. Some may even contact agencies to protect policies from political intervention by other actors and thereby *increase* policy durability in specific instances. Such contact happens, of course, when durability is threatened in the first place. Increased contact by political actors (though not necessarily interest groups), particularly after electoral turnover, usually indicates a threat to the policy and agency status quo. If political actors are unconcerned with agency activity, either because the agency and its programs are off the agenda or because the agency is doing what political actors prefer, there is little need for contact.[37] Contact by political overseers often reflects a desire to change agency policy or a concern for the choices of the agency in the future.

Congressional Influence over Personnel

One form of contact that could be influential is contact relating to personnel. The survey asked respondents about the influence of Congress in the selection of appointed and career executives in each agency. Specifically, the survey asked, "Please indicate your level of agreement or disagreement with each of the following statements about your job and work setting: Members of Congress regularly weigh in on the selection of appointed executives in my agency" and "Members of Congress regularly weigh in on the selection of career executives in my agency." Respondents were given fixed-choice responses of "strongly agree, agree, disagree, strongly disagree, not sure." Fifty percent of federal executives in commissions agreed or strongly agreed with the statement that Congress regularly weighed in on the selection of appointees compared to only 33% in executive branch bureaus. Unexpectedly, commission executives report that members and staff of congressional committees are less likely to weigh in on the selection of career executives than their counterparts in the departments and agencies (49% vs. 63%). Still, if appointees are the most policy-relevant actors on the commissions and Congress exerts a lot more influence over the selection of these officials, this is one explanation for why Congress exerts more influence over commissions than the White House. Unfortunately, the survey did not ask respondents about the influence of the White House over the selection of appointees.

Revolving Door

The results above indicate that interest group representatives exert less influence than either of the elected branches, but do exert about the same amount of influence in the commissions as in other agencies. Our expectation might have been that interest group representatives would exert less influence in commissions just as was the case for presidents and Congress. The question, then, is why is there so much interest group influence in commissions? One survey question that might help explain why interest groups are able to exert equal influence in the commissions is the following: "How often do former agency employees in the following groups accept jobs with firms that are regulated by your agency? [political appointees, senior civil servants]." Figure 9.5 graphs the responses for each type of executive (appointees, senior civil servants) by agency type. Commission respondents are significantly more likely to report that agency executives take jobs with firms regulated by the agency. Thirty-seven percent of commission respondents report that appointees take jobs in firms regulated by the agency regularly or frequently. In executive branch bureaus, only 25% of respondents report that appointees take these jobs regularly or frequently. Similarly, 27% of commission respondents report that senior civil servants take jobs with such firms compared to 19% in executive branch bureaus. The prospect of a job in a firm

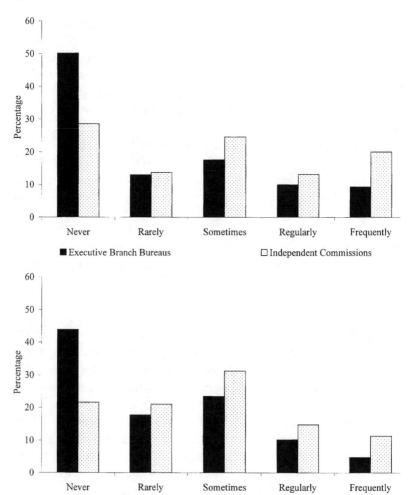

FIGURE 9.5. Revolving door practices for appointees and senior civil servants by agency type

Note: Question from the 2007–8 survey on the future of government service: "How often do former agency employees in the following groups accept jobs with firms that are regulated by your agency?" Don't-know answers are excluded.

regulated by one's agency can be an important influence on executive behavior. Without this additional motivation, it is possible that perceptions of interest group influence on commissions would be substantially lower.

The survey also asks a related question with the same format: "How often do former agency employees in the following groups accept jobs with firms that do business with your agency?" Responses to this question are less definitive than those described above. Forty-six percent of respondents in commissions report that appointees regularly or frequently take jobs with firms that do business with the agency compared to 43% of executive branch bureau respondents. Respondents in commissions, however, are less likely to report that senior civil servants regularly or frequently take jobs with firms that do business with the agency (30% vs. 36%).

When the set of commissions is restricted to just the better-known independent regulatory commissions, the results become more definitive across the board. Appointees and career executives in commissions are almost twice as likely to take jobs with firms regulated by their agencies. Appointed and career commission executives are also more likely to take jobs that do business with the agencies than their counterparts in executive branch bureaus. In total, the evidence suggests that interest groups may exert some influence due to the fact that senior agency executives regularly take jobs with the firms that the agencies regulate or do business with.

In total, patterns of contact, involvement in personnel selection, and the promise of future employment may be important explanations for the extra influence exerted by Congress and interest groups over the activities of independent commissions.

Caveat

While the evidence here is consistent and robust, showing that commissions are more insulated from political influence and that different actors have access to each type of agency, relying on survey data to measure political influence can be problematic for three reasons. First, it is an open question whether executives who share the views of political actors know whether influence is being exerted. Do agency officials who make policy according to their own views act of their own volition or in response to choices made by politicians to put them there in the first place? The preceding analysis attempted to partially account for this possibility by controlling for the political views of the respondents. If commission executives with different political views than the White House or Congress also report relatively less influence by the White House, Congress, and interest groups than their executive branch counterparts, this gives us confidence that commissions are more insulated than executive branch bureaus.

A second concern is how one should interpret an apparent lack of contact by political actors. If politicians do not need to contact an agency because the agency is doing what the politicians want, is influence being exerted and is that influence perceived by executives? It is possible that no contact is made and no influence is perceived because political actors have structured the agency and its laws to get exactly what they want without much day-to-day intervention.[38] If this is the case, no contact or influence would be reported, but a significant amount of influence would exist. Fortunately, in this case the survey was conducted when the two branches had significantly different political views. The differences in views of the two branches make it unlikely that an agency shared the same views as both branches. This helps mitigate the concern that agencies are doing exactly what the White House and Congress want.

The differences in views of the White House and Congress also help locate where bias would emerge, if it exists. For example, during the time of the survey Democrats controlled Congress and Democrats were found in greater numbers in the commissions (relative to executive branch bureaus). This implies that we should see *less* reported congressional influence in the commissions and more reported White House influence if executives do not accurately perceive influence. Yet, the data reveal that commission executives perceive *more* congressional influence than White House or interest group influence. This implies that, if anything, the analysis underestimates the extent to which Congress exerts influence over commissions. While in absolute terms the amount of reported political influence may be underestimated for both executive branch bureaus and commissions, there is little reason to believe that conclusions about relative amounts of political influence are in error.

Finally, top level agency officials may not accurately report what is happening in their agencies. Where surveys are employed to detect phenomena, there may be a gap between what is reported in the survey and what is actually occurring. There are numerous reasons for the gap, including perceptual biases, the desire to please the interviewer, and a genuine lack of knowledge about what is occurring. A number of steps have been taken in this analysis to account for perceptual biases and lack of information by including controls for respondent position, access, background, and ideology. Respondents were also reminded that their confidentiality was guaranteed so that responses would not be influenced by expectations of what other actors might expect them to say.[39] Still, respondents in independent commissions might plausibly be inclined to report less White House influence and more congressional influence because of perceptions that this is what they are expected to say or this is what they were taught. If this is the case, the analysis may overestimate the difference in executive versus legislative influence in executive agencies and commissions. While this may affect responses to questions about political influence, it is less likely to bias reports of more objective questions about the frequency of agency contact with different political actors or the frequency of executive departures to firms regulated by the agency. Answers to these questions generally support the overall argument about different levels of political insulation.

Discussion and Conclusion

A key concern for policymakers is how to ensure the durability of policies they have enacted. One tactic thought to enhance policy durability is to delegate responsibility for legislative implementation to independent commissions. This chapter has used data from a 2007–8 survey of federal administrators and program managers to evaluate whether independent commissions are more insulated than executive branch bureaus from political influence. The data indicate that independent commissions are more insulated from executive and legislative influence than executive branch departments. They also suggest that the relative influence of the White House, congressional committees, and interest groups differs by type of agency. Executive branch bureaus are most influenced by the White House, followed by congressional committees, and interest groups. Independent commissions are most influenced by congressional committees. Congress appears to exert more influence over commissions than executive branch bureaus because they are more likely to give input on the selection of appointed executives in these agencies. Interest groups arguably exercise more influence over commissions than we might otherwise expect because of the frequency with which former commission employees go to work for firms doing business with or regulated by the commission.

Several implications emerge from this analysis. First, delegating authority to independent commissions probably does enhance policy durability since commissions are less subject to political influence. The structures and processes associated with independent commissions influence the reported levels of political influence. This implies that policies delegated to independent commissions are less at risk to be influenced, amended, or terminated in the future. One possible reason why executives in commissions report less political influence is that commissions are producing policies that satisfy the political branches. This would be consistent with the arguments of Lewis that commissions produce policies closer to the congressional median, making them less subject to political termination.[40] A second reason why executives might report less political influence is that the structural features of the agency make it more costly to exert such influence. For example, presidents cannot remove commissioners, revise their budgets, or review their regulations easily relative to the executive branch bureaus. This makes it easier for commissions to resist presidential direction and, thus, less likely for the White House to pursue this strategy.

This research does not speak to other motivations for delegating to commissions or the consequences of doing so. Politicians delegate authority for many reasons other than durability, including expertise, blame shifting, or practical considerations about the timeliness of agency action.[41] The relative insularity of independent agencies does not guarantee their expertise or effectiveness.

Second, if threats do arise to policies implemented by commissions, they are most likely to come from Congress or interest groups rather than the White House. Independent commissions are most effective at limiting the president's influence. While administrators and program managers in the executive branch bureaus report that the White House has the most influence over agency decisions, those in independent commissions report that the White House has less influence than Congress. Indeed, the purpose of party-balancing limitations, fixed terms for appointees, and location outside the cabinet is to blunt the primary instruments of presidential influence—nominations, removals, and OMB review of budgets and regulations. With a few exceptions, Congress's primary means of influence—appropriations, lawmaking, confirmations, and direct contacts—are less influenced by the structural features that define these commissions. While these agencies are less subject to political intervention, the effects are most dramatic for presidents.

Finally, interest groups are equally influential in commissions and executive branch bureaus. While commissions are more insulated from influence by the political branches overall, interest groups maintain influence through the means suggested by theories of commission capture—regular contact and the revolving door. Federal executives report more contacts with interest groups and more regular moves from agency work to work for firms that do business with the agency or firms that are regulated by the agency. The prospects of future employment in these firms arguably make executives more sensitive to their concerns in agency policymaking.

APPENDIX A. **List of independent establishments**

IndCom	Agency Code	Agency
I	ACHP	Advisory Council on Historic Preservation
I	ADF	African Development Foundation
O	AMTRAK	Amtrak
I	ARC	Appalachian Regional Commission
O	ARMY	Department of the Army
I	BBG	Broadcasting Board of Governors
I	CCJJDP	Coordinating Council on Juvenile Justice and Delinquency Prevention
I	CFTC	Commodity Futures Trading Commission
I	CNCS	Corporation for National and Community Service
O	COM	Department of Commerce
I	CPSC	Consumer Product Safety Commission
I	CSHIB	Chemical Safety and Hazard Investigation Board
O	DHS	Department of Homeland Security
I	DNFSB	Defense Nuclear Facilities Safety Board
O	DOD	Department of Defense
O	DOE	Department of Energy
O	DOED	Department of Education
O	DOJ	Department of Justice
O	DOL	Department of Labor
O	DOT	Department of Transportation
O	DTRS	Department of the Treasury
O	DVA	Department of Veterans Affairs
I	EEOC	Equal Employment Opportunity Commission
O	EOP	Executive Office of the President
O	EPA	Environmental Protection Agency
I	EXIM	Export-Import Bank
I	FASAB	Federal Accounting Standards Advisory Board
I	FCC	Federal Communications Commission
I	FDIC	Federal Deposit Insurance Corporation
I	FEC	Federal Election Commission
I	FED	Federal Reserve System
I	FHFB	Federal Housing Finance Board
I	FMC	Federal Maritime Commission
I	FMSHRC	Federal Mine Safety Health and Review Commission
I	FRTIB	Federal Retirement Thrift Investment Board
I	FTC	Federal Trade Commission
O	GSA	General Services Administration
O	HHS	Department of Health and Human Services

(continues)

IndCom	Agency Code	Agency
0	HSTSF	Harry S. Truman Scholarship Foundation
0	HUD	Department of Housing and Urban Development
0	IMLS	Institute of Museum and Library Services
0	INT	Department of Interior
I	JMMFF	James Madison Memorial Fellowship Foundation
I	MKUSF	Morris K. Udall Scholarship Foundation
I	MMC	Marine Mammal Commission
I	MSPB	Merit Systems Protection Board
0	NARA	National Archives and Records Administration
0	NASA	National Aeronautics and Space Administration
0	NAVY	Department of the Navy
I	NCPC	National Capital Planning Commission
0	NFAH	National Foundation on the Arts and Humanities
I	NLRB	National Labor Relations Board
I	NMB	National Mediation Board
I	NRC	Nuclear Regulatory Commission
I	NREC	Neighborhood Reinvestment Corporation
0	NSF	National Science Foundation
0	OPM	Office of Personnel Management
I	OSHRC	Occupational Safety and Health Review Commission
0	OTH	Other
0	PCOR	Peace Corps
I	RRB	Railroad Retirement Board
0	SBA	Small Business Administration
I	SEC	Securities and Exchange Commission
0	SMTH	Smithsonian Institution
0	SSA	Social Security Administration
0	STAT	Department of State
0	USAF	Department of the Air Force
0	USAID	Agency for International Development
I	USARC	Arctic Research Commission
I	USCFA	Commission on Fine Arts
0	USDA	Department of Agriculture
I	USITC	International Trade Commission
0	USPS	Postal Service

Judicial Delimitation in the New Deal Era

Stuart Chinn

In line with the core theme of this volume, a quick glance at three of the most significant eras of reform in American political history suggests that the substance of new policies is hardly settled once initial reforms are successfully enacted. Indeed, when one examines various reform eras and their aftermath, one does not find complete continuity between the substance of momentous reforms and the substance of the new political orders; instead, one finds qualified continuity along with regular and striking *discontinuities*. For example, following Emancipation and the enactment of the Reconstruction Amendments, the new status quo that emerged with respect to southern race relations was a new form of racial subordination embodied in Jim Crow laws. Nearly a hundred years later, beginning with *Brown v. Board of Education* in 1954 and continuing through the 1960s, a second moment of transformative reform in race relations came to fruition as the Supreme Court and Congress worked in tandem to dismantle Jim Crow in the South. Yet, once again, the ambitions of reformers were curtailed as southerners pushed back by championing commitments to color blindness and neighborhood schools—a strategy that helped to pave the way for the continuation of de facto racial exclusions in the South, and especially in the North, in the post-*Brown* era.[1] Finally, consider a third example of this oddity, though

For helpful feedback and comments, thanks to Bruce Ackerman, David Mayhew, Stephen Skowronek, Eric Patashnik, and Jeff Jenkins.

notably, this is an example unrelated to race: The Wagner Act in 1935 brought to fruition the dismantling of an intricate system of social relations in the domain of labor. The statutory-based system of labor relations imposed by the Wagner Act replaced the old system of employer-employee relations governed by master-servant common law doctrines. Yet despite this transformative shift, many of the same employer prerogatives that defined the old order nevertheless enjoyed a resurgence in judicial rulings in the late 1930s that imposed sharp constraints on union activities. As events unfolded, these same prerogatives later became entrenched in the post–World War II system of labor relations as well.

These examples illustrate two related aspects about the nature of major institutional dismantlings in American politics where we find stratified systems of social relations being unraveled: First, they suggest that historically, there has been a consequential limit on how far political transformations of this type can be pushed. When the prerogatives of certain dominant social classes over subordinate classes are disrupted and dismantled in this fashion, we not surprisingly find the former eventually pushing back against the thrust of reform.

Second, these examples also suggest—in sympathy with several of the contributions to this volume—that a study focused solely on the major reforms of each of these eras, such as the Reconstruction Amendments, *Brown v. Board of Education* or the Civil Rights Act of 1964, or the Wagner Act, would be insufficient for any developmental account that sought to illuminate the foundations of the new, postdismantling political order. Any such account that bypassed the constraints on these new reforms, or the resilience of political losers, would offer a severely truncated view of the nature of political transformation in each of these three cases.

Thus, a more accurate account of how political transformations occur in American politics would have to acknowledge that even after reforms have been enacted, subsequent political developments will influence the scope and meaning of those initial reforms. Stated more broadly, it would be incumbent on an accurate developmental account to illuminate the precise processes by which the American polity has historically moved from a period of reform and disruption to a new political equilibrium or a new status quo; it would have to illuminate just how it is that new political orders, or new political equilibria, are constituted after dismantling reforms have been enacted.

In his chapter on tax reform and airline deregulation, Eric Patashnik emphasizes that "the most sustainable reforms *reconfigure* politics" by prompting institutional changes, prompting the rearrangement of interest groups, and stimulating investment in the new system.[2] While his argument strikes me as quite compelling, I would also emphasize that at least in the context of *reforms in social relations*, it is especially the case that these types of considerations are themselves often underdetermined by the initial reforms. As I discuss below, the Supreme Court has played a crucial role in the creation of social order precisely because its actions, prompted by political losers, are crucial in helping to determine just how much institutional change will occur, and how much coalitional fault lines may or may not be problematized, in the aftermath of reform.

Political Losers and Recalibration

One of the three claims that I advance in this paper is a general claim about dismantling reforms and American political development: Namely, I claim that extended processes of *institutional recalibration* are attendant on the occurrence of major political changes implicating the dismantling of systems of social relations. Political changes of this type simply cannot be unleashed within the larger political universe to then fit seamlessly with other preexisting institutional authorities.[3] Rather, major dismantlings require a subsequent period of adjustment during which the governing principles embodied in recent reforms are integrated within an enduring, resilient, already established institutional and legal fabric. These processes of "institutional recalibration" speak to the process of critical readjustment and accommodation between old and new governing principles. Thus, taking account of recalibration processes points us to a view of political development very much in line with the concept of "intercurrence" that Orren and Skowronek elaborate on. They assert that at any given moment in time, the polity is always composed of multiple institutional authorities, each operating according to different governing principles.[4] In line with their assertions, the perspective advanced here is that dismantling reforms cannot be self-contained within a given policy domain. Rather, to use the Orren and Skowronek terminology, it is an intercurrent dynamic—namely, the inherent frictions between new governing principles embodied in reforms and old governing principles in unreformed policy domains—that drives the pressures for integration and recalibration.

A second claim I advance is that political losers play a crucial role in driving the political momentum for recalibration processes. Indeed, the fact that losers remain significant portions of the electorate *after* the enactment of major reforms ensures that the scope of reform will be hotly contested. If losers have lost the central battle over reform, they still have enormously consequential openings to contest and shape the substance of political change at the margins, and to help establish the terms on which reform principles will be integrated with older, established governing principles. Stated in other words, the incongruities between new and old governing principles provide opportunities for political losers to potentially minimize the depth of political change.

Institutional recalibration is thus not a mere sideshow to the enactment of significant political reforms. Rather, the outcomes dictated by the former significantly determine the scope and the *very meaning* of the political change itself. Of course, other scholars have previously taken note of "Thermidorian Reactions" or "end of reform" periods.[5] But in contrast to previous efforts, I seek to place these dynamics within a comparative historical framework and to illuminate their institutional nature.

Recalibration and the Supreme Court

While drawing attention to general processes of institutional recalibration is the broader goal of this chapter, space constraints preclude anything approaching a comprehensive treatment of these processes.[6] My case study discussion below is thus offered as a preliminary examination of these processes as they have historically intersected with the Supreme Court and with the historical development of constitutional law.

Why focus on the judiciary, specifically, as an important site to investigate recalibration processes, and why approach recalibration from a legalistic perspective? After all, I have mentioned nothing up to this point to suggest that the judiciary would necessarily play a consequential role, or would necessarily play any role, in recalibration. Furthermore, one might expect that the dynamics of recalibration would likely encompass various social movement dynamics and developments in the elected branches as well. Without minimizing the potential significance of these other important sites of investigation, let me nevertheless offer three preliminary thoughts as to why we might expect the interests of political losers and the frictions of institutional recalibration to reliably register in the activities of the Supreme Court.

First, given the nature of the judicial function within the larger American governmental structure, there are sound reasons to think that a significant portion of the contestation that arises in the aftermath of a major dismantling of stratified social relations will find its way into litigation. This is an assertion that might sound familiar and in line with Alexis de Tocqueville's famous observation that "there is hardly a political question in the United States which does not sooner or later turn into a judicial one."[7] While Mark Graber has persuasively argued that Tocqueville may have overstated the point—in that many important political and constitutional issues seem to have escaped judicial resolution in the Jacksonian era[8]—Tocqueville's initial observation may nevertheless possess greater validity when it comes to the specific and peculiar context of political and legal questions that arise in the aftermath of such dismantlings.

Consider that if the historical examples discussed before are generally indicative of the nature of major institutional dismantlings in American politics, we should expect that in the aftermath of such an event, there will be a wholesale destruction of some set of individual rights, prerogatives, and responsibilities enjoyed by some previously dominant social class. In light of such sharp redistributions of power and authority, it seems more than plausible that for those social groups on the losing end of dismantling reforms, they will be energized, upset, and eager to contest these incursions on their individual rights and prerogatives. For disputes implicating the established prerogatives of a dominant social class that have been newly dismantled, what forum could possibly be more appropriate for these political losers to utilize than the judicial forum? Thus, the fact that these types of dismantlings implicate individual rights—combined with the fact that the judicial forum is peculiarly oriented toward adjudicating contestations of individual rights—gives rise to an expectation that the judiciary will very likely play an important role in postdismantling politics.

Of course, one might offer a counterargument at this point: namely, that there is no reason to necessarily expect the Supreme Court to issue decisive settlements or judgments in all of the matters that arise before it. Indeed, Alexander Bickel's normative theory of judicial review emphasized this point in endorsing the Court's use of various jurisdictional devices—such as standing and ripeness requirements—that would allow the Court to neither strike down nor legitimate laws. This style of adjudication—the "passive virtues"—would, according to Bickel, promote democratic political activity free of too much judicial intrusion.[9] As such, a skeptic might concede that while many facets of postdismantling political contestation may find their way into litigation and the judicial forum, there is no reason to think that the judiciary will necessarily do anything consequential in response to such legal disputes.

The preceding argument undoubtedly carries much validity in many political contexts. But this takes us to a second argument or justification for our focus on the judiciary, and it is a point that emanates from a concern about the nature of political order. I would suggest that in the specific context of those historical eras where new political orders are being created in some policy domains—that is, where new, stable allocations of institutional authority and individual rights are being entrenched in a given policy domain—there is a very real sense in which the Court *must* speak and offer settlement and guidance on these post-reform disputes: If an emerging, new reallocation of governing authority and individual rights is to become entrenched and sturdy enough to create a new order, its constitutionality or legality cannot remain ambiguous on fundamental principles. *If* a new political order is to be created after a dismantling, there would seemingly have to be some judicial statement regarding its constitutionality. So long as one's focus of inquiry was on those instances where a political order did arise, this would again suggest that processes of recalibration would seemingly have to run at least in part through the judiciary, and through the ultimate judicial authority of the Supreme Court.

A third and final reason for focusing on the judiciary as a valuable site for investigating institutional recalibration largely emanates from an understanding of the nature of the judicial role. As already noted, an institutional recalibration, at its core, deals with the integration, critical readjustment, and mutual accommodation between reforms on the one hand, and those institutions that have remained resilient in the face of reform on the other. For one interested in studying such processes of accommodation, a focus on the Court also seems particularly appropriate because this task—of blending old and new—is also a fair description of what the judicial role often entails. In particular, it has not been an unusual occurrence in American political history where we find legislatures making sweeping statements of change, and the judiciary subsequently taking the lead in clarifying how new constitutional amendments and statutes will be integrated within the wider fabric of the law encompassing old judicial precedents, old structural arrangements, and old constitutional amendments.[10] Institutional recalibration thus appears to be a task that looks peculiarly judicial at first glance. As such, again, where better to begin an investigation of it than with the Supreme Court?

Judicial Delimitation

As is discussed in the case study below, a close examination of Supreme Court behavior in the aftermath of the New Deal transformation of labor rights leads to the third core claim of this chapter: namely, that we find two notable dynamics regarding how the Court has historically interacted with the processes of recalibration. First, the Court has played a recurrent role in *delimiting* the scope of prior transformative reforms—that is, in clarifying and demarcating the outer boundaries of recent reforms. There has been a recurrence in the Court's function within broader processes of recalibration.

Second, the significance of the Supreme Court for processes of recalibration stems not just from the act or function of delimitation, but also from the substantive justifications or reasons that the Court has offered for delimiting reform. When judicial delimitation occurs, the Supreme Court has followed a historical pattern of "indirect opposition."[11] It has justified its delimitation of reform *not* by frontally challenging the core achievements of the dismantling, but instead by emphasizing the continuing legitimacy of tangential, yet resilient authorities that might be threatened if reins are not placed on reformist principles. As such, we see a pattern in the Supreme Court's opinions where it justifies delimitation by emphasizing the serious threat of allowing dismantling, reformist principles to spread further and further into the polity—which in turn could result in the destruction or weakening of other institutional authorities that still enjoy considerable legitimacy in broader society. Put simply, a slippery-slope rationale prominently underlies many of these judicial delimiting rulings. And indeed, as we see in the cases discussed below, the Court has occasionally lifted its "indirect" justifications for delimitation straight from the legal briefs of former political losers.[12]

To be sure, as these processes of recalibration have run through the Supreme Court, the end result has *not* been judicial rulings that constituted a reversal of prior political reforms in either form—as suggested by the indirect opposition dynamic—or in substance. A "recalibration" of reform is not a "reversal" of reform. What the former have constituted instead has been a clarification of the meaning and scope of the initial dismantling, in light of its integration within a broader political and legal fabric—and not a backtracking of earlier reforms.

Let me close this section by briefly addressing some qualifications to the claims just advanced. First, I am not making the claim that processes of institutional recalibration and delimitation implicate *only* the judiciary. It is generally the case that certain broader political conditions are necessary for particular judicial rulings to be politically efficacious.[13] I believe that this has been true as well for episodes of institutional recalibration after a dismantling. My focus on the judiciary is merely the consequence of having to limit my inquiry in this chapter to only a portion of a larger political process. Second, I am also not making the claim that during these eras of constitutional transformation, the judiciary is *only* capable of playing a delimiting or a conservative role. Indeed, in the aftermath of the civil rights revolution, the late Warren and early Burger Courts actually engaged in a short run of judicial activism in school desegregation cases, prior to the latter issuing judicial delimiting opinions with respect to constitutional equal protection.[14] I am, however, making a claim that whatever else the judiciary may be doing during these periods, it *is* the case that the judiciary regularly engages in delimiting behavior after the enactment of dismantling reforms.

In the sections that follow, I illuminate judicial delimiting behavior in the context of the New Deal transformation in labor rights. Through the Supreme Court's delimitation of reform, and its responsiveness to the legal claims of political losers, we will see one important aspect of how processes of recalibration shape American political development.

The New Deal and Judicial Delimitation

The New Deal saw the rise of a number of important political developments, such as the emergence of Keynesianism as the centerpiece of national fiscal policy,[15] and the triumph of federal governmental authority[16] validated by new Supreme Court interpretations of the Commerce

Clause.[17] But for the purpose of illustrating recalibration processes at work in the aftermath of dismantling reforms, only one aspect of the New Deal transformation fits the mold of encompassing a dismantling of a system of social relations: the New Deal era's transformation in labor relations.

With the legislative enactment and judicial validation of the Wagner Act, a complex, deeply entrenched system of legal rights and obligations was permanently dismantled. More specifically, what was dismantled was a hierarchical system of employer-employee relations that had been embedded in master-servant common law doctrines and enforced by the courts. Its replacement was a new regime of government-sponsored collective bargaining, established and to be overseen by Congress.[18] The similarities to Reconstruction, which also constituted an expansion of individual rights to be overseen by Congress, via section 2 of the Thirteenth Amendment, section 5 of the Fourteenth Amendment, and section 2 of the Fifteenth Amendment, are quite apparent. The full extent of the political change contemplated by the Wagner Act, however, was not apparent from the start. Uncertainty existed as to whether the new federal commitment to employee self-activity, as guaranteed in the text of the Wagner Act, might contemplate further federal incursions into the ownership rights of employers. At the most extreme transformative end, this latter institution stood in danger of being dismantled to an extent, in the same way that federalism had previously been implicitly threatened by the expansion of federal authority contemplated in the Reconstruction Amendments.

Thus, a crucial component of the developmental story of the New Deal transformation in labor rights lies specifically in tracing out the political processes by which the dismantling, carried out by the Wagner Act's passage in 1935, would be accommodated with other institutional authorities that remained standing. And once the dust had cleared from these processes of recalibration, it was apparent that while unionization was to be a permanent feature of the new political order, unions would also be constrained and hemmed in by the demands of employer and ownership prerogatives in the new order. The system of labor relations that ultimately took root in the post–World War II era—industrial pluralism—would have its genesis in these twin commitments to unionization and employer prerogatives. The first was rooted in a dismantling reform, and the second was rooted in the subsequent period of judicial delimitation.

My discussion of judicial delimitation in the New Deal era proceeds as follows: After a very brief discussion of the political context of the late 1930s, I examine, in turn, the three key Supreme Court cases that marked the judicial delimitation of the Wagner Act by establishing the definitive outer boundaries of the Act's protection of employees. With respect to each case, I first demonstrate how the legal outcome functioned to delimit the scope of the Wagner Act, and how this delimitation was accomplished by the Supreme Court in an "indirect" manner: namely, by emphasizing the significance of preserving industrial peace. Second, I discuss the briefs of the companies and corporations in these cases, to demonstrate how the goals and even the arguments of former "political losers" aligned with the Court's rulings—and to suggest that these briefs likely influenced the Court as well. Finally, after proceeding in this manner with each of the three Supreme Court cases, I conclude with a more general discussion of how these delimiting rulings contributed to the recalibration of the New Deal transformation in labor rights in helping to integrate the Wagner Act within the broader political and legal commitments of that era. The end result of this critical integration was a new order in labor relations: industrial pluralism.

Political Context

The political context surrounding judicial delimitation in the 1930s was set by the election of 1938, which was a pivotal moment in the politics of the later New Deal due to the stunning reversals suffered by the Democrats in the 1938 election. On top of Roosevelt's failed purge effort against conservative Democrats,[19] the election also saw Republicans gain eighty-one seats in the House, eight seats in the Senate, and thirteen governorships. The election did not suddenly put the Republicans in the driver's seat, nor did Republicans secure their wins with campaign promises to dismantle the New Deal—Democrats still held majorities in both the House and the Senate. But the election had put reformers in retreat. And the post-1938 environment would be one where Roosevelt would need at least some southerners or Republicans to form majorities.[20] A legislative stalemate, in effect, had set in: The next major piece of labor legislation to emerge from the elected branches would be the antilabor Smith-Connally Act or the War Labor Disputes Act, enacted over FDR's veto in 1943[21]—four years *after* the judiciary had offered its major statements on delimitation.

The politics of the later New Deal were also influenced by the judiciary as well. Judicial delimitation came in the form of three cases— *NLRB v. Mackay Radio & Telegraph Co.*,[22] *NLRB v. Sands Manufacturing Co.*,[23] and *NLRB v. Fansteel Metallurgical Corp.*[24]—that, oddly enough, do not figure prominently in standard historical works on the New Deal. Rather, these cases tend to remain topics of discussion among labor historians and labor law historical scholars.[25] The reason for this is not too hard to guess: These decisions were nestled in the midst of many more judicial decisions that were actually sympathetic to labor's interests in the late 1930s.[26] Yet, as labor scholars have noted, this is an unfortunate and unwarranted oversight given the significant and negative consequences for labor that nevertheless followed from these three rulings.

NLRB V. MACKAY RADIO & TELEGRAPH CO.

The Supreme Court's Ruling. A consequential first step in the judicial demarcation of the outer boundaries of the Wagner Act occurred in *NLRB v. Mackay Radio & Telegraph Co.*, where the Court confronted the question of how far the Act's protection extended to workers engaged in an economic strike—that is, workers striking for higher pay or shorter hours, as opposed to striking prompted by an employer's unfair labor practices.[27] Ultimately, the Court ruled that the five strikers who brought the suit were employees under the Wagner Act, that the evidence indicated they had been discriminated against because of their union activities, that this discrimination was an unfair labor practice, and that the NLRB's relief of reinstatement for the workers was appropriate.[28] More notable for our purposes, the Court also explicitly rejected the idea that economic strikers were entitled to reinstatement as a general principle and concluded that economic strikers could lawfully be *permanently* replaced (in the absence of any antiunion discrimination by the employer). This latter point is the most notable aspect of the case for the present argument because it suggests the delimiting impulse at work in this ruling. The Court was not engaged in the task of repudiation with this ruling—its support of the NLRB's reinstatement of the five workers was wholly grounded in an analysis of the Wagner Act, and thus an implicit, unquestioned recognition of the Act's constitutionality. However, in stating where the protection of the Act would *not* extend—in this case, toward the general right of reinstatement for economic strikers— this case was also engaged in demarcating the outer boundaries of that Act's protection for employees.

Unfortunately, Justice Owen Roberts—who wrote for the Court—was not particularly verbose in reaching his conclusions on the general non-right of reinstatement. His most extended comment on this subject was the following passage:

> Nor was it an unfair labor practice to replace the striking employes [*sic*] with others in an effort to carry on the business. Although § 13 provides, "Nothing in this Act shall be construed so as to interfere with or impede or diminish in any way the right to strike," it does not follow that an employer, guilty of no act denounced by the statute, has lost the right to protect and continue his business by supplying places left vacant by strikers. And he is not bound to discharge those hired to fill the places of strikers, upon the election of the latter to resume their employment, in order to create places for them.[29]

The key phrases in this statement lie in Roberts's reference to the employer's "effort to carry on the business" and his "right to protect and continue his business" as justifications for bringing in permanent replacement workers. A similar view is expressed in the NLRB's reply brief as well: "The Board has never contended, in this case or any other, that an employer who has neither caused nor prolonged a strike through unfair labor practices, cannot take full advantage of economic forces working for his victory in a labor dispute."[30] These are statements that suggest a "business necessity" rationale behind rejecting a general right of reinstatement for economic strikers. That is, if this general right were extended to workers under the Wagner Act, it could in some fundamental way threaten the ability of a manager or employer to successfully run his or her business. Thus, the Court's argument was not driven by a direct opposition to the legitimacy of the Wagner Act; rather, I would assert that it was driven instead by an indirect opposition toward some of the Act's potential implications.

The Employer's Supreme Court Brief. While neither the Court nor the NLRB was particularly rigorous in unpacking the concerns behind this business necessity rationale, the company's brief (not surprisingly) was more illuminating on this matter. In examining this brief, it is clear that the business necessity idea—and its rejection of general reinstatement rights for economic strikers—was driven by a belief or concern that the extension of such a right would allow unionized employees to simply run amok. If the employer's right to fire workers was impaired to the point that economic strikers would have a general right of reinstatement, what could possibly function to check the demands and actions of employees?[31] "By guaranteeing a striker his job, where the strike was neither provoked nor prolonged by the refusal of the employer to negotiate or by any other unfair labor practice," argued the Mackay Radio brief, "peaceful negotiation would be discouraged and strikes would be encouraged."[32] Such an interpretation of the Act "*guarantees* their jobs to employees, upon whatever terms and conditions they may demand, unless the employer shall elect to give up his business."[33]

In addition, a bargaining terrain shaped so decidedly to the advantage of workers would have the effect of not only rendering employers impotent, but also perverting the system of economic bargaining that the Wagner Act had, by its own terms, protected and modified with its defense of employee rights to self-organize. As the company's brief argued, "it is the purpose [of the Wagner Act] to allow economic forces to have free play subject only to the requirement that employers must negotiate with the representatives of employees, and that they must not interfere with employees in their choice of representatives."[34] An interpretation of the Act guaranteeing reinstatement would "paralyze" one of these economic forces—namely the threat of employees losing their jobs—thus constituting an obstacle to "industry functioning and commerce moving" and collective bargaining itself.[35] Such a result would fail to be "in accord with the purposes of the Act, nor is it consistent with its philosophy."[36]

Again, as with Justice Roberts's ruling, one interesting aspect about the arguments by the company lies in the fact that they clearly bypassed any primary reliance on freedom of contract or property rights as protected by the Fifth Amendment.[37] While the arguments in the preceding paragraph were no doubt driven by concerns to protect employer rights with respect to property and managerial control, as they are presented, they also conceded the legitimacy of the Wagner Act's system of collective bargaining.[38] The arguments are pitched less in the idealistic terms of fundamental impairments to employer prerogatives and more in the pragmatic terms of threats posed to a well-functioning economy. In short, these were not arguments that purported to repudiate the Wagner Act. Their appeals to a well-functioning economy and healthy businesses were appeals to core goals articulated in the preamble to the Wagner Act itself: the goal of healthy industry and industrial peace. The language of delimitation is what we find here—that is, the employment of still-credible political ideals and values to accomplish not a frontal assault on the

Wagner Act but a delimitation of the Wagner Act's infringement on additional employer rights—and they clearly found favor on the Court.

If we were to read the quotation from Justice Roberts's opinion for the Court as informed by the company's brief, it is especially the case that his references to the employer's right to "carry on his business" take on a meaning that embodies something very distinct from just a Fifth Amendment individual rights protection for employers. Roberts's phrase might instead be interpreted as referring to how the maintenance and preservation of employers' rights was a valuable prerequisite of a well-functioning industrial system as well.

NLRB V. SANDS MANUFACTURING CO.

The Supreme Court's Ruling. One year later, the Court's ruling in *Sands* further demarcated the outer boundaries of the Wagner Act, though this time the focus was on the Act's section 8 (5). This provision stated, "It shall be an unfair labor practice for an employer—To refuse to bargain collectively with the representatives of his employees, subject to the provisions of Section 9 (a)."[39] The key question posed in *Sands* in this regard was, "How expansively would the Court interpret this duty of employers to bargain?"

The case arose due to a dispute between the employee's union—"Mesa"—and the company over hiring and seniority clauses in a labor agreement. Faced with a seeming standoff over the proper interpretation of a labor agreement between the two, the company posed the following choice to the shop committee: accede to the company's interpretation of the contract or have the plant shut down temporarily. The union chose the latter. As a result, the plant closed down on August 21, 1935. On August 31, Sands Manufacturing completed another contract with the International Association of Machinists—a union affiliated with the American Federation of Labor—and reopened on September 3. When Mesa demanded a meeting with company representatives on September 4, they were informed that their members had generally been discharged.[40]

Writing for the Court again, Justice Roberts conceded that employers do have a duty to bargain and meet with employee representatives regarding modifications or questions of interpretation of an existing contract—thus obviously recognizing the fundamental legitimacy of the Wagner Act. But he also found that Sands had met this duty or obligation. A key element in helping him reach this conclusion was his related conclusion that the company's interpretation of the contract was clearly the correct one.[41] As he stated:

> The contract provided for departmental seniority, in §§ 5 and 6, and § 7 did not create any ambiguity on the subject. Moreover, the record makes it clear that the committee which negotiated the contract on behalf of the union fully understood its terms in the same sense as did the respondent. In this situation how often and how long was the company bound to continue discussion of the committee's demand that the provisions of the contract should be ignored?[42]

The uncompromising stance of the union made further negotiation pointless, according to the Court. Furthermore, Mesa's threat of a strike, should the company proceed with its desired plans and according to its interpretation of the contract, amounted to a breach of the June 15, 1935, agreement. By repudiating their labor contract, the Mesa members were eligible to be discharged and to lose their employee status under the Wagner Act, and thus the company had no obligation under section 8 (5) to bargain with Mesa subsequent to the plant shutdown on August 21.[43] To quote from the Court:

> Respondent rightly understood that the men were irrevocably committed not to work in accordance with their contract. It was at liberty to treat them as having severed their relations with the company because of their breach and to consummate their separation from the company's employ by hiring others to take their places. The Act does not prohibit an effective discharge for re-pudiation by the employe [*sic*] of his agreement. . . . [44]

In other words, according to Justice Roberts, the Wagner Act did not provide for a robust employer duty to bargain over (what Roberts thought was) a contract modification. The result was a ruling that offered a second statement demarcating the outer reach of the Wagner Act's authority.

The Employer's Supreme Court Brief.   For the NLRB, Mesa's threat of a work stoppage did not divest their members of their employee status or relieve the company of its obligation to bargain with them.[45] For the Court, exactly the opposite was true. Why might the Court have been motivated to grant union activities less leeway and interpret the company's obligation to bargain less robustly? The *Sands* opinion, like the *Mackay Radio* opinion, was written by Justice Roberts, and its reasoning is even briefer than the latter's. But again, the key analytical pivot for the Court lay in finding a breach of contract—in this case, by Mesa. And pragmatic reasons for coming to this conclusion, in addition to the Court's interpretation of the textual provisions of the labor agreement, might be speculated on in light of the company's brief and the brief's treatment of these issues.

Sands Manufacturing asserted that the merits of the underlying contractual dispute had everything to do with dictating the extent of the employer's obligation to bargain. If it were the case that the union's interpretation of the contract was clearly wrong and that the union was essentially pressing for a modification or change to the contract (which the company argued was the case here and which the Court also believed), then the extent of the employer's obligation was simply to hear and consider the employees' position—and that was it.[46] The collective bargaining duty could not be any greater than this in the case of a clear-cut contract modification, or else unions would enjoy far too much of a bargaining advantage:

> The Government contends that in collective bargaining between an employer and his employees over a requested change in an existing contract, the merits of the dispute cannot affect the extent of the employer's obligation under Section 8 (5).
>
> This statement cannot be the law, else a strike by a group of employees during the term of a contract for the sole purpose of accomplishing a change in the contract between them and their employer, as, for example, an increase in the wage rates specified in the contract, would be lawful on the part of the employees, and filling their places unlawful on the part of the employer.[47]

The systemic consequences of this would be obvious:

> If the respondent employer did not have the right to stand on its contract and refuse to negotiate further on the MESA refusal to perform, then respondent's contract was worthless. Indeed, the value of every collective bargaining contract would be greatly lessened if the rule stated by the Board and by the Government were held to apply in such situations.[48]

Notably, this defense of contractualism did not wholly rest on some inherent normative value of the sanctity of contract. Rather, there is a strong pragmatic flavor to these arguments; after all, a core purpose of the Wagner Act's provisions lay in the promotion of labor contracts in order to promote industrial peace—a rationale that should sound familiar. It was precisely this goal that would be endangered if the Court interpreted the section 8 (5) duty to bargain to encompass midterm contract modifications as well. In short, if an employer knew it might always be obligated to bargain during the life of a contract, the motivation to reach agreement on the contract in the first place would be greatly lessened. As the company's brief stated:

> The Act does not compel collective bargaining looking toward a contract and at the same time invalidate the contract it has encouraged by permitting an interpretation to the effect that an employer can not use it as the measure of his conduct toward his employees and of their conduct toward him. The Act does not encourage the making of contracts the breach of which is to be considered immaterial. The Act does not permit such a conclusion and such was not the intent of Congress.[49]

The structural consequences of following such a wrong-headed conclusion would be clear:

> Stabilization of business conditions by collective agreements between employers and employees would also be a mere delusion if they be not held to impose mutually enforceable obligations. If, before the Board it is immaterial that the Complaining Employees had willfully violated their contract, then is disobedience of and disrespect for law thereby encouraged and constant strife, not peace, prescribed as our daily portion.[50]

In light of the Court's ultimate sympathy with the company's position, it seems reasonable to speculate that such "indirect" appeals to industrial peace and industrial health helped push the Court to delimit labor's rights by establishing a less robust employer duty to bargain under the Wagner Act.

NLRB V. FANSTEEL METALLURGICAL CORP.

The Supreme Court's Ruling.   Finally, we come to the Court's treatment of sit-down strikes. The employer, Fansteel Metallurgical Corp., was an Illinois company that manufactured and sold products made from rare metals. The NLRB had found that subsequent to employee attempts to unionize in the summer of 1936, the corporation had engaged in a number of unfair labor practices.[51] After the company's superintendent refused to bargain with the union on February 17, the union committee decided to engage in a sit-down strike by taking possession of two of the corporation's key buildings on the same day. They did so, work stopped in the two buildings, and work stopped in the rest of the plant. The occupying employees were eventually forcefully driven out on February 26.[52] The key question presented by this sequence of events implicated the same kinds of uncertainties confronted by the Court in the prior two cases: Namely, how far would the protective cover of the Wagner Act extend to aid and support unions?

The tone for Chief Justice Hughes's opinion for the Court was set early with the following assessment of the sit-down strike: "Nor is it questioned that the seizure and retention of respondent's property were unlawful. It was a high-handed proceeding without shadow of legal right."[53] Hughes asserted that "this conduct on the part of the employees manifestly gave good cause for their discharge unless the National Labor Relations Act abrogates the right of the employer to refuse to retain in his employ those who illegally take and hold possession of his property."[54]

Yet perhaps the corporation's violations of the Wagner Act might provide partial justification for the employees' use of the sit-down tactic? The Court did indeed affirm the NLRB's findings of the employer's unfair labor practices referred to above. The answer, however, was still no, according to Hughes. An employer's unfair labor practices simply do not justify an illegal act against its property in response:

> For the unfair labor practices of respondent the [Wagner] Act provided a remedy. . . . [R]eprehensible as was that conduct of the respondent, there is no ground for saying that it made respondent an outlaw or deprived it of its legal rights to the possession and protection of its property. The employees had the right to strike but they had no license to commit acts of violence or to seize their employer's plant.[55]

The Court was well on its way to a more restrained and limited interpretation of the NLRB's remedial power under sections 2 (3)[56] and 10 (c)[57] of the Wagner Act:

> We think that the true purpose of Congress is reasonably clear. Congress was intent upon the protection of the right of employees to self-organization and

to the selection of representatives of their own choosing for collective bargaining without restraint or coercion. To assure that protection, the employer is not permitted to discharge his employees because of union activity or agitation for collective bargaining. The conduct thus protected is lawful conduct. . . . There is thus abundant opportunity for the operation of § 2 (3) without construing it as countenancing lawlessness or as intended to support employees in acts of violence against the employer's property by making it impossible for the employer to terminate the relation upon that independent ground.[58]

By engaging in a sit-down strike, the employees "took a position outside the protection of the statute and accepted the risk of the termination of their employment upon grounds aside from the exercise of the legal rights which the statute was designed to conserve."[59] Hence reinstatement of these workers was not demanded by the Wagner Act.

Particularly notable in the language of the opinion was the Court's multiple references to threats of chaos and lawlessness, particularly as it related to infringement on the corporation's property rights: "To justify such conduct [as a sit-down strike] because of the existence of a labor dispute or of an unfair labor practice would be to put a premium on resort to force instead of legal remedies and to subvert the principles of law and order which lie at the foundations of society."[60] Further, to note an extended comment from the Court:

We repeat that the fundamental policy of the Act is to safeguard the rights of self-organization and collective bargaining, and thus by the promotion of industrial peace to remove obstructions to the free flow of commerce as defined in the Act. There is not a line in the statute to warrant the conclusion that it is any part of the policies of the Act to encourage employees to resort to force and violence in defiance of the law of the land. On the contrary, the purpose of the Act is to promote peaceful settlements of disputes by providing legal remedies for the invasion of the employees' rights. . . . We are of the opinion that to provide for the reinstatement or reemployment of employees guilty of the acts which the Board finds to have been committed in this instance would not only not effectuate any policy of the Act but would directly tend to make abortive its plan for peaceable procedure.[61]

Once again, then, the path toward delimitation here—in demarcating the limits of the Act's protection for sit-down strikers—did not lie through questioning the core ambitions of the Wagner Act; indeed, much of the opinion was concerned with matters of interpretation of the Act. Rather, defenses of employer prerogatives were aided in significant part by an indirect justification that emphasized the threat posed to the tangential commitment of industrial peace if the sit-down strikers were protected by the Wagner Act.

The Employer's Supreme Court Brief   Before discussing Fansteel's brief and illustrating the similarities between its arguments and those advanced by Hughes in the Court's opinion, it is worth emphasizing that the Court's ultimate conclusion in this case was by no means self-evident. The NLRB's brief offered a more expansive interpretation of the Wagner Act that would have allowed for the reinstatement of the sit-down strikers. The reasoning for this conclusion was that the strike was prompted by the corporation's own unfair labor practices and its flouting of the Wagner Act's requirements.[62] Yet, what of the concern, found compelling by Hughes, that this protection for employees was perhaps nullified by virtue of the employees' own illegal acts?

First, the NLRB brief offered an argument based on the statute's text. Section 10 (c) of the Wagner Act states, in part, that the NLRB, on finding the occurrence of an unfair labor practice, may "take such affirmative action, including reinstatement of employees with or without back pay, as will effectuate the policies of this Act." And the definition of "employee" in section 2 (3) states that the term applies to "any individual whose work has ceased as a consequence of, or in connection with, any current labor dispute or because of any unfair labor practice." The NLRB argued that the sit-down strikers retained their employee status given that their strike resulted from a current labor dispute and from the corporation's unfair labor practices; as a result, they were eligible for reinstatement under section 10 (c). To be sure, the Wagner Act's section 2 (3) specifies one way in which the employee status may be terminated: if the individual has "obtained any other regular and substantially equivalent employment." But it would be difficult to argue that this limitation applied to the present case.[63] Furthermore, the NLRB essentially put forth the position that once an employer had committed an unfair labor practice against employees, the expansive scope of the Board's remedial power under section 10 (c) was triggered and the employer had, as a result of its Wagner Act violation, made itself *potentially* subject to the Board's authority (including its authority to reinstate) regardless of whether alternative grounds may exist for discharging some of these employees for cause.[64]

Second, more pragmatically, the NLRB also argued that reinstatement of the strikers was necessary to achieve the larger aims of the Act as called for under section 10 (c). As its brief stated:

> Under the circumstances of this case, reinstatement was essential to restore the status quo and dissipate the effects of respondent's unfair labor practices, especially when it is remembered that none of the things respondent raises as a bar to reinstatement would have occurred but for respondent's violations of the law.[65]

Furthermore, reinstatement would be in keeping with the larger purpose of the Wagner Act in promoting industrial peace:

> So far as the National Labor Relations Act is concerned, the way to prevent and discourage sit-down strikes, as well as all strikes, is through collective bargaining, not by punishing strikers. It flies in the very teeth of the whole policy of the Act and its constitutional basis as a regulation of commerce to contend that, faced with clear violations of the Act, the Board must withhold the only remedy which can encourage collective bargaining in this case by dissipating the effects of respondent's unfair labor practices because, after such practices were committed, some of the strikers engaged in acts illegal under state law, for which they have been punished under that law.[66]

Fansteel's brief, not surprisingly, took issue with both the NLRB's textual and policy-oriented arguments. With respect to the former, the crux of the corporation's departure from the NLRB's position was precisely on the point of how expansively to interpret the Board's remedial power under section 10 (c). As noted above, the NLRB asserted that this provision, coupled with section 2 (3)'s definition of an "employee," gave the Board the right to potentially reinstate discharged employees "to effectuate the goals of the Act" once an unfair labor practice had occurred (even if an employee discharge was for cause). The corporation, however, saw this remedial power under section 10 (c) to be much more narrow in encompassing an authority for the NLRB to intervene and reinstate employees *only* when they had been discharged specifically for going on strike or for activities related to the right to unionize. With the exception of employee discharges for these reasons, however, the corporation's brief asserted that an employer's right to discharge for cause remained wholly intact subsequent to the Wagner Act's passage.[67] For the present case, this interpretation of sections 2 (3) and 10 (c) would mean that the corporation's discharge of sit-down strikers was legitimate, being a discharge for cause and *not* for protected activities such as employee self-organization and collective bargaining.[68] As noted in the previous section, this more stingy interpretation of the NLRB's remedial powers is a conclusion that the Court ultimately agreed with.

Fansteel also departed from the NLRB's position on policy or pragmatic grounds. In the corporation's eyes, allowing the sit-down strikers to be reinstated would have precisely the opposite effect claimed by the NLRB and would undercut the core Wagner Act goal of promoting industrial stability by encouraging lawlessness and chaos[69]—again, a familiar argument we also find employed in the Court's ruling:

> The [Wagner Act] was designed to promote industrial peace by encouraging collective bargaining and to provide an orderly process for enforcing the employees' right to self-organization. The reinstatement of discharged employees guilty of the property destruction and lawlessness portrayed in this record cannot advance either the immediate objective of peaceful collective bargaining or the ultimate end of industrial peace.[70]

The corporation's brief, like Justice Hughes's opinion, was not short on rhetoric emphasizing the moral threat posed by the sit-down tactic: "The Board cannot brush aside and wipe out the property destruction, lawlessness and discharge, and treat the situation as if these events had never occurred."[71] Two pages later, it stated again, "Self-help, with force, has no place in organized society. Neither high moral purpose nor integrity of objective can condone or justify the substitution of violence for the orderly processes of government."[72] By the corporation's assessment, the sit-down strike in itself constituted a fundamental affront to the Wagner Act:

> The Board ignores, as did the men who seized the Respondent's plant, the legal, orderly remedies available under the law. The statutory right of collective bargaining may be enforced either by a proceeding before the Board or by a

peaceful strike. . . . Without waiting for the outcome of their legal proceeding, the men took the law into their own hands. They determined to settle the
matter by force and violence "according to their own sense of right" without
regard to either the federal or the state laws.[73]

Perhaps more obviously than with *Mackay Radio* or *Sands Manufacturing*, the Supreme Court in *Fansteel* was certainly influenced by arguments pressed by the corporation that justified a delimitation of the
Wagner Act's reach—and that defended pre-Wagner employers' rights in
their private property and in their right to discharge employees—by emphasizing the potential for disorder with the sit-down tactic. The "indirect" appeal to industrial peace to justify delimiting the Wagner Act was
once again successfully employed in this dispute by legal advocates for
an employer.

Recalibration and Industrial Pluralism

A new system of labor relations—with a central commitment to voluntary arbitration as the primary means to manage labor disputes—would
later begin to take hold during World War II, and would subsequently
receive the Supreme Court's blessing in 1960. This system of "industrial
pluralism" was, in turn, truly the successor status quo in labor relations
to the pre-Wagner master-servant common law system.[74] But as a matter
of political development, there is no straight and direct line that takes us
from the Wagner Act's commitment to unionization to industrial pluralism's commitment to voluntary arbitration. Rather, the rise of industrial
pluralism only begins to make sense once we recognize the developmental significance of this period of judicial delimitation in the late 1930s,
for the system of social relations constituted by industrial pluralism was
really the synthesis of governing principles established in both the initial reform *and* judicial delimiting rulings. Industrial pluralism reflected
both the reform commitment to collective bargaining—in the former's
emphasis on mutually agreed-on grievance procedures between labor
and management—*and* the principle of restraining aggressive unionism embodied in the judicial delimiting rulings of the late 1930s—in industrial pluralism's commitment to channeling and managing industrial
conflict in an orderly, bureaucratic manner. Recognizing judicial delim-

itation as a component of processes of recalibration is what allows us to bridge the developmental gap between the dismantling of the Wagner Act and the substance of a new political order in labor relations.

Conclusion

The aspiration of this chapter is to point toward a view of political change that illuminates how the meaning of legal enactments is subject to contestation long after their initial passage. An analysis of institutional recalibration indicates that new legislation and new constitutional amendments encompass only a portion of the constitutive politics that will actually define the new order. In line with the arguments of many legal scholars, the case of judicial delimitation in the New Deal era suggests that much of the substance of major shifts in constitutional development have occurred independently of the formal processes of constitutional and statutory lawmaking.[75] Furthermore, in recognizing the more drawn-out nature of political and legal change, we are also led to an understanding of the unique political functions of the Supreme Court during these processes. Much recent work in political science has highlighted how the judiciary has filled in the gaps of electoral governance in certain political contexts, often at the behest of elected politicians themselves.[76] My case study demonstrates, in a sympathetic vein, how the Court has played a crucial role in the context of delimitating and recalibrating dismantling reforms. Finally, and more broadly, the theory also explains how political losers can be resilient after major legislative losses and why post-reform results so often hold such great disappoint for reformers looking back in hindsight: Contestation over where reform will be delimited, and how it will be integrated with older, established values and institutional authorities, allows political losers to play a major role in influencing these crucial components of the new order.

The Significance of Policy Failures in Political Development: The Law Enforcement Assistance Administration and the Growth of the Carceral State

Vesla M. Weaver

By the millennium, the United States broke the world record for having the highest incarceration rate, imprisoning one out of every one hundred adults. Compared to other advanced industrialized nations, the United States imprisons at least five times more of its citizens per capita. In fact, U.S. prisons and jails hold more inmates (over 300,000 more) than the total inmate populations in twenty-six European countries combined (1,842,115).[1]

Correctional growth in the United States played out across three main periods of policy change. The last two are well known—the "war on drugs" era characterized by harsh mandatory minimum drug sentences in the 1980s and the "truth-in-sentencing" campaign of the 1990s, best embodied by the Clinton crime bill of 1994, which expanded crimes triggering the death penalty and lavished federal funds on states that promised to increase the time served of offenders. These episodes were preceded by a first period of growth that was widely appreciated at the time but has since been largely forgotten. Without it, later crime wars would hardly have been possible.

This chapter argues that to understand the unbridled expansion of imprisonment in the United States, the policy changes of the war on drugs, and the growth of an unprecedented government role in crime control, we must go back to the creation of a major federal crime bureaucracy, the Law Enforcement Assistance Administration (LEAA), by controversial omnibus legislation in 1968—the Safe Streets and Crime Control Act.

It was here that the modern criminal justice system took its first breaths, creating the structure and capacity for later campaigns and fostering a new and durable criminal justice constituency, which would develop into a powerful coalition that regularly lobbies Congress. Later outcomes would have been much less likely without this legislative achievement; Safe Streets accomplished the initial fertilization of the criminal justice field by providing a massive infusion of federal funds that engendered bureaucratic growth, policy innovation, and dramatic changes in criminal codes. It also professionalized parochial and disconnected local law enforcement and corrections agencies and converted them into interest groups, inspired the development of new technologies like 911 call centers and bullet proof vests, and established the tradition of criminal justice financing by the federal government. By the time of the drug war, mandatory minimums, determinate sentencing, sentence enhancements, and habitual offender laws were flourishing, and the weight of two decades of explosive growth in manpower, technology, and new prisons secured the institutional supports for later initiatives. Safe Streets provided the initial foundation on which later ideas, policies, and state-federal relationships would rest.

Yet, scholars have almost completely ignored Safe Streets because it was deemed a failure and the LEAA ultimately dismantled it. By resurrecting its importance for understanding crime policy and punitive developments in the United States, this chapter locates a missing piece of the puzzle of why, despite declining crime and drug abuse, the prison population would increase for thirty-eight consecutive years.

The argument I make here is that the Safe Streets legislation made a deep imprint on the later functioning, limits, and possibilities of the carceral state. While the policy was short lived, its implications for criminal justice infrastructure and crime policy were not. Once implemented, Safe Streets set off several policy feedback loops that transformed state capacity and infrastructure and reinforced the punitive path. Federal grants generated spoils for state and local agencies, creating strong incentives for them to invest heavily in criminal justice and increase the scope and penalties of offenses. The billions of dollars in federal aid attracted a powerful constituency, mollified previous opponents wary of federal intrusion into a state issue, and recast the terms of debate in ways that favored those with institutional loyalties to law enforcement and criminal justice. In short, as the "war on crime" campaign waned, it left enduring institutions, ideas, and organizational incentives. The strong policy feedbacks created by this policy, in turn, meant that the institutions and reach of the criminal justice system would expand in times of decreasing crime, when the public was concerned with other issues, and even when pressures for reform bubbled.

My argument both reinforces and complements themes developed by other contributors to this volume. Like the chapters by Eric Patashnik and Stuart Chinn, my chapter examines what happens after the dramatic moment of legislative enactment.[2] Chinn explores the history of efforts to dismantle major institutions governing social relations including Jim Crow and oppressive labor relations, and shows how the losers from reform can often be resilient after major legal changes as they find new defenses and seek to minimize the gains of their opponents. Chinn uncovers a fascinating dynamic of institutional recalibration, whereby reforms are subject to moves by the U.S. Supreme Court to delimit their impact on the ground. In contrast, the developmental story offered here traces how the initial scope of a policy can *expand* over time through the creation of supportive interests and institutions. We are both focused on downstream effects of reform, but in my case, certain features helped propel the policy change, not constrain its development. While for Chinn, the central actor is the interests (political losers) that rise up again after defeat to reclaim their ground, the motor in my account is the organizational interests, bureaucratic institutions, and state capacity changes that spring up from policy innovation.

Along with Patashnik, I employ concepts of policy feedback and path dependence as a guiding perspective to trace the key developments in the aftermath of Safe Streets. Specifically, policy-centered and state-centered analyses are attentive to how policies can shape the formation and goals of interest groups, the capacity of institutions, and the beliefs, identities, and engagement of mass publics. These "feedbacks" can lead to enduring political arrangements by providing the policy learning and material incentives that become self-reinforcing, making drastic alterations to the policy direction much less likely. Patashnik's analysis uncovers several important characteristics necessary for strong feedback dynamics to take hold. However, as my chapter points out, the institutional legacies of *policy failures* can often be important in reshaping later policy development. The effects of legislation can and often do survive the demise of the policy. Thus, the political landscape often inherits important interests, ideas, and institutions from past policies, even those that were ultimately dismantled.

Understanding Policy Durability and Feedback

To understand the punitive developments of the last several decades, we need to understand not just how the policies were arrived at—the moment of change—but also why they stayed—their institutional and policy legacies. Central to that story is the notion that policies can become enduring through self-reinforcing mechanisms of policy feedback.

Specifically, there are three major paths through which policies can reshape the political landscape in ways that make later outcomes more likely. Policies can influence the presence, goals, and capacities of interest groups; confer political lessons and influence public opinion; and bolster state capacity and grow new institutions. Because they shift the ideas of what is desirable or even possible, these "feedbacks" can narrow the menu of possibilities in later rounds of policymaking and may make deviations from the path costly, even when the original conditions and causes no longer obtain.[3]

First, by delivering benefits and goods, policies give incentives to beneficiaries to organize to ensure benefits continue. For example, the creation of an early pension system for veterans of the Civil War gave rise to a network of veteran's groups that worked to expand benefits, and ultimately inspired other American workers to work for a wider work-based pension system for all.[4] In much the same way, the G.I. Bill enhanced the civic engagement of World War II veterans.[5] Where policies generate constituencies that have a vested interest in the continuance of a policy, it will be extremely hard to retract them.

Second, policy arrangements can stimulate policy learning and have several interpretive effects. Just as public preferences shape policy choices, government policy transmits information back to the public, cultivating new understandings of issues and shaping public expectations of what is feasible for government intervention. In the words of two scholars: "Policies can set political agendas and shape identities and interests. They can influence beliefs about what is possible, desirable, and normal. . . . They can convey cues that define, arouse, or pacify constituencies."[6] Ideas give rise to institutions that may further reinforce the ideas on which they rested.

Finally, policies can transform state capacity, create new institutional structures, and shape the relationship between levels of government. State structures in turn shape the strategies and preferences of actors and the availability of courses of action.[7] Future policies must fit with the preexisting institutional matrix, which can itself become a barrier to reform.[8]

This policy feedback process carries several implications. First, policies that were hotly contested at one time often become durable policy arrangements later on.[9] Second, through mechanisms of reinforcement and path dependence, policies can be maintained long after the original motivation and initial conditions have disappeared. Third, small initial differences in policy designs can have large effects on future possibilities as later choices that reinforce the earlier decision accumulate.[10] Self-reinforcing mechanisms that serve to maintain a policy are not inevitable, however. As Patashnik points out in chapter 8, many major legislative achievements have "petered out" over time. Key features of policy can condition the extent and possibilities of feedback. In a recent paper, Patashnik and Julian Zelizer locate three significant factors for understanding when policy feedback will not occur or will be anemic, and thus, when a policy will diminish over time: where policy design is weak, where a policy lacks institutional supports, and when a policy's timing is poor.[11]

Characteristics of the specific crime control legislation enacted in the late 1960s limited later policy choices and embedded existing arrangements. Chief among these was federalism. By wielding plentiful grant money above them, the federal government communicated its policy aims and priorities to state governments, giving incentives for certain types of state crime and sentencing policy reform. Because the policies required state government and groups receiving funds to commit to criminal justice, these agencies and associations intensified mobilization to protect that investment. By the time the grant money had run out, lower levels of government had already invested heavily in their current course and made a long-term commitment to crime control. Criminal codes had been changed, technology had improved in light years, agencies were born and prison facilities constructed. State governments themselves became an interested constituency that would further promote policy initiatives. Paul Pierson reminds us that "as social actors make commitments based on existing institutions and policies, their cost of exit from established arrangements generally rises dramatically."[12] Furthermore, the policies activated groups whose livelihood depended on benefits from the policies and created formal channels for political activity of these groups. Crime policy also became the site of intense political mobilization for a new and influential set of interest groups, as policies like the Safe Streets Act presented a windfall of resources to criminal justice agencies and associations.

After an overview of the legislation, I begin with a detailed description of the incentives created by the policies, then connect these to organizational growth and state capacities, moving to the representation of interests at legislative hearings for extension, and finally end up at state policy changes in criminal justice. Together, these paths had the cumulative effect of substantially ratcheting up the investment in punishment and the development of a criminal justice infrastructure, increasing the probability and success of subsequent crime initiatives.

Background of Safe Streets Adoption

Prior to 1960, federal involvement in crime and law enforcement was quite limited. The Department of Justice (DOJ) was a small entity that, with its emaciated budget, basically prosecuted only Internal Revenue Service (IRS) cases. The only anticrime legislation that passed in the decade before Safe Streets concerned specific incidents—gambling and racketeering, crime in planes, obscene mail, and drunk driving. Federal anticrime legislation was rare, and the operation of criminal justice was chiefly a state and local concern.

That changed in the mid-1960s, as violence at home and abroad catapulted crime into the national agenda and President Lyndon Johnson announced a war on crime. After a two-year journey through Congress, the Safe Streets and Crime Control Act was passed and signed into law by a recalcitrant President Johnson, who saw the legislative proposal he initiated in 1967 become the prize of conservatives, who remade several provisions that directly contradicted LBJ's proposal. In addition to issuing major changes in criminal procedure and the rights of the accused, relaxing prohibitions on wiretapping and electronic surveillance, and regulating the sale of handguns, Safe Streets began a massive anticrime program by the federal government. Title I of the law authorized a major program of federal aid to assist state and local law enforcement and created a national agency in the DOJ, the Law Enforcement Assistance Administration (LEAA), to administer the grants.

Safe Streets and Its Legacies

Resources and the Expansion of the Crime Control Bureaucracy

Given only a two-year authorization and beginning with a meager budget of $63 million, the LEAA was not intended as a permanent agency, and its grants were originally designed to be seed money to aid cities confronted with civil disorders and states in upgrading their criminal justice system to better deal with the problem of crime. Attorney General Nicholas Katzenbach, in designing the original grant system, stated plainly that "a massive federal subsidy program is, in my judgment, undesirable."[13] However, each time the original act was amended or reauthorized, the LEAA was expanded financially and given greater reach over the workings of criminal justice at lower levels of government. The inaugural allocation in 1969 was multiplied tenfold by 1972 to be almost $700 million, and its appropriations increased by a factor of seven in the first seven years. LEAA became the fastest growing federal agency in the 1970s, spanning five presidential administrations over fourteen years and $28 billion dollars (in 2005 dollars). By the eve of the program's disbanding, 155,720 grants had been disbursed to states, counties, cities, and nonprofits for a total of 80,000 projects that ranged from victim assistance to police hardware to new career criminal bureaus.

Criminal justice became a major new role for the federal government, and in turn, federal financing became a very significant source of criminal justice expenditure, on which states came to rely. The proportion of state and local criminal justice expenditures originating from the federal government increased from just 3% in 1971 to over 12% in 1976, a substantial change given that crime control had been the province of state and local government.[14] During this time, the federal share of spending on criminal justice was double the federal share of elementary and secondary schools.[15] At the start of the LEAA program, only 16% of the federal government's crime spending went to assisting states; two years later the percentage of federal crime outlays for state assistance had increased to 41.[16] As a result, expenditures for criminal justice tripled from 1968 to 1985, rising more steeply than other government spending.

These federal commitments made the state status quo virtually impossible. Not only was a large bureaucracy in the federal government created, the block grant legislation created spoils for state and local government, generating momentum at the state level for dramatic investments in punishment and the creation of an even larger state-level criminal justice bureaucracy.

Transformation of State Capacity

By the end of 1968, the newly created state planning agencies submitted their first application to the LEAA for a planning grant, and within a few months, all comprehensive plans were approved and local governments submitted their claims for funds. The grants commenced, with about three thousand grants disbursed the first year, and criminal justice agencies accounted for 60% of the awards.

Once state and local agencies had fed from the LEAA cash cow, they grew significantly in size and professionalism. To appreciate the changes, one must contrast the situation compared to what criminal justice looked like in 1960, prior to the Safe Streets Act. State corrections, courts, and law enforcement agencies were fragmented, untrained, underfunded, and uncooperative across jurisdictions. While systematic data prior to the LEAA are scant, the information that does exist paints a patchwork of parochial agencies with little training and manpower. One survey found that 90% of local governments had police forces that employed fewer than ten full-time police officers, and those outside of metropolitan areas had a meager average of one police officer per locality.[17] Standards of training and education were consistently low. One-fourth of police agencies did not require a high school diploma, and under 1% required some college, according to a study by the International Association of Chiefs of Police. The Crime Commission similarly found that half of the nation's police had less than 12.4 years of schooling and little training. "The average barber receives 4,000 hours of training. The average policeman receives less than 200 hours," noted the report issued by the National Advisory Commission on Criminal Justice Standards and Goals in 1973.[18] Less than half of the states required more than 200 hours of police training.[19] Cooperation among local police departments was almost nonexistent, encroachment was treated with suspicion, and innovation was uncommon. The situation was little better in courts and corrections, where 40% of correctional facilities had no training personnel on staff, most states had no inspection of jails and prisons, and only eighteen states had unified court systems.[20] Most experts agree that a criminal justice *system* did not exist.

This situation began to change rapidly in 1968, after Safe Streets went into effect. A planning bureaucracy was immediately created as a result of the requirement that in order to receive Safe Streets funds, each state must form a state planning agency (SPA). Only ten SPAs had been established in the year before Safe Streets passage; by the end of 1968, the year Safe Streets became law, they had been created in all states.[21] Their staffs grew from just over 400 people to 1,425 in 1975, "creating in many state and local jurisdictions an entirely new category of civil servant, known as planners."[22] Soon after, state supervisory boards were established to oversee the SPAs and regional planning units to coordinate activities across states. State supervisory boards had an additional staff of 1,400, and regional and local supervisory boards included another 9,000.[23] There were 456 regional planning units across 44 states with 861 people on the professional staff. By close of 1971, 33 of the largest 50 cities had criminal justice coordinating councils (CJCC). In short, Safe Streets quickly created a large network of agencies designed to plan and oversee the operations of the criminal justice system and a cadre of professional planners.

Local agencies that had been largely disconnected and dependent on state and local funding came to have a significant new source of financial support. Not surprisingly, the distribution of grants was immediately followed by significant growth in manpower, bureaucratic organization, and professionalization uncommon prior to LEAA. In the ten-year period when LEAA was actively distributing grants, 6,350 new criminal justice agencies were fashioned. Expansion was most pronounced in the area of law enforcement, which grew from 14,806 to 19,298 agencies in this decade; given that many police forces were consolidated during this period, this growth is noteworthy.[24] As one critic rightly opined, "the net effect of the 'no strings-attached' distribution of funds has been a heavy emphasis on building up the material resources of the police."[25] Figure 11.1 charts the growth in the financial and manpower resources of the police and correctional agencies over time. Particularly in expenditures, there is

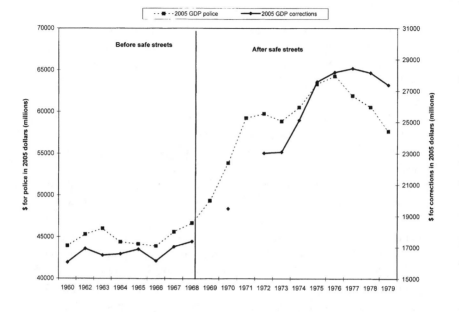

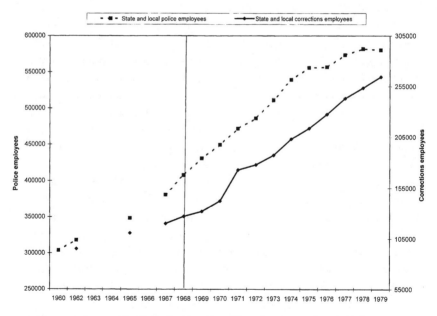

FIGURE 11.1. State and local criminal justice employees and expenditures (police and corrections), 1960–79

Source: *Statistical Abstract*, various years. Compiled by author and converted into 2005 constant dollars using the GDP.

a clear distinction between the time period before and after Safe Streets, characterized by tremendous expansion. Nationally, police forces doubled and correctional employees tripled from 1960 to 1980.

Changes occurring throughout the agencies of criminal justice were consistent with the timing and distribution of grants. National spending on police protection increased by a factor of eight from 1964 to 1974, and local police forces expanded by 21%. The Los Angeles force doubled in size, and Chicago's manpower grew by two-thirds during that decade.[26] Almost all states issued training and education standards. Professional associations formed and grew larger around these agencies. The International Association of Chiefs of Police (IACP) had been a small organization functioning on a small budget and with only three thousand members prior to passage of Safe Streets; by 1970, it had a budget of $2.5 million and membership of eight thousand.

This explosion in manpower is by far the most obvious result of LEAA funds, but the LEAA grants not only spurred growth in police muscle, but they also directly advanced the professional credentials of previously underdeveloped police forces. Prior to the LEAA, it was difficult to find programs for criminal justice and law enforcement in college. Only 3% of prison guards had a college degree, and a national crime commission poll of over six thousand police found only 7.4% had a college degree.[27]

Safe Streets established the National Institute of Law Enforcement and Criminal Justice for the specific purpose of providing academic assistance and coordinating the research of all aspects related to the criminal justice system. One of its capstone initiatives was the Law Enforcement Education Program (LEEP), which provided tuition assistance for law enforcement employees by giving colleges and universities funds to make loans and grants to students. LEEP grants gave thousands of dollars in tuition loans to police and helped spawn the creation of the first-ever criminal justice programs and departments at universities. In 1974, the year when the program reached its height, $44 million was disbursed to over a thousand schools to fund higher education for 95,000 students with careers in law enforcement.[28] This academic assistance helped professionalize criminal justice agencies, and from 1970 to 1974, 100,000 more police had some college education.[29] By the time LEAA began its decline in 1977, over 595,000 students, two-thirds of whom were police, had benefited from LEEP educational assistance, and $340 million in loans and grants had been awarded.

In pursuit of federal dollars, hundreds of universities and colleges initiated criminal justice curriculum and degree programs. In 1966–67, before Safe Streets, there were 184 colleges and universities with programs and criminal justice–related degree programs; by 1980, there were 1,500.[30] Gordon Misner, then president of the Academy of Criminal Justice Sciences, remarked, "When I started teaching there were 27 institutions in the United States giving degree programs. Now there are 1300 with their hand out for LEEP money."[31] Seven universities were given funds to start doctoral programs in criminal justice.

Organizational Growth and Mobilization

In addition to growing the bureaucracy and physical manpower of the police and corrections, newly available resources from policies and the incentives they bring can "influence the positions of interest groups, government elites, and individual social actors in politically consequential ways."[32] Safe Streets had important consequences for the patterns of group development and the structuring of those groups' interests. Specifically, the policy created a double-barreled incentive for groups first to mobilize to receive grants, and second, to mobilize to keep "the golden goose"—to ensure the survival of the agency responsible for the new source of funds. Safe Streets and the LEAA created a new trough from which local and state agencies could drink, in turn ensuring these groups would be supportive of federal government involvement and the LEAA. This new opportunity helped aid the creation of a broad network of criminal justice agencies and groups, which formed a coalition important in later policy debates.

Indeed, groups that had been ambivalent or hostile to federal crime legislation came to be tenacious supporters of further federal funding and expansion and lobbied extensively to keep the LEAA. The initial proposals to expand federal involvement in crime met with resistance from the potential constituency of the grant program, including the police. The precursor to the LEAA was a small pilot program initiated by President Johnson when he submitted his first crime program to Congress in 1965. The Law Enforcement Assistance Act of 1965 created a very small categorical grants-in-aid program intended to give local governments incentives to initiate innovative crime fighting programs. When the Office of Law Enforcement Assistance (OLEA) was proposed, there was no constituency to speak of; very few police, corrections, or court officials testified in support of the OLEA grant program. In fact, after president Johnson sent the crime message to Congress announcing the program, the IACP issued a resolution expressing explicit opposition to state and federal "encroachment" into local law enforcement at its annual convention.[33] State and local agencies had deep misgivings about the federal government usurping its constitutional powers to police and stepping outside their jurisdiction.[34] Still, the 1965 law establishing the OLEA grants, the initial legislation in Johnson's war on crime, was considered over the course of one day of debate, with only eight witnesses, three of whom were members of Congress.[35] In short, potential beneficiaries did not much care about the program's fate in Congress, but their orientation would quickly change once they became recipients of new and generous federal funds.

The structure of the fledgling OLEA was the model for its successor, the mammoth LEAA bureaucracy. Under it, the DOJ gave each state that desired it $25,000 to develop a state planning committee. The OLEA ultimately authorized 426 grants to fund 356 projects; half of the funding went to criminal justice agencies, 29% were distributed to universities, and 21% went to associations and organizations.[36] While it had a meager budget of $7.5 million a year and was ultimately replaced by the LEAA, the OLEA grants helped whet the appetites of local agencies for outside resource contributions. In response to the newly available grants, the OLEA received $85 million in requests from 1,200 separate projects by 1968. The OLEA committed the federal government to be involved in state systems of criminal justice and gave legitimacy to, and even the expectation of, federal assistance. The grants were also essential in forming a supportive constituency, relieving the taboo of federal encroachment into a state realm. The police received two-thirds of the OLEA grants; $800,000 was channeled to the IACP, and $1.5 million went to the Washington, D.C., police.[37] The OLEA thus accomplished the initial cultivation of groups that would be pivotal beneficiaries and have a critical stake in their continuance. According to a staff attorney for the Crime Commission, "one of the most important strategy decisions made by the Office of Law Enforcement Assistance was to pump funds into the [IACP] in the hopes that it would emerge as a force for reform."[38] By the time Safe Streets was being debated in 1967, local police and police groups like the IACP and Police Foundation, once ardently opposed to or ambivalent toward federal crime control assistance, were active participants in urging the legislation's passage. In short, the police became a supportive constituency of the legislation.

Once passed, the Safe Streets Act promoted two types of group activity through the cash register of the law, the Law Enforcement Assistance Administration. The grants not only helped existing criminal justice–related groups grow more prominent and bolster organizational strength, but also helped plant the seedlings of new groups. The presence of national groups related to criminal justice grew in temporal consistency with the initial passage of the LEAA and later expansions. Based on my analysis of the Encyclopedia of Associations, group density around criminal justice increased, quadrupling from 1959 to 1979.

This crude measure captures only trends in the formation of national groups rather than state and local groups, for which we should expect the most growth based on the structure of the block grants.[39] It also likely underestimates group formation and activity because many national groups not specifically formed around crime nonetheless began crime-related projects during this period to receive LEAA money. For instance, groups like the Jaycees without an explicit criminal justice mandate were enticed by the grants and began crime programs during this time, but there is no way to account for this growth.

Safe Streets grants almost immediately stimulated an interest in maintaining and extending the policy. By providing benefits and rewards, policies (and the agencies created through their enactment) can generate the conditions for their maintenance over time. As interests and groups become aware that the receipt of funds that might be crucial to their own organization's survival are contingent on the health of the original legislation and agencies, there are great incentives to support its existence and expansions that benefit the constituency. The landscape of actors and groups involved in the creation and the maintenance stages of the legislation likely will be different and have different goals. Organizations grown by a new policy with substantial material incentives can therefore become a critical mechanism for maintaining the policy direction and expansion in benefits.

The two major crime control policies responsible for federal assistance to states activated and coalesced a set of groups whose goals were directly tied to the maintenance of the policies and their affiliated agencies. I analyzed the more than two dozen hearings that concerned the extension or amending of Safe Streets from 1970 to its dissolution in 1980, and compared the activity of groups at the hearings to the presence and interests of groups during the initial passage of Safe Streets in 1967. There were 464 witnesses who gave testimony at hearings subsequent to Safe Streets, as well as 118 witnesses at the hearings considering the original act and its predecessor, the Law Enforcement Assistance Act, in 1965. Contrasting the interest representation at both stages, we observe a significant shift in representation and the emergence of a robust constituency at hearings related to the LEAA and Safe Streets reauthorization.

Almost half of the testimony in the formulation of Safe Streets was by members of Congress and separate individuals working in criminal justice fields, with a sprinkling of other groups and experts. In contrast, groups with only a moderate presence during the 1967 deliberations dominated all subsequent discussion in the 1970s. More than half of the testimony in the hearings related to Safe Streets after LEAA grants had commenced was from groups that were beneficiaries of the program. The groups that most stood to benefit from LEAA grants, and thus, the extension of the Safe Streets legislation, became active participants in later hearings related to the LEAA. Once a prominent voice, individual criminal justice agents—a local sheriff, a court official, or a parole officer—were largely replaced with associations representing the agencies of criminal justice and governments, which were also the groups that received LEAA funds.

Qualitatively, old arguments about the dangers of a national police force that had characterized the hearings around the initial passage disappeared and were replaced with testimony urging extension. In addition, the later hearings were dominated by groups that had stated interests in the form and maintenance of LEAA. The hearings were preoccupied with attention to "how to slice the pie" rather than program components or policy directions. In each and every instance that LEAA was up for reauthorization or amendment, groups and agencies were vocal in the hearings, claiming they were not receiving a fair share of the federal aid. With few exceptions, the amendments attached to the legislation later reflected the initiative by some group or set of groups that believed it could be better served by the inclusion of special priorities. For example, the National Legal and Defender Aid Association lobbied extensively, arguing that too big a portion of the grants were allocated to police to the exclusion of the courts. An amendment for a percentage of the funds to be specifically reserved for court function followed. Groups representing city interests lobbied for the grants to be distributed directly to their city halls, while groups like the National Governors Association countered with force that the funds were having the most impact as block grants to the states. Each amendment widened participation and earmarked funds for specific purposes, and this usually followed testimony by one or more interests advocating on their behalf.

Before moving on, three things stand out in the examination of hearings. First, the groups that were represented were the beneficiaries of policies, not those citizens directly affected by the policies, including victims or those having been directly impacted by crime and criminal justice.[40] Second, the testimony at the hearings revolved around how to divide and distribute the monetary benefits and not the substance of reform of criminal justice policies or how best to reduce crime. To quote two criminal justice experts: "Participation rather than purpose, distribution rather than reform, have become the bureaucratic routines in which these new structures administer the provisions of the Safe Streets Act."[41] Third, because the grants were targeted toward agencies of criminal justice (as opposed to early crime prevention legislation being directed by the Department of Housing, Education, and Welfare), agencies and groups with clear vested interests in maintaining their own operations (from SPAs to police departments) became the sole voice in discussions of crime policy. As the *Nation* observed in 1970, "The result is that reform of the criminal justice system has become the responsibility of persons with institutional loyalties to the existing system."[42] These tendencies would have implications for the path of criminal justice at the state level, to which I turn now.

State Changes in Sentencing Policy

So far this chapter has documented how federal policies triggered the growth of a criminal justice bureaucracy surrounded by a network of professional associations that became a supportive constituency, which led to the articulation of interests at key points when the continuance of LEAA was up for debate. But this is not only a national-level story. LEAA grants were an engine of change for state sentencing policy and practice.

Prior to enactment of Safe Streets, states had rarely engaged in criminal justice reform, and criminal codes were archaic; penalties often stood unamended for decades. Indeterminate sentencing, where judges have ultimate discretion in the punishment to assign for an offense, had been the leading practice since the early 1900s, and sentencing reforms had generally not been considered. However, newfound wealth from

Safe Streets (carefully attached to federal categorical requirements) promoted waves of change in state criminal codes and increased the importance of criminal justice on state agendas. With the expectation of future
funds, states made critical and long-standing investments to criminal justice. The widespread reform that resulted utterly transformed the criminal justice landscape.

The Safe Streets legislation superimposed on the states a massive federal allotment, extending the incentives for states to marshal resources
toward criminal justice. Grants disbursed from LEAA to the states
ranged from $1 million in Vermont to over $40 million in California in
1972. In many states, revenue from the federal government represented
over 15% of state and local spending on criminal justice.[43] While states
were not totally dependent on federal aid and these grants represented
only 5% of what was spent on criminal justice by state governments,
prior to the LEAA, states could expect very little outside assistance.
Rather than being the primary source of state spending on criminal justice, then, the federal grants were a special coupon, discounting the cost
of additional outlays and subsidizing and underwriting state efforts. It is
very unlikely that states could have made a major investment in criminal
justice around the time they did without the veritable boost of federal assistance. This was captured by a report by the state governments:

> Safe Streets monies represent almost the only funds available to criminal jus-
> tice for experimentation. These resources have permitted system-wide crimi-
> nal justice planning, directing responses to crime in urban areas, establishing
> standards for criminal justice personnel and operations, drafting major legis-
> lative changes including criminal code revisions, and introducing innovative
> programming. Without the infusion of federal funds under the Safe Streets
> Act, States and localities would be able to do little more than maintain their
> existing operations.[44]

At the same time as states could take advantage of this carrot, however, many features of the legislation ensured that states would independently increase their financial commitment to criminal justice through
the stipulations attached to the grants. Specifically, states were required
to (1) contribute one-fourth of their own money for projects supported
by LEAA grants; (2) expand their criminal justice budget by 5% a year
to receive LEAA funds; (3) demonstrate a "willingness" to assume the
costs of projects after federal assistance ended; (4) agree that no grant

money would be spent on functions that the state would have spent on anyway; and (5) allocate funds to localities according to "level of effort" (the proportion of criminal justice spending by local governments), unleashing a strong incentive for local governments to increase their own criminal justice spending. These requirements guaranteed expansion and innovation, and ultimately that states would commit more of their own resources to the cause of reforming criminal justice. And that is indeed what happened almost as soon as the first grants were issued; state and local spending on criminal justice increased from $9.5 billion to over $16 billion from 1971 to 1976, and the portion of state expenditures from the LEAA swelled from 4% to 12%.

Programmatic expansion was not short lived. Many states assumed responsibility for continuing the projects and reforms initiated by the grants, which were kept alive even after their grant expired, indeed after the dissolution of the LEAA itself. A report by the National Conference of State Criminal Justice Planning Administrators (NCSCJPA) estimated that an average of "64 percent of the projects initiated with Safe Streets monies have been assumed by State and local governments."[45] A Congressional Budget Office report found that 84% of the over three thousand projects that concluded in 1978 were continued by state and local government.[46]

In the lead-up to the passage of Safe Streets, the Senate Judiciary Committee report stated, "We don't want this bill to become the vehicle for the imposition of Federal guidelines, controls, and domination."[47] While in theory the LEAA gave states wide latitude for criminal justice programming in their borders, the grants were soon tethered to federal policy priorities through several subsequent amendments to the legislation (or "creeping categorization" in the words of critics).[48]

Perhaps the most heavy-handed of these was in the area of corrections. As part of its move to aggressively support the construction of more prisons, the Omnibus Crime Control Act of 1970 created Part E funds specifically designated for prison construction and renovation, and offered to pay for 75% of the cost of prison projects with federal dollars and obligated states to give at least 20% of all block and discretionary funds to the area of corrections. Because the amendment included a restriction against using funds to replace existing corrections funding, states were implicitly forced to enlarge their spending on prisons. Immediately after this directive, corrections spending increased and plans for new prisons were designed. State LEAA spending on corrections increased from \$2 million to \$134 million in just two years from 1969 to 1971.[49] A larger proportion of funding for corrections—traditionally a state domain—came from the federal government as a result of Safe Streets grants; the proportion of funding for corrections contributed at the state level decreased from 67% to 57% from 1967 to 1977.[50] As is discussed later in this chapter, the 75% contribution for prison construction by the federal government helped states build hundreds of new facilities in the next decade.

In addition to the amendments and guidelines, another way the grants influenced state criminal justice was through the creation of a SPA that would submit a comprehensive plan for improving law enforcement, corrections, courts, and all aspects of the criminal justice system in that state, which meant that the LEAA grants could potentially affect more than programs initiated by grant money. As one expert noted, "By the late 1970s planning offices were not just influencing the five percent of the local justice budget that was federal in origin, they were providing information, research, coordination activities, technical assistance, and analysis" for the "other 95 percent."[51]

The grants enabled states to take greater interest in comprehensive planning of criminal justice in their borders, which can be traced to a series of long-lived changes in sentencing policy. The NCSCJPA had a legislation committee that would develop recommendations for state legislation and promote specific reforms. Part of the explicit function of the SPAs was to participate in legislative reform, and the majority of SPAs had legislative study commissions. A report concerned with how the grants were affecting state systems of criminal justice reported that more than 80% of the SPAs had designed legislative proposals on criminal justice, and 60% were actually given responsibility for drafting bills.[52] Almost half of the proposals designed by SPAs were ultimately enacted. With few exceptions, SPAs "identify and track legislation" and "advise the legislature on pending proposals."[53] The report further found that the SPAs had materially and substantively contributed to criminal code revision in forty-nine states.[54] Thus, the newly created state bureaucracies became political actors in the formulation of crime policy in their own right. While data that would indicate what proportion of the grants were used for criminal code revision and policy changes are not available, there are numerous examples of states using LEAA money to overhaul their criminal justice systems, drafting legislative proposals, and reviewing pending legislation. For example, Missouri developed a state parole and probation system from a block grant.[55] Cases where the grants were used to change criminal laws are also prevalent. For example, the SPA in Wyoming was the sponsor of eighteen bills that passed in 1973,[56] while in Kentucky the SPA proposed a twelve-point package of legislation to the General Assembly in 1972, most of which was passed.[57] Colorado used an LEAA grant to hold a Conference on Sentencing and Corrections; based on the conference, the governor passed on recommendations to the legislature, which passed three bills for community corrections, habitual offender legislation and mandatory minimum sentences, and victim restitution.[58] The Florida SPA participated in that state's major judicial reform package, which included a mandatory sentence enhancement for crimes involving guns.[59]

More than acting as a conduit for funds to states, then, the federal government shaped state priorities related to criminal justice, and while not directly controlling the local operations, it came as close to setting crime policy as it could without actually changing state criminal law.

The LEAA appointed a commission to recommend that states commit to uniform criminal justice standards. It issued an unflinching directive to states in 1971: "States whose criminal codes have not been revised in the last decade should initiate revisions; these revisions should be complete and thorough, not partial, and the revision should include where necessary a revamped penalty structure."[60] While it acknowledged that the federal government could not force sentencing policy on the states, in a section labeled "Federal Encouragement" it also gently threatened states, saying that if in reviewing their annual comprehensive plans they did not address the standards of the Commission, the LEAA could withhold funds.[61] By promising to slow the receipt of funds to states or require them to amend their annual plans to receive action and discretionary grants, the LEAA pushed states to act on sentencing policy.

It appears that states heeded this threat. Criminal code revision was uncommon prior to the federal intervention in the mid-1960s. In the three decades prior to the Safe Streets grants, only sixteen states had revised their criminal codes. In the five years immediately following Safe Streets, eleven SPAs sponsored revisions of their criminal codes.[62] In one of the states, Maine, it was the first time the criminal code had ever been rewritten. One report documented that SPAs had "provided staff and financial support to legislative study commissions which have contributed to modifications in the criminal codes of no less than 49" states, including a total overhaul in Arkansas and North Carolina.[63]

While a lack of adequate time-series data prevents a systematic overtime examination of how Safe Streets grants influenced state reforms, the data that do exist reveal a pattern not seen before 1968. In 1985, the National Institute of Justice (NIJ) published a detailed report documenting sentencing reform in the fifty states from 1971–81, a period in which the LEAA actively disbursed hundreds of thousands of grants to hundreds of agencies and groups charged with updating criminal justice system in the states. In those ten years, every single state altered its sentencing policy in some fashion. Half of the states preformed a major revision of their criminal codes (fifteen of these were characterized as "sweeping"), while fifteen others had piecemeal revisions; in only eleven states was there no revision.[64]

Given the absence of more detailed time-series data on state changes in crime and sentencing policy, I turn to a source long forgotten and rarely used, the *Governmental Responses to Crime Project*,[65] which tracked changes in sentencing policy in a sample of nine states from 1948–78.[66] While it covers only nine states, it is the only study to date that examines year-by-year change in criminal sanctions and policy, allowing comparisons of state changes to sentencing before and after the omnibus legislation.[67] Based on my analysis of the original data, there were 425 changes across the nine states over the three-decade period. An examination of the timing of the reforms reveals a noticeable increase in the volume of enactments over time. Figure 11.2 plots the number of enactments in the states over time, separating out the changes by whether the law involved a change in the substance of the law or penalty assigned or both of these.[68] With the exception of the 1952 session, there is a clear upward trend in activity on sentencing policy by the states over time. The timing and volume of enactments is consistent with the enactment of the federal Safe Streets legislation in 1968. Until 1966, the number of enactments across the nine states hovered around twenty per year. By 1968 and in every year thereafter, states made at least thirty changes, and the number of enactments reached its zenith in the last year of the data collection when over fifty changes were enacted.

The federal commission that urged states to overhaul their criminal codes did not promote a "get tough" orientation to these changes. In practice, however, the clear direction of change in the states was to in-

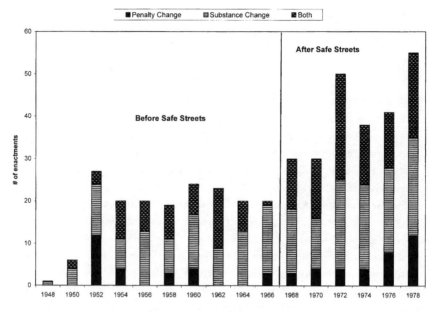

FIGURE 11.2. STATE CRIMINAL LAW ENACTMENTS BY TYPE, 1948–78
Source: Calculated by author from the *Governmental Responses to Crime Project, 1948–1978.*

crease penalties, define more acts as criminal, reduce parole, and pass special sentence enhancements for crimes involving drugs or guns. Of the penalty changes made by states, just under three-quarters were changes that increased penalties compared to only 28% where the penalty was decreased or there was no net change. Along with the expanded penalties, criminalization—the addition of new behaviors as offenses—also increased. Of the changes that altered the number of acts considered offenses, 63% increased the scope of the law, 31% decreased the scope, and the remaining 5% saw no change. In short, the frequency of sentencing laws increased, its content became more punitive, and its reach more extensive.

The data from the NIJ report echoes this pattern. A summary of the state changes from 1971 to 1981 (shown in figure 11.3) shows that penalties were increased in a majority of states and decreased in none; the majority of states passed habitual offender laws or increased their severity; every state except two enacted mandatory minimum sentences; half of the states restricted parole eligibility, and parole was completely eliminated in eight states[69]; and "good-time" provisions for early release were decreased in twelve states. By 1981, fifteen states had abandoned indeterminate sentencing for determinate, fixed sentences, and seven had initiated sentencing guidelines. Another study found that by 1976, thirty-five states had passed capital punishment laws, and fourteen had passed legislation for victim restitution.[70]

While there is variation across the states (and not all states adopted harsh reforms), which I do not deal with here, the major thrust was toward a pronounced increase in punitiveness. For example, California enacted a major criminal code revision, increased the severity of its habitual offender laws, altered provisions for offenders' appeal of sentences, eliminated parole boards, increased penalties, and was one of the first states to adopt a major determinate sentencing law that cut judicial discretion and included harsh sentence enhancements. The California sentencing law was made retroactive, affecting all prisoners, which meant that the number of incarcerated felons rose by 12% within the first year of its implementation. The NIJ report concluded: "Our analysis of the commonality of the reforms indicates that when sentencing laws were

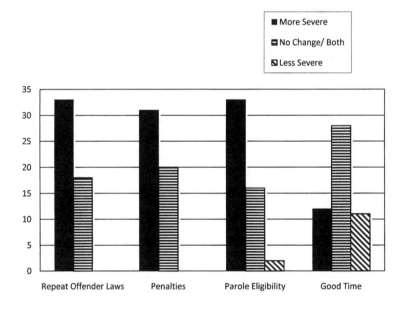

FIGURE 11.3. Sentencing reforms in the fifty states, 1971–81
Source: Sandra Shane-DuBow, Alice P. Brown, and Erik Olsen, *Sentencing Reform in the United States: History, Content, and Effect*. US Department of Justice, National Institute of Justice, Office of Development, Testing, and Dissemination. August 1985.

changed, penalties, almost entirely, were increased, mandatory minimum terms enacted, repeater or habitual criminal laws enacted or tightened or eliminated altogether."[71] The LEAA era witnessed tremendous
reform by states, and the content of those reforms bent in a more punitive direction.

Safe Streets did not directly make penalties more severe. Its significance lies in enabling states to undertake significant reform through
a consistent and plentiful flow of federal resources, in sending important signals to states about desired reforms (through categorical requirements), and in renewing state initiative in sentencing policies through
the help of a parent bureaucracy and federally funded SPAs, which
were given the staff and resources to overhaul their criminal codes. In
the years immediately after Safe Streets passage when states were receiving thousands of grants to update and improve their criminal justice systems, there was an unprecedented level of punitive reform. States
experimented with sentencing guidelines, increased the scope of their
habitual offender laws, and enacted time-served requirements and sentence enhancements for crimes involving drugs and weapons. Although
one must be cautious in drawing causal attributions between Safe Streets
and the numerous changes taking place—there were many other factors
at work—the major thrust of policy change in the crime arena was at the
very least consistent with the increasing capacity bestowed on it by a major federal block grant program initiated by the Safe Streets and Crime
Control Act of 1968.

Rapid state sentencing changes were not inevitable. To the contrary,
they were highly improbable given that few states had bothered themselves with the criminal code in the recent past. Moreover, many of
these reforms were enacted despite falling crime rates. While concur-
rent changes in sentencing ideology from indeterminacy to determinacy
are also important, it is difficult to imagine that state legislatures would
impose a much harsher sentencing structure and reforms intended to
strain current capacity on strapped, unprofessionalized state and local
agencies without a guarantee of generous and plentiful federal funds.
It is unlikely, therefore, that without Safe Streets, states would have independently pursued this widespread change and taken the initiative to
overhaul their criminal justice systems simultaneously. Instead, these innovations in state operations must be viewed alongside the timing and
structure of incentives from federal legislation, which had direct par-

allels with the acceleration and content of reforms being passed in the states.

While states were increasing penalties across the board, reducing parole, limiting good time and enhancing sentences distributed for crimes involving certain characteristics, no single state performed an evaluation of the potential impact of these reforms for prison capacity.[72] The need for more prisons was not mentioned in the 1967 Crime Commission report, and the National Advisory Commission noted that "there are more than enough [correctional] facilities at hand" and urged states to "refrain from building more State institutions for adults for the next 10 years except when total system planning shows that the need for them is imperative." The Commission instead promoted community-based supervision and alternatives to incarceration.[73] However, the effects of state reforms began to be seen in increasing correctional populations. After declining for eight years during the 1960s, the prison population began its monumental increase. By the mid-1970s, virtually every state was facing overcrowding, and the LEAA grants offered to pay for 75% of the cost of prison construction through its 1973 amendment. The LEAA gave $170 million in grants specifically for corrections from 1969 to 1977, $75 million of which was solely for construction of correctional institutions.[74]

The Task Force on Corrections, part of the President's Commission on Law Enforcement and Criminal Justice, authored a report in 1967 in the run-up to the 1968 legislation. Based on this report, in 1965, there were 358 state adult correctional institutions in operation.[75] By 1970, the number of state prisons counted by the Census Bureau was 578.[76] The first official Census of State Adult Correctional Facilities was initiated in 1974 and was performed again five years later. From 1974 to 1979, about 200 new prisons were built, bringing the number of state adult correctional facilities from 592 to 791.[77]

The LEAA was effectively dismantled in 1980 after twelve years of existence, but not before it had expanded police departments, spent billions on helping states construct new prisons, created huge bureaucracies, stimulated state-level policy change, and expanded the universe of criminal justice–related interest groups. Rather than simply providing money for crime control, this act established a large crime control bureaucracy; led to unparalleled growth in police and correctional financing and manpower; unified criminal justice agencies and local operations under SPAs; coalesced interests; and prompted state policy changes, innovation, and reform in the local operations of criminal justice. In short, the institutional context it left behind after its demise was a completely different criminal justice system than in the 1960s when Safe Streets was passed. This discussion ends with a consideration of the effects of the massive crime entitlement program. My purpose here is not to give a detailed account of the policies in the 1980s and 1990s; that is done better elsewhere. It is to speculate on how the way crime was addressed and how the criminal justice system was established and fortified during this time mattered not just then, but now.

"Pulling the Plug Did Not Kill the Patient": Enduring Effects of the LEA

Its designers and administrators insisted that LEAA was a neutral participant, providing resources only to those who needed them: "LEAA is not an enforcement agency. It makes no arrests, conducts no investigations, prosecutes no cases."[78] But in pumping federal money into the states and providing "leadership"—making the grants conditional on stringent requirements that reflected federal policy priorities—it effected widespread change throughout criminal justice. The LEAA created a network of practitioners, planners, universities, and associations; it inspired technological change through all levels of criminal justice; it cultivated greater interest in criminal justice policy making at the state level and enhanced the infrastructure to carry the policy changes through; it institutionalized system-wide criminal justice planning. After more than a decade of sustained infusion of federal dollars into underfunded law enforcement agencies, a criminal justice system emerged and the parochial system that existed prior to 1968 became extinct. In a retrospective on Safe Streets, one expert summarized the fourteen-year experiment this way: "LEAA shook the system up."[79]

Safe Streets and other policy changes produced initial shifts that were ultimately institutionalized and transformed the criminal justice system. Initially what was a small change (by today's standards) led to strong feedbacks that grew the initial investment and changed the institutional map for later actors.

While the implications of Safe Streets and the LEAA are many, three were important for embedding the path of criminal justice: shifting state capacity, initiating policy learning, and mobilizing organized interests.

These policy consequences together made it unlikely that the path of criminal justice would reverse course, returning to its pre-LEAA situation. Instead, the policy direction and criminal justice expansion persisted, enabled by vast state capacity and powerful interests.

First, as is now clear, one of the biggest effects of the policy was to immediately grow the agencies and capacity of the criminal justice system. By funneling billions of dollars into underfunded agencies, state and local criminal justice went from primitive to professionalized within a decade, advances that altered the institutional supports for the later path of criminal justice: Police had more education and training, and more hardware and better technology; courts were unified; criminal justice planning was regularized; and prisons were constructed. Through aid to police, courts, and corrections, LEAA created the capacity to arrest more, convict more, and imprison more. Later state and federal initiatives would not have to build criminal justice capacity and infrastructure—it was already in place. These critical investments expanded criminal justice infrastructure in ways that would encourage later initiatives.

Second, Safe Streets changed the organizational landscape, goals, and capacities of groups related to criminal justice. Later crime proposals would have to negotiate with powerful coalitions of organized interests, which had a very clear incentive to maintain their financial resources and prospects for further expansion. While Safe Streets did not change penalties directly, it "ensured that a constituency of grant-getting entrepreneurs for a newly nationalized policy concern would be immediately developed."[80] Adapted to new realities of federal funding, LEAA helped convert a vast number of local groups and agencies into interest groups, cultivated their influence in Congress, and regularized channels between local groups and national policy. This newly mobilized coalition of criminal justice agencies, state and local government officials, and professional associations that had come to rely on federal assistance remained after the LEAA. Groups like the International Association of Chiefs of Police and the Police Foundation and the American Correctional Association—groups that grew in size and influence with grant money—now regularly lobby Congress. The policy networks between agencies and associations survived the demise of LEAA. While it bolstered a new political constituency, LEAA marginalized some once important voices in criminal justice. Because the LEAA and SPAs had little representation from social service agencies and other agencies that might have offered proposals that did not center around further criminal justice expansion, potential opponents were cut out of key channels of influence. For instance, the California Council on Criminal Justice Los Angeles Board had no minority members and no members from the community. Opposing voices that may have emerged did not have a chance to develop and did not have access to key positions of influence. Before Safe Streets, the small, unconnected criminal justice agencies and few criminal justice related associations rarely lobbied Congress because there were no incentives. Feedback increased the asymmetry between the social handling of crime and the dominance of criminal justice agencies, leading to a lasting advantage of criminal justice agencies and interests in affecting crime policy.[81]

Third, Safe Streets and the large bureaucracy it began in the LEAA changed expectations of criminal justice actors, setting a firm precedent for federal assistance, priming the pump for later federal initiatives, and legitimating its role as the parent figure to states, providing guidance and direction in crime control. The aftermath of the dissolution of the LEAA saw a resurgent commitment to the path Safe Streets had begun. Past experience with over a decade of LEAA grants shaped the federal role going forward, even after the agency became a memory. Prior to Safe Streets, federal financial assistance for state and local criminal justice did not exist; spending for this function was zero in 1962.[82] States and localities had to rely on their own sources of revenue to maintain crime control in their borders. By initiating the concept of federal assistance to state and local criminal justice, Safe Streets began a new era of federal financial commitment, widely accepted and even expected by lower levels of government, which "had come to view these LEAA funds as a right."[83]

Through these investments and new arrangements, the menu of options in later policymaking changed, increasing the likelihood of certain outcomes and diminishing the probability of others. The key changes established at this moment would alter the path of criminal justice policy and practice. Later decisions were in the framework, organizational field, and structural constraints imposed by LEAA. While crime faded from the political agenda and become less salient as a political issue, a massive criminal justice system had been put in place that would alter the possibility and success of later crime initiatives. So when Reagan announced a war on drugs in spite of declining drug abuse, not only was there established precedent for federal intervention in crime and criminal justice but also the institutional capacity at lower levels of government to carry it out. Later crime campaigns were not predicated on crime but depended on institutional frameworks set by the LEAA.

Later crime policy debates effectively built on the well-tread terrain set in the 1970s LEAA experiment. Crime policies and criminal justice initiatives during the 1980s and 1990s were patterned after Safe Streets and continued the policy direction it began. Not only did federal crime legislation during the later decades grow out of the earlier Safe Streets episode and depend on the institutions left behind from LEAA grants, but it expanded the federal role even further, building on important precedents set by LEAA.

The LEAA grant system of federal aid to state crime control soon resurfaced in later crime legislation. The 1984 Crime Control Act began a new grant program, this time not out of the LEAA, but administered by its replacement, the Office of Justice Programs. The four omnibus crime bills that followed Safe Streets continued the trend of greater federal involvement and aid and rested largely on the LEAA model. The Anti-Drug Abuse Act of 1986 included matching grants for state and local law enforcement, which were further expanded in the Anti-Drug Abuse Act of 1988. Continuing the trend of its predecessors, the Crime Control Act of 1990 included $220 million in matching grants for state prisons and the $900 million Edward Byrne Memorial State and Local Law Enforcement Assistance block grants; the omnibus crime bill in 1994, the Violent Crime Control and Law Enforcement Act, extended the reach of federal grants still further, incorporating a block grant program of *$10 billion* and establishing a Violent Crime Reduction Trust Fund to set aside money for grant programs; part of the new trust fund would go to funding state grants for prison construction financed through saving money from reductions in over 250,000 federal jobs. Federal assistance aided in the building of over two hundred prisons during this decade.

So although the LEAA was not extended, federal assistance was far from over. Federal expenditures for the justice system multiplied twelve-fold in the two decades after Safe Streets.[84] As federal discretionary spending in general was declining, criminal justice was one of the only areas spared from cuts, and actually increased. While federal assistance to state and local government or crime control dropped immediately after LEAA failed to be reauthorized, by 1987 federal assistance had returned and would soon exceed LEAA levels, doubling from 1986 to 1995 and quintupling from 1994 to 1996 (as a result of the 1994 bill). As one scholar observes, "By 1997, local crime prevention took a bigger slice of the Justice Department's budget than the FBI, DEA, or Immigration and Naturalization Service."[85] The experiment that intended only to provide seed money to help jump-start sluggish states in improving crime control became an expected and normal part of government's crime control efforts. According to the Congressional Budget Office, "the 1994 Violent Crime Control and Law Enforcement Act represents not a major change from recent trends, but a continuation of a pattern that has seen federal justice spending more than sixfold in real terms since 1962 and almost double since 1986."[86]

The expansion of federal involvement established by Safe Streets was not limited to financial assistance. Federal influence had become so commonplace and accepted that when in the early 1980s the federal government passed sentencing guidelines, states largely adopted the approach. Relying on important precedents set in the LEAA era, the federal government more aggressively legislated criminal law at lower levels of government by tying the receipt of federal cash to major policy priorities. While remaining the junior partner in sheer spending, the national government wielded monetary carrots if states complied with policy mandates. For example, the 1994 law gave states grants for building more prisons if the states changed their sentencing policies to ensure that violent criminals served at least 85% of their sentences behind bars or if the state increased the sentence length and incarceration rate for violent felons and decreased early release and good-time provisions. These supports tied to guidelines not only expanded federal power over state and local sentencing policy but also reduced the incentive for states to experiment with other policy options and reforms.

In addition to making some outcomes more likely, the innovations, capacity, and group incentives inspired by the behemoth LEAA constrained the range of policy options. Early decisions changed the circumstances that later policymakers faced. Because we had built up criminal justice agencies, constructed new prisons, centralized the role of actors related to criminal justice in the policy process, and underwrote state reform that increased penalties, the once reasonable and popular "root causes" approach to crime was increasingly remote as time passed, and it ultimately dropped from the discussion altogether. Reformers were forced to seek changes at the margins of the already well-established criminal justice system. Instead of arguing for scaling back, they focused their efforts on much narrower disputes over the death penalty and gun control and sought changes at the margins of policy and practice. Common observers and scholars have attributed the expansions brought by the drug initiatives of the 1980s as the catalyst for expansion. The truth is that by the time of Reagan, abandoning these institutions or radically changing course would have been quite difficult. The Department of Housing, Education, and Welfare was defunct, the federal government had established its role as financier of criminal justice at lower levels of government, and police and corrections had a decade of sustained investment in their professional and institutional capacities. Once hotly debated, federal financing of state and local criminal justice, electronic surveillance, and mandatory minimums, to name just a few, had a taken-for-granted quality. Later criminal justice initiatives, including the policies forming the war on drugs, operated within a framework established by Safe Streets.

I am not arguing that Safe Streets alone accomplished all this, nor that LEAA single-handedly transformed the carceral state, but that this development gave criminal justice a major push in the long shadow of complacency about crime policy. Instead, this account suggests that these changes would not have occurred when they did and with the same intensity without the massive infusion of federal dollars and priorities. Safe Streets made a deep imprint on the later functioning, limits, and possibilities of the carceral state. Appreciating what LEAA and Safe Streets did to the criminal justice landscape helps us understand the massive effort in the later crime wars. Initiatives in the 1980s, so often the focus of reflections on criminal justice growth, did not begin the trend of federal involvement and sentencing changes but extended a path begun earlier, one that has been largely forgotten but without out which we would not have had the changes we did. In the absence of LEAA, progress would have been slower, criminal justice would still be in its infancy, cooperation would have been a novelty, and the legislation in the 1980s would be difficult to conceive and push onto state and local agencies used to non-interference. Had Safe Streets not been enacted, we might still have seen some development, but it would not have been as quick or urgent or uniform. This policy failure was hugely consequential for building and fortifying the modern criminal justice system.

PART III
Reflections

CHAPTER TWELVE

Lawmaking as a Cognitive Enterprise

David R. Mayhew

Inspired is the volume that can combine, as this one does, so many illuminating takes on an important subject. They are a pleasure to read and ruminate about. I would like to add an additional view that builds on and reacts to these presentations.

It is that lawmaking, whatever else it may be, is a cognitive enterprise. At least it is that very often. It was wise to position William Novak's chapter on the crafting of the legislative state a century ago as the keynote to this volume. Note Novak's language: Law in modern times would be "a product of conscious and increasingly determinate human will." There would be "policymaking efficacy." We would see "instrumental aims . . . achieved by a modern sovereign state passing positive laws." We would see "active, instrumental, and inventive statecraft."[1] Key to these ends would be an embedding of instrumental rationality in government. In the right kind of legislative processes, problems would be identified, causal connections would be examined, solutions would be devised. Lawmaking would not consist of just updating the common law, enacting feel-good rhetoric, or adding wish lists to the statute books.

That was heady exhortation. Yet to switch to a positive (that is, explanatory) mode, the idea of lawmaking as a reach for instrumental rationality, in the minds of the Progressive reformers—or, for that matter, the Romans or Alexander Hamilton before them—has an obvious component of good sense. An X is put on the books to achieve a Y. This idea has such obvious good sense that as analysts we tend to assume it and overlook it. Not that it lacks appreciation entirely. Eric Patashnik is this volume writes of "nonincremental, efficiency-oriented legislation"—an especially ambitious exercise of instrumental rationality, or, to use another term, design.[2] At a workaday level of lawmaking, Keith Krehbiel has theorized legislative activity in general to be a quest for the right information needed to achieve with maximum effectiveness the policy aims of the median legislator.[3]

It is a matter of emphasis. Other size-ups can be given to legislative processes. They can be seen, for example, as venues where values are expressed, constitutionality is interrogated, or tastes or interests are registered in more or less brute fashion. Here I emphasize a cognitive size-up. In theory and empirics, that means an alertness to perceptions of problems and searches for solutions. Not necessarily implied is a pattern of smoothly greased paths to consensual decisions. As an empirical matter, lawmaking often amounts to vigorous combat between advancers of perceptions and causal stories that clash. Yes, a problem exists. No, a problem doesn't exist. This bill in front of us, once enacted, will cause gratifications A, B, and C. Not so fast! It won't do that, and instead it will cause disasters D, E, and F. This kind of disputation is intrinsic to legislative activity as we, the society, see it. It accommodates an embracing of the society at large, not just the members of a legislature, into ongoing, interactive considerations of what the social realities are out there and what they might be made to be. There is a touch of John Dewey.

Again, it is a matter of emphasis. In congressional studies today, a particular alternative exists to the thrust I am arguing for here. I have employed it elsewhere myself. It is represented in this volume in the skilled analyses by Christopher Berry, Barry Burden, and William Howell, and Forrest Maltzman and Charles Shipan.[4] It is an analytic frame with three parts. First, lawmaking is a contestation between ideological or partisan tastes of, for analytic purposes anyway, a timeless quality. Second, policy outcomes vary with the arithmetic shares of elective politicians (including presidents) bearing those tastes. Third, the society sends its policy signals to Washington, D.C., only through biennial elections, thus structuring for a while those taste-bearing shares. This kind of frame can bring a large sweep of convincing illumination. The point is not at issue. Yet a good deal of dark territory remains. Here, I would like to complement, not contradict, this frame of taste-bearing shares in taking up a frame of cognition.

In a developmental treatment of lawmaking, two distinct questions arise: How and why do laws get enacted in the first place? What happens to them after that? On the first question, I see three good reasons for paying attention to the cognitive side.

First, a campaign to pass a law, which might end in the passage of one, very likely owes to somebody's perception that a problem exists. Note that very little insight into the existence, perception, or solution of problems is available in the arithmetic of partisan or ideological shares. Problems, once they surface, may *map onto* these never-ending cleavages or dimensions (although not always; voting rights for African Americans in the 1940s through the 1960s did not), but that is all. To get a good view of the political life of the society, a more sensitive empiricism is needed. Hence, for example, the value of Jeffrey Cohen and Matthew Eshbaugh-Soha's chapter, which looks into White House legislative agendas since 1799.[5] Presidents are major perceivers, or at least proclaimers, of problems. I recommend a close inspection of their figure 3.1, which shows an enormous expansion of White House legislative requests starting in the mid-1940s. In all of U.S. history, nothing matches that surge, which seems to have had little to do with the preceding New Deal. This pattern jibes with other contemporary scholarship pointing to those war-ending years as a hinge-point in many respects, no doubt at least because they were seen to be saturated with problems. Policy historians would do well to expand their focus from the 1930s to the 1940s.

A surge in the perception of a problem can raise a legislative issue from nowhere, or least from the back pages, into a prominent long-running sequence of attempted or successful lawmaking. Much of U.S. legislative history in recent decades has followed this pattern. The lessons of World War II, registering in sync with Cohen and Eshbaugh-Soha's figure 3.1, seem to have had this effect for civil rights, public housing, national health insurance, and federal aid to education.[6] A surge in crimes worries, as discussed by Vesla Weaver in her chapter, triggered the Safe Streets and Crime Control Act of 1968 and a line of follow-up measures.[7] Activists or intellectuals can generate a sense of problem. Note thus the consumer, feminist, and environmentalist critiques that sparked a burst of regulatory legislation in the late 1960s and 1970s, and the efficiency arguments voiced by economists that levered a quarter-century-long series of industry-specific deregulatory laws beginning in the mid-1970s— including airline deregulation, as discussed by Patashnik in chapter 8. An energy crisis brought responsive legislation under Nixon and Carter. Deficit reduction owing to seemingly out-of-control budgets was a chronic mission from 1981 through 1997. Concern over rising illegal immigration brought a quarter century of legislative drives, and some laws, starting in 1986. For U.S. officialdom, the Middle East erupted into a new kind of problem area around 1990, yielding such measures as—these were legislative instruments, too—the Persian Gulf Resolution of 1991 and the Iraq Resolution of 2002. Even taxation is not just a constant concern: The tax cuts of both Reagan in 1981 and Bush in 2001 followed on postwar peaks, which were no doubt experienced by taxpayers, in total federal revenue take.

In the instances cited here, note that any voter signals sent in elections were at best a contributing cause, and sometimes a vanishingly recessive one, of legislative activity. Signals that politicians may anticipate in future elections are another matter, but that case can be tenuous. The proximate spurs, at least, to legislative action have often come between or independent of elections.

Second, approached from a cognitive standpoint, a new law is often an experiment or a gamble. Who can guarantee the effects of adding words to parchment? For one thing, the causal stories that animate a measure may grip into reality, or they may not. A promising new law is not all that different from a promising new commercial product (although it is easier to get rid of products). Going back in U.S. history, Reconstruction of the South, discussed in this volume by Stuart Chinn, was a gamble.[8] As of 1867, given the uncertain horizons of opinion, costs, and resistance, who could know whether military occupation of that region could achieve its aims? The Eighteenth Amendment authorizing the prohibition of liquor comes down to us as a "noble experiment." In the Depression crisis of 1933, Franklin D. Roosevelt called exactly for experimentation. During recent decades, a list of enactments of an experimental cast might include the National Security Act of 1947 (was that an apt way to reconfigure the high military?), the Atomic Energy Act of 1954 (could a viable private industry be coaxed into existence by law?), the Civil Rights Act of 1957 (would it really help to ensure the vote?), the antipoverty act of 1964 (would its effects bear out its label?), the Kennedy tax cut of 1964 (would it really spur the economy?), model cities in 1966 (could some cities serve as showcases for the rest?),[9] the Emergency Petroleum Allocation Act of 1973 (how would that plan play out?), the Earned Income Tax Credit of 1975 (would that kind of idea "take" as a welfare-state device?), airline deregulation in 1978 (an invitation to disorder, as described by Patashnik), the synfuels program of 1980 (could coal liquefaction be an energy winner?), and banking deregulation in 1999 (we are still arguing about its effects). At their own lofty level of gamble are the war resolutions: Tonkin Gulf in 1964, Persian Gulf in 1991, Iraq in 2002.

Third, to press an earlier point, struggles over causal stories are often at the center of drives to enact legislation. The stories need to be merchandised—not only on Capitol Hill but before the general public. Congress may be stumbling block enough: Nixon's Family Assistance Plan, for example, was judged not to compute once its likely incentive effects were examined in Senate hearings. But the public is there, too. When a proposal reaches a question-mark point in public opinion—when its stories about felicitous effects are not selling—it risks serious trouble on Capitol Hill. Clinton's plan for health-care reform ran into that barrier in 1994, as did George W. Bush's plan to partly privatize Social Security in 2005. Sour public opinion of this sort may not be fatal for a bill, but it is not helpful. For political scientists, although not journalists, this is an underinvestigated topic of legislative studies.

So much for the process of initial enactment. Once measures are on the books, how can a cognitive frame illuminate their subsequent history? I find it hard to get around the idea that at least some laws are judged to be successes or failures. As Patashnik writes, "It matters whether policies work when set on the ground." Laws can work or not work. An X is causing or not causing agreeable Ys. This is an imprecise assertion. It is not clear who might be doing the judging. It is not clear what the criteria might be. The aims and causal stories associated with a measure at birth might supply the yardstick, yet experience afterward might bring additional or replacement yardsticks. Still, little is more central to the proceedings of a democratic society than an evolving sense that its laws are working or not working.

Let me start with a broad brush and some contrasting examples and then proceed to some particular arguments.

Since World War II, setting aside the exact meaning of the question, although the view of the median voter is one aspect, what are some especially plausible instances of successful legislative measures? Here are some candidates: the Taft-Hartley Act of 1947 (as a remedy for the incessant strikes of that decade),[10] the Marshall Plan in 1948, the creation of the National Science Foundation in 1950, the Federal Highway Act of 1956, food stamps in 1964, Medicare in 1965, the Voting Rights Act of 1965, the Clean Air Act of 1970, Pell grants in 1972, airline deregulation in 1978 (all else aside, consumer benefits did ensue), 14k pensions in 1978, the Persian Gulf Resolution of 1991, welfare reform in 1996, the Children's Health Insurance Program (CHIP) of 1997, possibly the omnibus deficit-reduction measures of 1990, 1993, and 1997.

At the other extreme, certain statutes have been iconic failures. Cases in earlier history would include the Kansas-Nebraska Act of 1854 (it aided slavery, alienated the North, and helped trigger the Civil War) and the Smoot-Hawley Tariff of 1930 (it helped ruin the world economy), not to mention the Eighteenth Amendment. In recent times, Three Mile Island ended the ambitions of the Atomic Energy Act of 1954. Dynamite administered to huge buildings in Chicago and St. Louis ended the aspirations of a lineage of public housing enactments. Gas lines undermined the energy regulation of the 1970s. A resonant fiction of "welfare queens" came to tag the Aid to Families with Dependent Children section of the Social Security Act of 1935 as it evolved to its close in 1996. Senior citizens beating up on Congressman Dan Rostenkowski's car brought down the Catastrophic Health Insurance Act of 1988. The Silverado collapse came to symbolize the savings-and-loans crisis invited by the banking deregulations of 1980 and 1982. Perhaps the helicopters on the Saigon roof were a coda to the Tonkin Gulf Resolution of 1964.

Short of iconic but still viewed as failures might be the "maximum feasible participation" sector of Johnson's antipoverty program (it generated controversy and died away); Nixon's revenue-sharing program (it didn't catch hold); the War Powers Resolution of 1973 (it hasn't worked); the Magnuson-Moss product warranty act of 1974 (it didn't take); the anti-tax-breaks thrust of the Tax Reform Act of 1986 (see Patashnik's chapter 8); the immigration reforms of 1986, 1990, and 1996 (they are widely seen as proof that illegal immigration cannot be restricted by statute); and agriculture deregulation in 1996 (it didn't last long).

Some enactments bring on disputes about their effects that never seem to end. The arguments become staples of partisan politics. They energize intellectuals. They take root in competing think tanks. What were the long-term consequences of the Reagan tax cuts of 1981?

Insofar as a cognitive approach can pertain to postenactment histories, what are the implications for analysis? I see seven.

First, from the standpoint of what U.S. society might be interested in, there does not exist any simple, clipped, or sure indicator of the future fortunes of an enactment. Formal amendments or repeals are worth tracking, but they stop well short of a full account. For one thing, other formal correctives such as court decisions and appropriations decisions can apply. As Maltzman and Shipan write, there exist "alternative vehi-cles for changing the law." For another thing, new statute B can impinge on the equilibrium of existing statute A without formally altering A. As Patashnik writes, "We need to examine the impact of the full *range* of policy changes than can affect a policy's durability over time, and not only the influence of formal amendments." In addition, beyond these formal terrains, I do not believe that there is any substitute for a sensi-tive attention to context. Statistics need to be framed by stories. What-ever the formal record might say, we should not be ignoring Three Mile Island, the downslope of the trajectory of synfuels, or the dynamiting of the big housing projects. In another consideration, a statute might "fail" in terms of its authors' aspirations yet continue to occupy a niche in the attic of government programs, as so often happens. That is a kind of fail-ure in which X has not caused Y.

Second, as a coding matter, there is good reason to differentiate among statutes in tracking their future fortunes—perhaps into categories of progressive (in the sense of a progressive research design), stable, or regressive change. Amihai Glazer notes in this volume that support for a law once it is enacted can dramatically increase or decrease.[11] Patashnik argues that "it is crucial to distinguish between the *existence* and the *di-rection* of [postenactment] change." Any such coding requires judgment. It cannot be done routinely. But it is worth the effort. What has it meant to "amend" the Social Security Act of 1935? Leaving aside welfare re-form in 1996, this amending has been overwhelming progressive. It has supplied one of the signal lawmaking patterns of the last three-quarters of a century. Data from it should not be allowed anywhere near a cod-ing regimen that implies, or that a reader might take to imply, that pol-icy change means policy reversal. The distinction is critical. Expansion implies a judgment of success. The Ys that X has been generating are so pleasing that we should have more of their kind.

Third, again from the standpoint of what U.S. society might be inter-ested in, there is good reason to code for, or otherwise attend to, the *im-portance* of statutes. Regarding the late 1860s and early 1870s, for ex-ample, Americans might have said, "Tell me about the postenactment effects of the Reconstruction statutes, and you can forget about the rest." This is an extreme example, but it makes the point. Also, it is not clear whether, or to what degree, the trajectories of statutes of high impor-tance or salience can be reflected in the workings of large-N data sets.

Fourth, a cognitive interpretation can figure in Berry, Burden, and

Howell's exceptionally interesting figure 5.1. This is their exhibit of "program hazard functions" clocking the likelihood of any spending program's mutation or death across several postenactment decades. That likelihood rises for eight years or so and then begins a long unending decline. Here is an intuition. To the degree that we look on laws as wait-and-see, trial-and-error enterprises that call for monitoring and assessment, eight years seems to make ballpark sense as a rethink peak. Consider the policy environment of 2010. Comment on the Sarbanes-Oxley Act of 2002 regulating the accounting industry had been mounting. In light of the 2008 election, the campaign finance reform act of 2002 was dwindling to irrelevance. Criticism of the No Child Left Behind Act of 2002 seemed to be climaxing as Diane Ravitch, a leading promoter of the original act, made up her mind that it wasn't working: "Scholar's School Reform U-Turn Shakes Up Debate."[12]

Fifth, changes in problem perception can shape the fortunes of enactments. Classic examples are afforded by national security crises. On the upswing, to cite an interpretation by Richard A. Posner centering on 9/11: "The USA Patriot Act, which civil libertarians abhor, was passed within weeks of those attacks; it would never have passed, or in all likelihood even have been proposed, had the attacks been thwarted." But then what? In the wake of such crises, Posner argues, U.S. history in general has brought mirroring downswings as "the relative weights of liberty and safety" have come to be traded off differently. "Every time civil liberties have been curtailed in response to a national emergency, whether real or imagined, they have been fully restored when the emergency passed—and in fact before it passed, often long before."[13] Accordingly, since 2001, congressional management of the Patriot Act has offered a textbook case of what might be called cut-point drift. Safety concerns have abated, opposition to the original act has blossomed, and constraints have been loosened (although not ended). But these changes do not owe, or they do not owe chiefly, to renovations in the taste-bearing shares of power enjoyed by parties, politicians, and ideologies in Washington, D.C. Even if support for the Patriot Act mapped originally, and if the coalitional patterns regarding it have mapped since, onto a standard ideological dimension related to party, the important pattern has been a cut-point shift by actors along that dimension engendered by changes in problem perception.

Sixth, Maltzman and Shipan reach a nice result in their finding that, everything else equal, "divisiveness" in the enactment of a statute makes a difference. The greater the roll-call opposition at that original point, regardless of its coalitional ingredients, the dicier the record of postenactment stability. This is intuitive. Large opposition might either index troubles that are likely to be lasting, or cause them. On the latter count, I see a case for a particular additional coding. How divisive was the original roll-call decision in *partisan* terms? As a theoretical and empirical matter, party versus party—especially when the opposing parties approach unity—might generate a special follow-up scenario. A party (as opposed to a cross-party coalition) is an organization built exactly to generate messages and mobilize voters. A party that loses on a congressional issue, if it was unified in that confrontation and stays angry, may have an incentive to keep the conflict going. There is a cognitive side. "We told you so" can supply a drumbeat of criticism as ex ante arguments about Xs causing or not causing Ys are continually brought out during the postenactment years. The reactive activity of losing parties, whether or not it follows this cognitive blueprint, is an underinvestigated topic. In fact, in political science it is embarrassingly underinvestigated. During the health-care debate of 2009–10, probably most of us were asked by journalists, "What does political science have to say about the postenactment fortunes of major statutes placed on the books over the unanimous (or nearly so) objections of opposition parties?" The answer: virtually nothing. Systematic work seems to be lacking.

Seventh, there is the line of analysis offered by Glazer and, in the case of airline deregulation, Patashnik. One reason that statutes stay in place is that consumers and firms adapt to them, get stuck in their adaptations, and resort to politics if necessary to protect those adaptations. This is convincing stuff. It occurs to me that there is a particular cognitive angle. All statutes are efforts to shape future behavior. Thus, all statutes incorporate, at least implicitly, X causes Y plans. If it is astutely crafted, an instrument such as airline deregulation will *plan for* future adaptations by consumers and firms. Those adaptations will be, in a removed but nontrivial sense, intended. To be sure, they will not be foreseen with precision. In 1978, possibly nobody saw a hub-and-spoke system coming. But it was hoped and envisioned that a system of spirited competition among airlines would ensue, and, the ways of firms not being a mystery, it was probably envisioned that the airlines (possibly some new ones, to be sure) would scramble to adapt themselves to their political and economic environments the way American firms ordinarily do. With luck a viable and, on balance, favorable economic sector of a familiar sort would kick into place. The lawmakers' crystal ball in 1978 was clouded but not opaque. To be sure, many statutes have postenactment stories that are not reached by this kind of analysis. The postenactment trajectories can overwhelm the in-going plans. Yet it is interesting to probe for eyes-open anticipations of adaptation.

A major attraction of this volume is its synergistic variety of approaches, tastes, data sources, and methodologies. One polarity is between case studies and large-N data sets. In general outlook, I tilt toward the latter pole. Yet in reading these chapters, I came out somewhere between the poles. I kept having an urge to embellish data points with empirical or historical information.

CHAPTER THIRTEEN

The Politics of the
Policymaking State

Sidney M. Milkis

This volume could not come at a better time. It arrives in the aftermath of the enactment of the Patient Protection and Affordable Care Act, potentially the most important social welfare legislation since the 1935 Social Security Act. As dramatic as the political conflict over this legislation proved to be, the most important lesson conveyed by the preceding chapters is that the story of health-care reform might have just begun. If the past is prologue, members of Congress, interest groups, and political parties will continue to mobilize and fight with one another over health-care policy. At the same time, a select few within the executive branch, congressional committees, and trade and advocacy groups will attend to routine matters of the legislation without much intense political conflict or public awareness. This compound of political conflicts and sub-rosa administration is likely to result in a story of policy development no less interesting and critical than the enactment of the landmark health-care reform legislation. As Jeffery Jenkins and Eric Patashnik observe in their introduction, "legislation is a living, breathing force in American politics."[1]

The Rise of the Policymaking State

In treating laws as a tale of policy development, the authors in this volume highlight three themes that contribute to our understanding of

American politics and government. First, many of the chapters show explicitly or implicitly that the United States has undergone a fundamental shift from a political order that restrained the national government's programmatic responsibility and enforced decentralized administration to one where, to use James Q. Wilson's refrain, the "legitimacy barrier" has been lowered considerably, if not removed entirely. Since the 1960s, especially, the timeless question of whether the federal government had the authority to devise a policy solution to social and economic problems has become a nonissue: Virtually any area of American life is now a legitimate issue on the national policy agenda.[2]

This transformation is the subject of William Novak's chapter, which traces the origins of the policymaking state to the latter part of the nineteenth century, when natural rights and laissez-faire were overwhelmed by a sui generis American version of state building that breached the wall of separation between the national government and society.[3] Not until the creation of the New Deal political order, however, did the three factors cited by Novak—the rise of legal positivism, the redefinition of liberalism, and a new conception of the national government's power—form the foundation of a policymaking state. Faced with domestic and international crises of the first order, Franklin D. Roosevelt was the first president to clearly give voice to a new, positive form of liberalism. In his justly famous "four freedoms" speech, delivered as the 1941 State of the Union address, Roosevelt pronounced two new freedoms to "supplement" traditional ones such as speech and religion: freedom from want, which would be embodied by the welfare state; and freedom from fear, institutionalized by the national security state.[4]

The data of Jeffrey Cohen and Matthew Eshbaugh-Soha on presidents' submissions of legislative proposals to Congress and the issues areas that have appeared on the White House's legislative agenda appear to confirm the development of an executive-centered administrative state by the end of World War II.[5] With the creation of the White House Office and the Executive Office of the President, the Second World War gave rise to new policy concerns that went beyond "social security"—to issues such as civil rights, housing, and health care that would command the attention of the liberal coalition through the end of the twentieth and beginning of the twenty-first centuries. That Cohen and Eshbaugh-Soha find evidence only of a "domestic" modern executive is most likely an artifact of their focus on *legislative* proposals. The institutionalization of the modern presidency gave rise not just to more legislative proposals but also to policies that could be advanced through administrative avenues—executive orders and administrative regulations—that proved to be especially important for national security policy.

Although Roosevelt and his New Deal political allies presupposed that the modern executive would be the center of the policymaking state, traditional fears of centralized power and the complexity of American government ensured that national administration would be shared by plethora of actors. As the chapters by Patashnik, Stuart Chinn, and Vesla Weaver show, with the explosion of government responsibilities during the 1960s and 1970s, the development of laws and policies would take place amid sprawling institutional arrangements that saw Congress, courts, states, and advocacy groups participate in the details of administration.[6] Indeed, Patashnik's story of airline regulation and deregulation suggests how American state building led to the expansion of national administration, even as executive power was circumscribed. From the 1930s to the 1970s, airline fares and routes were governed by the Civil Aeronautics Board (CAB), an independent regulatory commission, the type of administrative agency that, as David E. Lewis argues in his chapter, was designed to be free of direct presidential influence.[7] Moreover, the elimination of the CAB, the key institutional change that resulted from the deregulatory law enacted in 1978, did not cut the Gordian knot that linked government and the airline industry; rather, it "reconfigured" the administrative politics that affected the airline industry, dispersing influence to a new array of actors: government agencies responsible for consumer protection and antitrust policy, states and localities that became the sites of a new hub-and-spoke system, new entrepreneurial airlines like JetBlue and Southwest, and new lobby groups representing the interests that have benefited from the "fortress" hub operations that were constructed at airports around the country.

Like Patashnik's examination of airline deregulation, Weaver's study of the "carceral state" reveals how national policy entrepreneurs have deployed the states and localities to advance their objectives. Ironically, this far-flung bureaucracy became rooted throughout the country and carried out a dramatic change in policy, even though the organic statute— the 1968 Safe Streets and Crime Control Act—and federal bureaucracy it created—the Law Enforcement and Assistance Administration (LEAA)—were eliminated in 1980. Equally striking, Weaver shows how an ostensibly decentralized administrative structure was forged into a *national* policymaker that not only sustained but greatly expanded the reach of law enforcement. By funneling billions of dollars into under-funded agencies and mandating that states form coordinating planning agencies before its demise, the LEAA forged the creation of a widely dispersed but regnant carceral state: Amateur police forces were expanded and professionalized, fragmented courts were unified, and cooperation was achieved across agencies and levels of government. This "crime control bureaucracy" spurred a transformation of policy, establishing more severe penalties, defining more acts as criminal, reducing parole, and enacting special sentence enhancements for crimes involving drugs or guns. Consequently, whereas conventional wisdom has viewed the federal system as an obstacle to state building, the enlistment of states and localities in national crime policy placed America at the vanguard of law and order enforcement: Compared to other advanced industrial nations, the United States imprisons at least five times more of its citizens per capita.

Just as policy entrepreneurs used the federal system to expand national policy, so Chinn's chapter argues that their opponents have used the courts to constrain programmatic ambition. In the case of airline deregulation, Patashnik shows how a statute can reconfigure politics in a manner that serves the law's proponents. Chinn argues that, at least with respect to certain major changes, the Supreme Court has been the principal agent of an "institutional recalibration" that assuages the losers of policy conflict—indeed, that leads to a form of political and administrative pluralism. The policy area he examines in his chapter—labor—shows how the Supreme Court interpreted the National Labor Relations (or Wagner) Act, a pillar of the New Deal political order, during the late 1930s so as to restrain certain militant labor practices, for example, the sit-down strike. The Supreme Court cases he cites, Chinn argues, did not directly roll back the New Deal constitutional revolution that sanctified the right of collective bargaining, but they sharply delimited the power of the National Labor Relations Board to support aggressive union tactics. He does not say whether the "industrial pluralism" fostered by the Court laid the groundwork for subsequent statutory amendments such as the 1947 Taft-Hartley Act, which proscribed the closed shop. But the meaning is there. More to the point, Chinn shows that the Court plays a critical part in the policymaking state, not through constitutional ruling but through statutory interpretation that thrusts the judiciary into the details of administration.

The Patashnik and Weaver chapters suggest that state and localities risk severely compromising their institutional integrity—becoming agents of national administration—in shaping the development of laws and policies. In contrast, Chinn argues that the Supreme Court justices do not denigrate the "cult of the robe" in moderating reform and arbitrating conflict between winners and losers. Rather, the judiciary plays a critical role in codifying major political developments and thus fortifying new political orders with the rule of law. "If an emerging, new reallocation of governing authority and individual rights is to become entrenched and sturdy enough to create a new order," he claims, "its constitutionality or legality cannot remain ambiguous on fundamental principles." And yet, once the policymaking state fully emerged, the courts engaged in statutory interpretation, not just in labor law but also in critical policy areas like civil rights, environmental and consumer protection, and campaign finance, that seemed to defy clear constitutional or legal principles. R. Shep Melnick, for example, has shown how a "civil rights state" formed during the 1970s that largely eschewed the pronouncement of abstract rights and clear legal obligations; instead, the courts became imbedded in dense institutional structures that defined the meaning of such key terms as *discrimination* and *equal opportunity*, established detailed guidelines for the many public officials and private parties subject to civil rights laws, monitored their compliance, and imposed sanctions on those who failed to comply. Although the elaboration of civil rights law was not completely done on a case-by-case basis, many court decisions, especially those at the appellate and district court levels, immersed the Court in the level of policy detail that blurred rather than codified legal principles.[8]

Policy Development and the Rule of Law

The fascinating case studies authored by Patashnik, Weaver, and Chinn point to a second important theme of this volume: the relationship between administration and law. Does Novak's concept of the "legislative state" disguise a political order where administration has trumped law in the development of many important policies? Or does the important role that Congress, the states, and the courts play in national administration indicate that the United States has grappled seriously, if not always effectively, with the challenge of reconciling administrative aggrandizement and settled standing law? Lewis's chapter on agency design sheds additional light on these questions. The creation of independent regulatory commissions to shape policy in critical areas such as financial regulation, labor law, and consumer protection is another feature of the sui generis American bureaucratic structure dedicated to joining administration and the rule of law. Surveying federal administrators and program managers, Lewis provisionally concludes that these commissions, in contrast to regular executive agencies and departments, have the luxury to deliberate about policy issues and formulate regulations independently of the vagaries of presidential ambition, partisan conflict, and predatory interest. By logical extension, independent regulatory commissions are more likely to make policy that will endure. And yet, as Patashnik's evidence on the CAB suggests, such commissions might not truly be independent, but, instead, forums for "rent seeking." In fact, some of Lewis's survey evidence also seems to suggest that the CAB is not uniquely vulnerable to interest group influence, and that regulatory commissions might have been freed from presidential or partisan influence only to suffer the indignity of serving the particular interests of regulated industries. If indeed the policy of commissions persists, are we to take this as a sign of "neutral competence" or, as Theodore Lowi charges, "interest group liberalism."[9]

Lewis's ideal of agency autonomy might depend on the commission's grant of authority. The Federal Trade Commission (FTC), for example, has broad policy responsibility to police deceptive and unfair business practices, a mandate that might make it less subject to capture than industry-specific agencies like the CAB. Like many federal agencies, the FTC has been buffeted since the late 1970s by conflict between self-styled "public interest" advocates and champions of the market. But most commissioners and a substantial part of the professional staff appear to take pride in the FTC's ability to remain free of the ideological struggles that roil many executive departments and agencies. They relish working as an "island of sanity," as one staffer put it, in a sea where many regulators, prodded by Congress, the White House, or powerful interest groups, have pursued ideological agendas that seek to accomplish through rulemaking and enforcement actions (or inaction) policies that never could have been accomplished through legislation.[10]

Managing to stay above the fray, the FTC has consistently pursued a pragmatic program of consumer protection over the past three decades. This policy has been informed by a conceptual framework that reflects a skeptical view of government intervention in the marketplace but acknowledges a legitimate role for social regulation in protecting the public from market externalities like health hazards and fraud. George W. Bush's choice to head the FTC, Timothy Muris, as well as his two predecessors, Janet Steiger, appointed by George H. W. Bush, and Robert Pitofsky, a Clinton appointee, all effectively deployed the agency's commitment to intrepid professional policy development, thus gaining the praise of those inside and outside the Beltway for aggressively protecting consumers, even as their initiatives achieved strong bipartisan consensus. The FTC's most celebrated policy of recent years, the 2003 Do-Not-Call Rule, is a dramatic example of the agency's effectiveness. It prohibited telemarketers from calling consumers who had placed their names and/or telephone numbers on a centralized registry maintained by the Commission. Muris, a conservative Republican economist, pushed the Do-Not-Call Rule through in the face of fierce opposition from telemarketers, resistance from his own party in Congress, and limited support from the White House. That he was able to do so testified to the ability of FTC commissioners and staff to artfully reconcile government regulation and private rights. As Muris himself acknowledged, he built on the Pitofsky Commission's efforts "to put privacy issues on the map," most notably an aggressive effort to curb telemarketing fraud. As Patashnik shows, consumer advocates and conservative economists agreed at a critical moment on the beneficence of a market approach to airline fares. To a surprising extent, the FTC has provided a shelter for an ongoing institutional partnership between these normally rival camps that ultimately established one of the most successful and durable policies of recent history. As the *Washington Post* reporter Steven Pearlstein wrote in tribute to Muris's leadership of the FTC, "in terms of touching the lives of Americans, nothing is likely to rival the do-not-call registry that shields about 60 million households from unwanted telemarketing calls."[11]

And yet, the development of bureaucratic policymaking suggests that the FTC experience is, if not unique, rare. The expansion of national administrative power has increasingly made it difficult for government departments and agencies to achieve bureaucratic autonomy. In fact, with respect to certain highly charged issues such as tobacco regulation, the FTC has been unable to achieve a solid middle ground and has seen its authority to regulate the marketing practices of tobacco shifted to the more politicized Food and Drug Administration and the National Association of State Attorneys General.[12] Indeed, Daniel Carpenter has argued that since the inception of a professional bureaucracy in the late nineteenth century, bureaucratic autonomy has depended less on agency design than it has on the art of administrative politics. In a number of agencies—most notably the U.S. Department of Agriculture, the Social Security Administration, and the Environmental Protection Agency of the 1970s—"entrepreneurial bureau chiefs created administrative 'communities' of experts and officials who slowly refashioned policies to their liking." The programs shaped by these innovative administrators, moreover, are among the most significant and enduring policies of the twentieth century.[13] Even the highly successful consumer protection policy of the FTC has its origins not in the work of neutral experts, but rather in the effective administrative leadership of James Miller, appointed by Ronald Reagan to head the agency in 1981, who enlisted the support of politically savvy economists like Muris to steer the commission away from the controversial policies it had pursued during the 1970s that were dedicated to restructuring the economy and reforming consumer preferences.[14]

No program better illustrates the art of political administration better than Social Security. Although much of the work on the role of the bureaucracy in policymaking contrasts administration and law, the Social Security program demonstrates that policies are most likely to become integrated into the fabric of American politics when a well-conceived organic statute is prudently administered. The original 1935 statute was compromised both by the need to bow to the power of the southern wing of the Democratic Party and the policy experts' concern to ensure the long-term solvency of old-age pensions. Consequently, it did not cover agricultural, domestic, or hotel workers, thus leaving most African Americans and women outside the Social Security system. And yet, entrepreneurial bureaucrats nurtured the organic statute so that it became the framework for an expanding and popular entitlement—"the gilded lily of U.S. public policy."[15] Policy was long dominated by the Social Security Board, which was insulated to a remarkable degree from partisan politics, interest group influence, and competition from other administrative agencies. The agency, in turn, was dominated by program advocates who selected and trained personnel so that clerks, as well as higher-ups, were bound by a strong "clientele serving ethic." The commitment to advocacy among program officers was largely attributable to its executive leaders' tactical circumvention of routine civil service procedures in order to assemble a staff of exceptional competence and religious dedication to the cause of reform. These achievements created a political environment that encouraged presidents and Congress, caught between favorable public opinion and the expertise of leading bureaucrats, to bestow bipartisan legitimacy on the program.[16] Significantly, it was Dwight Eisenhower, the first Republican president of the New Deal era, who presided over the expansion of Social Security in 1954, so that the program covered most of the workers left out of the original statute.

Underwriting the success of Social Security was a subtle but profound shift in American political culture—the emergence of what Novak terms *positive liberty*, which FDR effectively joined to a new understanding of rights. In fact, Roosevelt committed the government in 1935 to an uncompromising policy of financing Social Security by payroll taxes rather than by general revenues, believing that such a policy would make the protection an earned right. To those who complained of the regressive nature of financing Social Security by a contributory program, Roosevelt stressed the *political* importance of linking welfare programs as closely as possible to the traditional principles and practices of American constitutional government. As he put it to one such critic, "I guess you are right on the economics, but those taxes were never a problem of economics. They are politics all the way through. We put those payroll contributions there so to give the contributors a legal, moral, and political right to collect the pensions. . . . With those taxes in there, no damn politician can scrap my social security program."[17] The idea of entitlement did not extend to all social welfare policies, especially to those measures that targeted the less advantaged. But, as Patashnik has demonstrated in his earlier work, the linking of policies as far afield as Medicare and transportation to a "trust fund," which attempts to put budget actors under future obligation, has frequently been an effective strategy for embedding policies enduringly in American political life. "Promise keeping," Patashnik claims, "is at the heart of democratic politics."[18]

The Policymaking State and Party Politic

But how democratic is the policymaking in contemporary American politics? The development of the Social Security law and a number of policies examined in this volume raise a third important theme—the relationship between imbedded policy and self-government. Martha Derthick's seminal study of the social security program, for example, is a poster child for path dependency theory. Social Security policymaking created political dynamics that inoculated the program from major culture, economic, and social changes. As FDR's commitment to the wage tax reveals, this was no accident: The architects of Social Security "sought to foreclose the options of future generations by committing them irrevocably to a program that promises benefits by right as well as those particular benefits that have been incorporated in an ever expanding law. In that sense they designed social security to be uncontrollable."[19] That such an important policy domain has been characterized for most of its history by "constricted participation, doctrinal rigidity, and extreme inertia," Derthick concludes, raises serious questions about the viability of American representative democracy. She appeals for a more open and combative politics that might generate a wider array of policy choices.[20]

Although their chapters cover different political terrain and explore a policy landscape far more sprawling than the one Derthick discovered in studying the incipient New Deal political order, the chapters of Patashnik and Weaver also emphasize how policies can take on lives of their own. Patashnik shows how airline deregulation reconfigured political interests and recast institutional arrangements in a form that sustains the essence of the 1978 law, even though the market mechanisms unleashed have directly or indirectly led to growing public discontent with service and increased concern among policymakers about anticompetitive behavior. Similarly, Weaver depicts the seemingly ineluctable growth of a carceral state that has transmuted the states, localities, and courts into principal agents of a large crime control bureaucracy. Even the 1986 tax reform law, Patashnik's example of a road not taken, hardly illustrates the sort of public debate and resolution Derthick prescribes for the infirmities of insulated policy communities. The Tax Reform Act was never repealed; instead, it died the death of a thousand cuts. Presidents after Reagan, joined with alacrity by Congress, have viewed "tax expenditures"—doling out "tax goodies" to business clienteles and earmarking tax benefits for causes such as individual retirement accounts and education—as a more politically viable way to engage the policymaking state than direct government subsidy or visible state building. These developments have not only been demoralizing to many reform supporters but also have greatly expanded government obligations in a form that, no less than path-dependent policies like Social Security and criminal justice, may severely constrain political possibilities and public accountability.

The case studies of Patashnik and Weaver reveal that policies and the politics they make are powerfully influenced by interest groups. Just as tax reform proved ephemeral because it failed to uproot the prevailing pressure group politics that preyed on the tax code, so airline deregulation prevailed because it encouraged new interests to invest in the "fortress" hub operations that were constructed in airports around the country. The Safe Streets and Crime Control Act reverberated long after its demise in no small part because the Office of Law Enforcement Assistance pursued policies that strengthened and professionalized police groups such as the Association of Chiefs of Police and the Police Foundation that formed a supportive constituency of an expanding criminal justice system. Similarly, as R. Kent Weaver has argued, the persistence of the Social Security policy regime has followed not only from artful administrative statecraft but also from the powerful interest group it spawned. The American Association of Retired Persons (AARP) claims a membership of 35 million Americans age fifty and above—nearly three times the membership of the AFL-CIO. The large size and ideological diversity of its membership make it difficult for AARP to lobby aggressively for policy change; "but it is very well positioned to resist policy initiatives that attempt to impose losses on all or part of its constituency."[21]

Still, the policymaking state, combining elaborate administrative protocol and vested interests, is not merely, as E. E. Schattschneider feared, "pressure group politics." Schattschneider thought that the expansion of national administration "provided the raw materials for testing the organizational assumptions of two contrasting politics, *pressure politics* and *party politics*."[22] And yet, several chapters in this volume suggest that political parties play a critical role in the enactment of laws and innovative administration as well as the development of these policies over time. Although the work of Gailmard and Jenkins, Maltzman and Shipan, and Berry, Burden, and Howell highlight different features of partisan conflict, each of these chapters suggests that the rise and fall of party coalitions are very important to policy durability and change. Moreover, these chapters, covering different periods of time, suggest how parties have changed over time in ways that affect the development of laws and policies.

Spanning the broadest time period—1789 to 2002—Sean Gailmard and Jeffery A. Jenkins suggest that policy innovation and development dovetail with the fortunes of party coalitions.[23] As Walter Dean Burnham's seminal work on party realignments has shown, programmatic breakthroughs, which are rare in a constitutional order that sets ambition against ambition, rely on critical elections that install a strong party coalition with the capacity to overcome the *vis inertiae* of American political life.[24] Like Burnham, too, Gailmard and Jenkins find that policy innovation declines as a party coalition ages, a result they attribute to arriving at what Keith Krehbiel dubs a "gridlock region."[25] More broadly, the enervation of party coalition might follow from the constraints on government action for much of American history. The Constitution, embodying an understanding of "natural rights" that restrains government action, has generated a cyclical dynamic to political life in the United States, such that episodic shifts in policy give way, as Warren G. Harding famously put it, to "normalcy."[26] Stephen Skowronek's classic ordering of presidential power, although it places more emphases on "endogenous" factors than Burnham's realignment theory, also shows that the high energy of "reconstructive presidents" gives way to executives tasked with juggling received commitments and uneasy coalition partners.[27]

Because their data analysis controls for party systems, Gailmard and Jenkins cannot show how laws and their fate might vary across party regimes. Nor can it be discerned, as David Mayhew suggests, whether the election of unified party coalitions outside of realigning periods might lead to similar, and perhaps more impressive, policy innovation.[28] But their findings detect a secular development that, when cast against Novak's idea that a more positive liberal tradition emergences in the twentieth century, is very interesting indeed. Since 1969, they show, legislative innovation has declined while amendments to extant legislation have increased. "This confirms an impressionistic sense about policy innovation in Congress," Gailmard and Jenkins observe, that has "transitioned away from a period in which Congress takes up broad new categories of public policy that it had not previously touched, and entered one in which Congress's major policy work tends to alter the legislative infrastructure already in place." More fundamentally, this striking finding might confirm the emergence of a powerful but widely dispersed administrative state by the end of the Great Society that subordinates foundational politics to the more prosaic, albeit critical task of amending and administering existing programs. The positive state, it seems, makes policymaking routine—conservatives, no less than liberals, as Hugh Heclo has observed, are now "policy minded"—but major programmatic departures less likely.[29] Gailmard and Jenkins thus might detect from the vantage of Congress what Patashnik and Weaver highlight in their examination of the bureaucracy-interest group nexus: the development of policy arenas dominated by a relatively constricted and autonomous set of actors with a strong sense of proprietorship in their respective programs.

And yet, since the 1980s, political parties have engaged in a contentious, sometimes rancorous contest for control over the policymaking state. The election of Ronald Reagan in 1980 signaled the fracturing of what Arthur Schlesinger Jr. once optimistically termed the "vital center" and the emergence of jarring partisan clashes over policy.[30] Gailmard and Jenkins show that policy conflict has always roiled party politics in the United States. What is new about contemporary policy factionalism, as Heclo observes, is that it has "shaped itself around a governmental presence that is doing so much more in so many different areas of life."[31] Democrats and Republicans are currently polarized not only on social issues like abortion and same-sex marriage, which get so much attention from the press, but also on policies at the core of the welfare and national security state. Even "the gilded lily of U.S. public policy" has become contentious, so much so that Derthick, who once thought more partisan combat might "enlarge the possibilities of choice," has recently invoked the aphorism, "be careful what you wish for." The bipartisan consensus that reverberated through the 1970s, she wrote in 2004, "has yielded to sharp partisan divisions that make differences hard to reconcile. Democrats proclaim the sanctity of the social contract and the responsibility of citizens to care for one another, while many Republicans argue for individual ownership of retirement assets."[32]

The policy consequences of this sharp partisan divide remain unclear, however. Despite the Democrats' and Republicans' fundamentally different perspectives on the idea of entitlement, there have been virtually no changes to the essentials of the Social Security since the "rescue bill" of 1983, which stabilized the program's finances through the dawn of the twenty-first century with a combination of benefit cuts, taxation of benefits for upper-income recipients, and a gradual increase in the age at which full Social Security retirement benefits are received from sixty-five to sixty-seven.[33] Indeed, the fundamentals of the Social Security program remain popular enough—even though dramatic demographic shifts and dire forecasts about its viability have made the public anxious—that both Democrats and Republicans tend to be expansionists. Consider, for example, the bipartisan support for a Medicare prescription drug program and the failure of George W. Bush to gain any traction on privatization.[34]

It may be, then, as Gailmard and Jenkins suggest, that partisan disagreements over existing policy is now interstitial rather than foundational. But interstitial politics can be driven by important ideological differences. It would be interesting to explore more deeply, for example,
the argument of Maltzman and Shipan that unified party government
gives presidents and Congress the opportunity to enact organic statutes
that are immunized from subsequent legislative attacks; and by logical
extension, to investigate whether the incentive to inoculate policy from
future emendations has grown as parties have become more polarized
during the past three decades. Similarly, it would be valuable to unpack
the legislative amendments they measure to discern how much partisan
conflict has shaped the development of policies over time. Significantly,
Berry, Burden, and Howell find that changes in the partisan composition
of Congress affect not only the probability that programs will be eliminated but also the much more frequent examples of policy "mutation."

The evidence uncovered in these chapters jives nicely with work
that Jacob Hacker has done on the "the hidden politics of policy retrenchment." Hacker argues that relatively rare formal policy change,
such as the elimination of the Aid for Families with Dependent Children (AFDC), shows only one face of significant program development.
Building on the work of Eric Schickler, he identifies a second dominant pattern of change, "layering, in which proponents of change work
around institutions that have fostered vested interests and long-term expectations by adding new institutions rather than dismantling the old."
More to the point, Hacker claims that layering best describes conservatives' use of openings in the early 1980s (due to Reagan's election), the
late 1990s (due to the GOP's capture of both chambers of Congress), and
the first six years of the George W. Bush presidency (due to unified GOP
control of the White House and Congress) to "privatize risk"—to create
tax breaks and government regulations that encouraged individualized
private benefits that compete with public programs. Even the prescription drug program that the Republicans enacted with some Democratic
support in 2003 strengthened the role of private insurance companies
in the development of Medicare policy, an effort at layering that origi-
nated in demonstration projects first pursued by the Reagan administration. Consequently, although a few conservative Republicans opposed
the prescription drug policy, most supported it in the hope that the traditional program, as Newt Gingrich candidly put it, would "wither on the
vine."[35]

Social Security also has been the target of conservative state building. Scholars of Social Security such as Derthick and Kent Weaver argue that the tug of war between proponents of privatizing and socializ-
ing risk has not had any serious policy consequences; but congressional
Republicans and conservative think tanks such as the Cato Institute and
the Heritage Foundation have championed tax subsidies and other policies, privileging IRAs and 401(k) plans, that have diminished the importance of Social Security as a source of retirement funds. As Stephen
Teles has persuasively demonstrated, "conservatives have slowly built up
counter-institutions, counter-experts, and counter-ideas [in] an attempt
to solve the political problem of social security privatization." The core
of this counter strategy, Teles concludes, was a "to carve out a competing policy path, one that would slowly undermine support for Social Security and preserve the idea of privatization for the day when it was politically ripe."[36]

The struggle for the soul of the policymaking state appeared to come
to a head in the battle over the Patient Protection and Affordable Care
Act. Although previous major entitlements can be rightfully characterized as Democratic programs, they achieved considerable Republican
support: A majority of Republicans in the House and Senate voted for
the 1935 Social Security bill; more than half of the House Republicans
and thirteen of the thirty-two GOP senators voted for Medicare. The
2010 health-care reform bill is the first major entitlement to pass without a single Republican vote. The path to its enactment, moreover, which
saw the Democrats circumvent the Senate filibuster rule, brought to
mind the sort of partisan discipline and strategy usually associated with
a parliamentary system. Finally, unlike the layering strategies that characterized partisan maneuvers over social welfare policy prior to 2008,
the recent struggle over health-care reform took place before a deeply
interested, if not actively engaged, public.

If Maltzman and Shipan are right, the Democrats took advantage of
their control of the White House and Senate to enact legislation that is
immunized against future legislative and administrative assault. But previous landmark legislation has endured not merely because of effective
legislative statecraft, but also because such programs eventually enjoyed
strong bipartisan consensus. It remains to be seen, however, whether contemporary parties—more national and programmatic than was the case
at previous critical junctures of policy change—will so readily achieve a
modus vivendi over national health care. This "new" party system may

deprive President Barack Obama of a successor—like Eisenhower—who bestows bipartisan legitimacy on the changes he brings about.[37] What future GOP president, with bipartisan support in Congress, will proclaim that national health care is here to stay? To the contrary, many Republican leaders and conservative intellectuals, spurred on by an insurgent Tea Party movement, anticipate regaining power so as to repeal it. In celebrating the politics of repeal, they invoke the popular example of the repeal of Eighteenth Amendment, when a thirsty country changed its mind about banning sale of alcoholic beverages.

Like past major legislative enactments, the story of the 2010 healthcare reform bill is only the first vital step in what is likely to be a long journey. The question is whether the policymaking state has reached a new, more contested stage of development that has fundamentally changed the rules of policy development. Given that partisan polarization might yield a more open policy process that generates serious debate about a wider array of choices, the struggle over health care and other issues might be good for American democracy. Of course, the American people, who have never been comfortable with raw and disruptive party conflict, may become so alienated from current partisan warfare that they force Democrats and Republicans to seek pragmatic solutions to the country's present discontents. One suspects, however, that policy has come to affect so many of our lives so deeply that it is no longer possible, for better or worse, to substitute "enlightened administration" for fundamental conflict over the future path of laws and programs.

Notes

Chapter One

1. Carl Huse and Robert Pear, "Sweeping Health Care Plan Passes House," *New York Times*, November 7, 2009, A1.

2. Robert Pear, "Senate Passes Health Care Overhaul on Party-Line Vote," *New York Times*, December 25, 2009, A1.

3. On the capacity of unexpected developments to shape political outcomes, see David R. Mayhew, "Events as Causes: The Case of American Politics," in *Political Contingency: Studying the Unexpected, the Accidental, and the Unforeseen*, ed. Ian Shapiro and Sonu Bedi (New York: NYU Press, 2007), chap. 4.

4. Robert Pear and David M. Herszenhor, "Obama Hails Vote on Health Care as Answering 'the Call of History,'" *New York Times*, March 22, 2010, A1. Several days later, Congress passed a Reconciliation Act to ratify the political bargain. Among other things, the Act closed the Medicare Part D "donut hole," increased tax credits to help low-income people afford health care, raised federal Medicaid payments to states, and rescinded the Medicaid deal that Senator Ben Nelson had struck (the "Cornhusker Kickback") to secure his vote on HR 3590.

5. For a crisp history of the development of the Patient Protection and Affordable Care Act, see Lawrence R. Jacobs and Theda Skocpol, *Health Care Reform and American Politics: What Everyone Needs to Know* (Oxford: Oxford University Press, 2010).

6. One element of the health-care law, requiring citizens to purchase health insurance, has already been struck down in federal district court after a challenge by the secretary of state of Virginia. See Kevin Sack, "Judge Voids Key Element of Obama Health Care Law," *New York Times*, December 14, 2010, A1.

7. On the sustainability risks of the health law, see Henry J. Aaron and

Robert D. Reischauer, "The War Isn't Over," *New England Journal of Medicine* 362 (2010): 1259–61; and Jacobs and Skocpol, *Health Care Reform*, chap. 5.

8. William N. Eskridge Jr. and John Ferejohn, *A Republic of Statutes: The New American Constitution* (New Haven, CT: Yale University Press, 2010).

9. Woodrow Wilson, *Congressional Government: A Study in American Politics* (New York: Houghton Mifflin, 1885), 297.

10. Ibid.

11. For a review of the literature, see Nelson W. Polsby and Eric Schickler, "Landmarks in the Study of Congress Since 1945," *Annual Review of Political Science* 5 (2002): 333–67.

12. David B. Truman, *The Congressional Party: A Case Study* (New York: Wiley, 1959); Donald R. Matthews, *U.S. Senators and Their World* (New York: Vintage, 1960).

13. See Richard F. Fenno Jr., *Congressman in Committees* (Boston: Little, Brown, 1973); David R. Mayhew, *Congress: The Electoral Connection* (New Haven, CT: Yale University Press, 1974); Morris P. Fiorina, *Representatives, Roll Calls, and Constituencies* (Lexington, MA: D. C. Heath, 1974).

14. The major works include Barry R. Weingast and William Marshall, "The Industrial Organization of Congress," *Journal of Political Economy* 96 (1988): 132–63; Keith Krehbiel, *Information and Legislative Organization* (Ann Arbor: University of Michigan Press, 1991); Gary Cox and Mathew D. McCubbins, *Legislative Leviathan: Party Government in the House* (Berkeley: University of California Press, 1993).

15. David R. Mayhew, *Divided We Govern: Party Control, Lawmaking, and Investigations, 1946–1990* (New Haven, CT: Yale University Press, 1991).

16. Some scholars questioned whether a raw count of major laws provided an accurate measurement of legislative productivity, and argued instead that a ratio of major laws to major law *opportunities* better captured the phenomenon. See Sarah A. Binder, *Stalemate: Causes and Consequences of Legislative Gridlock* (Washington, DC: Brookings Institution Press, 2003). Others argued that failed legislation, as well as successful legislation, needed to be considered in order to assess the impact of divided government and other variables. See George C. Edwards III, Andrew Barrett, and Jeffrey Peake, "The Legislative Impact of Divided Government," *American Journal of Political Science* 41 (1997): 545–63; John J. Coleman, "Unified Government, Divided Government, and Party Responsiveness," *American Political Science Review* 93 (1999): 821–35; Charles R. Shipan, "Does Divided Government Increase the Size of the Legislative Agenda?" in *The Macropolitics of Congress*, ed. E. Scott Adler and John S. Lapinski (Princeton, NJ: Princeton University Press, 2006), 151–70. Still other scholars lengthened Mayhew's major law time series back to Reconstruction or adopted alternative coding schemes. See Sean Q. Kelly, "Divided We Govern? A Reassessment." *Polity* 25 (1993): 475–84; William Howell, Scott Adler, Charles

Cameron, and Charles Riemann, "Divided Government and the Legislative Productivity of Congress, 1945–94," *Legislative Studies Quarterly* 25 (2000): 285–312; R. Eric Petersen, "Is It Science Yet? Replicating and Validating the Divided We Govern List of Important Statutes" (paper presented at the Annual Meeting of the Midwest Political Science Association, Chicago, IL, 2001); Steven W. Stathis, *Landmark Legislation, 1774–2002* (Washington, DC: CQ Press, 2002); Joshua D. Clinton and John S. Lapinski, "Measuring Legislative Accomplishment, 1877–1994," *American Journal of Political Science* 50 (2006): 232–49. Recently, Mayhew has extended his own time series by a dozen years. See David R. Mayhew, *Divided We Govern: Party Control, Lawmaking, and Investigations, 1946–2002*, 2nd ed. (New Haven, CT: Yale University Press, 2005).

17. Keith Krehbiel, *Pivotal Politics: A Study of U.S. Lawmaking* (Chicago: University of Chicago Press, 1998); Binder, *Stalemate*.

18. David Epstein and Sharyn O'Halloran, *Delegating Powers: A Transaction Cost Politics Approach to Policy Making Under Separate Powers* (Cambridge: Cambridge University Press, 1999); Charles M. Cameron, *Veto Bargaining: Presidents and the Politics of Negative Power* (Cambridge: Cambridge University Press, 2000); William G. Howell, *Power Without Persuasion: The Politics of Direct Presidential Action* (Princeton, NJ: Princeton University Press, 2003).

19. Hugh Heclo, "A Political Science Perspective on Social Security Reform," in *Framing the Social Security Debate*, ed. R. Douglas Arnold, Michael J. Graetz and Alica H. Munnell (Washington, DC: Brookings Institution Press, 1998), 65–94.

20. Charles C. Y. Wang and Yi David Wang, "Explaining the Glass-Steagall Act's Long Life, and Rapid Eventual Demise," December 8, 2010, http://ssrn .com/abstract=1722373.

21. Chapter 4 by Gailmard and Jenkins is also an example of this approach.

22. Political economist Amihai Glazer in chapter 7 uses an approach that is similar to historical institutionalism in political science.

23. Theda Skocpol, *Protecting Soldiers and Mothers: The Political Origins of Social Policy in the United States* (Cambridge, MA: Belknap Press of Harvard University Press, 1992), 58 and 232.

24. Although there are significant differences in emphasis, the importance of institutions is stressed in both the historical-institutional and rational choice literatures. For reviews of the vast literature, see R. A. W. Rhodes, Sarah A. Binder, and Bert A. Rockman, eds., *The Oxford Handbook on Political Institutions* (New York: Oxford University Press, 2006); and Robert E. Goodin, ed., *The Theory of Institutional Design* (New York: Cambridge University Press, 1996). For a direct comparison of the two approaches, as well as how they might complement one another, see Ira Katznelson and Barry R. Weingast, eds., *Preferences and Solutions: Points of Intersection Between Historical and Rational Choice Institutionalism* (New York: Russell Sage, 2005).

25. See, for example, Karen Oren and Stephen Skowronek, *The Search for American Political Development* (New York: Cambridge University Press, 2004).

26. See Terry Moe, "The New Economics of Organization," *American Journal of Political Science* 28 (1984): 739–77.

27. See E. E. Schattschneider, *Politics, Pressures and the Tariff* (New York: Prentice-Hall, 1935), 288.

28. Over the past fifteen years, a number of scholars have produced careful empirical studies of positive feedback. In their analyses of Social Security and the GI Bill of Rights, respectively, Andrea Campbell and Suzanne Mettler produce compelling statistical evidence of the impact of policy legacies on public attitudes and political behavior. Campbell shows that Social Security significantly expanded civic participation among the elderly, especially among less affluent individuals who were most reliant on the program. Mettler shows that the GI Bill had long-term effects on the democratic involvement of participants, leading veterans who took advantage of the GI Bill to become far more active in civic life than nonparticipating veterans with similar education levels. See Andrea Louise Campbell, *When Policies Make Citizens: Senior Political Activism and the American Welfare State* (Princeton, NJ: Princeton University Press, 2003); and Suzanne Mettler, *Soldiers to Citizens: The G.I. Bill and the Making of the Greatest Generation* (New York: Oxford University Press, 2005).

29. See Theodore J. Lowi, "American Business, Public Policy, Case-Studies, and Political Theory," *World Politics* 16 (1964): 677–715; and James Q. Wilson, *Political Organizations* (New York: Basic Books, 1973).

30. In a penetrating 1993 review essay, Paul Pierson suggested that policies can generate two kinds of feedback. First, policies can produce *resources and incentives* that may influence political action. Pierson argued that these effects can include material resources as well as access to public authority. In addition, Pierson argued that policies can generate *interpretive* effects that shape how actors make sense of a complex political world. Policies can convey information that influences actors' awareness of government activities. Policies can also serve as sources of meaning that help construct the political identities and define the perceived social statuses of constituent groups, shaping their willingness to engage in civic participation. See Paul Pierson, "When Effect Becomes Cause: Policy Feedback and Political Change," *World Politics* 45 (1993): 595–628.

31. An important conceptual difference, then, between the chapter by Maltzman and Shipan and the chapters by Glazer and Patashnik is that the former examines the factors that increase or decrease the likelihood that a law will be amended after enactment, while the latter probe the factors that allow a legislative project to become embedded. In other words, Maltzman and Shipan investigate the *probability* of a subsequent change (durability), while Glazer and Patashnik look at its *direction* (sustainability).

32. Michael E. Levine, "Regulation, the Market, and Interest Group Cohesion: Why the Airlines Were Not Reregulated," in *Creating Competitive Markets: The Politics of Regulatory Reform*, ed. Marc K. Landy, Martin A. Levin, and Martin Shapiro (Washington, DC: Brookings Institution Press, 2007), 215–46. See also Eric M. Patashnik, *Reforms at Risk: What Happens After Major Policy Changes Are Enacted* (Princeton, NJ: Princeton University Press, 2008), chap. 7.

33. Eric M. Patashnik and Julian E. Zelizer, "When Policy Does *Not* Remake Politics: The Limits of Policy Feedback" (paper prepared for presentation at the 2009 Annual Meetings of the American Political Science Association, September 3–6, Toronto, Canada).

34. Mayhew, *Congress*, 232–36.

35. Patashnik, *Reforms at Risk*.

Chapter Two

1. Jeremy Bentham, *A Fragment on Government* (1776; Cambridge: Cambridge University Press, 1988); William Blackstone, *Commentaries on the Laws of England* (1765–69; Chicago: University of Chicago Press, 1979).

2. Roscoe Pound, "Common Law and Legislation," *Harvard Law Review* 21 (1908): 383–487; Roscoe Pound, "Legislation as a Social Function," *American Journal of Sociology* 18 (1913): 755–68; Roscoe Pound, *Outlines of a Course on Legislation* (Cambridge, MA: Harvard University Press, 1934); Ernst Freund, *Standards of American Legislation* (1917; Chicago: University of Chicago Press, 1965); Ernst Freund, "Tendencies of Legislative Policy and Modern Social Legislation," *International Journal of Ethics* 27 (1916): 1–24.

3. James Willard Hurst, *Law and Social Order in the United States* (Ithaca, NY: Cornell University Press, 1977), 25; James Willard Hurst, *Dealing with Statutes* (New York: Columbia University Press, 1982); see also the remarkable compendiums of Robert Luce, *Legislative Assemblies: Their Framework, Make-Up, Character, Characteristics, Habits, and Manners* (Boston: Houghton Mifflin, 1924); *Legislative Principles: The History and Theory of Lawmaking by Representative Government* (Boston: Houghton Mifflin, 1930); and *Legislative Problems: Development, Status, and Trend of the Treatment and Exercise of Lawmaking Powers* (Boston: Houghton Mifflin, 1935).

4. Jeremy Waldron, *The Dignity of Legislation* (Cambridge: Cambridge University Press, 1999); Jeremy Waldron, *Law and Disagreement* (Oxford: Oxford University Press, 1999).

5. William N. Eskridge Jr., *Dynamic Statutory Interpretation* (Cambridge, MA: Harvard University Press, 1994); William N. Eskridge Jr., Philip P. Frickey, and Elizabeth Garrett, *Cases and Materials on Legislation: Statutes and the Cre-*

ation of Public Policy, 4th ed. (St. Paul: Thomson/West, 2007); Samuel Issacharoff, Pamela S. Karlan, and Richard H. Pildes, *The Law of Democracy: Legal Structure of the Political Process* (Westbury, NY: Foundation Press, 1998); William N. Eskridge Jr. and John Ferejohn, *A Republic of Statutes: The New American Constitution* (New Haven, CT: Yale University Press, 2010).

6. Eskridge, *Dynamic Statutory Interpretation*, 8. As Guido Calabresi put it in 1982, "The last fifty to eighty years have seen a fundamental change in American law. In this time we have gone from a legal system dominated by the common law, divined by courts, to one in which statutes, enacted by legislatures, have become the primary source of law." Guido Calabresi, *A Common Law for the Age of Statutes* (Cambridge, MA: Harvard University Press, 1982). Grant Gilmore less graciously referred to this era's "orgy of statute making." Grant Gilmore, *Ages of American Law* (New Haven, CT: Yale University Press, 1977), 95. See also Cass R. Sunstein, *After the Rights Revolution: Reconceiving the Regulatory State* (Cambridge, MA: Harvard University Press, 1990).

7. William Letwin, *Law and Economic Policy in America: The Evolution of the Sherman Antitrust Act* (Chicago: University of Chicago Press, 1954); David J. Langum, *Crossing Over the Line: Legislating Morality and the Mann Act* (Chicago: University of Chicago Press, 1994); Charles and Barbara Whalen, *The Longest Debate: A Legislative History of the 1964 Civil Rights Act* (Santa Ana: Seven Locks Press, 1985).

8. William N. Eskridge Jr. and John Ferejohn, "Super-Statutes," *Duke Law Journal* 50 (2001): 1215; David Vogel, "The New Social Regulation in Historical and Comparative Perspective," in *Regulation in Perspective: Historical Essays*, ed. Thomas K. McCraw (Cambridge, MA: Harvard University Press, 1981); Sunstein, *Rights Revolution*; David R. Mayhew, *Divided We Govern: Party Control, Lawmaking, and Investigations, 1946–2002*, 2nd ed. (New Haven, CT: Yale University Press, 2005).

9. Charles M. Andrews, *The Colonial Period of American History*, 2nd ed. (New Haven, CT: Yale University Press, 1964); Francis Newton Thorpe, *The Federal and State Constitutions, Colonial Charters, and Other Organic Laws of the States, Territories, and Colonies Now or Heretofore Forming the United States of America* (Washington, DC: Government Printing Office, 1909).

10. David P. Currie, *The Constitution in Congress: The Federalist Period, 1789–1801* (Chicago: University of Chicago Press, 1997), 3.

11. Charles M. Cook, *The American Codification Movement: A Study of Antebellum Legal Reform* (Westport, CT: Greenwood Press, 1981).

12. Theodore Sedgwick, *A Treatise on the Rules Which Govern the Interpretation and Application of Statutory and Constitutional Law* (New York: John S. Voorhies, 1857); E. Fitch Smith, *Commentaries on Statute and Constitutional Law and Statutory and Constitutional Construction* (Albany, NY: Gould, Banks, & Gould, 1848); Thomas M. Cooley, *A Treatise on the Constitutional Limita-*

tions which Rest upon the Legislative Power of the States of the American Union (Boston: Little, Brown, 1868); Francis Lieber, *Legal and Political Hermeneutics* (St. Louis: F. H. Thomas, 1880). For a fuller discussion of some of these themes, see William J. Novak, "Common Regulation: The Legal Origins of State Power in America," *Hastings Law Journal* 45 (1994): 1061–97.

13. Max Weber, *The Theory of Social and Economic Organization* (New York: Oxford University Press, 1947), 154–56; Max Weber, *Economy and Society: An Outline of Interpretive Sociology*, ed. Guenther Roth and Claus Wittich, trans. Ephraim Fischoff et al. (Berkeley: University of California Press, 1978), 1:217–20. For an excellent presentation, see Reinhard Bendix's discussion of Weber's view of "The Modern State and Its Legitimacy," in Bendix, *Max Weber: An Intellectual Portrait* (Garden City, NY: Anchor Books, 1962), 417–23.

14. C. K. Allen, *Law in the Making*, 7th ed. (Oxford: Oxford University Press, 1964), 606.

15. David R. Mayhew, "Lawmaking as a Cognitive Enterprise," chap. 12 in this volume.

16. Léon Duguit, *Law in the Modern State*, trans. Frida and Harold Laski (London: George Allen & Unwin, 1921), xxxv.

17. Roscoe Pound, "The Need of a Sociological Jurisprudence," *Green Bag* 19 (1907): 607.

18. The key secondary works on this intellectual transformation are Morton White, *Social Thought in America: The Revolt Against Formalism* (Boston: Beacon Press, 1957); Morton J. Horwitz, *The Transformation of American Law, 1870–1960: The Crisis of Legal Orthodoxy* (New York: Oxford University Press, 1992); John Henry Schlegel, *American Legal Realism and Empirical Social Science* (Chapel Hill: University of North Carolina Press, 1995); Laura Kalman, *Legal Realism at Yale, 1927–1960* (Chapel Hill: University of North Carolina Press, 1986); and Edward A. Purcell Jr., *The Crisis of Democratic Theory: Scientific Naturalism and the Problem of Value* (Lexington: University Press of Kentucky, 1973).

19. Donald R. Kelley's wonderful synthesis, *The Human Measure: Social Thought in the Western Legal Tradition* (Cambridge, MA: Harvard University Press, 1990), xi, provides a good measure of the early legal roots of this tradition.

20. As Roscoe Pound noted, "In common with sociology, sociological jurisprudence has its origin in the positivist philosophers in the sense that each subject has a continuous development from Comte's positive philosophy." Pound, "The Scope and Purpose of Sociological Jurisprudence, III," *Harvard Law Review* 25 (1912): 489. For an excellent brief synopsis of Comte's contribution, see Raymond Aron, "Auguste Comte," in *Main Currents in Sociological Thought* (Garden City, NY: Anchor Books, 1968), 1:73–143.

21. John Austin, *Lectures on Jurisprudence, or The Philosophy of Positive Law*, ed. Robert Campbell (London: John Murray, 1869).

22. John Chipman Gray, *The Nature and Sources of the Law* (New York: Columbia University Press, 1909); Henry T. Terry, *Some Leading Principles of Anglo-American Law: Expounded with a View to its Arrangement and Codification* (Philadelphia: Johnson, 1884), 87–101; Albert Kocourek, "The Century of Analytical Jurisprudence Since John Austin," in *Law: A Century of Progress 1835–1935*, vol. 2 (New York: New York University Press, 1937). On Hohfeld, see Joseph William Singer, "The Legal Rights Debate in Analytical Jurisprudence from Bentham to Hohfeld," *Wisconsin Law Review* (1982): 975.

23. Gray, *Nature and Sources of the Law*, 86–87.

24. Morris R. Cohen, "John Austin," in *Encyclopaedia of the Social Sciences* (New York: Macmillan, 1930), 2:318.

25. John Austin, *The Province of Jurisprudence Determined* (London: John Murray, 1832), 1.

26. Oliver Wendell Holmes Jr., "The Path of the Law," *Harvard Law Review* 10 (1897): 475; Roscoe Pound, "The Scope and Purpose of Sociological Jurisprudence I," *Harvard Law Review* 24 (1911): 594–95.

27. Felix S. Cohen, "The Problems of a Functional Jurisprudence," *Modern Law Review* 1 (1937): 8.

28. See, e.g., John Dewey, "Austin's Theory of Sovereignty," *Political Science Quarterly* 9 (1894): 31–52; John R. Commons, *A Sociological View of Sovereignty* (New York: Reprints of Economic Classics, 1965).

29. Julius Stone, *The Province and Function of Law* (London: Stevens, 1947), 70–71; Roscoe Pound, *Social Control through Law* (New Haven, CT: Yale University Press, 1942), 94.

30. Gray, *Nature and Sources*, 63.

31. Westel Woodbury Willoughby, *An Examination of the Nature of the State: A Study in Political Philosophy* (New York: Macmillan, 1896); Westel Woodbury Willoughby, *The American Constitutional System: An Introduction to the Study of the American State* (New York: Century, 1904); Westel Woodbury Willoughby, *The Constitutional Law of the United States* (New York: Baker, Voorhis, 1910); Westel Woodbury Willoughby, *The Fundamental Concepts of Public Law* (New York: Macmillan, 1924); see also John Mabry Mathews and James Hart, eds., *Essays in Political Science in Honor of Westel Woodbury Willoughby* (Baltimore: Johns Hopkins University Press, 1937).

32. Willoughby, *Examination*, 180.

33. Willoughby, *American Constitutional System*, 33.

34. Pound, "Scope and Purpose of Sociological Jurisprudence I," 595; Gray, *Nature and Sources*, 87.

35. Austin, *Lectures on Jurisprudence*, 1:298; Dewey, "Austin's Theory," 33.

36. Rudolf von Jhering, *Law as a Means to an End*, trans. Isaac Husik (Boston: Boston Book, 1913); Rudolf von Jhering, *The Struggle for Law*, trans. John J. Lalor (Chicago: Callaghan, 1879).

37. Association of American Law Schools, *Rational Basis of Legal Institutions*, ed. John H. Wigmore and Albert Kocourek (New York: Macmillan, 1923).

38. Ibid., xx, xxix.

39. Walter Lippmann, *A Preface to Politics* (1913; New York: Macmillan, 1933), 202.

40. Herbert Spencer, *Social Statics, Abridged and Revised; Together with The Man Versus the State* (London: Williams and Norgate, 1892), 357.

41. Lester Frank Ward, "The Laissez Faire Doctrine Is Suicidal," *Man* 4 (1884), in *Glimpses of the Cosmos* (New York: Putnam, 1913), 3:301–5.

42. John Dewey, "Individualism, Old and New," in *The Later Works, 1925–1953*, ed. Jo Ann Boydston (1929; Carbondale: Southern Illinois University Press, 1988), 5:41–123; John Dewey, "Liberalism and Social Action," in *The Later Works, 1925–1953*, ed. Jo Ann Boydston (1935; Carbondale: Southern Illinois University Press, 1991), 11:1–65.

43. Albert Venn Dicey, *Lectures on the Relation Between Law and Public Opinion in England During the Nineteenth Century*, 2nd ed. (London: Macmillan, 1914), liii–lv. Oliver Wendell Holmes's famous dissent in *Lochner* aimed not only at Spencer's *Social Statics* but at Mill's harm principle in precisely this way: "The liberty of the citizen to do as he likes so long as he does not interfere with the liberty of others to do the same, which has been a shibboleth for some well-known writers, is interfered with by school laws, by the Post Office, by every state or municipal institution which takes his money for purposes thought desirable or not, whether he likes it or not." Lochner v. New York, 198 U.S. 45, 75 (1905).

44. Roscoe Pound, "Liberty of Contract," *Yale Law Journal* 18 (1909): 456–57, 460, 484.

45. Roscoe Pound, *Outlines of Lectures on Jurisprudence*, 2nd ed. (Cambridge, MA: Harvard Law School, 1914), 58.

46. Thomas Hill Green, "Liberal Legislation and Freedom of Contract," in *The Political Theory of T. H. Green*, ed. John R. Rodman (New York: Appleton-Century-Crofts, 1964), 51–52; Green, *Lectures on the Principles of Political Obligation* (London: Longmans, Green, 1895).

47. Green, "Liberal Legislation," 53.

48. Novak, *People's Welfare*.

49. John Dewey and James H. Tufts, *Ethics* (New York: Henry Holt, 1909); John Dewey, *The Public and its Problems* (New York: Henry Holt, 1927).

50. Walter Lippmann, *Drift and Mastery: An Attempt to Diagnose the Current Unrest* (New York: M. Kennerley, 1914); Herbert Croly, *The Promise of American Life* (New York: Macmillan, 1909).

51. Jane Addams, *A New Conscience and an Ancient Evil* (New York: Macmillan, 1914), Walter Weyl, *The New Democracy: An Essay on Certain Political, and Economic Tendencies in the United State* (New York: Macmillan, 1913), 160–61.

52. Weyl, *New Democracy*, 159.

53. Elihu Root, "Address to the American Law Institute," *American Law Institute Proceedings* 1 (1923), 49. I cover some of this same material in "Police Power and the Transformation of the American State," in *Police and the Liberal State*, ed. Markus Dubber and Mariana Valverde (Stanford, CA: Stanford University Press, 2008), 54–73.

54. Charles E. Merriam, "Government and Society," in *Recent Social Trends in the United States: Report of the President's Research Committee on Social Trends*, one vol. ed. (New York: McGraw-Hill, 1933), 1515; R. F. Fuchs, "Quantity of Regulatory Legislation," *St. Louis Law Review* 16 (1930): 52.

55. John Maurice Clark, *Social Control of Business* (Chicago: University of Chicago Press, 1926), 4.

56. James W. Garner, *Introduction to Political Science: A Treatise on the Origin, Nature, Functions, and Organization of the State* (New York: American, 1910), 318–20.

57. For insight into this fundamental ambiguity in early modern English law, see the work of Charles Howard McIlwain, *The High Court of Parliament and Its Supremacy: An Historical Essay on the Boundaries Between Legislation and Adjudication in England* (New Haven, CT: Yale University Press, 1910); Charles Howard McIlwain, *Constitutionalism: Ancient and Modern* (Ithaca, NY: Cornell University Press, 1947); see also J. W. Gough, *Fundamental Law in English Constitutional History* (Oxford: Clarendon Press, 1955); J. G. A. Pocock, *The Ancient Constitution and the Feudal Law: A Study of English Historical Thought in the Seventeenth Century* (Cambridge: Cambridge University Press, 1957). On the ambiguity in early American jurisprudence, see Gordon S. Wood, *The Creation of the American Republic, 1776–1787* (Chapel Hill: University of North Carolina Press, 1969), esp. 259–305; Julius Goebel Jr., "Constitutional History and Constitutional Law," *Columbia Law Review* 38 (1938): 555; Christine A. Desan, "The Constitutional Commitment to Legislative Adjudication in the Early American Tradition," *Harvard Law Review* 111 (1998): 1381–1503.

58. Roscoe Pound, "Common Law and Legislation," *Harvard Law Review* 21 (1908): 383.

59. Francis Lieber, *Legal and Political Hermeneutics: Or, Principles of Interpretation and Construction in Law and Politics* (Boston: C. C. Little and J. Brown, 1839); Sedgwick, *Interpretation and Application of Statutory and Constitutional Law*; Joel Prentiss Bishop, *Commentaries on the Written Laws and Their Interpretation* (Boston: Little, Brown, 1882); see also Smith, *Commentaries on Statute and Constitutional Law*; G. A. Endlich, *A Commentary on the Interpretation of Statutes* (Jersey City: Frederick D. Linn, 1888).

60. Cooley, *Constitutional Limitations*; Christopher G. Tiedeman, *A Treatise on the Limitations of Police Power in the United States: Considered from Both a*

Civil and Criminal Standpoint (St. Louis: F. H. Thomas, 1886). For an excellent discussion, see Clyde E. Jacobs, *Law Writers and the Courts: The Influence of Thomas M. Cooley, Christopher G. Tiedeman, and John F. Dillon upon American Constitutional Law* (Berkeley: University of California Press, 1954).

61. Eskridge, *Dynamic Statutory Interpretation*, 2, 7.

62. For a general indication of the overall dimensions of this trend, see the four-volume encyclopedic synthesis of Robert Luce under the general series title "The Science of Legislation." Robert Luce, *Legislative Procedure: Parliamentary Practices and the Course of Business in the Framing of Statutes* (Boston: Houghton Mifflin, 1922); Robert Luce, *Legislative Assemblies: Their Framework, Make-up, Character, Characteristics, Habits, and Manners* (Boston: Houghton Mifflin, 1924); Robert Luce, *Legislative Principles: The History and Theory of Lawmaking by Representative Government* (Boston: Houghton Mifflin, 1930); Robert Luce, *Legislative Problems: Development, Status, and Trend of the Treatment and Exercise of Lawmaking Powers* (Boston: Houghton Mifflin, 1935).

63. Pound, "Common Law and Legislation," 384.

64. See generally Novak, *People's Welfare*.

65. Ernst Freund, *The Police Power: Public Policy and Constitutional Rights* (Chicago: University of Chicago Press, 1904); Ernst Freund, *Standards of American Legislation* (Chicago: University of Chicago Press, 1917); Ernst Freund, *Administrative Powers over Persons and Property: A Comparative Survey* (Chicago: University of Chicago Press, 1928); Ernst Freund, *Legislative Regulation: A Study of the Ways and Means of Written Law* (New York: Commonwealth Fund, 1932). In addition to his legal writings, Freund was active in progressive Illinois and Chicago politics, drafting a charter for the city of Chicago, participating in the National Conference of Commissioners on Uniform State Laws, and working on such reform issues as child welfare and immigration. For a serviceable introduction to Freund's career and writing, see Oscar Kraines, *The World and Ideas of Ernst Freund: The Search for General Principles of Legislation and Administrative Law* (Tuscaloosa: University of Alabama Press, 1974).

66. Francis A. Allen, "Ernst Freund and the New Age of Legislation," in *Standards of American Legislation*, by Ernst Freund (Chicago: University of Chicago Press, 1965), vii–xlvi; Ernst Freund, "The Problem of Intelligent Legislation," *Proceedings of the American Political Science Association* 4 (1907): 70.

67. Freund, *Legislative Regulation*, 12; Ernst Freund, *Jurisprudence and Legislation* (St. Louis: Congress of Arts and Science, Universal Exposition, 1904), 11.

68. Freund, *Police Power*; W. G. Hastings, "The Development of Law as Illustrated by the Decisions Relating to the Police Power of the State," *Proceedings of the American Philosophical Society* 39 (1900): 359–554; Alfred Orendorff,

"Public Policy and the Police Power of the State," *Chicago Legal News* 14 (1882): 256–57; B. J. Ramage, "Social Progress and the Police Power of a State," *American Law Review* 36 (1902): 681–99; J. M. Blayney Jr., "The Term 'Police Power,'" *Central Law Journal* 59 (1904): 486–92; Walter Wheeler Cook, "What Is the Police Power?" *Columbia Law Review* 7 (1907): 322–36; Thomas Reed Powell, *The Supreme Court and State Police Power, 1922–1930* (Charlottesville: Michie, 1932).

69. Freund, *Police Power*, 5–6 (italics in original).

70. Lewis Hockheimer, "Police Power," *Central Law Journal* 44 (1897): 158.

71. Bacon v. Walker, 204 U.S. 311, 317–18 (1907); see also Chicago, Burlington & Quincy Railway Co. v. Drainage Commissioners, 200 U.S. 561 (1906). For statements to similar effect concerning the police power and general welfare, see also Barbier v. Connolly, 113 U.S. 27 (1885); and Manigault v. Springs, 199 U.S. 473 (1905). See also the general discussion in Scott M. Reznick, "Empiricism and the Principle of Conditions in the Evolution of the Police Power: A Model for Definitional Scrutiny," *Washington University Law Quarterly* (1978): 31–32.

72. Harrison H. Brace, "To What Extent May Government in the Exercise of Its Police Power, Take, Destroy or Damage Private Property Without Giving Compensation Therefor?" *Chicago Legal News* 18 (1886): 341; B. J. Ramage, "Social Progress and the Police Power of a State," *American Law Review* 36 (1902): 698.

73. Samuel P. Hays, "The Social Analysis of American Political History, 1880–1920," *Political Science Quarterly* 80 (1965): 391.

74. Leonard D. White, "Public Administration," in *Recent Social Trends in the United States*, 1394.

75. United States v. Dewitt, 76 U.S. 41 (1870).

76. Charles Evans Hughes, "New Phases of National Development," *American Bar Association Journal* 4 (1918): 93–94.

77. Ernst Freund, "The New German Constitution," *Political Science Quarterly* 35 (1920): 181; Walter Thompson, *Federal Centralization: A Study and Criticism of the Expanding Scope of Congressional Legislation* (New York: Harcourt, Brace, 1923), 10.

78. Robert Eugene Cushman, *Studies in the Police Power of the National Government* (Minneapolis: Minnesota Law Review, 1919–20), 291; James A. Lyons, "Development of a National Police Power," *Tennessee Law Review* 14 (1935): 11–20.

79. Austin F. MacDonald, *Federal Aid: A Study of the American Subsidy System* (New York: Thomas Y. Crowell, 1928); Harry N. Scheiber, "Federalism and the American Economic Order, 1789–1910," *Law and Society Review* 10 (1975): 57–118.

80. Thompson, *Federal Centralization*.

81. Duguit, *Law in the Modern State*, 51.

Chapter Three

1. Frank Baumgartner and Bryan D. Jones, *Agendas and Instability in American Politics* (Chicago: University of Chicago Press, 1993); Jeffrey E. Cohen, "Presidential Rhetoric and the Public Agenda," *American Journal of Political Science* 39 (1995): 87–107; Jeffrey E. Cohen, *Presidential Responsiveness and Public Policy-Making* (Ann Arbor: University of Michigan Press, 1997); George C. Edwards III and B. Dan Wood, "Who Influences Whom? The President, Congress, and the Media," *American Political Science Review* 93 (1999): 327–44; Matthew Eshbaugh-Soha and Jeffrey S. Peake, "Presidential Influence Over the Systemic Agenda," *Congress and the Presidency* 31 (2004): 181–201; Matthew Eshbaugh-Soha and Jeffrey S. Peake, "Presidents and the Economic Agenda," *Political Research Quarterly* 58 (2005): 127–38; Kim Quaile Hill, "The Policy Agendas of the President and the Mass Public: A Research Validation and Extension," *American Journal of Political Science* 42 (1998): 1328–34; John W. Kingdon, *Agendas, Alternatives, and Public Policies* (Boston: Little, Brown, 1984); B. Dan Wood and Jeffrey S. Peake, "The Dynamics of Foreign Policy Agenda Setting," *American Political Science Review* 92 (1998): 173–84; Garry Young and William B. Perkins, "Presidential Rhetoric, the Public Agenda, and the End of Presidential Television's 'Golden Age,'" *Journal of Politics* 67 (2003): 1190–1205.

2. Jon R. Bond and Richard Fleisher, *The President in the Legislative Arena* (Chicago: University of Chicago Press, 1990), 31–32, 230; Cary R. Covington, J. Mark Wrighton, and Rhonda Kinney, "A 'Presidency-Augmented' Model of Presidential Success on House Roll Call Votes," *American Journal of Political Science* 39 (1995): 1001–24; Charles M. Cameron and Jee-Kwang Park, "A Primer on the President's Legislative Program," in *Presidential Leadership: The Vortex of Power*, ed. Bert A. Rockman and Richard W. Waterman (New York: Oxford University Press, 2008), 45–79; George C. Edwards III and Andrew Barrett, "Presidential Agenda Setting in Congress," in *Polarized Politics: Congress and the President in a Partisan Era*, ed. Jon R. Bond and Richard Fleisher (Washington, DC: CQ Press, 2000), 109–33; Paul C. Light, *The President's Agenda: Domestic Policy Choice from Kennedy to Carter* (Baltimore: Johns Hopkins University Press, 1982); Bryan W. Marshall and Brandon C. Prins, "Strategic Position Taking and Presidential Influence in Congress," *Legislative Studies Quarterly* 32 (2007): 257–84; Charles R. Shipan, "Does Divided Government Increase the Size of the Legislative Agenda?," in *The Macropolitics of Congress*, ed. E. Scott Adler and John S. Lapinski (Princeton, NJ: Princeton University Press, 2006), 151–71.

3. Matthew N. Beckmann, *Pushing the Agenda: Presidential Leadership in U.S. Lawmaking, 1953–2004* (New York: Cambridge University Press, 2010).

4. See Light, *President's Agenda*.

5. Bryan D. Jones and Frank R. Baumgartner, *The Politics of Attention: How Governments Prioritize Problems* (Chicago: University of Chicago Press, 2005).

6. However, the work of Baumgartner and Jones is aimed explicitly at the question of durability and change in agendas in general. Their research tends to focus on either policy subsystems or on governmental agendas in general, but not presidential agendas in much detail. See Baumgartner and Jones, *Agendas and Instability*; and Jones and Baumgartner, *Politics of Attention*.

7. Kingdon, *Agendas, Alternatives, and Public Policies*; Baumgartner and Jones, *Agendas and Instability*, 241.

8. Jones and Baumgartner, *Politics of Attention*.

9. Light, *President's Agenda*, 52–60.

10. Using decision-making terminology, assume that each issue presents the president with a benefit, B, but also costs, C. Benefits may be electoral, coalitional, etc., while costs include decision making (time, staff, information collection, etc.), transaction, and opportunity costs (i.e., allowing one issue onto the agenda may deny access to another, working on one issue will limit the time, etc., to work on another). Presidents calculate the relative net benefit (B – C) across issues and select issues with the highest net benefit until they have selected as many issues as they can deal with.

11. Charles O. Jones, *The Presidency in a Separated System* (Washington, DC: Brookings Institution Press, 1994), 164–68, quotation from p. 168.

12. Bryan D. Jones, Heather Larsen-Prince, and John Wilkerson, "Representation and American Governing Institutions," *Journal of Politics* 71 (2009): 277–90.

13. Brandice Canes-Wrone, *Who Leads Whom? Presidents, Policy, and the Public* (Chicago: University of Chicago Press, 2006); Cohen, *Presidential Responsiveness*; Light, *President's Agenda*.

14. Morris P. Fiorina, *Retrospective Voting in American National Elections* (New Haven, CT: Yale University Press, 1981); James A. Stimson, Michael B. MacKuen, and Robert S. Erikson, "Dynamic Representation," *American Political Science Review* 89 (1995): 543–65.

15. Patricia Conley, *Presidential Mandates: How Elections Shape the National Agenda* (Chicago: University of Chicago Press, 2001).

16. Bond and Fleisher, *President in the Legislative Arena*; Cameron and Park, "Primer on the President's Legislative Program"; Matthew Eshbaugh-Soha, "The Politics of Presidential Agendas," *Political Research Quarterly* 58 (2005): 257–68; Marshall and Prins, "Strategic Position Taking."

17. Cameron and Park, "Primer on the President's Legislative Program"; Keith Krehbiel, *Pivotal Politics* (Chicago: University of Chicago Press, 1998); Light, *President's Agenda*, 161–62. But see Mark A. Peterson, *Legislating Together: The White House and Capitol Hill from Eisenhower to Reagan* (Cam-

bridge, MA: Harvard University Press, 1990), who argues otherwise, that presidents do not calculate expected success in submitting legislation to Congress.

18. Richard E. Neustadt, *Presidential Power and the Modern Presidents* (New York: Free Press, 1990).

19. See Christopher R. Berry, Barry C. Burden, William G. Howell, "The Lives and Deaths of Federal Programs, 1971–2003," chap. 5 in this volume; Forrest Maltzman and Charles R. Shipan, "Beyond Legislative Productivity: Enactment Conditions, Subsequent Conditions, and the Shape and Life of the Law," chap. 6 in this volume.

20. Krehbiel, *Pivotal Politics*; David W. Brady and Craig Volden, *Revolving Gridlock: Politics and Policy from Carter to Clinton* (Boulder, CO: Westview Press, 1998).

21. We combined two data sets: the Presidential Request file of the Historical Congressional-Presidential Database for requests from 1789 through 1992 and an update of presidential requests, provided by Professor Andrew Rudalevige of Dickinson College, for 1993 through 2002. There are 14,188 total requests; private bills and requests that focus on District of Columbia are excluded, leaving 13,800. Because of data limitations for some key independent variables, the analysis focuses on proposals from 1799 through 2002.

22. See Ira Katznelson and John Lapinski, "The Substance of Representation: Studying Policy Content and Legislative Behavior," in Adler and Lapinski, *Macropolitics of Congress*, 90–126, for details on their coding scheme and its underlying conceptualization. Coders focused on the primary area in the president's request. Intercoder and other reliability statistics are available from the authors. Jones and Baumgartner, *Politics of Attention*, provide another coding scheme, but the KL framework is broader and includes more historical issues, such as Indian–Native American removal, national boundaries, and admission of states to the Union. The JB scheme was developed for post–World War II era policies and thus misses policies like these.

23. However, others argue that the institutionalization of the presidency, the foundation necessary for high levels of presidential legislative activity, was only set in place firmly in the late 1940s or early 1950s; Richard E. Neustadt, "Presidency and Legislation: The Growth of Central Clearance," *American Political Science Review* 48 (1954): 641–71; Richard E. Neustadt, "Presidency and Legislation: Planning the President's Program," *American Political Science Review* 49 (1955): 980–1021; Lester G. Seligman, "Presidential Leadership: The Inner Circle and Institutionalization," *Journal of Politics* 18 (1956): 410–26.

24. Rudalevige is very good in this regard. See Andrew Rudalevige, *Managing the President's Program: Presidential Leadership and Legislative Policy Formation* (Princeton, NJ: Princeton University Press, 2002).

25. Fred I. Greenstein, *Leadership and the Modern Presidency* (Cambridge, MA: Harvard University Press, 1988).

26. Here a "presidential agenda" consists of all proposals submitted during a natural, two-year Congress.

27. Adam Cohen, *Nothing to Fear: FDR's Inner Circle and the Hundred Days that Created Modern America* (New York: Penguin, 2009), 279.

28. Neustadt, "Presidency and Legislation: The Growth of Central Clearance"; Neustadt, "Presidency and Legislation: Planning the President's Program"; Seligman, "Presidential Leadership"; Rudalevige, *Managing the President's Program.*

29. Sidney M. Milkis and Michael Nelson, *The American Presidency: Origins and Development, 1776–1998* (Washington, DC: CQ Press, 1999).

30. The correlation between deleted and added issue areas is negative and statistically significant (Pearson's $r = -.32$, $p = .001$). The mean for deletions = 7.0 and the mean for additions = 7.3.

31. We average together these figures for the two years of a natural Congress to get these figures.

32. We also looked at a number of other indicators of political change: change in seat ratios in Congress, whether party control of Congress changed hands, and whether a new president of the same party as the previous party came to office. None proved to be statistically significant.

33. John R. Petrock, "Issue Ownership in Presidential Elections, with a 1980 Case Study," *American Journal of Political Science* 40 (1996): 825–50.

34. Tracy Sulkin, *Issue Politics in Congress* (New York: Cambridge University Press, 2005).

35. The wars are War of 1812, Mexican American, Civil War, Spanish American, World War I, World War II, Korea, and Vietnam. The Persian Gulf War is not included because of its brief duration.

36. We obtained these from EH.Net, maintained by Miami University and Wake Forest University at http://eh.net/hmit/. The interest rate series begins with 1799. As these data are annualized, we average across the two years of a Congress to get Congress specific measures.

37. The average of the first and second years in a Congress produces similar results. Economic indicators for the second year of a Congress, lagged, are not statistically significant.

38. The filibuster pivot is important because it reduces the effective range of policies that can beat the status quo by requiring a supermajority for passage.

39. Valerie Heitshusen and Garry Young, "Macropolitics and Changes in the U.S. Code: Testing Competing Theories of Policy Production," in Adler and Lapinski, *Macropolitics of Congress*, 129–50; Gregory J. Wawro and Eric Schickler, *Filibuster: Obstruction and Lawmaking in the U.S. Senate* (Princeton, NJ: Princeton University Press, 2006), 92–96.

40. The Augmented Dickey-Fuller test for Change, with a trend and a constant, reports a test statistic of -6.64 against a criterion value of -4.04 (.01 level).

For Stability, the Augmented Dickey-Fuller test, with a trend and constant term, produces a test statistic of -11.61 against a criterion value of -4.04 (.01 level).

41. Richard McCleary and Richard Hay, *Applied Time Series Analysis* (Beverly Hills, CA: Sage, 1980).

42. There are numerous other factors that could explain agenda durability and change, factors that could alter the story we tell here. First, the longer the president is in office, the more his agenda should reign and thus encourage greater durability and limit change. Second, the House and Senate could affect agenda durability and change differently, depending on which party is in control. If the president's party is in control, this may encourage agenda change. We coded time in office as a count of the number of years into the president's tenure and coded bicameral differences as a simple dummy variable for whether the president's party controls that house of Congress. We incorporated each in an alternative model specification, and none has a statistically significant impact on either change or durability.

43. Jones, *Presidency in a Separated System*.

44. For a classic statement, see Gregory L. Hager and Terry Sullivan, "President-Centered and Presidency-Centered Explanations of Presidential Public Activity," *American Journal of Political Science* 38 (1994): 1079–1103, who find support more for the presidency than president perspective. But see Matthew Eshbaugh-Soha, "Presidential Press Conferences over Time," *American Journal of Political Science* 47 (2003): 348–53, who finds support for the president perspective.

45. See, e.g., Greenstein, *Leadership and the Modern Presidency*.

46. Andrew W. Barrett and Matthew Eshbaugh-Soha, "Presidential Success on the Substance of Legislation," *Political Research Quarterly* 60 (2007): 100–112.

Chapter Four

1. David R. Mayhew, *Divided We Govern: Party Control, Lawmaking, and Investigations, 1946–1990* (New Haven, CT: Yale University Press, 1991).

2. See, e.g., ibid.; Sean Q. Kelly, "Divided We Govern? A Reassessment," *Polity* 25 (1993): 475–84; George C. Edwards III, Andrew Barrett, and Jeffrey Peake, "The Legislative Impact of Divided Government," *American Journal of Political Science* 41 (1997): 545–63; Gregory R. Thorson, "Divided Government and the Passage of Partisan Legislation, 1947–1990," *Political Research Quarterly* 51 (1998): 751–64; John J. Coleman, "Unified Government, Divided Government, and Party Responsiveness," *American Political Science Review* 93 (1999): 821–35; Sarah A. Binder, "The Dynamics of Legislative Gridlock, 1947–96," *American Political Science Review* 93 (1999): 519–33; William Howell, Scott

Adler, Charles Cameron, and Charles Riemann, "Divided Government and the Legislative Productivity of Congress, 1945–94," *Legislative Studies Quarterly* 25 (2000): 285–312; Sarah A. Binder, *Stalemate: Causes and Consequences of Legislative Gridlock* (Washington, DC: Brookings Institution Press, 2003); David R. Mayhew, *Divided We Govern: Party Control, Lawmaking, and Investigations, 1946–2002*, 2nd ed. (New Haven, CT: Yale University Press, 2005).

3. See, e.g., David P. Baron and John Ferejohn, "Bargaining in Legislatures," *American Political Science Review* 83 (1989): 1181–1206; Craig Volden and Alan E. Wiseman, "Bargaining in Legislatures over Particularistic and Collective Goods," *American Political Science Review* 101 (2007): 71–92.

4. See, e.g., Keith Krehbiel, *Pivotal Politics: A Theory of U.S. Lawmaking* (Chicago: University of Chicago Press, 1998); Charles M. Cameron, *Veto Bargaining: Presidents and the Politics of Negative Power* (Cambridge: Cambridge University Press, 2000).

5. Krehbiel, *Pivotal Politics*.

6. Binder, "Dynamics of Legislative Gridlock"; Binder, *Stalemate*.

7. Stephen W. Stathis, *Landmark Legislation, 1774–2002* (Washington, DC: CQ Press, 2002).

8. The Stathis data include major acts and treaties. We focus only on major acts in this chapter.

9. William Shadish, Donald Campbell, and Thomas Cook, *Experimental and Quasi-Experimental Designs for Generalized Causal Inference* (Boston: Houghton Mifflin, 2002).

10. See, e.g., Joshua D. Clinton and John S. Lapinski, "Measuring Legislative Accomplishment, 1877–1994," *American Journal of Political Science* 50 (2006): 232–49.

11. Studies that apply the Stathis data to various other law-related questions include Anna Harvey and Barry Friedman, "Ducking Trouble: Congressionally-Induced Selection Bias in the Supreme Court's Agenda" *Journal of Politics* 71 (2009): 574–92; Anthony J. Madonna, "Institutions and Coalition Formation: Revisiting the Effects of Rule XXII on Winning Coalition Sizes in the U.S. Senate," *American Journal of Political Science* 55 (2011): 276–88; Keith E. Whittington and Tom C. Clark, "Ideology, Partisanship, and Judicial Review of Acts of Congress, 1789–2006" (typescript, Princeton University, 2007).

12. We include party system indicators because there may be mean shifts in legislative productivity in each system that are not captured by a time trend, but that might be correlated with the mean time a party spends out of power or unified government.

13. The conversion between Congresses and years is $1787 + 2*(\text{Congress \#})$. So, for example, the first year of the fifth party system (1933) corresponds to the 73rd Congress: $1933 = 1787 + 2*73$.

14. Because the party system indicator variables are roughly speaking time dummies, it may seem redundant to include both the time trend and the party system indicators. Therefore, we also estimated the model without the time trend. We exclude the results for brevity, but for the coalition structure variables they are essentially indistinguishable from the results reported in table 4.1. The main difference is that with the time trend excluded, each party system appears more productive than its predecessors because of the time trend in the major acts data. This seems spurious so we prefer the specification reported in table 4.1 with both the party system dummies and the time trend.

15. We comment below on results from a negative binomial model of this count data, and simply note for the moment that the negative binomial results are very similar to the OLS results.

16. We prefer OLS with a standard error correction for a non-IID error process over a GLS estimator for serially correlated data such as Prais-Winsten because the former gives unbiased estimates of model coefficients even if the model of the error process is incorrect, whereas the latter is at best consistent, and only if the error correlation is modeled correctly.

17. Krehbiel, *Pivotal Politics*.

18. A Poisson model is rejected because the conditional variance of the dependent variable exceeds the mean.

19. Nolan McCarty, "The Policy Effects of Political Polarization," in *The Transformation of American Politics: Activist Government and the Rise of Conservatism*, ed. Paul Pierson and Theda Skocpol (Princeton, NJ: Princeton University Press, 2007), 223–55. For his main analysis, McCarty uses data from Mayhew, *Divided We Govern*, 2nd ed. For robustness checks, McCarty incorporates data from Howell et al., "Divided Government"; R. Eric Petersen, "Is It Science Yet? Replicating and Validating the *Divided We Govern* List of Important Statutes" (paper presented at the Annual Meeting of the Midwest Political Science Association, Chicago, IL, 2001); and Clinton and Lapinski, "Measuring Legislative Accomplishment."

20. The data source for this time series is "Congressional Bills and Resolutions: 1789–2000," contributed by John P. McIver, *Historical Statistics of the United States*, Millennial Edition Online, ed. Susan B. Carter, Scott S. Gartner, Michael R. Haines, Alan L. Olmstead, Richard Sutch, and Gavin Wright (Cambridge: Cambridge University Press, 2006).

21. Joseph A. Schumpeter, *Capitalism, Socialism, and Democracy* (New York: Harper, 1942).

22. Even restricting attention to 1932 and later, the post-1969 period has witnessed many more amendments on average; in this range of years the t statistic on the pre- and post-1969 difference is 9.43.

23. The null hypothesis of the Poisson model that the conditional mean equals the conditional variance is rejected at the .01 level in a likelihood ratio test.

24. Logit and linear probability (OLS) models yield essentially the same qualitative findings.

25. This is substantively similar to the estimated marginal effect in a logit and linear probability (OLS) model with Newey-West standard errors.

26. While outside the scope of this study, future work on coalition structure and lawmaking might extend beyond the spatial modeling (pivotal politics) approach and consider alternative theoretical accounts. A behavioral model, for example, might suggest that a burst of legislative activity provokes, over time, a reaction among the public so that the public mood, which might have initially been quite favorable to the governing coalition, turns against its policy aims. See, e.g., Robert S. Erikson, Michael B. Mackuen, and James A. Stimson, *The Macro Polity* (Cambridge: Cambridge University Press, 2002). Alternatively, a historical-institutional model might predict that more legislative success is achieved at the earliest moments of a new policy regime because those moments tend to represent a break with the previous regime; over time, however, presidents and their adherents become increasingly constrained by the gradual accretion of policy commitments. See, e.g., Stephen Skowronek, *The Politics Presidents Make: Leadership from John Adams to George Bush* (Cambridge, MA: Harvard University Press, 1993).

27. Forrest Maltzman and Charles R. Shipan, "Beyond Legislative Productivity: Enactment Conditions, Subsequent Conditions, and the Shape and Life of the Law," chap. 6 in this volume; Christopher R. Berry, Barry C. Burden, and William G. Howell, "The Lives and Deaths of Federal Programs, 1971–2003," chap. 5 in this volume.

Chapter Five

1. Harold Lasswell, *Politics: Who Gets What, When, and How* (Cleveland: Meridian, 1936).

2. Jon R. Bond and Richard Fleisher, *The President in the Legislative Arena* (Chicago: University of Chicago Press, 1990); George C. Edwards III, *At the Margins: Presidential Leadership in Congress* (New Haven, CT: Yale University Press, 1989); John Frendreis, Raymond Tatlovich, and Jon Schaff, "Predicting Legislative Output in the First One-Hundred Days," *Political Research Quarterly* 54 (2001): 853–70; Andrew Rudalevige, *Managing the President's Program: Presidential Leadership and Legislative Policy Formation* (Princeton, NJ: Princeton University Press, 2002).

3. Sarah A. Binder, *Stalemate: Causes and Consequences of Legislative Gridlock* (Washington, DC: Brookings Institution Press, 2003); Joshua D. Clinton, "Lawmaking and Roll Calls," *Journal of Politics* 69 (2007): 455–67; Joshua D. Clinton and John S. Lapinski, "Measuring Legislative Accomplishment, 1877–

1994," *American Journal of Political Science* 50 (2006): 232–49; Keith Krehbiel, *Pivotal Politics: A Theory of U.S. Lawmaking* (Chicago: University of Chicago Press, 1998).

4. John H. Coleman, "Unified Government, Divided Government, and Party Responsiveness," *American Political Science Review* 93 (1999): 821–35; William Howell, Scott Adler, Charles Cameron, and Charles Riemann, "Divided Government and the Legislative Productivity of Congress, 1945–94," *Legislative Studies Quarterly* 25 (2000): 285–312; Sean Q. Kelly, "Divided We Govern? A Reassessment," *Polity* 25 (1993): 475–84; David R. Mayhew, *Divided We Govern*, 2nd ed. (New Haven, CT: Yale University Press, 2005).

5. Brandice Canes-Wrone, William G. Howell, and David E. Lewis, "Toward a Broader Understanding of Presidential Power: A Reevaluation of the Two Presidencies Thesis," *Journal of Politics* 70 (2008): 1–16; Jeffrey E. Cohen, "A Historical Reassessment of Wildavsky's 'Two Presidencies' Thesis," *Social Science Quarterly* 63 (1982): 549–55; George C. Edwards III, "The Two Presidencies: A Reevaluation," *American Politics Quarterly* 14 (1986): 247–63; Brandon Prins and Bryan Marshall, "Congressional Support of the President: A Comparison of Foreign, Defense, and Domestic Policy Making during and after the Cold War," *Presidential Studies Quarterly* 31 (2001): 660–78; Aaron Wildavsky, "The Two Presidencies," *Trans-Action* 4 (1966): 7–14.

6. Eugene Bardach, *The Implementation Game: What Happens after a Bill Becomes a Law* (Cambridge, MA: MIT Press, 1977).

7. For reviews, see James P. Lester, Ann O'M. Bowman, Malcolm L. Goggin, and Laurence J. O'Toole Jr., "Public Policy Implementation: Evolution of the Field and Agenda for Future Research," *Review of Policy Research* 7 (2002): 200–16; Laurence J. O'Toole Jr., "Research on Policy Implementation: Assessment and Prospects," *Journal of Public Administration and Theory* 10 (2000): 263–88.

8. But see Eric Patashnik, *Reforms at Risk: What Happens after Major Policy Changes Are Enacted* (Princeton, NJ: Princeton University Press, 2008).

9. Joshua D. Clinton and John S. Lapinski, "Measuring Significant Legislation, 1877–1948," in *Process, Party, and Policymaking: Further New Perspectives on the History of Congress, Volume 2*, ed. David W. Brady and Matthew D. McCubbins (Palo Alto: Stanford University Press, 2007), 361–78; Clinton and Lapinski, "Measuring Legislative Accomplishment"; Mayhew, *Divided We Govern*.

10. Rui J. P. de Figueiredo, "Electoral Competition, Political Uncertainty, and Policy Insulation," *American Political Science Review* 96 (2002): 321–33; Terry M. Moe, "The Politics of Bureaucratic Structure," in *Can the Government Govern?*, ed. John E. Chubb and Paul E. Peterson (Washington, DC: Brookings Institution Press, 1989), 267–329.

11. Eric Patashnik, "After the Public Interest Prevails: The Political Sustainability of Policy Reform," *Governance* 16 (2003): 204; see also Patashnik, *Reforms at Risk*.

12. Patashnik, "After the Public Interest Prevails," 226.

13. Janet E. Frantz, "Reviving and Revising a Termination Model," *Policy Sciences* 25, no. 2 (1992): 175–89; Keith J. Mueller, "Federal Programs to Expire: The Case of Health Planning," *Public Administration Review* 48 (1988): 719–25; Robert Behn, "Closing the Massachusetts Training Schools," *Policy Sciences* 7 (1976): 151–71.

14. Herbert Kaufman, *Are Governmental Organizations Immortal?* (Washington, DC: Brookings Institution Press, 1976).

15. Ibid., 64.

16. See Stephen Coate and Stephen Morris, "Policy Persistence," *American Economic Review* 89 (1999): 1327; Mark R. Daniels, *Terminating Public Programs: An American Political Paradox* (Armonk, NY: M. E. Sharpe, 1997), 5.

17. Peter deLeon, "Public Policy Termination: An End and a Beginning," *Policy Analysis* 4 (1978): 369–92.

18. Herbert Kaufman, *Time, Chance, and Organizations: Natural Selection in a Perilous Environment*, 2nd ed. (Upper Saddle River, NJ: Pearson, 1995), 67.

19. Kevin J. Corder, "Are Federal Programs Immortal? Estimating the Hazard of Program Termination," *American Politics Research* 32 (2004): 3–25; David E. Lewis, "The Politics of Agency Termination: Confronting the Myth of Agency Immortality," *Journal of Politics* 64 (2002): 89–107.

20. Kenneth N. Bickers, "The Programmatic Expansion of the U.S. Government," *Western Political Quarterly* 44 (1991): 891–914.

21. Robert M. Stein and Kenneth N. Bickers, *Perpetuating the Pork Barrel: Policy Subsystems and American Democracy* (New York: Cambridge University Press, 1995).

22. Forrest Maltzman and Charles R. Shipan, "Change, Continuity, and the Evolution of the Law," *American Journal of Political Science* 52 (2008): 252–67; Forrest Maltzman and Charles R. Shipan, "Beyond Legislative Productivity: Enactment Conditions, Subsequent Conditions, and the Shape and Life of the Law," chap. 6 in this volume; Alison E. Post and Paul Pierson, "How a Law Stays a Law: The Durability of U.S. Tax Breaks, 1967–2003" (paper presented at the Annual Meeting of the American Political Science Association, Washington, DC, 2005); Jordan M. Ragusa, "The Lifecycle of Public Policy: An Event History Analysis of Repeals to Landmark Legislative Enactments, 1951–2006," *American Politics Research* 38 (2010): 1015–51; Daniel P. Carpenter and David E. Lewis, "Political Learning from Rare Events: Poisson Inference, Fiscal Constraints, and the Lifetime of Bureaus," *Political Analysis* 12 (2004): 201–32; Lewis, "Politics of Agency Termination."

23. Maltzman and Shipan, "Change, Continuity, and the Evolution of the Law"; Post and Pierson, "How a Law Stays a Law."

24. Carpenter and Lewis, "Political Learning from Rare Events."

25. Recognizing that programs may be transferred to another agency when

the original agency is terminated, Carpenter and Lewis recommend that scholars turn their attention to programs rather than agencies. As they put it, "focusing on the termination of government programs or responsibilities as opposed to bureaus or agencies may be a more fruitful avenue for future research." Ibid., 226. Moreover, as Carpenter demonstrates elsewhere, tremendous programmatic innovation can take place within agencies even when their institutional structure appears to be unchanged. See Daniel P. Carpenter, *The Forging of Bureaucratic Autonomy: Reputations, Networks, and Policy Innovation in Executive Agencies, 1862–1928* (Princeton, NJ: Princeton University Press, 2001).

26. Paul Pierson, *Politics in Time: History, Institutions, and Social Analysis* (Princeton, NJ: Princeton University Press, 2004).

27. Ibid.; Kathleen Thelen, *How Institutions Evolve: The Political Economy of Skills in Germany, Britain, the United States, and Japan* (New York: Cambridge University Press, 2004).

28. Eric Schickler, *Disjointed Pluralism: Institutional Innovation and the Development of the U.S. Congress* (Princeton, NJ: Princeton University Press, 2001).

29. Scott James, "Historical Institutionalism, Political Development, and the Presidency," in *The Oxford Handbook of the American Presidency*, ed. George Edwards and William Howell (New York: Oxford University Press, 2009), 54.

30. Whether by examining the number of districts that receive aid from individual programs (Stein and Bickers, *Perpetuating the Pork Barrel*), or the overall dollars that districts receive from all federal programs (Christopher R. Berry, Barry C. Burden, and William G. Howell, "The President and the Distribution of Federal Spending," *American Political Science Review* 104 [2010]: 783–99), the distribution of federal programmatic benefits does not conform to basic notions of universalism. In 2003, for instance, the programs examined in this chapter distributed aid to an average of ninety-two different House districts, with a standard deviation of 107. Our approach nonetheless permits some programs to be created by large coalitions. The natural variation in coalition size at enactment may explain some of the variation in durability.

31. Steven Levitt and James D. Snyder, "Political Parties and the Distribution of Federal Outlays," *American Journal of Political Science* 39 (1995): 958–80.

32. Brandice Canes-Wrone, David Brady, and John Cogan, "Out of Step, Out of Office: Electoral Accountability and House Members' Voting," *American Political Science Review* 96 (2002): 127–40.

33. Carpenter, *Forging of Bureaucratic Autonomy*.

34. Bryan D. Jones, Tracy Sulkin, and Heather A. Larsen, "Policy Punctuations in American Political Institutions," *American Political Science Review* 97 (2003): 151–69.

35. John W. Kingdon, *Agendas, Alternatives, and Public Policies*, 2nd ed. (Upper Saddle River, NJ: Pearson Education, 1995).

36. John B. Gilmour and David E. Lewis. "Does Performance Budget-

ing Work? An Examination of the Office of Management and Budget's PART Scores," *Public Administration Review* 66 (2006): 742–52.

37. Kaufman, *Time, Chance, and Organizations.*

38. As noted in the CFDA, "a 'Federal Domestic Assistance Program' may in practice be called a program, an activity, a service, a project, a process, or some other name, regardless of whether it is identified as a separate program by statute or regulation" (CFDA 2005, I). The *Catalog* is published by the General Services Administration. The current edition is available online at https: //www .cfda.gov.

39. CFDA 2005, I.

40. Specifically, "Assistance includes, but is not limited to grants, loans, loan guarantees, scholarships, mortgage loans, insurance, and other types of financial assistance, including cooperative agreements; property, technical assistance, counseling, statistical, and other expert information; and service activities of regulatory agencies" (CFDA 2005, I). Military spending and defense procurement programs are not included. In addition, the *Catalog* excludes foreign activities of the federal government, procurement for goods and services used by the federal government itself, and the activities of quasi-governmental entities such as the U.S. Postal Service and Fannie Mae.

41. Any given authorization, though, may establish more than one program.

42. Bickers, "Programmatic Expansion of the U.S. Government"; Kenneth N. Bickers and Robert M. Stein, *Federal Domestic Outlays, 1983–1990: A Data Book* (Armonk, NY: M. E. Sharpe, 1991); Stein and Bickers, *Perpetuating the Pork Barrel.*

43. For example, see Robert C. Lowry and Mathew Potoski, "Organized Interests and the Politics of Federal Discretionary Grants," *Journal of Politics* 66 (2004): 513–33.

44. The fate of each program in each year is reported in the following year's CFDA. Hence, to update the data through 2003, we relied on editions of the CFDA through 2004.

45. There are instances when programs mutate or die in one year only to be reborn in another. The hazard models estimated below account for this eventuality. Mutations and deaths, as defined here, could in principle be treated as competing events, recommending the estimation of a competing hazard or multi-episode model (see Hans-Peter Blossfeld, Aldred Hamerle, and Karl Mayer, *Event History Analysis: Statistical Theory and Application in the Social Sciences* [Hillsdale, NJ: Lawrence Erlbaum, 1989], 57–64, 75–79). For three reasons, however, this is not feasible. First, conventional multi-episode models have well-defined units—tracking, for instance, individual transitions into and out of full employment, partial employment, and unemployment. Mutations, though, typically involve consolidations and splits of programs, which wreak havoc on this underlying assumption. Second, and related, mutations in our data are treated

as terminal nodes. While we can identify the exact year when a program transitioned states, we do not know how long it remained in the latter. The final issue concerns the definition of an episode. Though a mutation signifies an important change in a program's structure, there does not exist a clear and finite set of episodes in and out of which programs transition.

46. Specifically, the graph presents the estimated hazard functions using a kernel density smoother.

47. One might be tempted to infer that the higher frequency of mutations and deaths in the first decade of a program's life is the result of preprogrammed sunsets, demonstration programs with short lives, or expired authorizations. But this appears not to be the case. Though the role of sunset provisions in program demise warrants further inquiry, we have no reason to believe that the omission of this factor threatens the validity of our analyses. Because partisan seat change results from inherently unpredictable election outcomes that occur after sunset provisions are in place, the two variables should be uncorrelated, and therefore omitted variable bias of this sort is not a concern for the models presented below. Future work on sunset provisions, though, might test for temporal discontinuities in the hazard, as discussed in Daniel P. Carpenter et al., "Deadline Effects in Regulatory Drug Review: A Methodological and Empirical Analysis" (unpublished manuscript, 2008).

48. Our data are never left censored, since we are considering only those programs that were created after 1971. The data, however, are right censored whenever programs either continue beyond 2003 or mutate since they can no longer be tracked. Our maximum likelihood estimates account for this right censoring.

49. Our approach of linking each program to the Congress that enacted it is akin to the common practice among judicial scholars of inferring the ideological orientation of justices from the partisan identification of the president who appointed them. An ideal approach might be to tie programs to the actual legislators who voted for their creation on the floor of the legislature, but this approach is impossible to implement. Programs are seldom created in one clean action such that supportive legislators can be identified. They are often embedded in larger pieces of legislation and then modified over time as parts of other legislative packages.

50. In the main models presented, we average the percentage gains and losses experienced by a majority party from the enacting to the current House and Senate. In some instances, the majority party may be different in the two chambers. As we discuss below, we also estimate separate models for each chamber.

51. Stein and Bickers, *Perpetuating the Pork Barrel*. Full descriptions of the funding schemes are available at http://www.polsci.indiana.edu/faad/codebook .txt. Categories are not mutually exclusive, so none of the dummy variables is excluded from the models.

52. GDP data were provided by the Bureau of Economic Analysis in the De-

partment of Commerce and are available at http://www.bea.gov/national/index
.htm#gdp.

53. As an alternative economic measure, one might include the federal budget balance under the assumption that large deficits tend to dampen spending
and surpluses would encourage it. We do not use this measure because of its en-
dogeneity with appropriations; spending is as likely to affect deficits as to be affected by them.

54. We identify the Vietnam War (though 1975), the Gulf War (1991), and the
conflicts in Afghanistan and Iraq (2002 onward).

55. This measure identifies whether either the House or the Senate is controlled by the opposite party as the president's. The core findings remain intact
when we focus on just the House or the Senate.

56. James A. Stimson, *Tides of Consent: How Public Opinion Shapes American Politics* (New York: Cambridge University Press, 2004).

57. Patricia Grambsch and Terry Therneau, "Proportional Hazards Tests
and Diagnostics on Weighted Residuals," *Biometrika* 81, no. 3 (1994): 515–26.
That is, rather than estimating the standard Cox proportional model specified
as $\lambda(t \mid x) = \lambda_0(t) \exp(B^t x)$, where $\lambda_0(t)$ identifies the baseline hazard, x is a vector of covariates, and B^t is a vector of coefficients, we instead estimate $\lambda(t \mid x) =
\lambda_0(t) \exp(B^t(t)x)$, where $B^t(t)$ now is a function of follow-up time. We lack strong
theory about the appropriate characterization of this function, and therefore we
have estimated a variety of specifications. The main results appear consistent
across these models. For ease of interpretation, we therefore focus on the results
from a linear representation. For more on the applications of nonproportional
hazard models in political science, see Janet M. Box-Steffensmeier, Dan Reiter,
and Christopher Zorn, "Nonproportional Hazards and Event History Analysis
in International Relations," *Journal of Conflict Resolution* 47 (2003): 33–53.

58. We note, however, that when dropping from the model the congressional
turnover variables, the effect of partisan change in the president appears positive and significant. Dropping the president variable does not alter the estimated
effects of congressional turnover.

59. We are hesitant, however, to make very much of this finding. When estimating models that include only measures of congressional turnover or only
measures of presidential turnover, we do not find any evidence that proportionality assumptions have been violated.

60. Because programs can belong to more than one of these categories, there
is no reference group.

61. We use appropriations rather than outlays as our spending measure. The
rationale for this approach is that Congress focuses its budgetary activity on setting appropriations levels, which are thought to be closely tied to actual spending
levels. Our statistical results below are actually stronger if we substitute actual

outlays as the dependent variable. All dollar amounts are measured in inflation-adjusted 2000 dollars.

62. The models below include only a linear expression of age. We have estimated models that include quadratic and cubed terms, though these variables are never statistically significant.

63. When adding to the model an interaction between change in the party of the president and a program's age, the main effect for presidential turnover is -0.08 ($p = .18$) and the interaction is 0.01 ($p = .02$), suggesting a modest initial decline in spending that fades over time. We do not find evidence, however, of a meaningful interaction between a program's age and measures of congressional turnover.

64. Steven D. Levitt and James M. Snyder Jr., "The Impact of Federal Spending on House Election Outcomes," *Journal of Political Economy* 105, no. 1 (1997): 30–53.

65. Stimson, *Tides of Consent*; Christopher Wlezien, "The Public as Thermostat: Dynamics of Preferences for Spending," *American Journal of Political Science* 39 (1995): 981–1000.

66. Robert S. Erikson, Michael B. MacKuen, and James A. Stimson, *The Macro Polity* (New York: Cambridge University Press, 2002).

Chapter Six

1. Christopher R. Berry, Barry C. Burden, and William G. Howell, "The Lives and Deaths of Federal Programs, 1971–2003," chap. 5 of this volume; Terry M. Moe, "The Politics of Bureaucratic Structure," in *Can the Government Govern?*, ed. John E. Chubb and Paul E. Peterson (Washington, DC: Brookings Institution Press, 1989), 267–329; Eric M. Patashnik, "After the Public Interest Prevails: The Political Sustainability of Policy Reform," *Governance* 16 (2003): 203–34; Eric M. Patashnik, *Putting Trust in the U.S. Budget: Federal Trust Funds and the Politics of Commitment* (New York: Cambridge University Press, 2000).

2. See Berry, Burden, and Howell, "Lives and Deaths of Federal Programs"; Eric M. Patashnik, "Why Some Reforms Last and Others Collapse: The Tax Reform Act of 1986 versus Airline Deregulation," chap. 8 in this volume; and David E. Lewis, "Policy Durability and Agency Design," chap. 9 in this volume. In addition, see David E. Lewis, "The Adverse Consequences of the Politics of Agency Design for Presidential Management in the United States: The Relative Durability of Insulated Agencies," *British Journal of Political Science* 34 (2004): 377–404; Patashnik, "After the Public Interest Prevails."

3. Paul Pierson, "Public Policies as Institutions" (paper presented at the Yale Conference on Crafting and Operating Institutions, New Haven, CT, 2003), 2–3.

4. Sean Q. Kelly, "Divided We Govern? A Reassessment," *Polity* 25 (1993): 475–84; Eric M. Patashnik, *Reforms at Risk: What Happens after Major Policy Changes are Enacted* (Princeton, NJ: Princeton University Press, 2008); Patashnik, *Putting Trust in the U.S. Budget.*

5. William Landes and Richard A. Posner, "The Independent Judiciary in an Interest-Group Perspective," *Journal of Law and Economics* 18 (1975): 875–911; see also Mathew D. McCubbins, Roger G. Noll, and Barry R. Weingast, "Structure and Process, Politics and Policy: Administrative Arrangements and the Political Control of Agencies," *Virginia Law Review* 75 (1989), 431–82.

6. Sarah A. Binder and Steven S. Smith, *Politics or Principle?* (Washington, DC: Brookings Institution Press, 1996); David Brady and Craig Volden, *Revolving Gridlock* (Boulder, CO: Westview Press, 1998); Keith Krehbiel, *Pivotal Politics* (Chicago: University of Chicago Press, 1998).

7. Rui J. P. de Figueiredo, "Electoral Competition, Political Uncertainty, and Policy Insulation," *American Political Science Review* 96 (2002): 321–33; John Ferejohn and Charles Shipan, "Congressional Influence on Bureaucracy," *Journal of Law, Economics and Organization* 6 (1990): 1–21; George Tsebelis, *Veto Players* (Princeton, NJ: Princeton University Press, 2002).

8. Sarah A. Binder, *Stalemate: Causes and Consequences of Legislative Gridlock* (Washington, DC: Brookings Institution Press, 2003); George Tsebelis and Jeanette Money, *Bicameralism* (New York: Cambridge University Press, 1997).

9. Patashnik, *Putting Trust in the U.S. Budget.*

10. Lewis, "Adverse Consequences."

11. Jacob S. Hacker and Paul Pierson, "Business Power and Social Policy: Employers and the Formation of the American Welfare State," *Politics and Society* 30 (2002): 277–35; Jacob S. Hacker, *The Divided Welfare State* (New York: Cambridge University Press, 2002).

12. See *Campaign Finance Reform: Hearings before Senate Comm. on Rules and Administration*, 106th Cong., May 17, 2000 (testimony of Spencer Abraham, U.S. Senator).

13. William Saletan, "The Money Jungle," *Slate*, March 22, 2001, http://slate.msn.com/id/102994.

14. See Scott E. Adler and John S. Lapinski, *The Macropolitics of Congress* (Princeton, NJ: Princeton University Press, 2006). Recent studies are also paying renewed attention to the policy content of legislation. See in particular Scott E. Adler, Michael Berry, Cherie Maestas, and John Wilkerson, "The Politics of Legislative Specialization: Issues and Considerations in Measurement, 96th–105th Congresses" (paper presented at the 2005 Annual Meeting of the Midwest Political Science Association, Chicago, IL, 2005).

15. See Binder, *Stalemate*; John J. Coleman, "Unified Government, Divided Government, and Party Responsiveness," *American Political Science Review* 93 (1999): 821–36; William Howell, Scott Adler, Charles Cameron, and Charles

Riemann, "Divided Government and the Legislative Productivity of Congress, 1945–94," *Legislative Studies Quarterly* 25 (2000): 285–312; David R. Mayhew, *Divided We Govern: Party Control, Lawmaking, and Investigations, 1946–2002*, 2nd ed. (New Haven, CT: Yale University Press, 2005).

16. William A. Niskanen, "A Case for Divided Government," *Cato Policy Report*, March/April 2003, 2.

17. See James Sundquist, "Needed: A Political Theory for the New Era of Coalition Government in the United States," *Political Science Quarterly* 103 (1988): 613–15.

18. Mayhew, *Divided We Govern*, 180.

19. Richard H. K. Vietor, *Energy Policy in America since 1945* (New York: Cambridge University Press, 1984).

20. Kent R. Weaver, *Automatic Government* (Washington, DC: Brookings Institution Press, 1988).

21. Sunset provisions can be viewed as either a causal factor that affects legislative durability or as a byproduct of legislative fragmentation. Our own view is closer to the latter—that is, these and other similar sorts of provisions are likely to be caused by the same factors that also determine legislative durability. Still, because sunset provisions certainly can represent attempts by legislators to increase the probability of significant revision, in our empirical analysis we will account for the effects of such provisions.

22. John D. Huber and Charles R. Shipan, *Deliberate Discretion?* (New York: Cambridge University Press, 2002); John D. Huber, Charles R. Shipan, and Madelaine Pfahler, "Legislatures and Statutory Control of Bureaucracy," *American Journal of Political Science* 45 (2001): 330–45; David Epstein and Sharyn O'Halloran, *Delegating Powers* (New York: Cambridge University Press, 1999).

23. See Thomas H. Hammond and Gary J. Miller, "The Core of the Constitution," *American Political Science Review* 81 (1987): 1155–77; Tsebelis and Money, *Bicameralism*.

24. Binder, *Stalemate*; Tsebelis, *Veto Players*.

25. Coleman, "Unified Government"; Howell et al., "Divided Government and Legislative Productivity"; Kelly, "Divided We Govern?"

26. Coleman "Unified Government"; Mayhew, *Divided We Govern*; James A. Stimson, *Public Opinion in America* (Boulder, CO: Westview Press, 1991).

27. Mayhew, *Divided We Govern*, 163.

28. John Kingdon, *Agendas, Alternatives, and Public Policies* (Boston: Little Brown, 1984), 153.

29. Jeb Barnes, *Overruled? Legislative Overrides, Pluralism, and Contemporary Court-Congress Relations* (Stanford, CA: Stanford University Press, 2004); William N. Eskridge Jr., "Overriding Supreme Court Statutory Interpretation Decisions," *Georgetown Law Review* 101 (1991): 331–455; George I. Lovell, *Legislative Deferrals* (Cambridge: Cambridge University Press, 2003); Charles R.

Shipan, "The Legislative Design of Judicial Review: A Formal Analysis," *Journal of Theoretical Politics* 12 (2000): 269–304; Joseph L. Smith, "Judicial Procedures as Instruments of Political Control: Congress' Strategic Use of Citizen Suits," *Legislative Studies Quarterly* 31 (2006): 283–305.

30. Lori Hausegger and Lawrence Baum, "Inviting Congressional Action: A Study of Supreme Court Motivations in Statutory Interpretation," *American Journal of Political Science* 43 (1999): 162–185; Theodore J. Lowi, "American Business, Public Policy, Case Studies, and Political Theory," *World Politics* 16 (1964): 677–715.

31. Complexity could, of course, be considered another aspect of the conditions at enactment, as the complexity of a law is determined at the time of enactment. Unlike divided government and interchamber agreement, however, complexity is not a specific feature of the political landscape during enactment, but varies by law, which is why we consider it here.

32. We begin our analysis with 1954 since the data we use to create two of our independent variables (judicial intervention and public mood) are not available prior to 1953. Nineteen treaties, resolutions, and proposed constitutional amendments that appeared on Mayhew's list were dropped from our analysis since they could not be amended after passage. We also dropped four bills—the Alaska and Hawaii statehood laws, the 1996 omnibus rescission bill, and the 2000 act normalizing relations with China—that could not have been amended after adoption because their primary purpose was completed on adoption. Finally, we independently went through the list and eliminated laws that technically were unlikely to be amended because they either authorized a public works project (such as the St. Lawrence Seaway Act of 1954) or were designed to address a temporary condition (e.g., the 1975 New York City bailout). In total, there were six additional "one-shot" laws. Elsewhere, we demonstrate that neither of these screens has a meaningful impact on our findings. See Forrest Maltzman and Charles R. Shipan, "Change, Continuity, and the Evolution of the Law," *American Journal of Political Science* 52 (2008): 252–67.

33. Mayhew's list excludes extensions and reauthorizations that "seemed to me [Mayhew] to offer little new" (Mayhew, *Divided We Govern*, 40). Although our decision to exclude amendments that did not make the Mayhew list establishes an admittedly high bar, it is a threshold that was established by Mayhew and his sources without consideration of the political conditions that created the underlying law. It also eliminates inconsequential amendments, which occur for virtually every law. If we treated every law (including inconsequential laws) that altered any provision of the underlying law as an amendment, our principal findings regarding the importance of enacting coalitions are, not surprisingly, not sustained.

34. Our statistical approach required us to drop the few laws that were amended during the same year that they were enacted.

35. Janet Box-Steffensmeier and Bradford S. Jones, "Time Is of the Essence: Event History Models in Political Science," *American Journal of Political Science* 41 (1997): 1414–61. We estimated the model using Stata 8.0's *stcox* routine and cluster by law.

36. For a description of the Binder measure, see Binder, *Stalemate*. For a discussion of alternative measures, see Maltzman and Shipan, "Change, Continuity, and the Evolution of the Law"; Michael A. Bailey, "Comparable Preference Estimates across Time and Institutions for the Court, Congress, and Presidency," *American Journal of Political Science* 51 (2007): 433–48; Sarah A. Binder, "Taking the Measure of Congress: Reply to Chiou and Rothenberg," *Political Analysis* 16 (2008): 213–25; Fang-Yi Chiou and Lawrence S. Rothenberg, "Comparing Legislators and Legislatures: The Dynamics of Legislative Gridlock Reconsidered," *Political Analysis* 16 (2008): 197–212.

37. For example, if a law was passed in 1974 and then amended in 1979, the *Subsequent divided government* variable would take on a value of 1 from 1974 through 1976, indicating divided government in those years, and then 0 from 1977 through 1979, due to the Democratic Party's control of the House, Senate, and presidency in those years.

38. The policy mood data set is available at http://www.unc.edu/~jstimson/.

39. For years prior to 1956, we use the preceding years back to 1953, which is the first year of data available in the Spaeth data set we employ (Harold J. Spaeth, "The Original Supreme Court Database," 2004).

40. We treated the percentage yea on a voice vote as a 100.

41. Finally, initial tests based on the analysis of Schoenfeld residuals revealed that two of our variables—*Chamber differences at enactment* and *Subsequent chamber differences*—are nonproportional. To address this issue, and to allow for nonproportionality in the effects of these covariates, we interact each of these variables with the natural log of time since enactment (i.e., *ln(t)*) and include these interactive terms as controls in our regressions. For a discussion of this approach, see Janet Box-Steffensmeier, Dan Reiter, and Christopher Zorn, "Nonproportional Hazards and Event History Analysis in International Relations," *Journal of Conflict Resolution* 47 (2003): 33–53.

42. We performed several tests that support the robustness of our results. First, our findings are not sensitive to the functional form that we use, with other hazard models, such as Weibull and complementary log-log, yielding similar results. Using logit also produced similar results. Second, we found no evidence of posttreatment bias: Our results for the enactment conditions hold up even when we vary the specification by omitting some of the postenactment variables. Third, because so many cases are censored, we calculated predicted values separately for the censored cases. The mean predicted values for the censored cases are higher than the noncensored cases, as would be expected, and both means make substantive sense. Fourth, regression diagnostics confirm the appropriate-

ness of our approach, with visual inspection of the Cox-Snell plot revealing the expected distribution of the residuals when compared to the hazard ratio.

43. Although there is no intuitive explanation for why the combined effect eventually falls to zero, we note that nearly three-quarters of our observations, and 96% of laws that are amended, fall into the category of fewer than twenty-five years (i.e., the point at which the combined effect of the variables is zero). Thus, there are very few observations after this year marker, and almost none of these observations fail.

44. We recognize three weaknesses that may limit our ability to find support for this hypothesis. First, our measure of judicial involvement is based exclusively on the decisions of the U.S. Supreme Court. Second, when Congress responds to Supreme Court decisions, the incubation period is often longer than the three-year threshold we employed. As demonstrated in Maltzman and Shipan ("Change, Continuity, and the Evolution of the Law"), our principal findings are robust if one excludes this variable. Third, we do not distinguish between litigation-prone statutes and those rarely litigated. Future work that categorizes laws on this dimension should be able to more accurately test for the effects of Court involvement.

45. To code this variable, we read the *Congressional Quarterly Almanac* for all laws that Epstein and O'Halloran identified as containing a sunset provision. For details, see Maltzman and Shipan, "Change, Continuity, and the Evolution of the Law."

46. William G. Domhoff, "Power at the Local Level: Growth Coalition Theory," *Who Rules America*, April 2005, http://sociology.ucsc.edu/whorulesamerica/power/local.html.

47. In model 1, an expenditure law dummy is turned on if the summary of the law, as reported in the *Congressional Quarterly Almanac*, reports any domestic projects or programs that require funding. In model 2, the dummy is coded as a 1 if the summary of the law, as reported in the *Congressional Quarterly Almanac*, reports any domestic projects or programs that require funding *or* contains a foreign policy project or program (e.g., the FREEDOM Support Act of 1992, a package of economic aid for the former Soviet republics). Note that if we include these variables separately, the results for the domestic variable are the same as reported in model 1, while the results for foreign projects are small and insignificant. In model 3, we rely on Mayhew's policy categories to identify laws that are distributive in nature. In particular, we identify the following policy areas as distributive: Agriculture, Cities, Housing, Nuclear Energy, Post Office, Public Lands, Transportation, Water Projects. Finally, in model 4 we employed an expenditure law dummy that was similar to model 1, except this variable takes on a value of 1 if the *Almanac* specifically mentions spending (and gives dollar amounts).

48. Such a finding contradicts the hypothesis that programs particularly de-

pendent on the appropriations process are amended via the budgeting process, rather than formal statutory amendments. Nevertheless, the fact that these programs contain prominent spending initiatives, and thus provide valuable credit claiming opportunities, may account for why Congress is more likely to revisit these laws.

49. V. O. Key Jr., *Politics, Parties, and Pressure Groups*, 5th ed. (New York: Thomas Crowell, 1964); E. E. Schattschneider, *Party Government* (New York: Holt, Rinehart, and Winston, 1942).

50. Bryan D. Jones and Frank R. Baumgartner, *The Politics of Attention* (Chicago: University of Chicago Press, 2005); Bryan D. Jones, Tracy Sulkin, and Heather Larsen, "Policy Punctuations in American Political Institutions," *American Political Science Review* 97 (2003): 151-70.

Chapter Seven

1. Eric Patashnik, "After the Public Interest Prevails: The Political Sustainability of Policy Reform," *Governance* 16 (2003): 203-34, gives a detailed analysis of how the Tax Reform Act of 1986 and the Federal Agriculture Improvement and Reform Act were effectively reversed. He discusses feedback effects related to those I discuss, and institutional reforms, which I do not. Neither shall I discuss here instabilities that can arise when parties compete for office by proposing policies along two or more dimensions.

2. Robert Erikson, "Would the Health Care Bill Become More Popular After Passage? The Lesson from Medicare," March 16, 2010, http://www.pollster.com/blogs/guest_pollster_would_the_healt.php.

3. Lena Winslott-Hiselius, Karin Brundell-Freij, Åsa Vagland, and Camilla Byström "The Development of Public Attitudes Towards the Stockholm Congestion Trial," *Transportation Research* A43 (2009): 269-82.

4. For an insightful analysis of another durable policy—airline deregulation in the United States—see Patashnik, "After the Public Interest Prevails."

5. See Hans Gersbach and Amihai Glazer, "Markets and Regulatory Hold-Up Problems," *Journal of Environmental Economics and Management* 37(1999): 151-64.

6. The creation of interest groups differs from the effects of investment in one important way. A policy may create interest groups that pressure government to adopt some policy, even if the policy is not one that a benevolent government, or one aiming to maximize the welfare of citizens, would favor. In contrast, investment can change the policy that a benevolent government would prefer.

7. Quoted in Richard E. Neustadt and Ernest R. May, *Thinking in Time: The Uses of History for Decision-Makers* (New York: Free Press, 1986), 102.

8. Kevin Corder, "Are Federal Programs Immortal? Reconciling Competing

Perspectives on Program Longevity" (working paper, Department of Political Science, Western Michigan University, 2003), provides data on program termination that is broadly consistent with the idea that support for a program increases the longer it has been in existence. He examines all federal credit programs from 1975 to 2001. Overall, the data indicate that programs face increasing hazards of failure in their first few years and lower risks of failure over the long run. Half of the observed terminations occurred when programs were in existence less than ten years, another 25% between ten and twenty years, and the remaining 25% more than twenty years.

9. Christopher R. Berry, Barry C. Burden, and William G. Howell, "The Lives and Deaths of Federal Programs, 1971–2003," chap. 5 in this volume.

10. Eric Patashnik, "Why Some Reforms Last and Others Collapse: The Tax Reform Act of 1986 versus Airline Deregulation," chap. 8 in this volume; see also Eric M. Patashnik, *Reforms at Risk: What Happens after Major Policy Changes Are Enacted?* (Princeton, NJ: Princeton University Press, 2008).

11. Forrest Maltzman and Charles R. Shipan, "Beyond Legislative Productivity: Enactment Conditions, Subsequent Conditions, and the Shape and Life of the Law," chap. 6 in this volume.

12. See Stephen Coate and Stephen Morris, "Policy Persistence," *American Economic Review* 89 (1999): 1327–36.

13. S. Lael Brainard and Thierry Verdier, "Lobbying and Adjustment in Declining Industries," *European Economic Review* 38 (1994): 586–95.

14. For a general discussion of credibility of policy, see Amihai Glazer and Lawrence Rothenberg, *Why Government Succeeds and Why It Fails* (Cambridge, MA: Harvard University Press, 2001).

15. See Robert W. Staiger and Guido Tabellini, "Discretionary Trade Policy and Excessive Protection," *American Economic Review* 77 (1987): 823–37; Kiminori Matsuyama, "Perfect Equilibrium in a Trade Liberalization Game," *American Economic Review* 80 (1990): 480–92; and Aaron Tornell, "Time Inconsistency of Protectionist Programs," *Quarterly Journal of Economics* 106 (1991): 963–74.

16. Robert Strotz, "Myopia and Inconsistency in Dynamic Utility Maximization," *Review of Economic Studies* 23 (1955–56): 165–80; Finn E. Kydland and Edward C. Prescott, "Rules Rather than Discretion: The Inconsistency of Optimal Plans," *Journal of Political Economy* 85 (1977): 473–91; Robert Barro and David Gordon, "A Positive Theory of Monetary Policy in a Natural Rate Model," *Journal of Political Economy* 91 (1983): 589–610; and Torsten Persson, "Credibility of Macroeconomic Policy: An Introduction and a Broad Survey," *European Economic Review* 32 (1988): 519–32.

17. Edmund S. Phelps, and Robert A. Pollak, "On Second-Best Saving and Game-Equilibrium Growth," *Review of Economic Studies* 35 (1968): 185–200.

18. Alberto Alesina and Guido Tabellini, "Credibility and Politics," *Euro-

pean Economic Review 32 (1988): 542–50; Guido Tabellini and Alberto Alesina, "Voting on the Budget Deficit," *American Economic Review* 80 (1990): 37–49.

19. Amihai Glazer, "Politics and the Choice of Durability," *American Economic Review* 79 (1989): 1207–13.

20. James H. Cassing and Arye H. Hillman, "Shifting Comparative Advantage and Senescent Industry Collapse," *American Economic Review* 76 (1986): 516–23.

21. Maurice Obstfeld, "Rational and Self-Fulfilling Balance-of-Payments Crises," *American Economic Review* 76 (1986): 73–81.

22. Dani Rodrik, "Policy Uncertainty and Private Investment in Developing Countries," *Journal of Development Economics* 36 (1991): 229–42.

23. Raquel Fernandez and Dani Rodrik, "Resistance to Reform: Status Quo Bias in the Presence of Individual-Specific Uncertainty," *American Economic Review* 81(1991): 1146–55.

24. This effect is discussed in Amihai Glazer and Kai Konrad, "The Evaluation of Risky Projects by Voters," *Journal of Public Economics* 52 (1993): 377–90.

25. See Robert A. Dur, "Why Do Policy Makers Stick to Inefficient Decisions?" *Public Choice* 13 (2001): 73–94.

26. Patashnik, "After the Public Interest Prevails," 203–34; and Daniel Shaviro, *When Rules Change* (Chicago: University of Chicago Press, 2000).

27. R. Kent Weaver and Bert A. Rockman, eds., *Do Institutions Matter? Government Capabilities in the United States and Abroad* (Washington, DC: Brookings Institution Press, 1993).

28. David Lewis, "The Politics of Agency Termination: Confronting the Myth of Agency Immortality," *Journal of Politics* 64 (2002): 89–107.

Chapter Eight

1. Hugh Heclo, "A Political Science Perspective on Social Security Reform," in *Framing the Social Security Debate*, ed. R. Douglas Arnold, Michael J. Graetz, and Alicia H. Munnell (Washington, DC: National Academy of Social Insurance, 1998), 71.

2. Ibid.

3. See, e.g., Martha Derthick and Paul J. Quirk, *The Politics of Deregulation* (Washington, DC: Brookings Institution Press, 1985); R. Douglas Arnold, *The Logic of Congressional Action* (New Haven, CT: Yale University Press, 1990).

4. Jeffrey H. Birnbaum, "Historic Tax Code Changes Eroded in Years Since 1986," *Washington Post*, June 7, 2004, A1.

5. See National Commission on Fiscal Responsibility and Reform, White House, December 2010, http://www.fiscalcommission.gov.

6. See Christopher R. Berry, Barry C. Burden, and William G. Howell, "The Lives and Deaths of Federal Programs, 1971–2003," chap. 5 in this volume.

7. For a related discussion, see William N. Eskridge Jr. & John Ferejohn, "Super-Statutes," *Duke Law Journal* 50 (2001): 1215–76.

8. Stephen Skowronek, *Building a New American State* (New York: Cambridge University Press, 1982).

9. See Terry M. Moe, "The Politics of Bureaucratic Structure," in *Can the Government Govern?*, ed. John E. Chubb and Paul E. Peterson (Washington, DC: Brookings Institution Press, 1990), 267–329; David E. Lewis "The Politics of Agency Termination: Confronting the Myth of Agency Immortality," *Journal of Politics* 64 (2002): 89–107.

10. Avinash K. Dixit, *Making Economic Policy: A Transaction-Cost Politics Approach to Politics Under Separate Powers* (New York: Cambridge University Press, 1999).

11. Frank R. Baumgartner and Bryan D. Jones, *Agendas and Instability in American Politics* (Chicago: University of Chicago Press, 1993).

12. Michael Bailey, Judith Goldstein, and Barry R.Weingast, "The Institutional Roots of American Trade Policy," *World Politics* 49 (1997): 309–38.

13. Paul Pierson, *Politics in Time* (Princeton, NJ: Princeton University Press, 2004).

14. Eric Schickler, *Disjointed Pluralism* (Princeton, NJ: Princeton University Press, 2001).

15. An early summary statement is Theda Skocpol, "The Origins of Social Policy in the United States," in *The Dynamics of American Politics*, ed. Lawrence C. Dodd and Calvin Jillson (Boulder, CO: Westview Press, 1994), 182–206. For an excellent literature review, see Suzanne Mettler and Joe Soss, "The Consequences of Public Policy for Democratic Citizenship," *Perspectives on Politics* 2 (2004): 55–73.

16. See Kathleen Thelen, "Historical Institutionalism in Comparative Politics," *American Review of Political Science* 2 (1999): 369–404.

17. Eileen Shanahan, "House Overwhelmingly OKs Tax Overhaul Bill," *Congressional Quarterly Weekly Report*, September 27, 1986, 2255; Eileen Shanahan, "Senate Clears Massive Tax Overhaul Measure, Technical Corrections Pose Minor Hang-up," *Congressional Quarterly Weekly Report*, October 4, 1986, 2344.

18. Timothy J. Conlan, David R. Beam, and Margaret Wrightson, "Policy Models and Political Change: Insights from the Passage of Tax Reform," in *The New Politics of Public Policy*, ed. Marc K. Landy and Martin A. Levin (Baltimore: Johns Hopkins University Press, 1995), 135.

19. Ronald Reagan, address before a Joint Session of the Congress on the State of the Union, January 25, 1984, in *Public Papers of the Presidents: Ronald Reagan, 1994* (Washington, DC Government Printing Office, 1986), 87.

20. R. Douglas Arnold, *The Logic of Congressional Action* (New Haven, CT: Yale University Press, 1990), 213.

21. Ibid., 218.

22. In fact, the CAB removed by policy statement and regulations virtually all entry restrictions within a few months of enactment.

23. Derthick and Quirk, *Politics of Deregulation*, 82.

24. Elizabeth Bailey, David R. Graham, and Daniel P. Kaplan, *Deregulating the Airlines* (Cambridge, MA: MIT Press, 1983), 32.

25. See Derthick and Quirk, *Politics of Deregulation*.

26. Richard H. K. Vietor, "Contrived Competition: Airline Regulation and Deregulation, 1925–1988," *Business History Review* 64 (1990): 82.

27. Bailey, Graham, and Kaplan, *Deregulating the Airlines*, 34.

28. Quoted in Steven Pearlstein, "Tax Reform Falling Prey to Tax Cuts," *Washington Post*, December 18, 1994, A1.

29. Quoted in David E. Rosenbaum, "Reform Taxes? Give Us a Break!" *New York Times*, December 25, 1994, sec. 4.

30. Gary Klott, "Rostenkowski Opposes Big '87 Tax Changes," *New York Times*, October 22, 1986, D2.

31. Michael J. Graetz, "Tax Reform Unraveling," *Journal of Economic Perspectives* 21 (2007): 70.

32. Barbara Bradley, "Tax Pruning Due Creates Opportunity," *Christian Science Monitor*, March 20, 1987, B6. In fiscal 1986, the federal deficit stood at 5% of GDP and the out years looked even bleaker.

33. Joseph White and Aaron Wildavsky describe the improbable triumph of tax reform as a "counterpoint" to the deficit wars of the 1980s and early 1990s. See White and Wildavsky, *The Deficit and the Public Interest: The Search for Responsible Budgeting in the 1980s* (Berkeley: University of California Press, 1989), chap. 21.

34. Quoted in Julian E. Zelizer, *Taxing America: Wilbur D. Mills, Congress, and the State, 1945–1975* (New York: Cambridge University Press, 2000), 19.

35. Michael J. Graetz, *The Decline (and Fall?) of the Income Tax* (New York: Norton, 1997), 142.

36. "America's Tax Laws, Vastly Simplified Three Years Ago, Are Slipping Back into Their Bad Old Ways," *Economist*, October 7, 1989, 16.

37. On the 1993 Act, see Paul Pierson, "The Deficit and the Politics of Domestic Reform," in *The Social Divide*, ed. Margaret Weir (Washington, DC: Brookings Institution Press, 1998), 126–80.

38. Steven Greenhouse, "Squaring Off on Taxes; Clinton Proposals Are Drawing Fire from Supporters of the 1986 Reform Law," *New York Times*, May 6, 1993, D1.

39. President's Advisory Panel on Federal Tax Reform, *Simple, Fair, and*

Pro-Growth: Proposals to Fix America's Tax System (November 2005), chaps. 2, 15, http://www.taxpolicycenter.org/taxtopics/upload/tax-panel-2.pdf.

40. Alison E. Post and Paul Pierson, "How a Law Stays a Law: The Durability of U.S. Tax Breaks, 1967–2003" (paper prepared for presentation at the Annual Meeting of the American Political Science Association, Washington, DC, September 1–4, 2005).

41. David S. Cloud, "Clinton Strategy Renews Debate over Investment Tax Credit," *Congressional Quarterly Weekly Report*, November 14, 1992, 3637.

42. Greenhouse, "Squaring Off on Taxes."

43. Leslie B. Samuels, "Clinton Won't Undo 1986 Tax Reforms, Treasury Nominee Tells Finance Panel," *Bond Buyer*, April 27, 1993, 1.

44. Anne Swardson, "Lawmakers Clamor Anew for Tax Breaks," *Washington Post*, April 17, 1988, H1.

45. Howard Gleckman, "Tinkering with Tax Reform: A Bad Idea that Will Just Get Worse," *Business Week*, November 6, 1989, 104.

46. Ibid.

47. Allen Schick, *The Federal Budget—Revised Edition* (Washington, DC: Brookings Institution Press, 2000), 151.

48. President's Advisory Panel, *Simple, Fair, and Pro-Growth*, 16.

49. U.S. General Accountability Office, *Government Performance and Accountability: Tax Expenditures Represent a Substantial Federal Commitment and Need to Be Reexamined*, GAO05–690 (September 2005), 22.

50. See Jill Barshay, "Corporate Tax Bills, Stuffed, Scorned—and Supported," *Congressional Quarterly Weekly Report*, June 26, 2004, 1540; Jonathan Weisman, "President Signs Corporate Tax Legislation," *Washington Post*, October 23, 2004, A10.

51. The TRA did not target any of the major existing social tax expenditures (e.g., the home mortgage interest deduction) for repeal; the provisions were considered too politically sensitive.

52. Quoted in Fred S. McChesney, *Money for Nothing: Politicians, Rent Extraction, and Political Extortion* (Cambridge, MA: Harvard University Press, 1997), 94.

53. Michael E. Levine, personal communication, April 1, 2005. This chapter was drafted prior to my correspondence with Levine, but the final version has benefited enormously from his comments and from reading his own writings on the topic.

54. Alfred E. Kahn, "Surprises of Airline Deregulation," *American Economic Review* 78 (1988): 316.

55. See, e.g., Adam Bryant, "Why Flying Is Hell," *Newsweek*, April 23, 2001, 34–37.

56. Steven A. Morrison and Clifford Winston, "The Remaining Role for Government Policy in the Deregulated Airline Industry," in *Deregulation of Net-*

work Industries: What's Next?, ed. Sam Peltzman and Clifford Winston (Washington, DC: Brookings Institution Press, 2000), 9.

57. Michael E. Levine, "Regulation, the Market, and Interest Group Cohesion: Why Airlines Were Not Reregulated," in *Creating Competitive Markets: The Politics of Regulatory Reform*, Marc K. Landy, Marin A. Levin, and Martin Shapiro (Washington, DC: Brookings Institution Press, 2007), 224.

58. Another air carrier known as Frontier Airlines was in existence between 1950 and 1986. The Frontier Airlines of the 1990s was founded by previous executives of this firm.

59. Dan Reed, "Low-Fare Carriers Service Bests Big Rivals," *USA Today*, April 5, 2004, 2B.

60. See, e.g., Stacey R. Kohl and Kenneth M. Lehn, "Deregulation and the Adaption of Governance Structure: The Case of the U.S. Airline Industry," *Journal of Financial Economics* 51 (1999): 79–117. I thank Amihai Glazer for bringing this study to my attention.

61. Elizabeth E. Bailey, "Airline Deregulation: Confronting the Paradoxes," *Regulation* 15, no. 3 (1992), http://www.cato.org/pubs/regulation/regv15n3/reg15 n3-bailey.html.

62. Ibid.

63. See "Airline Industry Problems," *CQ Researcher* 9, no. 36 (1999): 825–48.

64. See "Deregulation: Dethroning the Customer," *Consumer Reports*, July 2002, 30–35.

65. Carolyn Lochhead, "Fears of Monopolies in the Sky," *San Francisco Chronicle*, May 6, 1998, A1.

66. Frank Swoboda, "Airline Rules Put on Shelf," *Washington Post*, June 25, 1998, C05.

67. Greg Gordon, "Airline Panel Doesn't Clear Air," *Minneapolis Star Tribune*, July 31, 1999, 1D.

68. Frank Swoboda, "American's Tactics Against Discounters Legal, Judge Says," *Washington Post*, April 28, 2001, E1.

69. Statement of Carol B. Hallett, President, Air Transport Association, ATA Press Release, April 30, 1999.

70. David Armstrong, "Travelers Say Airline Reforms Are Way Behind Schedule," *The San Francisco Chronicle*, March 30, 2001, B1.

71. "Airline Industry Problems," 827.

72. Cited in "Reid Introduces Bill to Improve Airline Travel for Passengers," *Congress Daily AM*, January 30, 2001.

73. "GAO Report Questions Value of EAS Program," *Community Regional Airline News*, March 31, 2003, 1.

74. Lochhead, "Fears of Monopolies in the Sky."

75. *Hearings before the Subcomm. on Aviation of the House Comm. on Transportation and Infrastructure*, May 25, 2000 (testimony of John V. Coleman).

76. In 2003, the federal government gave the airlines another $3.8 billion in assistance, $2.3 billion of which was partial reimbursement for security-related taxes and costs incurred by the industry after the September 11 attacks.

77. Micheline Maynard, "New Scrutiny for Airline Bailout Plan Three Years After Sept. 11," *New York Times*, September 15, 2004, C1.

78. Kathryn A. Wolfe, "Senior Lawmaker Says Airlines Will Get No More Federal Aid," *Congressional Quarterly Weekly Report*, June 5, 2004, 1355.

79. Scott McCartney, "Airline Loan-Guarantee Deal Ends with a Profit," *Wall Street Journal*, May 30, 2006, D4.

80. Michael E. Levine, "Why Weren't the Airlines Reregulated?," *Yale Journal on Regulation* 23 (2006): 286–87.

81. See Tim Groseclose and Charles Stewart III, "The Value of Committee Seats in the House, 1947–1991," *American Journal of Political Science* 42 (1998): 453–74.

82. Jeffrey Milyo, "Electoral and Financial Effects of Changes in Committee Power: The Gramm-Rudman-Hollings Budget Reform, the Tax Reform Act of 1986, and the Money Committees in the House," *Journal of Law and Economics* 40 (1997): 105.

83. Graetz, *Decline (and Fall?)*, 289.

84. Levine, "Regulation, the Market, and Interest Group Cohesion," 225–26.

85. Ibid.

86. Ibid., 227.

87. Levine, "Why Weren't the Airlines Reregulated?," 286.

88. Paul Starobin, "Deregulation: New Doubts, Damage Control," *Congressional Quarterly Weekly Report*," July 11, 1987, 1489.

89. Carol Matlack, "Coming Unglued," *National Journal*, November 4, 1989, 2692.

90. Poll data cited in W. Lance Bennett and Erik Asard, "The Marketplace of Ideas: The Rhetoric and Politics of Tax Reform in Sweden and the United States," *Polity* 28 (1988): 14n55.

91. Forrest Maltzman and Charles R. Shipan, "Beyond Legislative Productivity: Enactment Conditions, Subsequent Conditions, and the Shape and Life of the Law," chap. 6 of this volume.

92. Derthick and Quirk, *Politics of Deregulation*, 163; Vietor, "Contrived Competition," 83.

93. Berry, Burden, and Howell, "Lives and Deaths of Federal Programs."

94. See Agis Salpukas, "Future of Airline Deregulation: Issue and Debate," *New York Times*, May 8, 1982, 29.

95. On layering, see Jacob S. Hacker, "Privatizing Risk Without Privatizing the Welfare State," *American Political Science Review* 98 (2004): 243–60.

96. Paul Pierson, "The Study of Policy Development," *Journal of Policy History* 17 (2005): 37–56.

Chapter Nine

1. See, e.g., Amihai Glazer, "Politics and the Choice of Durability," *American Economic Review* 79 (1989): 1207–13; Forrest Maltzman and Charles R. Shipan, "Change, Continuity, and the Evolution of the Law," *American Journal of Political Science* 52 (2008): 252–67; Forrest Maltzman and Charles R. Shipan, "Beyond Legislative Productivity: Enactment Conditions, Subsequent Conditions, and the Shape of the Law," chap. 6 in this volume; Terry M. Moe, "The Politics of Bureaucratic Structure," in *Can the Government Govern?*, ed. J. E. Chubb and P. E. Peterson (Washington, DC: Brookings Institution Press, 1989); Eric M. Patashnik, *Putting Trust in the US Budget* (New York: Cambridge University Press, 2000); Eric M. Patashnik, "After the Public Interest Prevails: The Political Sustainability of Policy Reform," *Governance* 16 (2003): 203–34; Eric M. Patashnik, *Reforms at Risk: What Happens After Major Policy Changes Are Enacted* (Princeton, NJ: Princeton University Press, 2008). Concerns about durability are particularly acute in the case of public interest legislation since the private interests adversely influenced by the public interest policies use their substantial resources and organizational advantages to delay, disrupt, or stunt the implementation of enacted policies during implementation. See, e.g., Marver Bernstein, *Regulating Business by Independent Commission* (Westport, CT: Greenwood Press, 1955); Terry M. Moe, "Political Control and the Power of the Agent," *Journal of Law Economics and Organization* 22 (2006): 1–29; Patashnik, "After the Public Interest Prevails"; Jason Webb Yackee and Susan Webb Yackee, "A Bias Towards Business? Assessing Interest Group Influence on the U.S. Bureaucracy," *Journal of Politics* 68 (2006): 128–39.

2. David Epstein and Sharyn O'Halloran, *Delegating Powers* (New York: Cambridge University Press, 1999); David E. Lewis, *Presidents and the Politics of Agency Design* (Stanford, CA: Stanford University Press, 2003); Mathew D. McCubbins, Roger Noll, and Barry Weingast, "Structure and Process, Politics and Policy: Administrative Arrangements and the Political Control of Agencies," *Virginia Law Review* 75 (1989): 431–82; Craig Volden, "A Formal Model of the Politics of Delegation in a Separation of Powers System," *American Journal of Political Science* 46 (2002): 111–33.

3. Lewis, *Presidents and the Politics of Agency Design*; David E. Lewis, "The Adverse Consequences of the Politics of Agency Design for Presidential Management in the US: The Relative Durability of Insulated Agencies," *British Journal of Political Science* 34 (2004): 377–404.

4. See Lewis, "Adverse Consequences." Of course, to argue that delegation to a commission increases a policy's durability assumes that commissions are sympathetic to goals of the statutes they are charged with implementing. There is no reason to believe, however, that commissions are systematically more likely than

executive branch bureaus to be opposed to the policies they are charged with implementing.

5. See, however, J. Kevin Corder, "Are Federal Programs Immortal? Estimating the Hazard of Program Termination," *American Politics Research* 32 (2004): 3–25; Maltzman and Shipan, "Change, Continuity, and the Evolution of the Law."

6. Lewis, *Presidents and the Politics of Agency Design*; Moe, "Politics of Bureaucratic Structure."

7. Lewis, *Presidents and the Politics of Agency Design*; Moe, "Politics of Bureaucratic Structure"; Terry M. Moe and Michael Caldwell, "The Institutional Foundations of Democratic Government: A Comparison of Presidential and Parliamentary Systems," *Journal of Institutional and Theoretical Economics* 150, no. 1 (1994): 171–95; Patashnik, *Putting Trust in the US Budget*.

8. McCubbins, Noll, and Weingast, "Structure and Process."

9. Epstein and O'Halloran, *Delegating Powers*; John Huber and Charles Shipan, *Deliberate Discretion* (New York: Cambridge University Press, 2002); George A. Krause and Ann O'M Bowman, "Adverse Selection, Political Parties, and Policy Delegation in the American Federal System," *Journal of Law, Economics, and Organization* 21 (2005): 359–87.

10. Daniel P. Carpenter, "Stochastic Prediction and Estimation of Nonlinear Political Durations: An Application to the Lifetime of Bureaus," in *Political Complexity: Nonlinear Models of Politics*, ed. D. Richards (Ann Arbor: University of Michigan Press, 2000); Daniel P. Carpenter and David E. Lewis, "Political Learning from Rare Events: Poisson Inference, Fiscal Constraints and the Lifetime of Bureaus," *Political Analysis* 12 (2004): 201–32; Corder, "Are Federal Programs Immortal?"; Herbert Kaufman, *Are Government Organizations Immortal?* (Washington, DC: Brookings Institution Press, 1976); David E. Lewis, "The Politics of Agency Termination: Confronting the Myth of Agency Immortality," *Journal of Politics* 64 (2002):89–107; Lewis, "Adverse Consequences."

11. Lewis, "Politics of Agency Termination."

12. Lewis, "Adverse Consequences."

13. Corder, "Are Federal Programs Immortal?" The bulk of federal credit programs, however, are located in independent agencies like the Small Business Administration that are organized like bureaus rather than commissions. This makes it difficult to determine whether programs housed in commissions are more or less durable. Devins and Lewis argue that the time it takes presidents to appoint majorities to independent commissions has been increasing over time, but that the commissioners appointed are more reliably partisan loyalists. Neal Devins and David E. Lewis, "Not-So Independent Agencies: Party Polarization and the Limits of Institutional Design," *Boston University Law Review* 88 (2008): 459–98; see also Daniel E. Ho, "Congressional Agency Control: The Impact of Statutory Partisan Requirements on Regulation" (unpublished

manuscript, Stanford University, February 12, 2007), http://dho.stanford.edu/
research/partisan.pdf.

14. Carpenter and Lewis, "Political Learning from Rare Events."

15. Maltzman and Shipan, "Beyond Legislative Productivity."

16. They do control for whether legislation includes a sunset provision and
find that laws enacted with sunset provisions are more likely to be amended.

17. Bernstein, *Regulating Business by Independent Commission*; J. Leiper
Freeman, "The Bureaucracy and Pressure Politics," in *Bureaucratic Power in
National Politics*, 2nd ed., ed. Francis E. Rourke (Boston: Little, Brown, 1972),
15–27; Theodore J. Lowi, *The End of Liberalism: The Second Republic of the
United States*, 2nd ed. (New York: W. W. Norton, 1979); Moe, "Political Con-
trol"; Francis Rourke, "Variations in Agency Power," in Rourke, *Bureaucratic
Power in National Politics*, 240–62.

18. R. Shep Melnick, "Strange Bedfellows Make Normal Politics: An Essay,"
Duke Law and Policy Forum 9 (1998):76.

19. Anthony Bertelli, Joshua Clinton, Christian Grose, David E. Lewis, and
David C. Nixon, "The Ideology of Federal Executives and their Agencies" (paper presented at the Annual Meeting of the Midwest Political Science Association, Chicago, IL, 2008).

20. The survey was web-based. Each potential respondent was sent a letter
on Princeton University letterhead inviting them to participate and giving them
options about how to do so. Potential respondents whose e-mail addresses were
available to the Princeton Survey Research Center (77%) were told that they
would receive an e-mail of the survey one week after the initial letter. They were
also told they could go to a website and log in immediately with a login and password included in the invitation letter. Potential respondents whose e-mail addresses were not available to the PSRC were asked to provide the PSRC with an
e-mail address or go to the website directly and use the login and password provided. The PSRC then scheduled a series of follow-up e-mails, letters, and ultimately, telephone calls. All respondents with valid e-mail addresses received
an initial letter (week of November 5, 2007), an e-mail invitation (November
14, 2007), three follow-up e-mail reminders (November 29, 2007; December 13,
2007; January 17, 2008), and a telephone call (December 2007–January 2008).
Respondents for whom the PSRC did not have an e-mail address received an initial letter (week of November 5, 2007), a follow-up letter (November 21, 2007), a
telephone call, and a final reminder letter (February 27, 2008).

21. The survey excludes executives who are not administrators or program
managers.

22. We obtained the contact information for the executives from Leadership
Directories, Inc., a firm that publishes the *Federal Yellow Book*.

23. The response rate from the original 7,448 names was 32%. When potential respondents who were included incorrectly are excluded (i.e., those who are

not employees of the federal government or not federal executives), the response rate in the text is produced. The original list included 461 potential respondents from the National Science Foundation because the firm incorrectly labeled NSF program officers as managers or executives. The original list also included 27 names of executives working for the Delaware River Basin Commission, National Gallery of Art, Susquehanna River Basin Commission, and Japan–United States Friendship Commission. Two of these agencies are multistate compacts and so not technically federal agencies. The National Gallery of Art is partially private, and the Japan–United States Friendship Commission is a multilateral agency with both Japanese and U.S. citizens working together.

24. Agency by agency, the lowest responders were the Executive Office of the President (11%), the Securities and Exchange Commission (17%), and the Department of the Treasury (19%). The highest responders were the Nuclear Regulatory Commission (55%), the Federal Trade Commission (65%), and the National Archives and Records Administration (75%).

25. An analysis of the early and late responders to the surveys shows generally that early responders look very similar to late responders with the exception that women responding late to the survey tend to be slightly less likely to be self-identifying Democrats. It is unclear how this might influence the results of this chapter.

26. The independent commissions include the following agencies with minor commissions denoted with an (m) and larger independent regulatory commissions denoted by *italics*: Advisory Council on Historic Preservation (m), African Development Foundation (m), Arctic Research Commission (m), Broadcasting Board of Governors, *Commodity Futures Trading Commission*, *Consumer Product Safety Commission*, Coordinating Council on Juvenile Justice and Delinquency Prevention (m), Corporation for National and Community Service, Defense Nuclear Facilities Safety Board, *Equal Employment Opportunity Commission*, Export-Import Bank, Federal Accounting Standards Advisory Board (m), *Federal Communications Commission*, Federal Deposit Insurance Corporation, *Federal Election Commission*, Federal Housing Finance Board, Federal Maritime Commission, *Federal Reserve System*, Federal Retirement Thrift Investment Board (m), *Federal Trade Commission*, Harry S. Truman Scholarship Foundation (m), James Madison Memorial Fellowship Foundation (m), Marine Mammal Commission (m), Merit Systems Protection Board, Morris K. Udall Scholarship and Excellence in National Environmental Policy Foundation (m), National Capital Planning Commission (m), *National Labor Relations Board*, National Mediation Board, National Transportation Safety Board, Neighborhood Reinvestment Corporation (m), *Nuclear Regulatory Commission*, Occupational Safety and Health Review Commission, Railroad Retirement Board, *Securities and Exchange Commission*, United States Chemical Safety and Hazard Investigation Board (m), U.S. Commission of Fine Arts (m), and the U.S. In-

ternational Trade Commission. I do not include the Institute of Museum and Library Sciences, Overseas Private Investment Corporation, Smithsonian Institution, or Tennessee Valley Authority as commissions because their boards are more advisory or like boards of directors rather than boards that are involved in day-to-day functioning of the agencies. I exclude the Pension Benefit Guarantee Corporation and the U.S. Interagency Council on Homelessness because they are not really independent. They are headed by directors who report to other presidentially appointed officials such as the secretaries of labor and commerce. The results reported below are robust to including or excluding minor commissions or examining only the major independent regulatory commissions. A full list of agencies and independent commissions is included in appendix A.

27. Lewis, *Presidents and the Politics of Agency Design.*

28. Don't know responses are excluded. The percentages for White House influence are 4.4%, 9.87%, 21.57%, 31.45%, and 32.69%. The percentages for members and staff of congressional committees are 3.77%, 7.27%, 29.51%, 37.80%, and 21.65%. The percentages for interest group representative influence are 7.53%, 22.3%, 42.22%, 21.86%, and 6.09%.

29. In the federal government, the bulk of federal administrators and program managers are either Senate-confirmed political appointees (5% of sample) or members of the Senior Executive Service (SES). The SES is a corps of seven to eight thousand federal managers who serve in management positions between PAS appointees and the traditional civil service. It is comprised of a mixture of career managers (53%) and political appointees (6%). Below the SES is the traditional civil service (26%). Schedule C appointees (1%) are another category of appointees who serve in policy and confidential positions that generally do not have managerial responsibilities, with a few exceptions. The omitted category in the analysis are those federal employees who serve in other personnel systems excepted from the traditional civil service system, including those serving in managerial roles in scientific or technical positions (7%). For a review of the federal personnel system, see David E. Lewis, *The Politics of Presidential Appointments: Political Control and Bureaucratic Performance* (Princeton, NJ: Princeton University Press, 2008), chap. 2. I also estimated models using pay levels rather than appointment authorities to measure location in the hierarchy. The results confirm what is reported here and are available on request from the author.

30. Omitting such variables could bias estimates on the commission indicator since commission employees, particularly those with fixed terms, serve longer tenures in their agencies on average.

31. Notably, while 54% of respondents overall, 60% of respondents working in independent commissions are Democrats.

32. Over the entire executive branch, agencies vary in size and importance from the Department of Defense to the Advisory Council on Historic Preser-

vation. To account for these differences I include controls for tiny independent agencies and those performing only advisory functions. Specifically, I code the Advisory Council on Historic Preservation, Federal Accounting Standards Advisory Board, James Madison Memorial Fellowship Foundation, Marine Mammal Commission, Morris K. Udall Scholarship and Excellence in National Environmental Policy Foundation, Neighborhood Reinvestment Corporation, United States Arctic Research Commission, and U.S. Commission of Fine Arts as minor independent agencies. I have also estimated models including the number of employees working for the respondent as a measure of agency size. The results are comparable to what is reported here, and I was not able to reject the null hypothesis that the number of civilian employees under the respondent was unrelated to perceptions of political influence.

33. One difficulty with these models is that the sample that responded to the survey may not be representative of the population as a whole. To account for this possibility a firm was hired to identify the home addresses of potential survey respondents. Once home addresses were identified for those potential respondents with a unique name, another firm was hired to check voter registration information. The percentage of Democrats in the sample falls well within the range of Democrats in the population. In other analysis, I also estimated a probit model with selection in order to model the selection equation directly. The estimates confirm what is reported here. Respondents in commissions are significantly less likely to report a good bit or great deal of policy influence by the executive or legislative branch. Details of these models and model estimates are available from the author.

34. Lewis, *Politics of Presidential Appointments*.

35. More troubling for inference is the possibility that unobservable sources of influence are correlated with observed sources of influence. This makes parsing out the unique influence of contact, personnel, and future job prospects difficult. There is no easy way around this problem except to note that each source of influence is arguably among the most important and solidly grounded in the existing literature about why presidents, Congress, or interest groups have influence over agency behavior.

36. The other groups mentioned were "Republicans in Congress and their staff," "Democrats in Congress and their staff," and "political appointees in your department or agency."

37. Mathew D. McCubbins and Thomas Schwartz, "Congressional Oversight Overlooked: Police Patrols Versus Fire Alarms," *American Journal of Political Science* 28 (1984): 165–77; Mathew D. McCubbins, Roger Noll, and Barry Weingast, "Administrative Procedures as Instruments of Political Control," *Journal of Law, Economics, and Organization* 3 (1987): 243–77.

38. McCubbins and Schwartz, "Congressional Oversight Overlooked"; McCubbins, Noll, and Weingast, "Administrative Procedures."

39. Survey respondents were informed, "We would like to remind you that your answers are completely confidential and that your participation in the survey is voluntary. The results of the survey will be reported as aggregate statistics so that it will be impossible to identify individual survey respondents. You should feel free to express your views openly and honestly. Of course, you are also free to refuse to answer any questions along the way."

40. Lewis, "Adverse Consequences."

41. Epstein and O'Halloran, *Delegating Powers*; Morris P. Fiorina, *Congress, Keystone of the Washington Establishment* (New Haven, CT: Yale University Press, 1977); Cornelius M. Kerwin, *Rulemaking: How Government Agencies Write Law and Make Policy*, 3rd ed. (Washington, DC: CQ Press, 2003).

Chapter Ten

1. Matthew D. Lassiter, *The Silent Majority: Suburban Politics in the Sunbelt South* (Princeton, NJ: Princeton University Press, 2006), 132, 244, 249, 304. On the persistence of de facto school segregation in many urban areas of the South, see ibid., 299–300. Despite the fact that the South has enjoyed relatively greater integration in its public schools than elsewhere in the nation, trends since the 1990s have nevertheless pointed toward heightened resegregation in southern schools. Gary Orfield, "Introduction: The Southern Dilemma: Losing *Brown*, Fearing *Plessy*," in *School Resegregation: Must the South Turn Back?*, ed. John Charles Boger and Gary Orfield (Chapel Hill: University of North Carolina Press, 2005), 7–11.

2. Eric M. Patashnik, "Why Some Reforms Last and Others Collapse: The Tax Reform Act of 1986 versus Airline Deregulation," chap. 8 in this volume.

3. Orren and Skowronek get at this point by conceptualizing the larger political universe as akin to "downtown Tokyo." As they state, "in historical construction, as in downtown Tokyo, empty lots are few and far between: building something new usually means disturbing something else." Karen Orren and Stephen Skowronek, *The Search for American Political Development* (New York: Cambridge University Press, 2004), 22–23.

4. *Ibid.*, 112–18.

5. See, e.g., Crane Brinton, *The Anatomy of Revolution* (New York: Vintage, 1965).

6. I offer a book-length treatment of the subject, however, in Stuart Chinn, "The Limits of Political Change:

The Recalibration of Reform and the Construction of Governance" (unpublished manuscript, 2011).

7. Alexis de Tocqueville, *Democracy in America*, trans. George Lawrence, ed. J. P. Mayer (New York: Harper Perennial, 1988), 1:270.

8. Mark A. Graber, "Resolving Political Questions into Judicial Questions: Tocqueville's Thesis Revisited," *Constitutional Commentary* 21 (2004): 485–545.

9. Alexander M. Bickel, *The Least Dangerous Branch* (New Haven, CT: Yale University Press, 1986), 69–72, 199–207.

10. Bruce Ackerman has elaborated on the "synthetic" nature of certain judicial rulings. Ackerman, *We the People: Foundations* (Cambridge, MA: Belknap Press, 1991), 88, 92–99, 113–15.

11. The morphing of reform opposition into new forms after a dismantling has occurred has also been insightfully discussed by Reva Siegel. She discusses how new forms of subordination always seem capable of resurfacing after older forms have been dismantled by major egalitarian reform efforts, in the context of race and gender. Siegel, "Why Equal Protection No Longer Protects: The Evolving Forms of Status-Enforcing State Action," *Stanford Law Review* 49 (1997): 1111–48. My discussion of judicial-indirect opposition also bears similarities, I believe, to Vesla A. Weaver's discussion of "frontlash" in the context of electoral politics surrounding mid-twentieth-century crime policy. Weaver, "Frontlash: Race and the Development of Punitive Crime Policy," *Studies in American Political Development* 21 (2007): 230–65.

12. The question of what motivates judicial actors to put forth delimiting opinions is a question that I address in significant depth in a separate paper. Stuart Chinn, "Race, the Supreme Court, and the Judicial-Institutional Interest in Stability," *Journal of Law (Law and Commentary)* 1 (2011): 95–184.

13. See, e.g., Mark A. Graber, "The Nonmajoritarian Difficulty: Legislative Deference to the Judiciary," *Studies in American Political Development* 7 (Spring 1993): 35–73; Keith E. Whittington, "'Interpose Your Friendly Hand': Political Supports for the Exercise of Judicial Review by the United States Supreme Court," *American Political Science Review* 99 (November 2005): 583–96.

14. E.g., Keyes v. School District No. 1, 413 U.S. 189 (1973); Swann v. Charlotte-Mecklenberg Board of Education, 402 U.S. 1 (1971); Green v. County School Board, 391 U.S. 430 (1968).

15. See, e.g., Alan Brinkley, *The End of Reform: New Deal Liberalism in Recession and War* (New York: Vintage Books, 1996).

16. Bruce Ackerman, *We the People: Transformations* (Cambridge, MA: Belknap Press, 1998), 257.

17. Wickard v. Filburn, 317 U.S. 111 (1942); United States v. Darby, 312 U.S. 100 (1941).

18. Karen Orren, *Belated Feudalism: Labor, the Law, and Liberal Development in the United States* (Cambridge: Cambridge University Press, 1999).

19. David M. Kennedy, *Freedom from Fear* (New York: Oxford University Press, 1999), 348; William E. Leuchtenburg, *Franklin D. Roosevelt and the New Deal* (New York: Harper and Row, 1963), 266–68.

20. Leuchtenburg, *Roosevelt and the New Deal*, 271–72; James T. Patterson, *Congressional Conservatism and the New Deal* (Lexington: University of Kentucky Press, 1967), 288–91.

21. Melvyn Dubofsky, *The State and Labor in Modern America* (Chapel Hill: University of North Carolina Press, 1994), 190–91; Brinkley, *End of Reform*, 216.

22. 304 U.S. 333 (1938).

23. 306 U.S. 332 (1939).

24. 306 U.S. 240 (1939).

25. *Mackay* and *Fansteel* are sometimes mentioned as early antiunion cases before the Court. They, and to a varying extent the topic of early conservative judicial rulings on the Wagner Act, are discussed, for example, in Karl E. Klare, "Judicial Deradicalization of the Wagner Act and the Origins of Modern Legal Consciousness, 1937–1941," *Minnesota Law Review* 62 (1978): 265–339; James B. Atleson, *Values and Assumptions in American Labor Law* (Amherst: University of Massachusetts Press, 1983), 19–34, 45; Christopher L. Tomlins, *The State and the Unions* (Cambridge: Cambridge University Press, 1985), 239–40 (discussing *Fansteel*); Paul Weiler, "Striking a New Balance: Freedom of Contract and the Prospects for Union Representation," *Harvard Law Review* 98 (1984): 388–89 (discussing *Mackay*).

26. Dubofsky, *State and Labor*, 164–66; Klare, "Judicial Deradicalization," 318–19.

27. 304 U.S. 333 (1938).

28. Ibid., 346–48.

29. Ibid., 345–46.

30. Reply Brief for the NLRB at 15–16, NLRB v. Mackay Radio & Telegraph Co., 304 U.S. 333 (1938).

31. Brief for Respondent at 27–29, NLRB v. Mackay Radio & Telegraph Co., 304 U.S. 333 (1938).

32. Ibid., 27.

33. Ibid., 39–40 (emphasis in original).

34. Ibid., 26.

35. Ibid., 28, 29.

36. Ibid., 27–28.

37. The company did also offer one "substantive due process"-sounding argument in its brief, but this was by no means the centerpiece of that brief. Ibid., 40–53.

38. Ibid., 27–28, 32.

39. 49 Stat. 449 (1935).

40. 306 U.S. at 338–39.

41. Ibid., 342–43.

42. Ibid.

43. Ibid., 343–44.

44. Ibid., 344.

45. Contrary to the Court's interpretation of events, the NLRB—not surprisingly—did not find a breach of contract in the actions of the employees. The NLRB noted that the proposal to stop work temporarily had in fact been proposed by the company. Brief for the NLRB at 32, 32 n.9, NLRB v. Sands Manufacturing Co., 306 U.S. 332 (1939).

46. Respondent's Brief at 43, NLRB v. Sands Manufacturing Co., 306 U.S. 332 (1939).

47. Ibid., 43–44 (citations omitted).

48. Ibid., 44.

49. Ibid., 56.

50. Ibid., 57.

51. 306 U.S. at 247–48.

52. Ibid., 249.

53. Ibid., 252.

54. Ibid.

55. Ibid., 253.

56. The Wagner Act states in section 2 (3) that the term "employee" shall include "any individual whose work has ceased as a consequence of, or in connection with, any current labor dispute or because of any unfair labor practice." 49 Stat. 449 (1935).

57. Section 10 (c) of the Wagner Act empowered the NLRB, when faced with the incident of an unfair labor practice, to "take such affirmative action, including reinstatement of employees with or without back pay, as will effectuate the policies of this Act." Ibid.

58. 306 U.S. at 255–56 (citations omitted).

59. Ibid., 256–57.

60. Ibid., 253.

61. Ibid., 257–58.

62. Brief for the NLRB at 35–38, NLRB v. Fansteel Metallurgical Corp., 306 U.S. 240 (1939).

63. Ibid., 40–41.

64. Ibid., 43–45; see also Reply Brief for the NLRB at 20–29, NLRB v. Fansteel Metallurgical Corp., 306 U.S. 240 (1939). Separately, the NLRB also asserted that its reinstatement power would be appropriate even if the strikers were not "employees" under the terms of the Wagner Act, given the possibility of interpreting the Board's remedial power under section 10 (c) more expansively to cover nonemployees as well. Brief for the NLRB at 45–49, NLRB v. Fansteel Metallurgical Corp., 306 U.S. 240 (1939). The NLRB had tried this argument in its brief for *Mackay Radio* as well. Brief for the NLRB at 49–54, NLRB v. Mackay Radio & Telegraph Co., 304 U.S. 333 (1938).

65. Brief for the NLRB at 49–50, NLRB v. Fansteel Metallurgical Corp., 306 U.S. 240 (1939).

66. Ibid., 58–59.

67. Brief for Fansteel Metallurgical Corp. at 24–25, 32–34, NLRB v. Fansteel Metallurgical Corp., 306 U.S. 240 (1939).

68. Ibid., 25–29.

69. Ibid., 35–45, 52.

70. Ibid., 35.

71. Ibid., 36.

72. Ibid., 39–40.

73. Ibid., 39.

74. Katherine van Wezel Stone, "The Post-War Paradigm in American Labor Law," *Yale Law Journal* 90 (1981): 1509–80; James B. Atleson, "Wartime Labor Regulation, the Industrial Pluralists, and the Law of Collective Bargaining," in *Industrial Democracy in America: The Ambiguous Promise*, ed. Nelson Lichtenstein and Howell John Harris (New York: Cambridge University Press, 1993), 146–50; Nelson Lichtenstein, "Industrial Democracy, Contract Unionism, and the National War Labor Board," *Labor Law Journal* 33 (1982): 524–31; Staughton Lynd, "Government Without Rights: The Labor Vision of Archibald Cox," *Industrial Relations Law Journal* 4 (1981): 483–95. The Court gave its blessings to industrial pluralism in Justice Douglas's three opinions in the *Steelworkers Trilogy: United Steelworkers of America v. American Manufacturing Co.*, 363 U.S. 564 (1960); *United Steelworkers of America v. Enterprise Wheel & Car Corp.*, 363 U.S. 593 (1960); *United Steelworkers of America v. Warrior & Gulf Navigation Co.*, 363 U.S. 574 (1960).

75. Ackerman, *We the People: Foundations*; Ackerman, *We the People: Transformations*.

76. Graber, "Nonmajoritarian Difficulty"; Whittington, "'Interpose Your Friendly Hand.'"

Chapter Eleven

1. PEW Center on the States, *One in 100: Behind Bars in America 2008* (Washington, DC: PEW Center on the States, 2008), http://www.pewcenter onthe states.org/report_detail.aspx?id=35904.

2. Eric M. Patashnik, "Why Some Reforms Last and Others Collapse: The Tax Reform Act of 1986 versus Airline Deregulation," chap. 8 in this volume; Stuart Chinn, "Judicial Delimitation in the New Deal Era," chap. 10 in this volume.

3. Paul Pierson, "When Effect Becomes Cause: Policy Feedback and Political Change," *World Politics* 45 (1993): 595–628.

4. Theda Skocpol, *Protecting Soldiers and Mothers: The Political Origins of Social Policy in the United States* (Cambridge, MA: Harvard University Press, 1992).

5. Suzanne Mettler, "Bringing the State Back in to Civic Engagement: Policy Feedback Effects of the G.I. Bill for World War II Veterans," *American Political Science Review* 96 (2002): 351-65.

6. Joe Soss and Sanford F. Schram, "A Public Transformed? Welfare Reform as Policy Feedback," *American Political Science Review* 101 (2007): 113.

7. Margaret Weir and Theda Skocpol, "State Structures and the Possibilities for 'Keynesian' Responses to the Great Depression in Sweden, Britain, and the United States," in *Bringing the State Back In*, ed. Peter B. Evans, Dietrich Rueschemeyer, and Theda Skocpol (Cambridge: Cambridge University Press, 1985), 107-63.

8. Eric M. Patashnik, "After the Public Interest Prevails: The Political Sustainability of Policy Reform," *Governance* 16 (2003): 203-34.

9. But not always; see ibid.

10. Jacob Hacker, *The Divided Welfare State: The Battle over Public and Private Benefits in the United States* (Cambridge: Cambridge University Press, 2002).

11. Eric M. Patashnik and Julian E. Zelizer, "When Policy Does Not Remake Politics: The Limits of Policy Feedback" (paper presented at the Annual Meeting of the American Political Science Association, Toronto, Ontario, Canada, 2009).

12. Paul Pierson, "Increasing Returns, Path Dependence, and the Study of Politics," *American Political Science Review* 94 (2000): 259.

13. Quoted in John K. Hudzik, *Federal Aid to Criminal Justice: Rhetoric, Results, Lessons* (Washington, DC: National Criminal Justice Association, 1984), 12.

14. Congressional Budget Office, *The Law Enforcement Assistance Administration: Options for Reauthorization* (Washington, DC: Government Printing Office, 1979).

15. Sarah C. Carey, *Law and Disorder IV: A Review of the Federal Anti-crime Program Created by Title I of the Omnibus Crime Control and Safe Streets Act of 1968* (Washington, DC: Center for National Security Studies, 1976).

16. U.S. Advisory Commission on Intergovernmental Relations (ACIR), *Making the Safe Streets Act Work: An Intergovernmental Challenge* (Washington, DC: Government Printing Office, 1970).

17. National Advisory Commission on Criminal Justice Standards and Goals, *A National Strategy to Reduce Crime* (Washington, DC: Government Printing Office, 1973).

18. Ibid., 83.

19. Ibid.

20. ACIR, *State-Local Relations in the Criminal Justice System: A Commission Report* (Washington, DC: Government Printing Office, 1971).

21. ACIR, *Making the Safe Streets Act Work.*

22. Robert L. Smith, "LEAA and Corrections," in *Federal Aid to Criminal Justice: Rhetoric, Results, Lessons,* ed. John K. Hudzik (Washington, DC: National Criminal Justice Association, 1984), 298.

23. National Conference of State Criminal Justice Planning Administrators (NCSCJPA), *State of the States on Crime and Justice: A Report of the National Conference of State Criminal Justice Planning Administrators* (Washington, DC: Government Printing Office, 1976).

24. Though there are no time-series data to analyze this trend, the LEAA had established a criminal justice agency directory in 1970. The database was maintained through the decade and another count done at the end of the decade. A rough evaluation based on these endpoints suggests many more agencies in 1980 than in 1970, near the beginning of LEAA's implementation. Excluding courts and federal and tribal agencies, there were 32,924 criminal justice agencies in 1970 compared to 39,274 in 1980. I exclude courts because the 1970 file included courts related to family relations and probate courts and did not include federal and Indian tribal agencies.

25. Lawyers' Committee for Civil Rights Under Law and National Urban Coalition, *Law and Disorder III: State and Federal Performance under Title I of the Omnibus Crime Control and Safe Streets Act of 1968* (Washington, DC: National Urban Coalition, 1973), 9.

26. Carey, *Law and Disorder IV,* 3.

27. Ibid., 15.

28. Twentieth Century Fund Task Force on the Law Enforcement Assistance Administration, *Law Enforcement: The Federal Role* (New York: McGraw-Hill, 1976).

29. Hudzik, *Federal Aid to Criminal Justice,* 234.

30. Ibid., 217.

31. Quoted in Matthew Neary, *Higher Education for Police* (New York: American Academy for Professional Law Enforcement, 1977), 14.

32. Pierson, "When Effect Becomes Cause," 610.

33. Gerald Caplan, "Reflections on the Nationalization of Crime, 1964–1968," *Law and the Social Order* 3 (1973): 594.

34. Malcom M. Feeley and Austin D. Sarat, *Policy Dilemma: Federal Crime Policy and the Law Enforcement Assistance Administration* (Minneapolis: University of Minnesota Press, 1980); Virginia Gray and Bruce Williams, *The Organizational Politics of Criminal Justice: Policy in Context* (Lexington, MA: Lexington Books, 1980).

35. Another hearing on the research, statistics, and training components of OLEA took up three days of debate with thirteen witnesses testifying.

36. ACIR, *Safe Streets Reconsidered: The Block Grant Experience 1968–1975* (Washington, DC: Government Printing Office, 1977).

37. Barry Mahoney, "The Politics of the Safe Streets Act, 1965–1973: A Case Study in Evolving Federalism and the National Legislative Process" (PhD diss., Columbia University, 1976).

38. Caplan, "Reflections on the Nationalization of Crime," 620.

39. There is no source of data for local groups, which, based on the LEAA newsletter, were a major part of the organizational growth around changes in crime policy.

40. Other work has also demonstrated this tendency of criminal justice bureaucrats to dominate political debate: "Since 1970, criminal justice agents have constituted almost one-third or more of all witnesses at congressional crime and justice hearings in all but one Congress (1971–2)." Lisa L. Miller, "Rethinking Bureaucrats in the Policy Process: Criminal Justice Agents and the National Crime Agenda," *Policy Studies Journal* 32 (2004): 576.

41. Feeley and Sarat, *Policy Dilemma*, 59.

42. Joseph C. Goulden, "The Cops Hit the Jackpot," *Nation*, November 2, 1970, 525.

43. U.S. Department of Justice, Bureau of Justice Statistics, *Report to the Nation on Crime and Justice: The Data* (Washington, DC: Government Printing Office, 1983), 91.

44. NCSCJPA, *State of the States on Crime and Justice*, 24.

45. Ibid., 42.

46. Ibid, 23.

47. Hudzik, *Federal Aid to Criminal Justice*, 24.

48. In their analysis of LEAA, Gray and Williams also find that "LEAA has successfully used a dependence strategy to encourage SPAs to allocate money for national priority innovations." *Organizational Politics of Criminal Justice*, 292. The 1971 amendment required states to allocate funds to corrections, allocate greater funding to high-crime areas, and establish local coordinating councils. The Crime Control Act of 1973 included a "pass-through" mandate, requiring states to relinquish a certain percentage of grant funds directly to localities and urban areas. The Juvenile Justice and Delinquency Prevention Act of 1974 issued a directive for special funds to go to youth crime programs. The Crime Control Act of 1976 earmarked funds for community anticrime projects, court planning, narcotics, and elderly crime victims.

49. Law Enforcement Assistance Administration, *Safe Streets . . . The LEAA Program at Work* (Washington, DC: Government Printing Office, 1971), 11.

50. Charles M. Gray, Virginia Gray, and Bruce Williams, "Federalism, Policy, and Innovation in Corrections," *Review of Policy Research* 1 (1981): 288.

51. Hudzik, *Federal Aid to Criminal Justice*, 214.

52. Ibid.

53. Ibid, 32.

54. Ibid., 45. An earlier report stated that more than half of the states had

unified their courts and revised their criminal codes. Congressional Budget Office, *Federal Law Enforcement Assistance: Alternative Approaches* (Washington, DC: Government Printing Office, 1978), xii.

55. NCSCJPA, *State of the States on Crime and Justice: An Analysis of State Administration of the Safe Streets Act*, (Washington, DC: Government Printing Office, 1973).

56. NCSCJPA, *State of the States on Crime and Justice*.

57. National Advisory Commission on Criminal Justice Standards and Goals, "National Strategy to Reduce Crime," 33.

58. "Colorado Passes Comprehensive Sentencing and Corrections Laws," *LEAA Newsletter*, June 1976, 5.

59. NCSCJPA, *Halting the Invasion of Categorization in the Crime Control Act Program: Why the Block Grant?* (Washington, DC: Government Printing Office, 1977), 31.

60. National Advisory Commission on Criminal Justice Standards and Goals, "National Strategy to Reduce Crime," 137.

61. Ibid., 148.

62. NCSCJPA, *State of the States on Crime and Justice*.

63. NCSCJPA, *Halting the Invasion*, 30.

64. Sandra Shane-DuBow, Alice P. Brown, and Erik Olsen, *Sentencing Reform in the United States: History, Content, and Effect* (Washington, DC: U.S. Department of Justice, National Institute of Justice, Office of Development, Testing, and Dissemination, August 1985).

65. Herbert Jacob, "Governmental Responses to Crime in the United States, 1948–78" [computer file], conducted by Herbert Jacob, Northwestern University, 2nd ICPSR ed. (Ann Arbor, MI: Inter-university Consortium for Political and Social Research [producer and distributor], 1985).

66. Originally compiled to examine the responses of urban governments to crime, using a sample of ten cities during the years 1948–78, it also collected and documented changes in criminal law in each of the nine states where the cities were located using state criminal codes. The states included in their study were Arizona, California, Georgia, Indiana, Massachusetts, Minnesota, New Jersey, Pennsylvania, and Texas. While the study investigators made no claim to representativeness, they did point out that the cities were selected to "represent distinct clusterings on particular dimensions of cities" including black representation, political nature of police force, governing structure, financial strength, and disadvantage. Anne M. Heinz, *Legislative Responses to Crime: The Changing Content of Criminal Law* (Washington, DC: U.S. Department of Justice, National Institute of Justice, 1982), x.

67. A Vera Institute of Justice project is undergoing research to compile these data, but it has not been formally released.

68. The data were combined into two-year points to smooth extremes associated with legislative sessions.

69. Another source reports that by 1984, twelve states had abolished parole. Samuel Walker, *Taming the System: The Control of Discretion in Criminal Justice, 1950–1990* (New York: Oxford University Press, 1993), 139.

70. ACIR, *Safe Streets Reconsidered*.

71. Shane-DuBow, Brown, and Olsen, *Sentencing Reform in the United States*, 279.

72. Shane-DuBow, Brown, and Olsen, *Sentencing Reform in the United States*.

73. National Advisory Commission on Criminal Justice Standards and Goals, "National Strategy to Reduce Crime," 121.

74. General Accounting Office, *Overview of Activities Funded by the Law Enforcement Assistance Administration: Study* (Washington, DC: Government Printing Office, 1977).

75. Task Force on the Administration of Justice, The President's Commission on Law Enforcement and Criminal Justice, *Task Force Report: Corrections* (Washington, DC: Government Printing Office, 1967), 179.

76. Based on data faxed by James Stephan of the Bureau of Justice Statistics, April 4, 2007.

77. *Statistical Abstract*, Nos. 292, 328, "State Prisons—Selected Characteristics, by Type of Institution: 1974 and 1979."

78. Law Enforcement Assistance Administration, *The Law Enforcement Assistance Administration: A Program for a Safer, More Just America* (Washington, DC: Government Printing Office, 1970), 1.

79. Hudzik, *Federal Aid to Criminal Justice*, 195.

80. Diana R. Gordon, *The Justice Juggernaut: Fighting Street Crime, Controlling Citizens* (New Brunswick, NJ: Rutgers University Press, 1990), 204.

81. Lisa L. Miller, *The Perils of Federalism: Race, Poverty, and the Politics of Crime Control* (Oxford: Oxford University Press, 2008).

82. Congressional Budget Office, "Trends in Federal Spending for the Administration of Justice," August 1996, https://www.cbo.gov/ftpdocs/6xx/doc602/justice.pdf.

83. Hudzik, *Federal Aid to Criminal Justice*, 106.

84. Congressional Budget Office, "Trends in Federal Spending."

85. Daniel Richman, "Past, Present, and Future of Violent Crime Federalism," *Crime and Justice* 34 (2006): 400.

86. Congressional Budget Office, "Trends in Federal Spending," 44.

Chapter Twelve

1. The first quotation is from Roscoe Pound. The third and fourth exhibit ideas attributed to respectively Oliver Wendell Holmes Jr. and Walter Lipp-

mann. See William J. Novak, "Making the Modern American Legislative State," chap. 2 in this volume.

2. Eric M. Patashnik, "Why Some Reforms Last and Others Collapse: The Tax Reform Act of 1986 versus Airline Deregulation," chap. 8 in this volume.

3. Keith Krehbiel, *Information and Legislative Organization* (Ann Arbor: University of Michigan Press, 1991).

4. Christopher R. Berry, Barry C. Burden, and William G. Howell, "The Lives and Deaths of Federal Programs, 1971–2003," chap. 5 in this volume; Forrest Maltzman and Charles R. Shipan, "Beyond Legislative Productivity: Enactment Conditions, Subsequent Conditions, and the Shape and Life of the Law," chap. 6 in this volume.

5. Jeffrey E. Cohen and Matthew Eshbaugh-Soha, "Durability and Change in the President's Legislative Policy Agenda, 1789–2002," chap. 3 in this volume.

6. In the 1930s, none of these four concerns was the subject of a major legislative drive by the Roosevelt administration. Senator Robert Wagner pressed the first three with mixed success during the years before World War II. The war changed the context. It brought, among other things, arresting new data on health and literacy deficiencies among military recruits, a huge housing crisis, and the shame of fighting against the Nazis while practicing racism at home. In 1944 came Roosevelt's important speech advancing an "economic bill of rights." Soon afterward came Truman's Fair Deal program.

7. Vesla M. Weaver, "The Significance of Policy Failures in Political Development: The Law Enforcement Assistance Administration and the Growth of the Carceral State," chap. 11 in this volume.

8. Stuart Chinn, "Judicial Delimitation in the New Deal Era," chap. 10 in this volume.

9. This program began in the White House as an unusually well-planned experiment, although it shed much of its original blueprint on Capitol Hill as the members nudged it toward a customary something-for-everybody distributive instrument. See R. Douglas Arnold, *Congress and the Bureaucracy: A Theory of Influence* (New Haven, CT: Yale University Press, 1979), 165–69.

10. Viewed in this way, the Taft-Hartley Act shared a key aspiration with the previous Wagner Act of 1935. Stuart Chinn points to "the core Wagner Act goal of promoting industrial stability." Chinn, "Judicial Delimitation in the New Deal Era," chap. 10 in this volume. An alarming brand of nationwide strike activity had peaked just beforehand in 1934. On the public's extreme discontent with the labor union strikes of the early and mid-1940s that helped trigger the Taft-Hartley Act, see Eric Schickler, "Public Opinion, the Congressional Policy Agenda, and the Limits of New Deal Liberalism, 1936–1945" (paper presented at the Annual Meeting of the American Political Science Association, Toronto, Ontario, Canada, 2009).

11. Amihai Glazer, "How Unpopular Policies Become Popular after Adoption," chap. 7 in this volume.

12. Sam Dillon, "Scholar's School Reform U-Turn Shakes Up Debate," *New York Times*, March 23, 2010.

13. Richard A. Posner, *Not a Suicide Pact: The Constitution in a Time of National Emergency* (New York: Oxford University Press, 2006), chap. 2, quotations at 46, 40, 44.

Chapter Thirteen

1. Jeffery A. Jenkins and Eric M. Patashnik, "Living Legislation and American Politics," chap. 1 in this volume.

2. James Q. Wilson, "New Politics, New Elites, Old Publics," in *The New Politics of Public Policy*, ed. Marc C. Landy and Martin A. Levin (Baltimore: Johns Hopkins University Press, 1995), 249–67; and Hugh Heclo, "Sixties Civics," in *The Great Society and the High Tide of Liberalism*, ed. Sidney M. Milkis and Jerome Mileur (Amherst: University of Massachusetts Press, 2005), 53–82.

3. William J. Novak, "Making the Modern American Legislative State," chap. 2 in this volume.

4. Franklin D. Roosevelt, *The Public Papers and Addresses of Franklin D. Roosevelt*, ed. Samuel I. Rosenman (New York: Random House, 1940), 9: 671–72.

5. Jeffrey E. Cohen and Matthew Eshbaugh-Soha, "Durability and Change in the President's Legislative Policy Agenda, 1789–2002," chap. 3 in this volume.

6. Eric M. Patashnik, "Why Some Reforms Last and Others Collapse: The Tax Reform Act of 1986 versus Airline Deregulation," chap. 8 in this volume; Stuart Chinn, "Judicial Delimitation in the New Deal Era," chap. 10 in this volume; Vesla M. Weaver, "The Significance of Policy Failures in Political Development: The Law Enforcement Assistance Administration and the Growth of the Carceral State," chap. 11 in this volume.

7. David E. Lewis, "Policy Durability and Agency Design," chap. 9 in this volume.

8. R. Shep Melnick, "The Great Debate over the Civil Rights State" (paper presented at the American Enterprise Institute, Washington, DC, May 12, 2010).

9. Theodore Lowi, *The End of Liberalism: The Second Republic in the United States*, 2nd ed. (New York: W. W. Norton, 1979).

10. Staff interview conducted by Sidney M. Milkis, for "The Federal Trade Commission and Consumer Protection: Regulatory Change and Administrative Pragmatism," *Antitrust Law Journal* 72 (2005): 911–41.

11. Interview with Timothy Muris, August 4, 2004; Steven Pearlstein, "An FTC Tenure Worthy of Praise," *Washington Post*, August 13, 2004, E1.

12. Martha Derthick, *Up in Smoke: From Legislation to Litigation in Tobacco Politics*, 2nd edition (Washington, DC: CQ Press, 2004).

13. Daniel P. Carpenter, "The Evolution of National Bureaucracy in the United States," in *The Executive Branch*, ed. Joel D. Aberbach and Mark A. Peterson (New York: Oxford University Press, 2005), 54, 58; Daniel P. Carpenter, *The Forging of Bureaucratic Autonomy, Reputation, Networks and Policy Innovation in Executive Agencies, 1862–1928* (Princeton, NJ: Princeton University Press, 2001).

14. Richard A. Harris and Sidney M. Milkis, *The Politics of Regulatory Change: A Tale of Two Agencies*, 2nd ed. (New York: Oxford University Press, 1996), chaps. 5, 8; Milkis, "Federal Trade Commission and Consumer Protection."

15. Martha Derthick, "Reflections on *Policymaking for Social Security*," *PS: Political Science and Politics* 37 (2004): 444.

16. Martha Derthick, *Policymaking for Social Security* (Washington, DC: Brookings Institution Press, 1983), 17–37.

17. Franklin D. Roosevelt, cited in ibid., 417.

18. Eric M. Patashnik, *Putting Trust in the U.S. Budget: Federal Trust Funds and the Politics of Commitment* (New York: Cambridge University Press, 2000), xii, 1.

19. Derthick, *Policymaking for Social Security*, 417.

20. Ibid., 12–13; Derthick "Reflections on *Policymaking for Social Security*," 443.

21. R. Kent Weaver, "Policymaking for Social Security: Past, Present, and Future," *PS: Political Science and Politics* 37 (2004): 436.

22. E. E. Schattschneider, *The Semisovereign People: A Realist's View of Democracy in America* (Fort Worth, IN: Harcourt Brace Jovanovich, 1960), chaps. 2, 3 (emphasis in original).

23. Sean Gailmard and Jeffery A. Jenkins, "Coalition Structure and Legislative Innovation in American National Government," chap. 4 in this volume.

24. Walter Dean Burnham, *Critical Elections and the Mainsprings of American Politics* (New York: W. W. Norton, 1970).

25. Keith Krehbiel, *Pivotal Politics: A Theory of U.S. Lawmaking* (Chicago: University of Chicago Press, 1998).

26. Burnham argues that realigning coalitions undergo a "midlife crisis" after about fifteen years, which is similar to the time Gailmard and Jenkins identify as when a unified party runs aground. See "Critical Realignment: Dead or Alive," in *The End of Realignment?*, ed. Byron Shafer (Madison: University of Wisconsin Press, 1991), 101–39.

27. Stephen Skowronek, *The Politics Presidents Make: Leadership from John Adams to Bill Clinton* (Cambridge, MA: Harvard University Press, 1997).

28. David R. Mayhew, *Electoral Realignments: A Critique of an American Genre* (New Haven, CT: Yale University Press, 2002).

29. Heclo, "Sixties Civics," 60–63.

30. Arthur Schlesinger Jr., *The Vital Center: The Politics of Freedom* (Boston: Houghton Mifflin, 1949).

31. Hugh Heclo, "The Emerging Regime," in *Remaking American Politics,* ed. Richard A. Harris and Sidney M. Milkis (Boulder, CO: Westview Press, 1989), 310.

32. Derthick, "Reflections on *Policymaking for Social Security,*" 443–44.

33. Weaver, "Policymaking for Social Security," 435–36.

34. Deborah Stone, "Martha Derthick as Paradoxical Postmodernist: A Quarter Century Reappraisal of *Policymaking for Social Security,*" *PS: Political Science and Politics* 37 (2004): 438.

35. Newt Gingrich (speech, conference of Blue Cross/Blue Shield, Washington, DC, October 24, 1995).

36. Jacob S. Hacker, "Privatizing Risk without Privatizing the Welfare State: The Hidden Politics of Social Policy Retrenchment in the United States," *American Political Science Review* 98 (2004): 243–60; Stephen Teles, "The Dialectics of Trust, Ideas, Finance, and Pension Privatization in the U.S. and U.K." (paper presented at the Annual Meeting of the Association for Public Policy Analysis and Management, New York, NY, October 29–31, 1998).

37. Sidney M. Milkis and Jesse H. Rhodes, "George W. Bush, the Republican Party, and the 'New' Party System," *Perspectives on Politics* 5 (2007): 461–88; Sidney M. Milkis and Jesse H. Rhodes, "Barack Obama, the Democratic Party, and the Future of the 'New' Party System," *Forum* 1, no. 1, art. 7 (2009).

Contributors

CHRISTOPHER R. BERRY
Harris School of Public Policy
The University of Chicago
Chicago, IL 60637

BARRY C. BURDEN
Department of Political Science
University of Wisconsin–Madison
Madison, WI 53706–1316

STUART CHINN
University of Oregon Law School
Eugene, OR 97403–1221

JEFFREY E. COHEN
Department of Political Science
Fordham University
Bronx, NY 10458

MATTHEW ESHBAUGH-SOHA
Department of Political Science
University of North Texas
Denton, TX 76203–5017

SEAN GAILMARD
Department of Political Science
University of California, Berkeley
Berkeley, CA 94720

AMIHAI GLAZER
Department of Economics
University of California,
Irvine Irvine, CA 92697

WILLIAM G. HOWELL
Harris School of Public Policy
The University of Chicago
Chicago, IL 60637

JEFFERY A. JENKINS
Department of Politics & Miller Center of Public Affairs
University of Virginia
Charlottesville, VA 22904

DAVID E. LEWIS
Department of Political Science
Vanderbilt University
Nashville, TN 37235–1817

FORREST MALTZMAN
Department of Political Science
George Washington University
Washington, DC 20052

DAVID R. MAYHEW
Department of Political Science
Yale University
New Haven CT, 06520–8301

SIDNEY M. MILKIS
Department of Politics & Miller Center of Public Affairs
University of Virginia
Charlottesville, VA 22904

WILLIAM J. NOVAK
The University of Michigan Law School
Ann Arbor, MI 48109–1215

ERIC M. PATASHNIK
Frank Batten School of Leadership and Public Policy & Department of Politics
University of Virginia
Charlottesville, VA 22904

CHARLES R. SHIPAN
Department of Political Science
University of Michigan
Ann Arbor MI 48109–1045

VESLA M. WEAVER
Department of Politics & Miller Center of Public Affairs
University of Virginia
Charlottesville, VA 22904

Index